MARRIAGE AND SLAVERY IN EARLY ISLAM

MARRIAGE AND SLAVERY IN EARLY ISLAM

Kecia Ali

Harvard University Press
Cambridge, Massachusetts
London, England
2010

Printed in the United States of America

Library of Congress Cataloging-in-Publication Data

Ali, Kecia.
Marriage and slavery in early Islam / Kecia Ali.
p. cm.
Includes bibliographical references and index.
ISBN 978-0-674-05059-4 (alk. paper)
1. Marriage (Islamic law) 2. Concubinage (Islamic law)
3. Slavery (Islamic law) I. Title.
KBP542.35.A45 2010
297.5'77—dc22 2010000937

Contents

Acknowledgments vii

Introduction 1

1 Transacting Marriage 29

2 Maintaining Relations 65

3 Claiming Companionship 97

4 Untying the Knot 133

5 Marriage and Dominion 164

Conclusion 187

Notes 199

Index 253

Acknowledgments

Numerous people and institutions have helped me during this project. I have benefited tremendously from correspondence and conversations with Karen Bauer, Jon Brockopp, Ayesha Siddiqua Chaudhry, miriam cooke, Vincent Cornell, Mohammad Fadel, Havva Guney-Rudenbacker, Ahmet Karamustafa, Bruce Lawrence, Ebrahim Moosa, Sara Omar, Kevin Reinhart, Behnam Sadeki, Omid Safi, Laury Silvers, Amira Sonbol, and others too numerous to name. My colleagues in the Feminist Sexual Ethics project at Brandeis University involved me in comparative discussions; Bernadette Brooten and Gail Labovitz were especially vital. The two anonymous readers for Harvard University Press were also extremely helpful, as was my editor, Sharmila Sen. Collectively, these people have saved me from many errors of fact and interpretation, but none of them bears any responsibility for remaining mistakes or my insistence on particular views.

I was fortunate to spend a year (2003–4) as a visiting scholar at the Harvard Divinity School's Women's Studies in Religion Program. Director Ann Braude and the other visiting scholars—Ana Maria Bidegain, Kelly Chong, Sharon Gillerman, and Hanna Herzog—read and commented on early versions of two chapters; my HDS seminar students read another and made helpful comments. I continued to work on the project at Brandeis University, where I held the Florence Levy Kay postdoctoral fellowship from 2004 to 2006. The latest revisions were completed at Boston University. I would like to thank my colleagues in the Department of Religion for their support and the Boston

University Humanities Foundation for providing me with a grant to cover the cost of Widener Library privileges.

Material from Chapters 1, 4, and 5 was first presented in lectures at Brandeis University, Harvard University, Princeton University, Stanford University, and the 1999 and 2008 Annual Meetings of the American Academy of Religion. I am grateful for the productive discussions that ensued.

My family has lived with this project for years. I would like to thank my children, Shaira, Saadia, and Tariq, for their understanding and enthusiasm, but that would be overstating the case; tolerance more accurately captures their attitude. They simply do not see the point of writing anything that has no dragons, sharks, princesses, wizards, fairies, vampires, or alien civilizations, although they do admit that it is kind of neat to see Mom's name on the cover of a book. Finally, it seems fitting that a book about marriage be dedicated to my husband: Shahan, this is for you.

MARRIAGE AND SLAVERY IN EARLY ISLAM

Introduction

WHILE writing this book, I have had numerous opportunities to explain its subject. One of my less successful attempts occurred several years ago, when an Algerian acquaintance enquired politely about my progress, adding, "Remind me what it's about." I answered that I was writing about marriage, divorce, and the reciprocal but gender-differentiated obligations of husbands and wives in ninth-century Islamic jurisprudence. I was focusing, I added, on three major issues: first, diversity of opinion in early legal thought; second, the influence of hierarchical social structures, including slave ownership, on the jurists' visions of marriage; and third, the vital role of polemical exchange in the refinement of legal doctrine. As I finished this summary, we were joined by a colleague of his, another North African Muslim. "Guess what?" said the first man enthusiastically, drawing the new arrival into the conversation. "She's writing a book on women's rights in Islam."

This exchange—funny only in retrospect—involved a series of miscommunications. My own inept, jargon-filled explanation deserves most of the blame. Incomprehensibility plagues academics. We have specialized knowledge that bears on contemporary topics but tend to be lousy at communicating it to people not initiated into our disciplinary mysteries. Although the time period with which this book is concerned is remote, its subject matter is of vital interest today, when women, gender, and Islamic law occupy center stage in debates about modernity and religious authenticity across the globe. I failed to show how my treatment of marriage, sex, and interpretive authority resonates deeply with contemporary discussions. But not all the blame for the misunderstanding was mine. Common habits of thought make it difficult for people to hear nuances, no matter how clearly expressed. Intricate ideas shrink to bite-sized platitudes. An analysis of gender and hierarchy in family and society dwindles to a simple matter of women's rights. An historical description of a particular era in Muslim legal thought morphs into a statement about a monolithic entity called Islam. Pernicious tendencies toward sweeping generalizations seem to increase exponentially when the subject involves both women *and* Islam.

Fortunately, the situation is better among scholars than among the general public. Though bestselling books on women and Islam tend toward sensationalistic memoirs or journalistic exposés, recent decades also have witnessed a spectacular surge of relevant academic studies, especially in law. We now have an impressive understanding of women's transactions (personal and proprietary) in much of the premodern Muslim world, especially the Ottoman Middle East, for which abundant court records and fatwa compilations exist.[1] Leslie Peirce's microhistory of a year in the sixteenth-century life of the Ottoman provincial court of Aintab notes, "Focusing on women at court has the benefit of highlighting the gap between normative prescription and actual practice—or perhaps, more accurately, highlighting the complicated relationship between the two." In the courts, actors including judges and litigants draw from available resources, which include "official" jurisprudence as well as customary practice, to arrive at the most favorable outcome. Courtroom observation by legal anthropologists across twentieth-century Muslim societies supplements historians' archival work. By focusing on the court as a sphere of negotiation and on the variety of resources that actors of all types brought into the court, historians such as Peirce and anthropologists such as Ziba Mir-Hosseini and Susan Hirsch are able to make women's voices—filtered and mediated though they may be—appear in a way that is nearly impossible with the textual sources of legal manuals and fatwas.[2] From Africa to Indonesia, Muslim women are not the silent victims of oppressive patriarchal regimes but active participants in their families and societies. Women own and manage property, claim and sometimes win custody of children, seek divorce and often get it, and generally stand up for themselves. Judges uphold female rights within the context of broader patriarchal patterns. Both in courtrooms and in daily life, women have managed to negotiate leeway in a variety of spaces.[3]

One major way in which studies of law have proceeded has been to "compare doctrine with the actual practice of the court."[4] As one scholar discussing scriptural and legal texts notes, "Social patterns were in great contrast to the 'official' picture presented by these 'formal' sources."[5] Studies often juxtapose flexible and relatively fair court outcomes with an undifferentiated and sometimes harshly patriarchal textual tradition of jurisprudence. We are shown proof of "the flexibility within Islamic law that is often portrayed as stagnant and draconian."[6] Given the shift within women's studies over the last decades of the twentieth century—from concern with documenting oppressive structures to retrieving evidence of women's agency and resistance—it is not surprising that the record of practice has been more attractive than the comparatively elitist and androcentric jurisprudential discourse.

As scholars emphasize diversity and contingency in contemporary and historical applications of the law, though, they often overlook diversity of doctrine within and between normative texts. At a very basic level, the existence of contradictory positions within the realm of jurisprudence considered mutually orthodox challenges the simplistic equation of "Islamic law" with revealed law. Instead of supporting a model whereby the jurists merely discover the *sharīʿa*—and sometimes disagree on minor points—close attention to jurisprudence reveals significant differences on important topics. At a minimum, one conclusion of this book, salient to Muslim reformers, is that Islamic legal rules are to a significant extent the product of human and therefore fallible interpretive processes, and thus are susceptible to reform. Human reason and agency have been involved deeply in the production of religio-legal rules, including those governing marriage and divorce. This is, as one early reader of this manuscript pointed out, jejune for scholars of Islamic legal history, but may well be a new idea for lay Muslims and others for whom Islamic jurisprudence equals *sharīʿa,* which is understood as immutable Divine law. Drawing this connection is of vital importance given the widespread appeals to *sharīʿa* in Muslim contexts today.

Revivalist groups call for the implementation of *sharīʿa* as the sine qua non of a truly Islamic society. But these contemporary appeals to reinstate *sharīʿa* involve "a grossly exaggerated sense of the practical application of Shariʾa as a comprehensive, self-contained and immutable normative system in the pre-colonial period."[7] Despite the conceptual importance of *sharīʿa,* "most premodern Islamic states maintained two or more parallel legal systems."[8] Scholars and rulers alike were less concerned with the purity of the legal system than its overall success at keeping order and ensuring a reasonable approximation of justice. The jurists were charged with constructing from the raw material of scripture, prophetic precedent, and (in interpersonal matters) local custom a set of regulations that would guide the behavior of individual believers and serve as a basis for adjudication by duly constituted authorities. From its inception, the implementation of law involved a series of compromises between secular, state-generated law (*siyāsa sharʿiyya* or, in Ottoman terms, *kanun*) and religiously grounded jurisprudence *(fiqh).*

Jurisprudence, then, is not reducible to law in its modern Western sense. It most closely parallels rabbinic law, *halakha,* in both scope and process. As with rabbinic discourse, Muslim jurisprudence was an open rather than a closed system. Jurists expounded, explained, debated, and justified their stances on legal matters both mundane and lofty, social and ritual. Opinions and arguments continued over time, and minority views remained part of a canon, available for later thinkers to draw on. Issues were seldom fully resolved. It remained fully permissible for jurists to derive fresh solutions to legal problems based on independent recourse to foundational texts *(ijtihād).* Of necessity, however, this innovation coexisted with a routine reliance on precedent. The need for stability and predictability meant that advisory legal opinions (fatwas) and judicial verdicts were based largely on dominant views within the legal schools.[9]

In the aftermath of European colonialism, legislative codes have supplanted jurisprudence as the primary fount of legal doctrine in nearly every nation with a Muslim majority.[10] There is no pretense of religious legitimacy for most areas of law such as commerce, crime, or international relations. Marriage and family, however, remain regulated by so-called personal-status laws. With the rise of political Islam, these laws have become an ideological battleground, with women's rights at center field. Inheritance, marriage, divorce, and sexual crimes have been the chief arenas in which claims are staked.[11] Even as its links to the historical tradition of jurisprudence become tenuous, the ideological heft of Islamic law has increased. Politicians and activists have fixated on women's status as a barometer of religious authenticity. Appeals to *sharīʿa* invoke a timeless, authentic past, even as the content and implementation of the laws in question diverge considerably from earlier regulations. As Judith

Tucker notes, "For the state to make 'Islamic' rules and then use modern means of repression to apply them to its population as part of a legitimating process does not, in terms of substance and procedure, find much support in traditional Islamic legal thinking."[12]

My point in highlighting divergences between classical Islamic jurisprudence and today's claims about Islamic law by various actors is not that modern claims to enact *sharīʿa* are unacceptable because they deviate from a pristine past. If anything, it is to make clear that there was no such pristine past. The early jurists were themselves engaged in a messy, complicated, human project of cobbling together from revealed and mundane sources a law that would be a pale reflection of the divine imperative and at the same time its closest earthly equivalent. Knowing how discourses on marriage have evolved allows a fuller understanding of ongoing normative discussions about marriage in Islam. My aim is not to debunk feminist claims with regard to Islamic law, nor to present what the Qurʾan or sunna (prophetic example) "really say" about how marriage should be structured. Instead, I offer an analysis of the jurists' conceptual system.

Although the jurists' doctrines do not directly govern Muslim lives today—and did not directly govern Muslim lives in the past, either—they remain deeply influential. This is true even though the jurists' project differed from the legal codes so vehemently debated today. In her recent survey of Islamic law as it pertains to women and the family, historian Tucker observes that the premodern "system and the doctrines it produced are no longer intact, but I submit that there is an embedded approach and a texture to gender issues that remain relevant to the ways in which those issues are being confronted today."[13] I would go further: core ideas about maleness, femaleness, sexuality, and power that structured marriage in the early jurists' thinking survive in myriad ways in today's discourses. Some of these ideas would be disclaimed if set out openly for approval—the parallel between wives and slaves being the most obvious—but they remain influential in contemporary discussions.

Modern discourses about women and marriage typically focus on women, as with my interlocutors' reframing of marriage as a question of women's rights. Christina de la Puente has suggested that "the woman is the true protagonist of the chapters dedicated to marriage law in the Islamic sources."[14] I am skeptical about this characterization of the decidedly androcentric early Muslim legal texts, but it certainly holds today, when the emphasis has shifted from men's duties and men's rights.

A related and equally vital change has taken place in the rhetoric associated with marriage. Modern Muslim authors, both clerics and laypeople, glorify female domesticity and maternal virtue. The family unit they idealize, with mother-housewife at its center, differs sharply from early jurists' visions of the normative family. Domestic duties of child rearing and housewifery serve as the rationale for support by the male husband-father-breadwinner. In some respects, this model is likely to have accorded more fully with the experience of nonelite women throughout history: domestic drudgery and responsibility for child care would have been primary concerns for many, if not most, women. But, as the chapters that follow will show, premodern Muslim legal writings presented a model of spousal relationships in which parental relations were peripheral and children were secondary. (This separation derives at least partially from the way that legal works are structured into chapters, with separate "books" addressing marriage and divorce.) Although in the practice of the courts other family duties might get a hearing, in the jurists' treatises, a wife's main duties to her husband were to obey him and be sexually available. In exchange, he fed, clothed, and housed her.

Hierarchy, tempered to a greater or lesser degree by affection, stood at the core of marriage. The jurists showed no hesitation in making analogies between wives and slaves or between marriage and commercial transactions. In fact, their central notion about marriage was that the marriage contract granted a husband, in exchange for payment of dower, a form of authority or dominion *(milk)* over his wife's sexual (and usually reproductive) capacity. The same term, *milk,* was used—though with a somewhat different semantic range—for ownership of a slave. It was the exclusive *milk* over a particular woman—as a slave or as a wife—that rendered sexual access licit. The implications of this basic idea, and the ways in which it affected the jurists' regulation of spousal rights while the marriage endured, are the subject of this book.

Discussing slavery in tandem with marriage will strike some readers as deliberately provocative. Ownership terminology and imagery may offend or bewilder. It would have been unexceptionable to early Muslim audiences, for whom both life and law were saturated with slaves and slavery. In this, Muslim societies were not unusual. Norman Cantor has estimated that "roughly one quarter of any major society in antiquity were human chattels—someone's property."[15] The percentages for Muslim societies varied, and precise figures are difficult to come by, but enslaved people formed a significant proportion of any population. Some specialized research has been done on specific legal doctrines concerning slavery.[16] Scholars have studied the elite slave soldiers of the Mamluk and Ottoman eras; others have shown that African as well as Turkic slaves were used for military purposes in the Abbasid era.[17] But references in legal and literary works do not provide a firm basis for assessing the proportion of slaves in any given population or determining their ethnic or occupational profiles. Eric Savage's assessment of the slave trade in eighth-century North Africa discusses the enslavement of captives in warfare and the use of slave girls and women. He suggests in passing, following Bernard Lewis, that the primarily domestic and military use of slaves portrayed in scholarship may reflect urban and other biases of the sources rather than any reality.[18] Slaves worked in agriculture in large numbers in some regions and at some times. Ibn Buṭlān's eleventh-century handbook refers to slaves employed in gold, salt, and copper mines.[19] These are not the types of slavery that preoccupied the jurists. Instead, their queries mostly treated domestic servants as well as slaves acting as commercial agents.

Domestic slavery was common. Frequent offhand textual references to household servants can be taken as evidence of their ubiquity. The omnipresence of slaves in legal texts owes not only to their social presence but also to their utility in legal discussion: slaves are useful to think with. Slaves appear not only in chapters devoted to subjects such as manumission but also interspersed throughout discussions of matters where slavery itself is marginal. For instance, discussions over the fine points of commercial transactions often take the purchase of a slave as their basic example. One reason is that a slave is a nonfungible (unique) commodity. Complicated legal issues can arise: what if a newly purchased slave has a defect that the seller did not disclose? What if a slave dies before delivery? The problem cannot be rectified, as it could with agricultural produce or other fungible goods, by substitution of an equivalent item. In these discussions, slaves serve as a placeholder for other types of commodities. Another reason is the nature of slaves as persons who could be freed. Vital issues arose about slaves as potentially free persons who were subject to future manumission, which could place limits on their salability.

Even prior to manumission, slaves were not only chattels. They could also be legal subjects—for instance, as parties to marriage contracts. Cases involving slaves introduced additional variables into legal queries. These issues sometimes involved core tenets of marriage, such as the right of a male slave to divorce his own wife or how the time of a female slave was to be divided when she had both a husband and a master. Slavery affected not only the particulars of how marriage could be practiced when one spouse was enslaved, but also the entire legal understanding of marriage itself.

But slavery was more than an occasion for technical virtuosity in details of marriage law: it was central to the jurists' conceptual world. In particular, it affected how marriage and gender were thought about. There was a vital relationship between enslavement and femaleness as legal disabilities, and between slave ownership and marriage as legal institutions. Slaves and women were overlapping categories of legally inferior persons constructed against one another and in relation to one another—sometimes identified, sometimes distinguished. Slavery was frequently analogized to marriage: both were forms of control or dominion exercised by one person over another. The contracting of marriage was parallel to the purchase of a slave, and divorce parallel to freeing a slave. Marriage and slavery intersected at the institution of concubinage *(milk al-yamīn)*, which legitimized sex between a man and his own female slave and made any resultant progeny free and legitimate.[20] Slave concubinage helped define marriage both by comparison and contrast. To discuss marriage in the premodern period without reference to slavery would fundamentally distort the jurists' ways of thinking; the one was bound up with the other, even more so in legal thinking than in actual practice.

Islam in the Context of Other Legal Systems

Every society must organize kin relations. Perhaps the most crucial question is how marriages will be formed and how children will be legitimated. What role do individuals, especially daughters, play in selecting their marriage partners? What claims could each spouse make on the other? What rules govern parental and filial rights and obligations? What possibilities for extramarital outlets do men and women have? Is polygamy permissible? What rights do husbands and wives have to dissolve their marriages? The combinations of solutions in various traditions cannot be reduced to a spectrum that runs from being most oppressive to women to most liberating. Rather, rules combined in distinctive ways, according to often unspoken requirements of logical coherence as well as social patterns and customs. Muslim jurists' answers to questions about kin, consent, property, sexuality, and progeny were drawn from a pool of available resources, including pre-Islamic Arab custom, scripture, precedent of the Prophet and other early Muslims, local custom in areas to which Islam spread, and other legal systems. These were also affected, I will argue, by the exigencies of legal reasoning itself.

Pre-Islamic Arab practice served as one vital source of law. Muḥammad and those who formed his community were born into an Arabia where Islam did not yet exist. Its rejected marriage customs are obscure, sometimes available only in Qur'anic and other polemical characterizations. But other customs were sanctioned, perhaps restricted or channeled or regulated in new ways. Broad questions of legal principle arise from the selective treatment of practice: are customary practices presumed permissible unless specifically forbidden? Or, to the contrary, do particular regulations serve as the foundation for an entirely new system? Qur'an and prophetic precedent are, of course, the best known sources of law. To a certain extent, they obviously reflect the practice of the time, and in that sense reinforce Arab custom.

As Islam spread from the Arabian peninsula—north and west as well as east, to territory previously governed by Sassanians, Romans, and Byzantines—Muslims encountered new local customs as well as extant legal systems. Just as Islam never existed in a vacuum, neither did its legal system. The extent of outside influence, especially Jewish and Roman, on the development of Islamic law is deeply contentious. In some cases, vital parallels seem to provide clear instances of borrowing or adaptation. For instance, certain Muslim rules about manumission of a slave by contract resemble Roman institutions. And, with regard to marriage settlements, one might speculate that the practice of breaking dower into prompt and deferred portions, which was at first rejected by Muslim legal thinkers but persistently practiced, might have some relation to norms of Roman Egypt. Some of these parallels likely arose out of independent interaction with local practice in the areas where Islam spread. In other cases, Muslim law may have been influenced more directly by legal systems; it makes sense that Muslim jurists would look to solutions to tricky problems formulated by their counterparts in other traditions. But Wael Hallaq has argued that "the ingenious process of assimilation, systematization, and Islamicization managed to dissipate all the indigenous features of legal institutions and to recast them in a fashion that is not in the least reminiscent of the older institutions."[21] Hallaq's "not in the least reminiscent" is perhaps an exaggeration, but his basic point holds: "Systematization in particular had a powerful effect on reshaping and reformulating whatever raw legal material Islam encountered. This systematization was given sharp expression in the profound desire of Muslim scholars for logical coherence, while at the same time they took into full consideration what they deemed to be divinely inspired propositions."[22]

There are critical similarities and vital differences among Roman, Jewish, and Islamic laws regulating marriage and slavery. The similarities illuminate the broader context of the ancient Near East and Mediterranean. All use terms related to acquisition or sale for some forms of marriage, but the rabbinic *kinyan,* acquisition, is central, while the Roman *coemptio,* a fictive sale, is marginal. The archaic Roman form of marriage known as *manus* refers to the husband's "hand" as a representation of his power, as do the Muslim terms *yad* (hand) and *milk al-yamīn* (ownership by the right hand), which refer to control over certain marital rights (by a husband or father) and to slave ownership, often concubinage. These coincidences of vocabulary are not necessarily indicative of doctrinal borrowing, but rather of a broader culture of legal understandings growing out of hierarchical social structures. A systematic comparative study of Roman and Islamic marriage law, with due attention to differences of period and possible influences (especially given Roman rule in Egypt) would be highly desirable. A similar study of Islamic jurisprudence and *halakha* is also much needed.[23] But rather than explore these similarities extensively, I have chosen to highlight those ways in which Muslim jurisprudence departs notably from its predecessors.

In particular, returning to Hallaq's notion of systematization, it is the particular way that Muslim thinkers frame the conceptual and legal relationship between marriage and slavery, hinging on the transfer of rights to licit sex, that constitutes its unique formulation. Premodern Muslims were typical rather than unique in having both patriarchal marriage and slaveholding. The two coexisted throughout the ancient Near East and Mediterranean as well as in pre-Islamic Arabia. Male-dominated marriage and patrilineal kinship predominated in Greek, Roman, biblical, rabbinic, Byzantine, and Sassanian law and practice, though specific contours of these systems varied and shifted over time both within and across civilizations. Kin relationships placed some women and men in dependent and subordinate positions to others, especially—but not exclusively—to fathers. Marriage in the ancient and late antique world was inseparable from other forms of control over women.[24] It is misleading to think that marriage subjugates an otherwise independent female to a husband. Rather, females (like subordinate males) were already enmeshed in webs of kin control and mutual obligation.

Treatment of slaves was one of the most unusual elements of Muslim law, generally, and marriage law, specifically. Enslavement of captives was widely practiced in antiquity. People were routinely bought and sold. Household slavery was common. Slaveholding, in practice nearly everywhere, included the sexual use of enslaved women and sometimes men. In some times and places, both were explicitly permitted by law; in others, sexual use of slaves happened despite legal strictures. Muslim rules were exceptional in light of prevailing regional practices in extending certain privileges and restrictions to slaves—especially contingent permission to marry and the expectation of adherence to the same sexual codes binding free people, though with lesser penalties for violations. Muslim distinctiveness surrounding the marriages and sexual conduct expected of enslaved people is crucial. Yet two factors militate against drawing too strong a contrast with other systems. First, rules surrounding the use of slaves in Muslim contexts were undoubtedly flouted in practice, especially the ones that (unlike Greek and Roman slavery) strictly forbade any sexual use of male slaves and prohibited all access by masters to married female slaves. Second, though other systems, such as the Roman, forbade formal marriages by slaves, a degree of social and even legal accommodation of slave unions developed.[25] In practice, then, there is likely to have been a good deal less difference than a strict law-to-law comparison would indicate.

If social practice perhaps did not differ greatly, we must ask why such distinctions were legally so vital. This returns us to the internal logic of the Muslim legal tradition. Rules regarding marriage and slavery were closely tied to definitions of both licit sex and legitimate paternity. Legitimacy had fewer implications in the Muslim system than in either the Jewish or Roman systems. Muslim jurisprudence did not preoccupy itself greatly with questions of "citizenship" or illegitimacy, apart from the latter's connection with illicit sexual relationships. Instead, it focused on licit conduct and extended the privilege and obligation of licit conduct to slaves as well.

Early Muslim jurists adhered to a bottom-line view of marriage as a transaction that conveyed to the husband, in exchange for a pecuniary consideration paid to the wife, a type of control, power, or dominion *(milk)* analogous to (but more limited than) a master's power over his female slave. It is this dominion over her that makes intercourse between them lawful. The connection between *milk* and lawful sexuality stands at the core of all regulation of marriage and divorce and by its absence marks discussions over punishment for illicit sex. Though Muslim jurists rarely consider the situation of a woman dallying with her male slave (whatever role it plays in literary works such as *Thousand and One Nights*), it is the absence of sexualized ownership by a female owner over her male slave that prevents them from having a licit relationship, even without the complication of a cuckolded husband.

Interlude

In the Arabian peninsula, a few years after the death of the Prophet Muḥammad, an audacious Muslim woman took one of her young male slaves as a bed partner. She mentioned having done so to the caliph ʿUmar, who inquired incredulously as to her justification. "I thought," she replied, "that ownership by the right hand made lawful to me what it makes lawful to men."[26] "Ownership by the right hand" (*milk al-yamīn,* also "property of the right hand") is a Qurʾanic euphemism for slavery. It appears in several verses that refer to "what your right hands own" alongside wives or spouses as lawful sexual partners.[27] This scriptural allusion went neither unnoticed nor unchallenged by ʿUmar ibn al-Khaṭṭāb, a notoriously stern figure.[28] Shocked and dismayed by her action as well as her implicit claim to have God's permission for it, he sought the advice of the Companions, those Muslims who had known Muḥammad during his lifetime and whose collective wisdom and judgment came to be considered by later Sunnis a vital source of legal precedent. Their verdict: "She has [given] the book of Exalted God an interpretation that is not its interpretation." Though ʿUmar refrained from punishing her for committing illicit sex, he forbade her from ever marrying any free man. Most importantly, in the account of this episode preserved in the *Muṣannaf* of ʿAbd al-Razzāq al-Ṣanʿānī (d. 211/827), ʿUmar put an end to the liaison by "order[ing] the slave not to approach her."

The *Muṣannaf,* a collection of reports from Companions and Meccan authorities, includes another version of this story, which agrees in some details and differs in others.[29] It reports that another ʿUmar, the later caliph ʿUmar b. ʿAbd al-ʿAzīz, was confronted by "a woman from the Bedouin who came to him with a Byzantine *(rūmī)* slave of hers." She complained of the meddling of her agnatic kin—her "father's brother's sons"—who objected to her relationship with her slave: "I have sought to take him as a concubine *(innī istasrartuhu)* and my kin have forbidden me." She explicitly states what the other woman merely implies: a woman should be able to have sex with her male slave by right of possession. In the first narrative, the female owner asserts her rights somewhat tentatively ("I thought [it] made lawful to me"), but this owner defiantly claims her due: "I am in the position of a man: he has a female slave and has sex with her."[30] ʿUmar retorts that her position is not that "of a man" but rather one "in ignorance." He avers that only her "ignorance" saves her from a *ḥadd* punishment, the stoning threatened though not carried out in the previous anecdote. He then commands a group of men, perhaps the aforementioned kin, to take the slave and "sell him to someone who will take him to a land other than hers."

ʿUmar's rebuke alludes to the pre-Islamic "age of Ignorance," the Jāhiliyya, the mores of which Muslim sources depict as wanton and promiscuous. Marriage patterns in pre-Islamic Arabia are necessarily obscure; our sources are Muslim and view many facets of that era through contemptuous eyes, especially practices dealing with sexual morality. In a famous account, Muḥammad's wife ʿĀʾisha describes four types of marriage that existed in Arabia before the coming of Islam. The first, the form of patriarchal marriage sanctioned by Islam, stressed female sexual exclusivity and male control over the marriage tie. The other three types allowed a woman multiple sexual partners, and sometimes—though not always—the power to choose or refuse them herself.[31] Presumably, ʿUmar's allusion to "ignorant" practices alludes to this female freedom to select and reject partners at will—a power one would expect to be wielded by the owner of a slave, but one that did not accord with later Muslim views.

In both anecdotes, a free woman asserts sexual rights over her male slave, and a group of free men reject her claim. The public nature of these incidents is notable. The anecdotes take for granted that the authorities, the woman's kin, or both have a stake in her sexual relationship with her slave, and thus the right to intervene. As they do so, they make no definitive pronouncement about women's right to take concubines, but they base their stance implicitly on a notion of fundamental gender difference: women do not have the same sexual prerogatives as men.

Though the woman's status as owner of the slave is unquestioned, her position is nonetheless ambiguous. The free men concur that she cannot make him her licit partner. But what then? The divergent resolutions reflect the unstable nature of the woman's position as owner once sexuality enters into the equation, as well as the equivocal agency of the male slave. Having the slave sold away recognizes the woman's control over her property, while the order to the slave not to approach her assumes that because of his maleness, he can control the sexual relationship, even though he is owned, not owner.[32]

It will be helpful to compare these passages from the *Muṣannaf* with a parallel text from the *Kitāb al-Umm* of Muḥammad ibn Idrīs al-Shāfiʿī (d. 204/820), roughly al-Ṣanʿānī's contemporary.[33] To my knowledge, this is the only other formative-period text in which the question of a woman taking her male slave as a sexual partner appears. The *Umm*, the most hermeneutically sophisticated of the ninth-century legal texts, is a magisterial collection of substantive law, refined and expanded by Shāfiʿī's students after his death.[34] In the course of a discussion of how many wives and concubines a man may have, the *Umm* briefly addresses the question of women taking male concubines. It is in this context of discussing licit sexual relationship among free people and slaves that Shāfiʿī digresses to debate with an interlocutor who "holds the view that a woman has ownership of the right hand, and says: Why does she not take her male slave as a concubine as a man takes his female slave as a concubine?" Shāfiʿī responds with a sweeping pronouncement about women, gender, and control in marriage and concubinage: "The man is the one who marries, the one who takes a concubine, and the woman is the one who is married, who is taken as a concubine. One cannot make analogies between things that are different."[35] The *Umm* appeals to fundamental gender differences that it deems vital to marriage, divorce, spousal prerogatives, and, ultimately, legal personhood. It also notably mentions analogy *(qiyās)*, a significant methodological development and one that is vital to understanding intersecting legal discourses about marriage, concubinage, and slavery. The jurists' recourse to analogy, unlike the way marriage and slavery are treated by the hadith scholars and exegetes, furthers the connection between marriage and slavery by drawing connections and extending verdicts systematically.

Legal Development

Shāfiʿī's treatment of a woman taking her male slave as a concubine both crystallizes and constitutes a culmination of the legal discussion of marriage, spousal rights, and lawful sex in the formative period. It demonstrates continuities with the era represented in the *Muṣannaf* as well as departures from the decision-making process it depicts. Slavery remained an unchallenged fact of social life. Authorities still forcefully rejected the notion that a (free) woman could take a (slave) concubine and took for granted (free) men's right to do so. Fundamentally, neither ʿUmar's companions nor Shāfiʿī could conceive of licit sex without male control, even if they expressed themselves differently and with varying degrees of self-awareness about the regulating endeavor in which they were engaged. Yet between the one and the other, vital shifts in Islamic legal thought occurred. Between the late eighth century, when key formative figures lived, and the early tenth century, when the eponymous schools of jurisprudence were established, doctrines became systematized, methods became more uniform, and a theoretically coherent notion of marriage and licit sexuality, centered on exclusive male dominion of female sexual capacity, emerged.[36] Some of these elements were already in place at an intuitive rather than systematic level in the *Muṣannaf*. There, ad hoc decision making prevailed. ʿUmar alludes to scripture in discussing the woman who takes a male concubine, but does not explicitly cite Qur'anic verses. No one was professionalized or formally authorized to render legal opinions. The compilation of the *Muṣannaf* more than a century later retrospectively affirms the precedential value of Companion verdicts alongside the legal opinions of early regional authorities (here, mostly Meccan), even as its transmission bears witness to the activity of a new class of specialists who report and record these earlier precedents.

Early legal texts display remarkable variety in form as well as content, ranging from compendia of reports like ʿAbd al-Razzāq's *Muṣannaf* to explicitly reasoned treatises and vigorous discussions of legal disagreements. Texts like the *Muṣannaf* served a different purpose from the *Umm*'s, and continued to be produced alongside more speculative works of jurisprudence. But even though there was no strict linear progression from one methodological stage to another, the overall trend was toward more formal arguments and scriptural evidence-based justifications for particular doctrines. Qur'an and prophetic precedent in the form of hadith were the primary sources utilized, though the opinions of earlier authorities, from the generation of the Companions to regional scholars, continued to carry weight.[37] Yet over the course of the formative period, the bounds of viable opinion on a variety of topics narrowed and justifications for specific positions were elaborated. Intergroup polemics helped strengthen evidentiary and logical standards. Certain types of arguments gained prominence while others tended to fade. In some instances, new doctrines developed. In other cases, jurists took established doctrines and kitted them out with scriptural proof texts and bolstered them with stronger logical defenses.

Analogy, *qiyās*, plays a central role in formative-period legal thought. Its use in the main texts of Mālikī, Ḥanafī, and Shāfiʿī thinkers is evident. Analogy comes to be a major component of the shared Sunni legal method, one of the four sources of law in the framework commonly if erroneously attributed to Shāfiʿī. Explicit reference to it in formative-period texts is tentative and sometimes erratic, though, mostly occurring when a doctrine deviates from the results that would be expected by it.[38] It is one of my core contentions that the use of analogy, in particular the analogy between marriage and slavery, is key to understanding Muslim marriage law. The strict gender differentiation of marital rights, the importance of women's sexual exclusivity, and above all the strict imposition of rules about unilateral divorce, however contested in practice, all facilitate and flow from the key idea that marriage and licit sex require male control or dominion. Analogy makes this possible.

In this book, I analyze early texts from what would become three major Sunni legal schools: the Mālikī, the Ḥanafī, and the Shāfiʿī. I have left out the Ḥanbalīs. Ibn Ḥanbal (d. 241/855), who knew Shāfiʿī, kept aloof from the types of debates taking place here. Though analogy eventually found a place in later Ḥanbalī legal theory, it was deeply suspect to Ibn Ḥanbal and his early associates. As Christopher Melchert writes, "He staunchly opposed the teaching of law apart from the transmission of *ḥadīṯ* reports, staunchly opposed the collection and transmission of juridical opinions from anyone later than the Companions and Successors—staunchly opposed, that is, both the practice of his rationalistic contemporaries, the nascent Ḥanafi school (also the nascent Māliki and Šāfiʿi schools), and the basis of *Sunnī* jurisprudence from the tenth century onwards."[39] Susan Spectorsky's translation of Ibn Ḥanbal's responsa on questions of marriage and divorce demonstrates topical overlap with the concerns of other jurists, but also a constant refusal to engage in the what-if scenario spinning that animated their disputations.[40]

The Mālikī, Ḥanafī, and Shāfiʿī schools, their major scholars, and their core texts require some elucidation. The Mālikīs originated in Medina, the Arabian city where the first Muslim community was situated. Named after Mālik ibn Anas (d. 179/795), the Mālikīs identify themselves as the record (and arbiter) of traditional Medinan "practice" *(al-ʿamal ʿindanā),* which they view as a vital source of law. The two foundational texts to be discussed here are the *Muwaṭṭaʾ*, attributed to Mālik, and the *Mudawwana,* attributed to Saḥnūn al-Tanūkhī (d. 240/855).[41] The *Muwaṭṭaʾ* presents the precedent of Muḥammad, the practice of the Medinan community, and often the opinions of respected Medinan jurists, sometimes with Mālik's own views included. A comparatively short work, the *Muwaṭṭaʾ* represents a quite early stage of Medinan/Mālikī jurisprudence, originally dating to the eighth century.[42] A much longer text, the *Mudawwana* provides an early ninth-century elaboration of Mālik's views and those of his predecessors and followers.[43] The *Mudawwana* purports to reflect conversations between Saḥnūn and Ibn al-Qāsim (d. 191/806), who had studied extensively with Mālik. A comparison of the *Mudawwana* with the *Muwaṭṭaʾ* on various points suggests that proponents of Medinan doctrines considered it necessary to substantiate and defend their positions in response to challenges by Iraqi jurists. The *Mudawwana* reflects these debates, but seldom explicitly.

If Mālik reflected and transmitted the juristic heritage of the Medinans, then Abū Ḥanīfa (d. 150/767) stands as the principal representative of the Iraqi school. Iraq was a hotbed of legal thought in the second/eighth century. Both Jaʿfar al-Ṣādiq—after whom the main Shiʿi legal school is named—and Abū Ḥanīfa, who studied with him, were based there, as was the Kufan jurist Ibn Abī Laylā (d. 148/765–766), a rival of Abū Ḥanīfa. Muḥammad b. al-Ḥasan al-Shaybānī (d. 189/805) and Abū Yūsuf (d. 182/798) were the preeminent disciples of Abū Ḥanīfa. These men transmitted and refined his doctrines, defending them against his Iraqi and Medinan opponents. Several expository and comparative or polemical works are more or less securely attributed to Shaybānī. In the former category are *al-Jāmiʿ al-Kabīr* and *al-Jāmiʿ al-Ṣaghīr*.[44] In the latter category are the *Kitāb al-Ḥujja*, a polemic against "the people of Medina," of whom Mālik was the most prominent representative, and a recension of Mālik's *Muwaṭṭaʾ*, known as the *Muwaṭṭaʾ* of Shaybānī *(Muwatta*ʾ *Shaybānī)*, which compares the views of Mālik, with whom Shaybānī studied for several years, to those of Abū Ḥanīfa, his later teacher.[45] Abū Yūsuf, whose *Kitāb al-Āthār* compiles juristic opinions in a manner like the *Muṣannaf*, also has attributed to him a similar text comparing the doctrines of Abū Ḥanīfa to those of his Kufan rival Ibn Abī Laylā *(Ikhtilāf Abī Ḥanīfa wa Ibn Abī Laylā)*.[46]

The importance of networks of scholarship can be even more clearly seen in the career of Shāfiʿī, whose *Umm* I discussed earlier. Shāfiʿī is a crucial figure in early Islamic jurisprudence, remembered primarily for his contribution to legal theory. Though Noel Coulson exaggerates when he calls him "the *deus ex machina* of his time," Shāfiʿī contributed signally to the compromise legal methodology that ultimately allowed Sunni scholars to integrate both prophetic traditions and various techniques of reasoning, including analogy.[47] After early study with important Meccan scholars, Shāfiʿī spent time learning from Mālik in Medina. He then traveled to Iraq, where he studied and debated with Shaybānī. After a period of study—and a return to Mecca, where he led a teaching circle—Shāfiʿī taught in Baghdad and composed works of jurisprudence. Shāfiʿī draws from both Mālikī and Ḥanafī traditions, here synthesizing, there rejecting his predecessors in developing his distinctive doctrines and increasingly systematic rationales for them. Toward the end of his life, he settled in Egypt, where he revised his works and taught additional students, who in turn taught others; the *Kitāb al-Umm*, compiled and polished after his death, and chiefly transmitted by al-Rabīʿ ibn Sulaymān al-Murādī (d. 270/884), represents his mature doctrines.[48] A more independently minded student, Ismāʿīl b. Yaḥyā al-Muzanī (d. 264/877–878), composed a widely circulated abridgement *(Mukhtaṣar)* of the *Umm*.[49] Modern editions of the *Umm* are printed with this *Mukhtaṣar* as well as several shorter treatises on particular legal-methodological issues or jurisprudential disagreements. These notably include *Ikhtilāf al-ʿIraqiyayn*, which records Shāfiʿī's responses to Abū Yūsuf's record of the "disagreement of the two Iraqis"—that is, Abū Ḥanīfa and Ibn Abī Laylā.

This brief sketch of the relationships between a handful of formative-era jurists hardly does justice to their overlapping connections or the broader networks of which they formed part. In the eighth and ninth centuries, boundaries between groups of jurists were porous rather than fixed; there were no formal legal schools (*madhāhib*, singular *madhhab*). Nurit Tsafrir notes, "It is not at all certain what the nature of a legal school in the second[/eighth] century was, and what it meant to be a follower of such a school."[50] And with regard to what to call them, Steven Judd refers to an "epistemological dilemma" of long standing: "In a world of diverse views held by thousands of scholars who travel frequently and borrow concepts from each other, how does one sort scholars and ideas into manageable categories?"[51] Naming schools after eponymous "founders" became standard in the ninth or tenth century, taking precedence over earlier categories based on "intellectual persuasion," "teacher," or "geography." To use eponymous school names rather than geographical ones before the tenth century is thus anachronistic: the *Ḥujja* refers to its opponents as "the people of Medina" and Shāfiʿī's comparative work treats "two Iraqis." But the labels Ḥanafī, Mālikī, and Shāfiʿī are useful so long as we remember that we are speaking, for instance, of a "nascent Mālikī school"[52] rather than a full-fledged classical *madhhab*. Mālikī, Ḥanafī, and Shāfiʿī serve as useful shorthand for identifying loosely affiliated clusters of jurists who (usually) congregated in certain areas and were engaged in both internal and external debates over legal method and doctrine. One must keep in mind the fluid nature of school boundaries, lest the terms become more a hindrance than a help. In referring to jurists throughout this book with eponymous labels, I intend something along the lines of Peter Hennigan's provisional use of the identifier Ḥanafī: "'Ḥanafī' defines a legal culture in which an identifiable group of jurists—who were later (re)-contextualized as 'Ḥanafīs'—cited to and disputed with one another."[53]

Reading Legal Texts

Hennigan's reference to citation and disputation highlights core practices of jurisprudential culture. Both left traces in the texts. References to respected predecessors helped trace the line of authority for a particular position, or supported a particular position in arguments with colleagues. Disputation could be internal (acknowledging differing opinions within a group, as with the various Medinan authorities cited in the *Mudawwana* or differences between Abū Ḥanīfa and Abū Yūsuf in the *Jāmiʿ al-Ṣaghīr*) or external (Abū Ḥanīfa's view against Mālik's, or that of Shāfiʿī against Shaybānī). Argumentative practices helped define the boundaries between groups of jurists. As Alasdair MacIntyre famously noted, traditions necessarily have external boundaries and internal divisions.[54] From an outsider's perspective, the Sunni jurists under study here constitute a single tradition. Engaged in a legal approach to regulating Muslim lives, they share certain assumptions, approaches, and values, as well as authoritative texts. Additional core agreements defined distinctively Mālikī, Ḥanafī, and Shāfiʿī traditions. Each has characteristic doctrines, particular themes, and concerns that emerge repeatedly. Internally, they engaged with issues of concern to their predecessors, and in conversation with them, in "an argument extended through time."[55] Jurists also engaged in conversation, debate, and argument with contemporaries outside of their increasingly self-contained schools.

Formative-period texts express and defend doctrines, sharing, disputing, modifying, adapting, and rejecting them both within and across geographical and chronological boundaries and across groups of adherents. Doctrines and supporting evidence emerge as fragments of a conversation. Sometimes we are able to hear both halves of it, but at other times we can only infer what the other portion must, or at least might, have been. Attending to this discursive nature of the legal tradition is vital to understanding it, even as the fixity of writing, especially near the end of the formative period, affected how composition and transmission occurred.

It is necessary to say a word about the relationship between legal texts and social practice. At one level, texts were the outcome of social processes. They were affected by the material conditions of their production. Patterns of thought were defined in part by who met whom, where information was transmitted and shared, who could travel in order to study with recognized authorities.[56] Networks of conversation across a deeply interconnected Muslim world, with strong circulation not only of goods but of people and ideas, led to locally inflected forms of Islam coming into contact with and being challenged by other norms and practices. The texts discussed here were produced from Andalusia to Iraq over the course of a century or two. Some of the differences among jurists' doctrines have been explained, in part, by social phenomena in their places of origin. Greater Mālikī rights for slaves, for instance, have been attributed to the relative egalitarianism of Medina, while Ḥanafī strictures on social equality in marriage have been linked to Kufan cosmopolitanism. Still, whatever regional differences existed, common traits affected legal scholarship. Economic stratification, ethnic hierarchy, and at least some degree of sex segregation were prominent features of the societies where these texts emerged.

We must say a bit more about the gendered settings in which legal texts were produced as well as the general climate of ideas and social practices of the time. Prescriptive texts advocating strict sex segregation did not fully describe reality, but jurisprudence was in practice a predominantly male enterprise. Women were not formally excluded from studying jurisprudence or attaining its highest ranks; some jurists even permitted, at least theoretically, women's appointment to judgeships. Within scholarly families, females might receive an education in jurisprudence, and some of these women taught students. (They did not, though, partake of the *riḥla,* the journey in search of knowledge that was de rigueur for most scholars of the time.) A few later female scholars became famous muftis, and their guidance was routinely sought. However, women are rarely cited as authorities for particular legal positions—Muḥammad's wife ʿĀʾisha is an exception—and none is recorded in these texts as the author of a work of jurisprudence. Women's voices in these legal texts are muted, though not uniformly silent.

Gendered patterns of segregation and female subordination not only marginalized women from the ranks of scholars but also shaped male jurists' doctrines. Leila Ahmed has argued that legal norms for marriage were colored by the "easy access" elite men had to female slaves, which led to a blurring of "the distinction between concubine, woman for sexual use, and object."[57] She links these shifts in "the ground of intersexual relationships" to the process whereby "it became the norm among the elites for men to own large harems of slave women."[58] One must not discount the influence of the sexual commodification of enslaved women on cultural production. Nonetheless, the practices of the courtly elite did not translate directly into law. First, harems were complex institutions, serving purposes other than the sexual gratification of rulers. Of the thousands of women in the early Abbasid caliph al-Mutawakkil's harem (estimates range from 4,000 to 12,000), only a small fraction were likely concubines.[59] Most would have been domestic drudges and personal servants, not only of the concubines but also of administrators, women of the family, young children, and so forth. A second consideration is that jurists were not truly part of the courtly elite with fabulous wealth and "large harems." Their experience of the sexual system was tempered both by their distance from the rock-star lifestyle of the caliph's court and by their consistent attempts to integrate theory and practice, text and life.

Slave ownership was not only for the filthy rich, though, and the jurists identified with slaveholders rather than with slaves. Some owned at least one enslaved concubine; both Shāfiʿī and Ibn Ḥanbal died leaving concubines who had borne them children *(umm walads)*.[60] One report declares that Mālik ibn Anas "purchased three hundred *sarārī* [concubines] and would spend one night a year with each of them."[61] Even if, as is likely, this report exaggerates, it makes clear that concubinage was a normal part of the sociosexual patterns of life in this era, as was domestic servitude more generally. Shāfiʿī—by no means a wealthy man—apparently had in his household two adolescent male slaves as well as an Andalusian wet nurse, who nursed the child born to his slave concubine. Stories about Mālik refer to a black female slave who answered knocks at his gate. In addition to illustrating the widespread nature of slaveholding, these anecdotes help us remember that their own status as slaveholders cannot help but have influenced the jurists' rulings. We can discern very little definitely about the ways that the women or slaves in male jurists' lives might have affected their scholarship beyond a few tantalizing hints in their texts.

Legal Norms and Social Practices

There was a complex, multilayered, and bidirectional relationship between the legal-discursive tradition and the social world. One must not "mistake medieval normative and legal texts for descriptive accounts of gender relations in medieval Islam."[62] Texts may unwittingly attest to social practices through their repeated condemnations of specific activities. For instance, a tirade by fourteenth-century Cairene scholar Ibn al-Ḥājj terming women's public presence a cause of social disorder inadvertently demonstrates women's persistence in appearing in public spaces.[63] Historian Amira Sonbol suggests that "the actual lives women led caused reactionary clergymen to interpret laws more conservatively. The 'looser' the women, the stricter the interpretation."[64] The norm of female seclusion was consistently subverted in practice.

But one cannot simply assume that texts merely presented a foil for resistance or that practice directly opposed doctrine. Legal writings, cautiously utilized, can serve as evidence for social history.[65] The prevalence of certain subjects in legal treatises sometimes reflects their actual importance and at other times is wildly disproportionate to their presence in real life. The focus on the validity of certain conditions in marriage contracts—such as those denying the husband the right to take additional concurrent wives—suggests that this was something brides routinely sought to negotiate. On the other hand, eunuchs and intersexed individuals occasioned a great deal of legal reflection but cannot have constituted more than a tiny minority of any population. Telling the difference between the two is sometimes a matter of guesswork, and sometimes can be backed up by other evidence, such as notarial manuals and court archives. Fatwas that include case particulars are more revealing than treatises; notarial manuals, which have a close connection to practice, are perhaps more useful still.[66] In evaluating specific cases mentioned in legal compendia, again one must assess whether they present historical fact or hypothetical cases.

My aim in this book is not to extract social history from prescriptive texts. I neither assess how closely these texts mirror real life nor speculate extensively about how actual behavior conformed to jurists' dictates. Rather, I try to explicate the jurists' surprisingly coherent vision of marriage and its gendered duties and, secondarily, explore the role of jurisprudential dispute in producing doctrinal development. Though the dominant ideology in the texts was contested in practice, understanding it remains beneficial. In fact, to the unknowable extent that the jurists' ideals went unrealized, the logical exigencies of the legal system—the things the jurists felt compelled to insist on even though they could not be enforced—are more sharply revealed. This book focuses on the jurists' conceptual worlds, using agreements and disagreements on marriage, divorce, and spousal rights to illuminate ideas about gender, ownership, and legal reasoning. How did legal rationales develop the way they did? What were the jurisprudential reasons as well as social assumptions behind the jurists' choices?

Understanding these discursive patterns poses challenges for readers today. As already noted, their authors shared unarticulated presuppositions unthinkable to many modern readers. Slavery, which they took for granted, is the clearest example, and I have already explained why it is inseparable from ideas about marriage. Less immediately obvious but perhaps even more significant are notions about property rights and bodily rights, individual freedoms, kinship structures, and systems of patronage. It is easier to point out what is obviously objectionable, such as some people's ownership of others or the apparent commodification of women's bodies, than to recognize the merely unfamiliar, such as the role of the family in marriage arrangements. Readers understandably focus on what is strange—noting unanimous juristic agreement on the right of the father to marry off his minor and/or virgin daughter without her permission—and bypass what was a highly significant reform in its own context: the insistence that a woman who had once been married could not be married off again without her spoken consent. Seeing through a modern lens, we risk overlooking the key issues that animated these legal discussions.

I have already noted two of the interrelated challenges that formative-period legal texts pose to modern readers. First, they are prescriptive rather than descriptive, with a complex relationship to the social contexts they reflect and address. Second, they assume certain things about men, women, and kinship that are no longer givens. A third challenging factor is their genre. These texts are addressed to an audience trained in a specific way of asking questions and interpreting answers. They use specialized terminology and rely on a wealth of assumed knowledge. Not only do they presume familiarity with religious source texts of the Qurʾan and hadith and specific legal doctrines and ideas, but they expect their audience to be conversant with broader ongoing legal discussions. Much remains unstated because it is obvious.

I will argue, moreover, that the rhythms or modes of argument characteristic of legal texts shaped the jurists' views. Conventions of legal argumentation led jurists to different conclusions from those of others equally steeped in the same scriptural and cultural milieu.[67] Legal thinkers were neither cut off from larger social patterns nor necessarily restricted to jurisprudential works in their intellectual output.[68] In works of poetry or scriptural exegesis, the same men might approach questions of marriage and gender quite differently. Jurisprudence is not merely an epiphenomenon of patriarchy. The law has a life and logic of its own. At some level, ideas are determinative of other ideas, or at least limited by the intellectual justifications that can be produced. The need to construct defensible arguments leads to a hardening of certain positions, including those denying the enforceability of certain wifely rights, such as those to sex.

We see this manifest directly in discussions of marriage and slavery. The critical conceptual links between marriage and slavery emerge from a core idea about sexuality and sexual licitness: licit sex was possible only when a man wielded exclusive control over a particular woman's sexual capacity. This view, implicitly shared at the outset of the formative period, was fuzzy with regard to female slaves and stronger with regard to free women. By the end of the formative period, among the legal thinkers discussed here, it was accepted that the same strictures would apply to slave sexuality. The jurists' comfort with the semantic overlap between marriage and slavery facilitated this process. Gail Labovitz, in a study of marriage in rabbinic thought, has proffered a model for understanding the relationship between wives, slaves, and other possessions.[69] Using the work of George Lakoff and Mark Johnson *(Metaphors We Live By)* as well as of Paul Ricoeur, she suggests that metaphor is a means of understanding, and indeed making, reality. In the case of the rabbinic treatment of marriage, the central metaphor is "women are ownable." But metaphor requires ambiguity: marriage "is" and "is not" ownership; both affirmation and negation are necessary to its function.

In the Muslim context, metaphor serves as a necessary backdrop for the central analogy between marriage and slavery and marriage and other forms of ownership. The analogy can function only because of the perception of an underlying similarity: if there was no way in which the wife was viewed as like a slave, it would not work. The fact that the comparison resonates unpleasantly to educated Muslim ears today suggests the extent to which the broader metaphorical ground has shifted. For the early jurists, however, analogies between marriage and slavery appear as if the parallels between these categories were "real or self-evident or in the nature of things."[70] From our vantage point, we see them instead as a "code specific to the praxis of [a] given social group," specifically, the jurists of premodern Muslim times.[71] A concern for descriptive efficiency, rather than a deliberate attempt at female subordination, helps explain frequent analogies between marriage and purchase or divorce and manumission.[72] But once analogies are in use, they are self-perpetuating. The continual approximation of wives and slaves, as well as husbands and masters, resulted in deeply entrenched ideas about male agency and female passivity in matters of marriage and sexuality.

Structure of the Book

The chapters of this book build a cumulative argument about jurisprudential understandings of marriage and slavery, men and women, and husbands and wives. It argues for understanding early Muslim legal texts as expressions of a technical discourse, bound by its own internal logic and need for systematization and consistency. The legal-methodological imperatives driving the production and defense of legal doctrine cannot be divorced from their end product: a hierarchical framework for marriage and sexuality that deals with competing pressures by allowing differences in women's legal personhood before and outside of marriage, but pressing for uniformity in the legal claims of wives. At the same time, an expansive vision of male marital privilege opens the rights and duties of husbands even to male slaves. Sexuality becomes the key realm for the construction of masculinity and femininity.

Chapter 1 addresses the basic parallel between contracting marriage and buying a slave. It discusses the extent of and limits on paternal and owners' power over the marriages of their charges and looks at the integration of slaves into an economy of kinship. Exploring varying legal views on women's legal personhood, it discusses women's capacity to contract marriage. The role of the ownership tie in establishing licit sexual access constitutes a major element of the conceptual relationship between marriage and slavery.

Chapter 2 treats interdependent claims established by marriage, focusing on the exchange of maintenance for sexual availability. It stresses the gender differentiation of marital rights and explores the differences introduced when a female slave is married. By looking at the way in which claims are divided between her husband and her master, it becomes possible to delineate with greater precision the core elements of the marital transaction.

Chapter 3 turns from the husband's rights to sex to the wife's rights to companionship. It investigates wives' claims on their husbands for sex and companionship, using jurists' discussions of a wife's right to an allotted portion of her husband's time. Both the division between wives and concubines and the crucial distinction between the wife's claims and the husband's claims are evident. I show how the jurists were trapped, to a certain extent, by their own insistence on logical consistency.

Chapter 4 looks at various modes of divorce, particularly the husband's unilateral right to repudiation, frequently analogized to manumission. With sustained attention to the establishment of consensus on the right of a male slave to alone wield the right of divorce over his wife, this chapter argues that the right to sever the marriage tie is essential to the jurists' vision of marriage—making a one-way right the basis for a two-person relationship.

Chapter 5 explores the parallels between marriage and slavery as forms of *milk,* utilizing the regulations surrounding the marriages of male and female slaves, as well as the institution of slave concubinage, to elucidate the rights of husbands and wives. It also returns to the subject of women taking male slaves as "concubines" to revisit the key idea of a man's exclusive dominion over a woman's sexuality as the basis for licitness in both marriage and slavery.

Note on Texts, Translation, and Transliteration

Recent scholarship has debated heatedly the authorship and chronology of particular works from the eighth and ninth centuries (the second and third *hijri* centuries). Scholars have argued over when texts such as the *Umm* and the *Mudawwana* came to exist in their current forms, who authored them, and when and how they circulated in oral and written form. Since I trace the lines of argument for certain doctrines, my conclusions must be regarded as provisional to the extent that they depend on assumptions about the chronology or authenticity of specific works. However, my main arguments about the structure of marriage and marital rights depend neither on the precise chronology of the texts nor on their attributions to particular individuals.[73]

Few Arabic legal texts have been translated into English or European languages. Of those used here, only the *Muwaṭṭaʾ Shaybānī* has had an adequate translation, which appeared after this book was substantially complete. Mālik's *Muwaṭṭaʾ* has had several full and partial nonscholarly translations, but none with sufficient attention to the nuances of the legal terminology. All translations from legal texts here are, therefore, my own unless otherwise noted. The notes provide book *(kitāb)* and chapter *(bāb)* titles so that those working with editions of the texts other than those I have cited will be able to locate the relevant passages.

Legal texts present special challenges for a translator. Islamic legal writings combine layers of allusion to scripture with technical legal terminology. My translations are usually as literal as possible, and I repeat key Arabic words frequently. Legal texts are also often brief and allusive rather than expository. Where necessary, extended clarifications appear in square brackets.

I follow a modified version of the transliteration system used by the *International Journal of Middle East Studies.* Terms that have passed into common English usage, such as *Qur'an, hadith, Sunni,* and *fatwa,* appear without diacritical marks or italics.

I have done my best to present these legal texts on their own terms and to assess their arguments accordingly. This book is engaged in thinking through what a group of scholars had to say. The jurists themselves closely scrutinized and criticized each other's works. I like to think they would not mind that I also engage with their claims and evidence, and attend closely to the ways in which they argue with each other.

1

Transacting Marriage

IN SEVENTH-CENTURY Arabia, a daughter was born to a Muslim named al-Musayyab ibn Najaba. He hastened to visit his cousin Quray'a bint Ḥibbān at her home to share the good news. Her innocuous reply—"May God bless you"—led Musayyab to an impetuous declaration: "I have married her to your son." Without hesitation, she responded: "I have accepted." The visit continued, but after a while Musayyab reconsidered his offer of marriage between his newborn daughter and his cousin's son, and he stated, "I was not serious; I was only joking." Quray'a, though, rejected his attempt to renege. "You offered marriage," she pointed out, "and I accepted." Unable to convince her to free him from his promise, Musayyab tried a new tack. Despite having originally viewed his cousin's consent as sufficient, he insisted that he would take the matter up with her husband, the father of the son whose marital fate was being arranged: "[It is] between me and 'Abd Allāh ibn Mas'ūd." Not long thereafter, Ibn Mas'ūd returned home and learned what had transpired in his absence. On ascertaining that Musayyab had really made the offer of marriage, Ibn Mas'ūd rejected his claim that a proposal made in jest could be withdrawn, repeating a prophetic dictum: "In marriage, seriousness and joking are the same, as in divorce seriousness and joking are the same."[1] When Musayyab remained unconvinced, Ibn Mas'ūd delivered the clincher: "Quray'a's word is valid, and she accepted."[2]

This story defending a woman's right to contract a valid marriage appears in the *Kitāb al-Ḥujja*, a ninth-century work whose full title translates as "The Book of Refutation of the People of Medina." It is attributed, with some debate, to Muḥammad al-Shaybānī, one of the two main disciples of eighth-century Iraqi jurist Abū Ḥanīfa. The *Ḥujja* defends Abū Ḥanīfa's views against his detractors, "the people of Medina," a group comprising that city's prestigious legal authorities, including Mālik ibn Anas. Abū Ḥanīfa held that women could contract marriages for their minor or enslaved charges, as agents for others, and on their own behalf. Other Sunni thinkers, including even Shaybānī elsewhere, hotly contested the notion that women could contract valid marriages. Rather, a woman had to be represented by her father or another marriage guardian *(walī)* drawn from her agnatic kin. Such was female incapacity that in the absence of a kinsman able or willing to act for her, a woman was obliged to seek out a public official, such as a judge, to act in her *walī*'s stead.

The incident with Musayyab's daughter and, more to the point, the way the *Ḥujja* draws upon it invite us into the prevailing culture of jurisprudential dispute. They also show how heated disagreements on specific points of law—here, an aspect of women's legal capacity—coexisted with crucial shared assumptions about marriage and kinship. A mother's guardianship was controversial, but neither the parties involved in the original incident nor the jurists whose views are explored in the *Ḥujja* question the legitimacy of marrying off infants. In examining the disputes we must not neglect the consensus over broader social arrangements. In texts that explore legal disputes, arguments often concerned issues that were relatively small compared to the universe of unspoken agreements. At the same time, seemingly minor disputes could hinge on major differences in jurisprudential methodologies.

This chapter treats consent to marriage and dower, areas around which formative-period Muslim authorities agreed and disagreed. I highlight assumptions about kin and household networks as well as about the legal personhood of free and enslaved males and females, both minors and majors. I discuss the marriage contract, considering who had the power to contract it and whose consent was necessary. Then, I turn to dower, the compensation due from a husband to a wife at marriage. I show significant points of agreement between the jurists and also their differences in method and approach. I argue for the significance of jurisprudential dispute to the formation and honing of doctrines and for the role of analogy—especially the linked analogies between wife and slave, and marriage and purchase—in shaping jurisprudence on marriage.

Consent and Coercion

Marriage was necessarily consensual. It required an agreement, expressed in terms of offer and acceptance, by the two contracting parties.[3] But these were not necessarily the bride and groom. Guardians and proxies abound in the legal sources, especially for brides. As with the case of Musayyab and his newborn daughter, the agreement of the spouses was not always required. Marriage was very much a family matter, and involvement of kin in arranging and concluding women's and girls' marriages was assumed. But parental—usually paternal—involvement was not limited to the marriage of daughters. Qurayʿa and Ibn Masʿūd's son was married off with no more say in the matter than Musayyab's daughter. In trying to weasel out of the impulsive marriage he had contracted for his daughter, it never occurred to Musayyab to challenge it on grounds that the infant groom could not give his consent. Rather, everyone agreed that fathers had the power of compulsion, *ijbār,* over children of both sexes. Yet the term *compulsion* gives a false impression of constraint; though occasionally the jurists discussed the permissibility of contracting such a marriage over a son or daughter's objections, for the most part minors were presumed too young to have any opinion.

Marrying off a minor child was not a Muslim innovation. It has parallels in other ancient legal systems and precedent in pre-Islamic Arabia, where parents might arrange marriages for their young children. Sometimes, as with Musayyab's daughter, both spouses were infants. At other times, one spouse was a child and the other an adult. The life of ʿĀʾisha, daughter of Abū Bakr and later wife of Muḥammad, reflects both practices. She was originally promised as a young child to a boy about her own age. That agreement was eventually dissolved by the two sets of parents—with apparent relief on the would-be groom's side, since ʿĀʾisha's family had converted to the new faith and they had not.[4] She was then, at age six or seven, married to the Prophet, though the marriage was not consummated for a few years. I will say more about this marriage shortly and return to it in the next chapter; for now, suffice it to note that it has since been invoked as precedent for topics ranging from when girls attain majority to whether compulsion of minors is permissible.

For free males, legal capacity was a simple matter: before majority they were subject to paternal compulsion; after it, they were not. As minors, they could not contract their own marriages; as majors, they could. (*Bulūgh*, majority, was usually constituted by puberty, normally menarche for a girl and first nocturnal emission for a boy, though other signs of physical maturation could be taken into account.) A father's right to marry off his minor sons was taken for granted, as was the cessation of this right when they attained majority. Any free male in his majority and of sound mind had free rein over his marital affairs, but the Muslim jurists did not think of this in terms of obtaining his consent. That would have implied assent to someone else's decision or actions, which was antithetical to their notion of the male agent. Instead, it is only with regard to enslaved males and females that serious discussion of consent, or lack thereof, occurs.

Even setting aside, for the moment, the argument in the *Ḥujja* over female capacity to contract marriage, free females' consent—that is, whether their consent was necessary in order for a valid marriage to be contracted for them—was a complicated subject. Virginity, not a consideration with regard to males or enslaved females, factored into decisions about compulsion of free females. The terms *thayyib* (previously married, non-virgin) and *bikr* (never married, virgin) are occasionally applied to males in connection with the application of more or less severe *ḥadd* punishments for illicit sex.[5] In connection with marriage, however, they are relevant only to females; for males, the key distinction is majority. Legal texts seldom discuss a female slave's virginity in the context of marriage, whether because of the presumption that she was unlikely to have remained a virgin until such time as she might be married off or because it was entirely irrelevant to her legal standing: she never had a say in her own marriage arrangements. For free females, both virginity and majority were of concern. Fathers could compel marriage of daughters who were both virgins and minors. On the flip side, those who were neither virgins nor minors could not be compelled but had to give their spoken assent to any proposed marriage. The intermediate categories—daughters who were either minors or virgins but not both—were the subject of disagreement. Never-married (and thus presumably virgin) daughters in their majority generated the most significant debate surrounding consent. Mālik and Shāfiʿī affirm the father's right to compel her, while Abū Ḥanīfa and his disciples reject it forcefully. I will turn to their rationales below.

The (marriageable) minor non-virgin appears seldom in these texts and is likely to have been rare in practice. A girl could be married then divorced or widowed before reaching majority since, as Chapter 2 shows, majority was not a criterion for consummation. Because it was theoretically possible, the jurists considered it. Mālik allowed the compulsion of a minor non-virgin while both Shāfiʿī and the Ḥanafīs rejected it, though for different reasons.

For Mālik, either virginity *or* minority allowed compulsion, so a minor non-virgin could be compelled.[6] A previous marriage, if unconsummated, did not remove a father's power of compulsion. A passage from the *Mudawwana* explores the limits of a father's authority over a previously married (but not minor) daughter: "[Saḥnūn] said: If a man marries off his virgin daughter and her husband divorces her or dies before consummating [the marriage] with her *(yabtanī bihā)*, may the father marry her off [again] as he would marry off a virgin according to Mālik? [Ibn al-Qāsim] said: Yes."[7] Because this marriage ended before consummation, the bride remained subject to paternal compulsion.[8] If the husband had consummated the marriage, however, "then she has more right to herself." A wife gains control of her own affairs *("malakat amrahā")* through consummation.[9]

Abū Ḥanīfa rejects compulsion at majority for all females, both virgin and non-virgin. Formative-period texts do not record his opinion or that of his major disciples on the case of the minor non-virgin, though later Ḥanafī texts explicitly state that majority is determinative: a *bāligh* female could not be coerced even if she was a virgin, but a minor could be, even if she was *thayyib.*[10] Shāfiʿī, though, objects not only to compelling the minor non-virgin into marriage but to marrying her off at all. A non-virgin could not be married off without her consent, and a minor could not give valid consent. Thus, a once-married minor could not be married again until she came of age.[11] One glimpses the particular preoccupations of the jurists in their treatment of this issue: Mālik's focus on paternal power, Abū Ḥanīfa's attention to female as well as male majority, and Shāfiʿī's concern for not voiding an individual's consent when that person has any characteristic requiring consent.

The disagreement over a virgin in her majority receives a great deal more attention. One hadith text takes center stage in the jurists' discussions of consent and compulsion. It declares that "a virgin is asked for her permission for herself, and the non-virgin has more right to herself *(aḥaqqu bi nafsihā)* than her marriage guardian." In exploring the jurists' use of this prophetic declaration as a proof text, it bears repeating that the question of bridal consent in marrying off virgin daughters generates dispute only when majority is brought into the equation: a father's power of compulsion over his virgin daughter is unquestioned so long as she is a minor. The application of the concept of majority to marriageable females competed with the categories of virgin and *thayyib* found in the hadith sources. The authorities mentioned in ʿAbd al-Razzāq's *Muṣannaf* under the heading "What is reprehensible in marriage and not permitted" touch on whether the father must consult virgins, non-virgins, or both; how their consent is expressed; and whether he can compel them over expressed objections.[12] Though several authorities ʿAbd al-Razzāq cites allowed the marriage of minors without consent, only two suggested that compulsion of *bāligh* virgins was permitted. Dozens took the view that a *bāligh* female, whether virgin or non-virgin, could not be married against her wishes.[13]

For Mālik and Shāfiʿī, the relevant issue was virginity, not minority. Unlike Abū Ḥanifa, they held the permission hadith to be compatible with paternal compulsion in marriage (though their interpretive strategies vary), even when the bride had arrived at her majority, so long as she remained virginal. Let us compare the treatment of this hadith in the *Muwaṭṭaʾ* and the *Mudawwana*. Where the permission hadith appeared in the *Muwaṭṭaʾ*, Mālik did not take it to mean that a father was bound to seek his virgin daughter's consent. Instead, the *Muwaṭṭaʾ* followed the hadith with an account of two companions who married off their virgin daughters without consulting them. Mālik affirmed that such contracts were binding and justified them as Medinan practice: "This is the way we do things."[14]

The *Muwaṭṭaʾ* here expresses a characteristic stance about the living example of the Medinan community: it constitutes an authoritative proof of correct practice. Rather than viewing the acts of ordinary Muslims as a potential competitor to the spoken transmission of Muḥammad's words and deeds, the customary practice of Medinans, passed down from many to many, is more reliably authentic than any individual hadith could be.[15] Thus, Mālik feels no need to reconcile these actions with the apparent sense of the Prophet's declaration that a virgin's permission must be sought. The *Mudawwana*, by contrast, prefaces these accounts with an explanation: when the Prophet ordered the marriage guardian to ask a virgin's permission to marry her off, he was referring only to a fatherless virgin girl *(al-bikr al-yatīma)*.[16] The term *walī*, "marriage guardian," was understood to exclude reference to fathers who served in this capacity.[17] In addition to repeating the anecdotes given in the *Muwaṭṭaʾ*, the *Mudawwana* presented further evidence of a father's right to marry off his daughters without their consent. It cites Ibn Wahb's report, ultimately depending on a narration from al-Ḥasan al-Baṣrī, that "the Messenger of God, may God's blessings and peace be upon him, married two of his daughters to ʿUthmān b. ʿAffān and did not consult them."[18] The *Mudawwana*'s provision of evidence and rationales, we may surmise, implicitly responds to competing Ḥanafī views; the assertion that such marriages were the practice in Medina was insufficient as a rebuttal, since Ḥanafī authorities did not recognize Medinan customary usage as a proof.

Both the *Mudawwana* and the *Umm* describe a father's power over his daughter in terms of her virginity rather than her age or maturity. The *Umm* characteristically seeks to reconcile the doctrine of compulsion with the seemingly obvious sense of the permission hadith.[19] As a first step, Shāfiʿī argues that exemplary Prophetic practice *(sunna)* granted a father the power of compulsion over his virgin daughters. Though the *Muwaṭṭaʾ* and *Mudawwana* presented anecdotes about Companions and the Prophet marrying off their daughters, the *Umm* focused on the Prophet's own marriage to ʿĀʾisha, concluded when she was six or seven (Shāfiʿī admits to uncertainty about her exact age) and consummated when she was nine.[20] In Shāfiʿī's view, she was still a minor when consummation occurred.[21] The binding nature of Muḥammad and ʿĀʾisha's union establishes fathers' power to contract binding marriages for their minor virgin daughters: "Abū Bakr's marrying ʿĀʾisha to the Prophet, may God's blessings and peace be upon him, when she was a girl of six and [the Prophet's] having sex with her when she was a girl of nine indicates that the father has more right over a virgin than she has over herself."[22]

This right of compulsion, Shāfiʿī claims, continues to apply when the daughter attains majority. Mālikī texts never explicitly argue that the father's power of compulsion continues, while the Ḥanafīs, discussed below, contend vigorously that it does not. Shāfiʿī directly enters the fray, explicitly engaging with the Ḥanafī view on majority, but insisting that the relevant categories are those of the Prophet, who distinguished between the virgin and the *thayyib* rather than between the minor and the *bāligh*. For him, there was no real difference between a minor and a *bāligh* female so long as she remained a virgin.[23] Shāfiʿī must then reconcile the potential contradiction between Muḥammad's reported speech (asking a virgin's permission) and his exemplary action (marrying someone whose permission was not sought). He does so by differentiating, as the legal theory he outlines in the *Risāla* calls for, between obligatory actions and recommended ones: the Prophet's "command to ask the virgin's permission for herself expresses a preference *(amr ikhtiyār),* not an obligation *(farḍ).* If it were the case that if she objected he could not marry her off, she would be like the non-virgin."[24] In his commentary on the *Ikhtilāf al-ʿIraqiyayn,* Shāfiʿī resolutely sides with Ibn Abī Laylā as to the validity of compulsory marriages by fathers: "he contracts the marriage for the *bāligh* virgin, and it is not rescinded even if she objects."[25] His logical rules dictate that he do so, especially where juridical disagreements are at stake and a dissenting view must be clearly articulated.

Nonetheless, in the *Umm,* where he has more scope to enlarge on his views, Shāfiʿī recommends strongly that daughters who have reached majority be consulted. He appeals to both ethical and pragmatic considerations in an attempt to modulate the exercise of patriarchal power.[26] Similarly, in Ḥanafī texts, the much later *Hidāya* suggests that though it is legally unnecessary, it is a sign of good breeding for a woman to use a *walī* to contract marriage on her behalf.[27] We might attribute the absence of this caveat from the formative-period sources to the fact that where they discuss women's agency in contracting marriage, they do so in arguments against others who hold divergent positions. Shared ideals about the nuances of good behavior are less salient in disputation than evidence and proof. When female capacity to contract marriage is not at issue, though, these same Ḥanafī texts frequently posit a male contracting marriage on behalf of a related female. It is impossible to ascertain what this indicates about customary practice, but it certainly demonstrates juristic comfort with the involvement of male kin.

Like Shāfiʿī's view in the *Ikhtilāf,* the Ḥanafī stance on noncompulsion of females in their majority appears already in tension with existing procompulsion views, primarily those of Mālikīs.[28] Once a male or female child matured, according to Abū Ḥanīfa, the father had to obtain consent for any marriage he wished to contract. A virgin daughter's arrival at *bulūgh* exempted her from forced marriage. Quoting the Prophet's words about consultation, Abū Ḥanīfa noted, "If she dislikes it *(in karihat)* the marriage is not permitted, because she has reached majority and taken control of her affair *(malakat amrahā)* and she is not coerced *(la tukrahu)* in [marriage]."[29] For Mālik, a woman took "control of her affair" after she had consummated a marriage, while for Abū Ḥanīfa her majority triggered this control.

The language with which the jurists addressed a female's control over her marriage merits attention. A female who cannot be compelled to marry is said to be *"aḥaqqu bi nafsihā,"* having more right to herself, or to have *"malakat amrahā,"* taken control of/owned her affair." In both cases what she has "more right to" or "controls" is her marital fate—the right to grant or withhold consent to a proposed match. And yet, as Gail Labovitz points out with regard to rabbinic discourse, "the fact that a woman who is becoming independent of male control is still linguistically and lexically subject to ownership, even if by her own self, is significant and telling. The moment at which a woman becomes a possessor, she does not entirely escape being the possessed."[30] We will see later that this language of rights and control plays out with slight variation in discussions of divorce.

Let us return to the *Kitāb al-Ḥujja* for another scenario. In this case, rather than a mother marrying off her infant son, here a father marries off his mature virgin daughter *(imra'a bikr)* "against her will *(wa hiya kāriha)*."[31] This unwilling bride complains to the Prophet, who separates her from her husband. Prophetic precedent shows that once a female reaches majority any marriage that takes place against her will is ineffective. Consent may be—as another hadith on ʿĀ'isha's authority avers—silent acquiescence, but spoken objections vitiate the marriage. The Ḥanafī divergence does not stop here. The *Ḥujja* also defends Abū Ḥanīfa's view that a *bāligh* female could contract her own marriage. Though Abū Ḥanīfa held females, like males, to be both free from compulsion at majority and capable of contracting marriage for themselves, he and his followers still considered it normal for a bride to be represented by a guardian from among her agnates.

The authority of kin, especially fathers, was critical for these thinkers. Paternal authority was not unique, but rather one instance of a broader phenomenon that encompassed other marriage guardians and slave owners. Mālik explicitly likens a father's power to that of a master: "No one may compel anyone to marry except the father in the case of his virgin daughter and his minor son, and [the master] in the case of his female slave and his male slave and the marriage guardian in the case of his fatherless ward *(yatīmihi)*."[32] Shāfiʿī similarly conjoins fathers and masters: "Any marriage guardian of a non-virgin or a virgin woman who marries her off without her permission, the marriage is void, except for the fathers of virgins and the masters of slaves *(mamālīk)*."[33] These statements do not equate children to slaves or paternal power to ownership so much as they frame all social relationships within hierarchical and patriarchal kinship structures.

Though most of the analogies under discussion here relate slavery to marriage, the "slaver/enslaved relationship"[34] is sometimes compared to a paternal/filial relation. The absence, probably inadvertent, of the word *master* in the *Mudawwana*'s discussion places the owner in a paternal relationship to his slaves: "the father in the case of . . . his female slave and his male slave." Just as a father may be like a master in the control he wields over his offspring's marital unions, a master is also something like a father: slaves are at least partially assimilated into an economy of kinship. Fluid and imprecise boundaries between kinship and ownership ties characterized other relationships in the Abbasid era, including those of clientage. As Paul Forand writes for that era, "one of the categories of symbolic thought in which the slave or freedman appears is that of offspring begotten by the master, their figurative father."[35]

Juxtaposing the control over marriage wielded by a father and that wielded by an owner can help us better understand the rules governing consent to marriage as well as the jurists' varying views on female legal capacity. First, though, we must make clear the crucial effect—at least theoretically—in the Muslim slave system of allowing slaves to marry, albeit with their masters' consent.[36] The ethos of sexual morality binding all believers, including slaves, was vital. A contrast to Roman marriage helps make the case more clearly. If "the purpose of Roman marriage was the production of legitimate citizen children,"[37] the purpose of Muslim marriage was licit sex. Roman marriage was limited to citizens or those who were granted "*ius conubii,* the right to contract a valid Roman marriage with Roman citizens."[38] For the Muslim jurists, procreation was an aim of marriage, to be sure, but neither licit sex nor legitimate offspring were limited to marriage. Concubinage—in a form quite different from its Roman practice—made sex lawful and legitimized any resultant children.

Muslim law allowed slaves of both sexes to marry with their owners' permission, and anecdotal evidence shows that they did. They could validly marry either other slaves or free persons, though never their own masters or mistresses. Men could have sexual access to their female slaves only as long as these slaves were unmarried. This attempt to impose sexual exclusivity for female slaves was rare in antiquity; in fact, to be a female slave was generally to have no claim to sexual exclusivity.[39] But for the Muslim jurists, slaves' liaisons fell under divine purview: marriage for slaves was a way of ensuring that they did not transgress the boundaries of moral conduct set forth by God. Allowing slaves to marry, however, risked jeopardizing their owners' authority and prerogatives to use their labor and oversee their movements. Owners' control was reaffirmed through regulating the formation and dissolution of marriages and by insisting on the rights of masters to control slaves' labor regardless of marital status.

In keeping with the integration of slavery into a hierarchical framework of kin relations, the supervisory role played by agnatic kin in marriages of free persons (especially females) was played by enslaved people's owners. Owners' scope of authority differed, like that of parents, depending on the slaves' characteristics. As with rules governing marriages of free people, regulations for slave marriage varied by gender and, in some cases, age. Slavery and femaleness were both legal disabilities. Merged in the person of the female slave, they aggravated one another; the disability could be mitigated by maleness in the case of the former or freedom in the case of the latter.

For free males, majority determined their scope for legal action in marriage, but majority might or might not make a difference for enslaved males. The nonconsensual marriage of minor male slaves, like minor sons, was universally accepted, though seldom discussed and presumably rare. A master would gain little by marrying his male slave off before maturity, whereas marrying off a female slave would give him the right to the dower thereby garnered, as well as ownership of any offspring she bore to her husband. Could an adult male slave be compelled to marry? On this point, jurists disagreed. An adult slave's maleness, which would have given him full and sole control over his marital destiny if he were free, stood in tension with his status as a slave. Mālik and his followers allowed an owner to marry off his male slave without the slave's consent; in this matter, slave men were like female slaves, virgin daughters, and minor sons.[40] Enslavement either feminized or infantilized the male with regard to consent. Formative-period Ḥanafī texts do not discuss explicitly whether male slaves could be married off without their consent, and later texts are split, though the dominant view favors compulsion.[41] Both Ḥanafī and Mālikī authorities held that though the owner's permission was required for the valid marriage of a male slave just as for a female slave, if a male slave married before obtaining permission, his master could either dissolve the marriage or authorize it after the fact.[42]

Shāfiʿī—concerned, as with the minor non-virgin, with making sure every legal claim was respected—diverged on both points. He disallowed the master's after-the-fact ratification of a slave's marriage. But not only was the master's permission vital for a valid contract, so was the slave's explicit consent: the contract was null if either had not consented in advance.[43] Gender interacted with enslavement to define a male slave's agency for Shāfiʿī. As a slave, he could not marry without his master's permission, but as a man, he could not be compelled to marry. A certain irreducible masculinity prevented an adult male slave from losing the right to sexual self-determination for Shāfiʿī; he explicitly contrasts the male slave with a female slave, who was perpetually subject to coercion.

In contrast to the male slave and the free female, sexual and marital self-determination was never available to an enslaved female. Her master's right of possession granted him licit sexual access to her, and if he married her off that right passed to her husband.[44] Occasional passages suggest that certain enslaved women had forceful opinions on the selection of their husbands. Ḥanafī authorities even countenance after-the-fact ratification of a slave woman's marriage.[45] The ultimate decision, however, rested with her master: as a matter of law, a female slave had no choice, regardless of whether she was in her majority or had been previously married. In contrast to free women, female slaves' virginity is seldom discussed in connection with their marriages, and where it does appear, its irrelevance is clear: "He may marry off his female slave without her permission whether she is a virgin or a non-virgin."[46]

The transition from virgin to *thayyib,* legally irrelevant in matters of marriage for female slaves and all males, was momentous for free females. *Thayyib* free women past the age of majority had to give their spoken assent to any marriage contracted on their behalf.[47] Sexual experience gave the bride a voice, as al-Shaybānī notes: "A virgin's permission is her silence, but a non-virgin's consent is spoken [*bi lisānihā*]."[48] The bride's speech acts not merely as token acquiescence but might potentially reflect a take-charge attitude: Ibn al-Qāsim states in the *Mudawwana,* in response to Saḥnūn's query as to whether silence on the part of a *thayyib* constitutes assent, "No, rather she must speak and delegate her *walī* to marry her off."[49]

The paradigmatic case for this type of female consent is that of Khansāʾ bint Khidhām. Having been previously married, Khansāʾ objected to a marriage concluded for her by her father. According to the *Muwaṭṭaʾ*'s account, "She went to the Messenger of God, may God's blessings and peace be upon him, and he rescinded the marriage."[50] Mālikī and Shāfiʿī texts cite her case as proof that a man loses the power to compel his daughter's marriage once she is a *thayyib.* Ḥanafī authorities stretch the lesson of Khansāʾ's case further, concluding that *any* woman who has reached majority escapes her father's power of compulsion. Muḥammad al-Shaybānī follows Khansāʾ's case in the *Muwaṭṭaʾ Shaybānī* with the declaration that "[neither] the non-virgin nor the virgin if she has reached majority should be married off except with her permission"; this is the case "whether her father or someone else is marrying her off."[51] Though she need not consent verbally, a mature virgin's implicit assent through silence is required. If a mature virgin expresses opposition, she cannot be considered to have consented to the marriage. The *Kitāb al-Ḥujja* recounts further instances in which a *bāligh* virgin was married off "without her consent *(bi ghayri riḍāhā)*"[52] or "against her will *(kāriha).*"[53] In each case, the Prophet revokes the marriage or declares it null.

Abū Ḥanīfa takes his view about females in their majority further still. Like his teacher Jaʿfar al-Ṣādiq, he holds that women can conclude marriage contracts. In Khansāʾ's case, as retold in the *Kitāb al-Ḥujja,* the Prophet separated her from the man to whom she did not wish to be married and "commanded her to marry" the man she wanted to marry. Abū Ḥanīfa interprets the prophetic grammatical imperatives to include the actual conclusion of the marriage contract.[54] (*"Jaʿala ilayhā ʿuqdat al-nikāḥ."*) Later Ḥanafī texts point to the use of the active verb form in Q. 2:232 to describe women "marrying" spouses as evidence for their position.[55] The *Ḥujja* restricts itself to sunna evidence, suggesting that Qurʾanic grammatical arguments about women's legal agency had not yet become part of the debates on this topic.

Though he departs from the view of the other jurists in ruling that women may conclude marriage contracts, Abū Ḥanīfa assumes, like his contemporaries, that families have a special stake in the marriage arrangements of their female members and that women should not marry beneath themselves. He permits women to contract their own marriages, though with restrictions that do not apply to men. For Abū Ḥanīfa, a woman must marry a man who is at least her social equal *(kufʾ)*. Though various criteria for suitability are given, the text notes pragmatically that "he is not an equal for her in any way if he cannot find the means for her dower or maintenance."[56] Indeed, the bride must specify the full dower appropriate to a woman of her family, status, and, where relevant, personal qualities. "If she selects a suitable match and does not settle for a reduced dower," Abū Ḥanīfa declares, "then the marriage is allowed."[57] Abū Ḥanīfa appeals to a statement attributed to the caliph ʿUmar ibn al-Khaṭṭāb: "A woman is not married except with the permission of her marriage guardian, someone of her family with sound judgment, or the constituted authority *(al-sulṭān)*."[58] If the marriage she contracts meets these criteria, she could herself be considered a "member of her family with sound judgment."[59] If it does not, her marriage guardian could challenge the marriage. Mona Siddiqui has suggested that the cosmopolitan and stratified society of Iraq was influential in the development of the Ḥanafī concept of suitability *(kafāʾa)*, which has a more prominent place than in the jurisprudence of more egalitarian Medina.[60] Reflection also suggests a legal rationale: granting women the power to contract marriage without the involvement of a guardian raises the need for a more extensive check than would be the case under Mālik's or Shāfiʿī's view, where no marriage can be contracted except through a guardian.[61]

Women's capacity to conclude marriage contracts divided the Ḥanafī authorities. The *Kitāb al-Ḥujja* defends Abū Ḥanīfa's view without dissent; in the *Muwaṭṭaʾ Shaybānī*, though, Shaybānī reports Abū Ḥanīfa's view but sides with Mālik, declaring, "There is no marriage without a marriage guardian."[62] A prophetic statement affirming that "if a woman marries without a marriage guardian, her marriage is void, her marriage is void, her marriage is void" serves as proof here, as similar statements do in Mālikī and Shāfiʿī texts. Many versions of this sentiment are found in the *Muṣannaf*s as well, though they do not appear in Ḥanafī texts apart from Shaybānī's *Muwaṭṭaʾ*. Thus, the Prophet's words about the non-virgin having "more right to herself" meant only that she could withhold her consent for any marriage and not be coerced, al-Shaybānī says, not that she could contract a marriage independently.[63]

At stake in all of these arguments is a basic question of female capacity, or rather incapacity. For the majority of these thinkers, a previously married woman might take a more direct role in the selection of potential grooms, perhaps "delegat[ing] to her marriage guardian,"[64] but she still required his permission to marry and he had to conclude the contract for her. If he was unwilling to do so despite the groom's suitability, a woman could seek intervention from a public authority or, perhaps, bypass a father's authority by having another (male) agnatic relative such as a brother marry her off—with her consent, of course.[65] Some Medinan authorities were willing to fudge the guardian issue in the case of "lowly" women, retroactively authorizing publicly celebrated marriages.[66] Shāfiʿī jurists objected; all marriages must have guardians, regardless of the economic and social status of the parties involved.[67] This is, in a way, an egalitarian stance. But if social class is irrelevant here for Shāfiʿī, gender is not: maleness is a prerequisite for contracting a marriage. As Shāfiʿī puts it, a woman "does not conclude a marriage contract *(lā taʿqidu ʿaqd al-nikāḥ)*"—or, more poetically, "does not tie the marriage knot."[68] In other words, a woman is bound by a tie she can neither establish nor sever of her own accord: she is tied up in the marriage in a way that her husband is not.

The case of female owners and their female slaves can help us see what is at stake in women's (in)ability to contract marriage as well as how marriage was different from other transactions. Free women in their majority could own and manage assets *(māl)*, just as free men could. A wife's legal personality was not subsumed by her husband's. Control over property was independent of marital status for women just like it was for men, except that Mālikī jurists granted a husband the right to oversee certain of his wife's transactions.[69] Cristina de la Puente argues that, in addition to the requirement for the husband's "express consent" to be given for certain acts, the husband's right to forbid his wife from leaving the home also amounts to an indirect restriction on her legal capacity.[70] But, in formal terms, marriage did not generally interfere with a woman's legal capacity to own, buy, sell, or manage property. Substantial evidence for economic activity by Muslim women of all social classes and marital statuses attests to the importance of these rules in practice, but my concern here is with the jurists' treatment of these rights.

The property over which women wielded control included both male and female slaves for whose marriages a free woman's consent was required. (Being married was a "defect" that could reduce the slave's commercial value, as the owner had to accommodate the slave's marital rights.) None denied the female owner's proprietary interest even as they disagreed over the scope of her powers over her slaves' marriages.[71] But could a woman marry off her own female slaves? The jurists' answers to this question show three distinct approaches to women's legal capacity and the nature of marriage as a contract and also illustrate the give-and-take process through which doctrines were refined. Mālik and his followers held that female owners had to appoint or delegate someone to contract the actual marriage. The agent had to be male, adult, Muslim, and not subject to restrictions on his legal capacity. Agnatic kinship was not required—that is to say, the agent need not be eligible to be the woman's own marriage guardian. In contrast, Abū Ḥanīfa believed that "there is no harm in a woman marrying off her female slave *(amatahā)* or her male slave *(ʿabdahā)*."[72] Because it was her consent as owner that was necessary, there is no point in making her delegate the actual contracting to a male. Shāfiʿī insists that both of these positions were flawed. He concurs with the Ḥanafī critique of Mālik's doctrine: "If she is not the slave girl's marriage guardian, no one can be a marriage guardian on her [i.e., the slave-owner's] account."[73] Delegation is a flimsy end run around the issue of female capacity to contract marriage. Shāfiʿī finds Abū Ḥanīfa's solution equally unpalatable. To avoid the pitfalls inherent in both opposing positions, Shāfiʿī declares that a female slave must be married off by her female owner's own marriage guardian. This effectively renders the slave woman's sexuality an extension of her owner's sexual capacity; it must be subject to the control of a responsible male, and not just any responsible male. If this guardian is unavailable or unwilling, the role defaults to the constituted public authority, as in the owner's own marriage.[74]

Jennifer Glancy, discussing Roman slavery, notes that slave bodies can serve as surrogates for their owners.[75] Here, in a sense, the female slave owner serves as a kind of body double for her slave. It is neither that her own status is reduced to that of slave, nor that the slave's status is elevated to hers. The simplest explanation is that when it comes to marriage, femaleness trumps other legal considerations. But the identification of the slave with her mistress is intriguing. Shāfiʿī does not, to my knowledge, address the parallel case of a woman marrying off her male slave. Must the owner's own guardian marry him off too? That one cannot formulate a model that answers this precisely points to some of the difficulties of women owning other persons but not having the capacity to conclude transactions that result in sexual legitimation.

Shāfiʿī's rationale for prohibiting a female owner from delegating the contracting of her female slave's marriage boils down to an unspoken difference between marriage and other contracts. Delegation itself posed no problem. A male slave owner, he says, could delegate the contracting of his slaves' marriage, "except that he may not appoint a woman as an agent," or a slave, a minor, someone who was not completely free, who was under interdiction,[76] or who had lost his reason, "because such people cannot be marriage guardians under any circumstances."[77] This list likens a free woman to individuals with restricted legal capacity, including unfree persons who cannot own property at all under Shāfiʿī doctrine and others who, because of interdiction, loss of rationality, or minority status, are temporarily unable to conclude any property transactions.[78] Neither the restriction on ownership nor that on making contracts normally applies to a free woman, but when marriage enters the equation, the female owner's legal capacity shrinks. Marriage of slaves thus poses a dilemma for Shāfiʿī. Otherwise at pains to insist on the inalienability of female property rights regardless of agnatic authority over female bodies, here Shāfiʿī restricts them in the same way he restricts women's ability to marry themselves off. In this instance, property rights and control over bodies intersect. He restricts a woman's property rights over her enslaved female in order to remove her possible role in any transfer of sexual rights. (Interestingly, she could sell her unmarried female slave to a man, and sexual rights would belong to the new master. One explanation for this potential contradiction is that these rights are somehow in abeyance when the owner is female. The slave woman's sexuality is not actually under the owner's control, precisely; the woman cannot use it herself nor does she really have dominion over it. She can sell it, but she is selling a potential along with the actual ownership of the slave. This is symbolized in the lack of *istibrāʾ*, a one-menstrual-period ban on sex with a newly purchased slave woman to make sure she is not pregnant, if sold by a trustworthy woman.)

For Shāfiʿī—though not for Abū Ḥanīfa—marriage is fundamentally distinct from the transactions involving purely commercial property that women were free to conclude, because marriage chiefly functioned to establish the sexual lawfulness of a woman who would otherwise be forbidden. The broader scope for involvement of women in their own marriages and that of others in Ḥanafī doctrine was not limited to contracting it, but also to witnessing it. Ḥanafī authorities allowed women as witnesses to marriage (albeit at a two-to-one ratio, as with sales, and only so long as one man was present), suggesting a view of marriage as similar to (other) property transactions. Others treated marriage as being unlike sales but rather like areas where women's testimony was uniformly forbidden, where God's claims were at stake, as with transgressions involving prescribed *(ḥadd)* punishments.[79] Marriage was intimately bound up not only with transfers of money but also with potentially dangerous sexual rights.

Those who believed that a woman could not conclude a marriage contract on her own behalf or for someone else linked this incapacity to the woman's inability to convey licit sexual access to herself or another woman through marriage. According to the *Mukhtaṣar* of al-Muzanī, "The [woman's] sexual organ is forbidden *(al-farj muḥarram)* before the contract and it is never made lawful except that the marriage guardian says 'I have married her to you.' "[80] The *Mudawwana* phrases its concern differently; a woman's marriage is valid only when concluded by her marriage guardian because the marriage guardian has a "share" in, or authority over, her *buḍʿ* (vulva, also the initiation of her marriage) and thus has an interest in seeing it properly transferred to a fit spouse.[81] He must prevent her from "marrying someone whose lineage *(nasab)* is deficient in comparison to her lineage."[82] Mālik's half-measure in the case of a female slave perhaps recognizes that lineage is not a concern in her case; this may parallel the relative unimportance of marriage guardians for "lowly" women. Despite their differences, then, all accepted a kin-based patriarchal system that invested free women's agnates with significant control over their bodies. Indeed, though his view on women's ability to conclude marriage contracts differed, Abū Ḥanīfa's shared concern for lineage was reflected in his opinion that a woman's marriage guardian could have her marriage annulled if she married beneath her station.

Gender was, then, the most enduring aspect of legal personality. Both slavery and minority were legal disabilities of a sort, as was—in a different respect—being non-Muslim. However, only femaleness permanently limited a person's legal capacity. A slave might be manumitted, a non-Muslim could convert, a child would reach maturity. A woman, however, would remain female, with the "whiff of disability" attached to her legal capacity.[83] In many respects, Muslim women were less constrained legally than their other near-Eastern counterparts, and certainly less than their later European sisters. Even though sweeping statements about premodern European women's low legal status have been substantially qualified or outright contradicted by archival research, the fully independent legal personality enjoyed by married Muslim women stands out as unusual, historically. With regard to the management of property in particular, despite the lingering restrictions under Mālikī thought, women retained capacity for many types of transactions. Marriage, however, was not one of them.

Gail Labovitz has pointed out that under Jewish law women, minors, and slaves had a different "relationship to commandedness" with regard to religious obligations.[84] She writes that "women and slaves are differentiated from children—and associated with each other—by their shared, paradoxical status as adults with conscious control over their activities who are nonetheless excluded from full religious participation."[85] The nexus differs somewhat in Muslim thought with regard to religious obligations: husbands and masters must allow the fulfillment of obligatory devotions precisely because wives and slaves, if Muslim, are required to fulfill them. On the other hand, they are allowed to prohibit supererogatory acts of worship if they might interfere with the performance of duties. Interestingly, no one ever seems to ask whether a parent can forbid a child from performing acts of worship: discussion centers on the parental obligation to teach children appropriately so that they are both capable of and willing to fulfill their obligations, especially prayer, once they reach the appropriate age.

Early Christian thinkers discussing maleness make a different connection between slavery and minority. Though in some respects slaves were treated like minors, Glancy notes that a minor "expects that he will eventually attain the status of manhood, but the slave does not." In first-century "Greco-Roman systems of gender" "the slave could not grow into the full status of a man." Because of his "subordinate status" he could not claim "the position or the prerogatives of manhood."[86] A comparison with Muslim law illustrates significant commonalities but also crucial differences. A male slave was most like a minor in the exercise of property rights (though minors could not transact property but could own it), and least like one in connection with marriage. The most characteristic element of enslavement—the inability to truly own property—was not, in the Islamic understanding, gendered. Because free women as well as free men have the legal capacity to own and transact movable and immovable property of virtually all types, property ownership never became a distinguishing criterion of manliness.

The enslaved male was infantilized insofar as his master controlled his marriage—at a minimum having to grant permission, and at a maximum being able to force a marriage over the slave's objections, as a father could with his minor sons. But, as later chapters will show, once he became a husband, he gained the full "prerogatives of manhood," which were not coextensive with those of freedom. Glancy notes that for the apostle Paul's first-century audience, the "sexual vulnerability of the slave" would have been assumed: "A slave's inability to master the borders of his own body was a corollary of his subordinate status and his permanent exclusion from the category of manhood into which the heir would grow."[87] Muslim jurists, by contrast, soundly insisted on the male slave's status as sexual agent, not sexual object. Despite abundant historical and literary evidence for the sexual use of male slaves in courtly and other contexts, early legal discourse firmly distinguished enslaved men from enslaved women—and indeed all women—through granting to them uniquely masculine prerogatives.

Dower

Bodies and sexual rights were not the only things transacted in marriage; money figured too. As in most societies through history, marriage transferred wealth. Dower—*mahr* or *ṣadāq*—was the primary male obligation resulting from marriage. Wealth given from the groom to the bride became legally her sole property, unless she was enslaved, in which case it belonged to her master.[88] Dower has historically served as an important source of economic capital for women, as well as a bargaining chip in negotiations with spouses and kin. The practical patterns of financial transactions associated with marriage did not always conform precisely to legal norms governing dower, in which the payment from groom to bride was the single necessary monetary transfer associated with marriage. Yossef Rapoport and Amalia Zomeño have shown that in both early Egypt and later Andalusia, reciprocal wealth transfers from the bride's family to the new household in the form of trousseaux were the norm.[89] Further, Rapoport has shown that early jurists opposed the deferral of part or all of the dower to death or divorce, although they eventually capitulated to this common practice.[90] Precisely because their doctrines did not merely replicate practice, the jurists' preoccupations with dower allow us see it as a key part of the logical system of marital rights. Early legal authorities said little about its practicalities. They were concerned instead with dower's role in legitimizing sexual intercourse and justifying *milk*. Beyond the social function of dower in marriage, a strong link is established in legal thought between financial compensation and sexual legitimacy, making clear connections between bodily and financial claims.

Discussions of dower depended on and furthered the conceptual relationship between marriage and sale. Juristic disagreement existed over whether a marriage could be contracted using terms for transferring ownership, giving a gift, purchasing, or selling. Mālik and Abū Ḥanīfa validated some or all of these figurative expressions. Shāfiʿī, though, allowed only the use of terms relating to *nikāḥ* or *tazwīj*. The latter, "espousal," has forms that relate both to marrying and to causing someone else to be married. The former, whose literal meaning is intercourse, takes on the legal meaning of a contracted marriage. (There is no parallel here to the "acquisition" of a woman through intercourse found in rabbinic literature; though a claim that the parties *thought* they were married can divert the punishment for illicit sex, such a claim can never establish a marriage without the proper offer and acceptance.)

Whether the terminology of sales can validly contract a marriage or not, the vocabulary of sale or purchase was already used metaphorically for other relationships, including those between human beings and the divine. A late nineteenth-century essay by Charles Torrey points out that "the theological terminology of the Koran contains a number of words which are primarily used to express some commercial relation."[91] Such usage neither trivializes nor concretizes the human-divine relationship. For instance, God is said to buy human souls, but no one understands this as a literal purchase. Likewise, the language of slavery is also applied to the human-divine relationship. The word for a male slave, *ʿabd*, also means a male worshipper: human beings are God's slaves. Indeed, in the profession of faith, Muslims bear witness that Muḥammad is God's *ʿabd* and messenger. Servitude of this form carries positive value. Yet to be enslaved to another human being is to be abased. When a wife is compared to a slave, or the marriage contract analogized to purchase, questions emerge about which connotations are most apt.

The jurists employ overlapping linguistic, conceptual, and legal parallels between marriage, slavery, and ownership. The contracting and dissolving of a marriage gave rise to the clearest parallels between matrimony and slavery or purchase. The centrality of *milk* (ownership, control, dominion) emerges as the tie joining the two parties is established or dissolved. These parallels "between the condition of servility and the condition of marriage in Islam" center on the sexual claims established by the marriage contract. In the words of John Ralph Willis, "A comparison is drawn between the dominion imposed by the husband through which his wife is caused to surrender her sexual self, and the sovereignty established by the master whereby the slave is compelled to alienate his right to dispose." Willis notes that marriage is "likened to a sale": "it is said that in the market the master buys his slave, whereas in marriage, the husband purchases his wife's productive part."[92] Yet the fact that the wife does not lose her "right to dispose"—that is, her control over property—distinguishes the transactions even as it highlights the sexual character of the ownership conveyed through marriage. More obvious even than parallels between marriage and purchase of a slave are jurists' frequent analogies between unilateral divorce *(ṭalāq)* and manumission.[93] Marriage, Willis says, enslaves a "woman's sexual self"[94] through the dower, as a slave comes to be owned through purchase; repudiation frees her just as manumission frees the slave

Despite these formal similarities, other scholars have focused on critical discontinuities between marriage and sale to argue that marriage is *not really* a sale and the wife is *not really* owned. Using Transoxanian Ḥanafī texts from the tenth through the twelfth centuries, Baber Johansen presents the most cogent defense of this position. Marriage, he argues, is a social rather than a commercial transaction.[95] In commerce *(tijāra)*, property *(māl)* is exchanged for property. In "social exchange," a symbolic status or relation is transferred in exchange for property. In the marriage contract, "an article of commerce"—that is, the dower—"serves as a means to acquire a social relation or a social status."[96] A wife, Johansen argues, grants certain rights in exchange for the dower she receives, meaning marriage cannot be understood as a commercial exchange. Most saliently, the husband does not, by paying dower, come to own his wife: he cannot sell her to someone else. But against Johansen we may note that the inability to alienate something is not, by itself, dispositive: Islamic law forbids masters to sell certain slaves (including female slaves who have borne them children) and landowners to dispose freely of certain real estate; the slaves and the land are, nevertheless, property in a very real sense.

The vexed question of marriage and ownership is not unique to Muslim legal sources. The question of whether—and to what extent—wives are property in rabbinic tradition has received a great deal of scholarly attention, most famously in Judith Romney-Wegner's *Chattel or Person?* as well as in numerous responses to her arguments. Labovitz, who surveys this literature, has argued that the "very direct and specific question: are women property in the rabbinic system of marriage?" is unanswerable as formulated.[97] Instead, she suggests that exploring the metaphors associated with acquisition ("the central model by which the rabbis construct their system of marriage and gender relations") and ownership provides a better way to think about rabbinic understandings of women and marriage.[98] She writes, "The metaphor of marriage as ownership and women as ownable is present and critically significant for the construction of gender and gender roles throughout the strata of rabbinic literature."[99]

Although a series of overlapping metaphorical associations between women, slaves, and (other) property characterizes Muslim legal discourse as well, the central presence of enslaved women alters the dynamic: we move beyond metaphor to analogy. Johansen's analysis, persuasive in key respects, fails to account for the way that the actual commodification of slave women's bodies prevents any simple bifurcation of commercial and social exchange in both concubinage and the marriage of enslaved women, who are both wives and property, albeit of different men. Marriage and slavery require tandem analysis. A "pervasive process of simultaneous assimilation and distinction"[100] between women and slaves, as well as between marriage and concubinage, structures legal discourse.

The frequent resort to analogy facilitates and furthers the association between marrying a wife and purchasing a female slave. Early controversies over the use of analogical reasoning aside, analogy became one of four basic sources of Sunni jurisprudence. The others are Qur'an and sunna, the two textual sources of the law, and consensus. Although consensus came to serve a key legitimating function, it did not play a prominent role for the early jurists. Analogy, however, filled a significant need. Many situations were not directly addressed by revelation or prophetic precedent. By allowing the extension of a ruling from one case to another via a shared underlying rationale *('illa, ratio legis)*, analogy extended the jurists' reach far beyond the texts while allowing them to conceptualize their project as applying revelation to life.

An analogy requires an essential similarity that allows for comparison, but it also requires difference: if things were actually the same, analogy would be unnecessary, as there would be *identity*. In this respect, analogy is much like metaphor. But the legal domain of analogy requires a more precise mapping of one decision onto another, often to the exclusion of other possible "targets." The fact that things are analogous in some respects does not mean that they are so in every respect. An example from the realm of divorce can clarify this. In a Ḥanafī discussion of a wife's option of divorce, beginning or resuming travel causes her to lose her right to choose. The jurists affirm, in their discussion of various modes of travel, that "a boat is like a house."[101] That is, the forward motion of the boat does not constitute a deliberate progression on the woman's part that implies a rejection of her choice.

To take this analogy to mean that a boat *is* a house or that all the regulations applying to houses also apply to boats would be ludicrous.

With marriage and sales, the question of how far the analogy stretches is trickier, in part because of the jurists' consistent recourse to comparisons. Despite the likening of marriage to purchase and a wife to a concubine, a wife was not—and could by definition never be—her husband's slave. Not only was she due marital rights far beyond those due to enslaved persons from their owners, though different from and lesser than those granted to her husband, but the two types of *milk* could not be combined. (This will be addressed further in Chapter 5.) Yet marriage and slavery both made a woman sexually lawful. Of particular significance is payment associated with a husband or master's dominion. Both dower and the purchase price of a female slave compensate for exclusive licit access to and control over a particular woman's sexual capacity. The obligation to pay dower correlates to sexual lawfulness in marriage, just as the purchase of a slave conveys sexual lawfulness—provided that other necessary criteria, such as proper consent and the absence of impediments, are also fulfilled.

Given the ubiquity of commercial terminology and the notion of sale as the paradigmatic transaction, comparisons between dower and price were practically inevitable. An outline of the basic rules governing dower will help clarify the underpinnings as well as the limits of legal parallel between dower and a purchase price. The jurists accepted a crucial distinction: marriage contracted for an unspecified dower was valid, whereas sale contracted without a fixed price was void. Nonetheless, they drew heavily on the regulations established for sales (especially of female slaves) to remedy this and other irregularities with dowers. In the frequent analogies made between marriage of a woman and purchase of a slave, the jurists likened the wife to a slave, the husband to the master, and the dower to the purchase price.

In one scenario reported in the *Mudawwana*, a man sends a representative to marry him to a woman for a dower of 1,000 dirhams. The representative dutifully contracts the marriage, but for twice that amount. Saḥnūn asks Ibn al-Qāsim whether in Mālik's view the husband owes the entire 2,000 dirhams.[102] Ibn al-Qāsim answers, in accordance with Mālik's logic, that the husband must pay the entire amount if he consummated the marriage despite knowing that his representative had set a higher dower. To justify his view, he makes a comparison to the purchase of a female slave. "Can you not see," he presses, "that if a man ordered [another] man to purchase so-and-so's slave girl for him for 1,000 dirhams, and [the representative] bought her for him for 2,000, and he knew [that his representative had paid 2,000] and he took her and had sex with her and had privacy with her, then he did not want to pay anything except the 1,000 for her, he could not do that?"[103] Ibn al-Qāsim clearly expects his questioner to accept his logic in the case of the female slave. He assumes that once the rule has been clarified for the purchase of a slave, its application to marriage will be self-evident. Al-Muzanī applies the same principle in reverse in his *Mukhtaṣar,* quoting a verdict in the case of marriage, which "indicates that" the same rule applies to the purchase of a female slave.[104]

Dower was both like and unlike (other) prices and, by extension, marriage was and was not like (other) commercial transactions. In an ideal scenario, a bride received a dower of a specific item or amount, agreed on in advance, of value equal to or greater than her fair dower *(mahr al-mithl),* which was calculated with reference to her female relatives as well as the standards of her premarital place of residence, and adjusted upward or downward to account for her personal qualities, such as beauty, virginity, and wealth. As usual, though, the legal texts deal mostly with departures from the ideal.

Three scenarios follow in which some legal flaw with the dower required remedy—the parties failed to specify a dower, the dower was set below the bride's fair dower, or the fixed dower was invalid. The varying treatments of these irregularities reveal hermeneutical strategies and assumptions, the limits of parallels between marriage and slavery, and the crucial connection between money and *milk* over the marriage tie.

The first type of irregularity—the lack of a fixed amount—presents the clearest contrast between marriage and sale. Failure to specify a dower at the time of contract had no bearing on the validity of the marriage contract.[105] (The spouses could either come to an agreement later or, if they could not agree, the wife would be due her fair dower if the marriage were eventually consummated; if they parted before consummation with no dower set, she would not receive anything except a "consolation" gift.)[106] In direct contrast, in the case of a sale, the lack of a specified price caused the transaction to be canceled. In characterizing marriage as *not* a sale, Yves Linant de Bellefonds seizes on Shāfiʿī's assertion that marriage is not like a sale because dower is not like a price: a sale without a specified price is always null and void, whereas a marriage that leaves the dower unspecified is generally valid.[107]

Though de Bellefonds is correct in saying that this is a clear instance of how marriage was not like sales (or *other* sales), juristic discussions began from the presumption of similarity rather than difference. Though "the marriage is permitted and she is due her fair dower," the *Kitāb al-Ḥujja* proclaims that had it been "a sale or some other type of pecuniary transaction *(wa law kāna fī bayʿ aw ghayrihi min al-ijārāt)* and a man purchased [something] without a price or leased [something] without a fixed compensation *(ajr)*, that [would] not be permitted."[108] For Shāfiʿī also, the sameness of dower and price needed no justification; rather, any departure from the application of the rules governing sales to marriages required explanation. Shāfiʿī defends his stance on the validity of marriage without a specified dower to an imagined interlocutor who points out that "you [i.e., Shāfiʿī] generally apply rules for sales to marriage *(wa anta taḥkumu fī ʿāmmat al-nikāḥ aḥkām al-buyūʿ)*." He explains his reasoning precisely when commercial rules are not applied.[109]

The second case, marriages contracted where the specified dower was too small, had no parallel in standard sales. Although some ordinary commercial transactions were restricted or regulated, such as those deemed speculative or potentially usurious, for the most part no attempt was made to set a minimum (or maximum) price for any goods or services. Any compensation satisfactory to both parties was adequate. Not so with dower. Though the agreement of the contracting parties, and possibly of the wife herself even if she was not making the contract, was important, the jurists disagreed as to whether such agreement also sufficed to determine a legally valid dower. Both Mālik and Abū Ḥanīfa considered a minimum dower necessary. Mālik, following earlier Medinan authorities, held that the minimum acceptable dower was one-quarter of a dinar, or three dirhams, while Abū Ḥanīfa and his followers fixed the minimum at ten dirhams.[110] In a notable difference between Islamic and rabbinic reasoning, there is no differentiation between virgin and non-virgin brides with regard to minimum dower amount. This minimum dower amount is sometimes linked to the lowest amount for which a thief's hand will be amputated. The rationale seems to be that there is an irremediable loss that occurs through consummation, for which the minimum dower compensates; however, the lack of differentiation between virgin and non-virgin brides means that this loss cannot be defined as the loss of an intact hymen.[111]

Against Mālik and Abū Ḥanīfa, Shāfiʿī opposed a minimum dower. Asked in the *Ikhtilāf Mālik wa ʾl-Shāfiʿī* about "the smallest permitted dower," Shāfiʿī's rebuttal to Mālik drew on a parallel to sale: "The dower is a price *(thaman)* among prices, so whatever they consent to as a dower that has a value *(qīma)* is permitted, just as whatever a buyer and seller *(mutabāʾiʿān)* of anything that has a value [agree to] is permitted."[112] Elsewhere, he directly compares marriage and the purchase of a female slave for sex: "Some of the companions of Abū Ḥanīfa said: We find it objectionable that a [woman's] sexual organ *(farj)* be made permissible so cheaply *(bi shayʾ yasīr)*. We said, What is your view if a man buys a slave girl for a dirham, is her sexual organ lawful to him? They said: Yes. We said: You have permitted a sexual organ and added [ownership of] the [slave girl's] body for a trifle."[113] Shāfiʿī's answer here relies on the sameness and the difference between a wife and a slave girl. The essential similarity between two otherwise different women hinges on the transaction conveying sexual licitness for compensation. Shāfiʿī's overt point in his argument against Abū Ḥanīfa is that there is no minimum amount for licit access to a woman's sexual organ. There is nothing inherently wrong with conveying sexual dominion cheaply if one can buy a slave girl for a dirham and be entitled to sex with her. But to accept his argument requires one to conclude that one acquires something more valuable in buying a slave girl than in marrying a wife. A slave's purchaser comes to own her entire body; a husband acquires substantially more limited access rights over his wife. If one pays only one dirham for a slave girl and gets not only rights to sex but also ownership of her body, access to a wife ought to be worth less than that. If one presumes that access to a wife is worth more than access to a slave, Shāfiʿī's argument does not hold up. In the last analysis, the success of this comparison rests on the interchangeability of women as sexual outlets.

Exchange marriage *(shighār)*, an irregular type of marriage specifying a "nondower," confirms a dower's legitimating function with regard to sex at the same time as it shows the jurists' concern with ensuring brides' property rights over and above their bodily rights. Apparently an accepted pre-Islamic practice, exchange marriage consisted of two men marrying their charges, usually daughters or sisters, to each other without a dower being paid to either woman.[114] Repeated references to exchange marriage in historical and anthropological literature in Turkey, Jordan, Israel, and Iran, spanning the period from the Ottoman era to the late twentieth century, suggest that exchange marriage has been both widespread and persistent, despite its clear illegality from the perspective of religious law.[115] It may be helpful to read the jurisprudential treatment of exchange marriage as a critique of social practice. At the same time, jurists offer specifically jurisprudential rationales for the prohibition, not limiting themselves to repeating that the Prophet forbade *shighār*. Jurists agreed that it was forbidden by the Prophet and that it constituted a legal basis for annulling either or both of the marriages since, as al-Shaybānī put it, "the marriage of a woman is not a dower" *(lā yakūnu ṣadāq nikāḥ imra'a)*.[116] The jurists frame their objections to exchange marriage in terms of how it does or does not meet the legal criteria for valid marriages, focusing first on faulty dower and, as a distant second, the possibility of improper consent. The lack of appropriate compensation is the key problem: as the *Mudawwana* put it in another context, a free woman "is due her dower, and her *buḍʿ* is not made lawful by anything except it."[117] One Medinan authority quoted in the *Mudawwana* stated, "Exchange marriage is that a man marries [another] man to a woman and that other man marries him to a woman, the *buḍʿ* of one of them for the *buḍʿ* of the other, without a dower, and [other practices which] resemble that.[118] In the *Umm*, the fact that "the dower of each of them will be the *buḍʿ* of the other and no [other] dower is set for either of them" defines exchange marriage.[119] Mālik objects to such marriages even if dowers are assigned to each woman, particularly if the dowers are identical; he refers to the cases of daughters as well as slaves. In addition to the general parallel between father and master here in terms of broad authority, these are both instances where the men in question would have access to the money involved; Mālik grants fathers extensive power to draw from their offspring's property holdings at will.[120]

Jurists explained the forbidding of exchange marriage in terms of its failure to fulfill the requirement of proper dower. In doing so, they raised the question of how consent to marriage relates to control over financial rights. There was a complicated relationship between bodily integrity and financial integrity. Exchange marriage involved the nonconsensual waiver of the bride's financial rights. However, even guardians with the right to marry women off without their consent did not necessarily have the right to waive the women's financial claims. This conflict sometimes arose outside of exchange marriage, when a proposed dower fell beneath the bride's fair dower (but above any necessary minimum). A female in her majority could accept a less-than-fair dower, though this might require the approval of her guardian or guardians.[121] But if a bride did not control her own assets because of minority or other incapacity, could her guardian marry her off for less than her fair dower? Mālik and Abū Ḥanīfa allowed a minor girl's father to do so, and Mālik extended this to a virgin in her majority who was married under compulsion: compulsion and financial control were coterminous. Mālik's treatment of a daughter's financial rights coheres with his overall stance granting fathers extensive rights to appropriate the property of their offspring—male or female, minor or major—at will. It also assumes goodwill on the father's part: any reduction of dower should be out of concern for the daughter and should not result in harm to her.[122]

Abū Ḥanīfa's disciples and Shāfiʿī object: a minor ought never be contracted in marriage for less than her fair dower.[123] The *Umm* argues that no one else has control over a female's property, regardless of her age, and so no marriage guardian can forgo her claim on her behalf. When she attains majority she can consent to a reduced dower, but as a minor she is not legally capable of making financial decisions and is thus unable to consent validly. (Shāfiʿī's argument here parallels his stance on the marriage of the minor non-virgin: her consent was necessary but she was incapable of giving it, so no marriage could take place.) Shāfiʿī's zealous defense of female property rights stands against his seemingly cavalier treatment of bodily integrity. A never-married woman's father could marry her off even over her objections, but could not alienate any portion of the compensation due her for the marriage.

The previous two types of dower irregularity—either failing to specify the dower or falling below a minimum amount—were problematic because of their potential interference with the wife's rights. The third and final type related to the dower itself. What happened if the particular goods specified as dower could not be delivered? If the goods were discovered to be unlawful, turned out to be defective, or were damaged before the handover, two remedies were possible. The husband could either pay the wife's fair dower or give her the goods' fair price. Both approaches draw heavily on the rules for the regulation of commercial transactions. At times, these comparisons point up differences, but more frequently they show similarities.

As with the case of the doubled dower, Ibn al-Qāsim appeals to another case involving the purchase of slaves in order to explain a verdict with regard to marriage. This explicit calling of attention to the fact of the parallel is noteworthy. More usually, the parallel is alluded to and the analogy drawn with the presumption that its relevance will be understood. But here the *Mudawwana* states that a man may marry a woman "for whichever of my two slaves" *she* wants, but if he specifies that she receive whichever of two slaves *he* wants, "there is no good in it." Justifying this decision, Ibn al-Qāsim offers, "Can you not see that if he sold one of the two [slaves] to a man for ten dinars and let [the buyer] choose [which one he wanted], there would be no problem with it, but if he says 'I will give you whichever of the two I want,' there would be no good in that?"[124] The commercial rule self-evidently applies to the negotiated dower. Ibn al-Qāsim's approach to this problematic dower, like his approach to the case where the husband's representative doubled the dower, illustrates the vitality and usefulness of commercial analogues in the property transfer associated with marriage. The parallel between dower and price may be effective only up to a point, but up to that point it is useful.

Where the strict correspondences break down, however, we see instability in the jurists' categories. In the case of the doubled dower confronted by Ibn al-Qāsim earlier, the wife is a seller and maybe also the object of sale. Where her role is parallel to that of a purchaser of one of two slaves, she is a buyer. Barter systems lead to these uncertainties: if one is not exchanging cash for goods, then a strict demarcation between buying and selling becomes impossible. The dower sometimes functions as a method of purchasing rights over the wife's sexuality. At other times, it appears as an asset that the wife acquires, paying for it with her *buḍʿ*. This fluidity of categories—the bride is sometimes akin to buyer, and her sexual capacity is the thing transacted or the object of the transaction—stands in the way of facile characterizations of marriage as a purchase of a woman's sexual capacity or a woman "selling herself."

Treatment of a similar issue, where dower goods were destroyed before a bride took possession of them, reveals diversity of opinion, change, and legal development. Dower, like any other salable good, had to consist of "ritually and legally clean" items with "legal value."[125] Salable goods were either fungible *(dayn),* such as cash or produce, or unique *(ʿayn).*[126] Problems with a fungible dower could be fixed simply by substituting its equivalent. With unique items such as real estate, livestock, and—most often—slaves, substitution was an inadequate remedy. In an ordinary purchase, destruction or damage to unique goods would cancel the transaction. If the defective goods were specified for dower, however, the marriage would not be invalidated. Rather, if a slave specified as dower turned out to be defective or free, the problem could be resolved in two ways, which we can term the *fair price approach* and the *fair dower approach*. In the former, the wife would collect the monetary equivalent of the invalid dower. In the latter, the specified dower would be ignored in favor of the wife's fair dower, whether that turned out to be more or less than the specified dower. The *Jāmiʿ al-Ṣaghīr* takes the example of a dower of a particular slave who turns out to be free. Because the wife may not, of course, take possession of the free man, Abū Ḥanīfa and Muḥammad al-Shaybānī resort to her fair dower.[127] Abū Yūsuf instead awards her the amount the man would have been worth as a slave, an approach shared by Mālik and his followers.[128]

Shāfiʿī texts express both views but ultimately favor the use of fair dower instead of the fair price model of Abū Yūsuf and Mālik. In one instance of the fair price approach, the *Umm* states that in the case of a defective slave fixed as dower, the wife is to receive his value "as in sales."[129] This view was not authoritative, however; al-Muzanī criticizes it as "an error *(ghalaṭ)*" in his *Mukhtaṣar,* which draws on a slightly different, and presumably earlier, body of Shāfiʿī doctrine than that preserved in the present-day text of the *Umm.*[130] Al-Muzanī's solution, the one ultimately adopted by Shāfiʿī, is that she "is due her fair dower instead."[131] One text in the *Umm* explicitly acknowledges both views in a case where the dower was destroyed before the wife took possession. The analysis lays bare the logic of the marital transaction: the wife barters her *buḍʿ* for a consideration *(ʿiwaḍ)* in the form of a dower. Shāfiʿī argues that the wife should get her own fair dower: "Rather than claiming the thing [i.e., the dower] that she came to own by her *buḍʿ,* she claims the *buḍʿ*'s price *(thaman al-buḍʿ).*"

At the liminal moment of the marriage, the wife is a purchaser, using her *buḍʿ* as payment. "This is," Shāfiʿī continues, "as if she bought something for a dirham and that thing was destroyed [before she took possession of it]." Her *buḍʿ* is equivalent to the dirham; the husband is the seller, and the dower the item being sold. As the goods sold (the dower) for the dirham (her *buḍʿ*) were destroyed, the wife is entitled to "claim what she gave him because he did not give her the consideration for the [one] dirham price." Once the marital transaction has been finalized, though, and payment must be corrected, the wife's *buḍʿ*—unlike a dirham—cannot be refunded. Instead of claiming her *buḍʿ* back from her husband, she can only claim back its value. In an analogous case, where the specified dower was a slave who turned out to be defective, Shāfiʿī states, "If she returns it, she claims her fair dower from him, because she has sold him her *buḍʿ* for the slave *(bāʿathu buḍʿahā bi ʿabd)*."[132] Seen retrospectively, the marital transaction positions the wife as the seller, even if what she has sold (i.e., her *buḍʿ*) was, in strict terms, a noncommodity.

With this example, we return to Johansen's model of commercial versus social exchange. He explains marriage as an exchange of a commodity (the dower) for a noncommodity, which is reasonable when the bride is free. But though what is being exchanged on the wife's part is noncommodified, the transaction can be understood in commercial terms. It differs from ordinary sales in that, with a few very limited exceptions, problems with the dower do not justify voiding a marriage.[133] Rather than view this as evidence that marriage is unlike sales, though, we see that it is like a sale in which the sold item perishes and hence cannot be returned. As Shāfiʿī puts it, "Marriage is not rescinded; it is like the sale of a consumable."[134] This view was implicit in the Mālikī view already presented, where "a man marries a woman for a specific slave," but, when the woman takes possession, "she discovers a defect in the slave." According to Mālik, "She returns [the slave] and she is due his price, and this is the same as in sales *(mithl al-buyūʿ sawāʾ)*."[135] A cash sale of a defective slave would have been entirely canceled and the purchase price refunded to the buyer. In marriage, though, the wife cannot claim back what she had paid (or traded to) the husband. Defective dower cannot cancel the marriage because transfer of authority or control has irrevocably taken effect with the contract, even before consummation. (This is also the case for Mālik, despite the fact that in other cases he admits some significance to consummation.) With regard to dower here, consummation merely finalizes some aspects of the husband's control and establishes the wife's right to the full amount of her dower.

Conclusion

The early jurists' treatment of issues such as kin involvement in marriages, the consent of brides, and the role and regulations surrounding dower have been transmuted, and in some cases radically transformed, over the centuries. Guardianship and dower still play key symbolic, and sometimes legal, roles in most Muslim marriages. In two key respects, though, modern discourses about contracting marriage depart significantly from their premodern juristic counterparts. The first main shift has to do with consent and the second with the use of commercial language to describe the contracting of marriage.

Contemporary conventional wisdom about Islamic law holds that female consent is always necessary for marriage. In modernity, Muḥammad's words in the permission hadith are commonly taken to forbid any marriage without the bride's consent. It is a truism among both lay thinkers and some scholars that "Islam requires" a woman's consent to marriage and forbids all compulsion. This use of the hadith reflects a broader tendency among many Muslims to take hadith texts and Qur'anic texts as literal guidelines wherever possible, not interpreting them through the lens of legal assumptions.[136]

Such interpretations are furthered by the near disappearance of marriages conducted before puberty among educated Muslims and in urban areas. Both the rising age of marriage required by national bureaucracies and the shifting social patterns that increase the usual age at marriage have led to a decline in marriages of minors. These reforms can also be the result of deliberate policy shifts, as with the Aga Khan's twentieth-century reforms raising the minimum marriage age for girls to fourteen in 1925 and sixteen in 1962.[137] Changing conceptions have linked legal majority not to puberty but to a "coming of age" that hovers around eighteen in most nations with a Muslim majority, though a slight disparity between boys and girls is often present. Even with such reforms, earlier marriage is often possible with parental consent and does occur, despite its illegality, in some regions and social strata.[138] Where the marriage age has been lowered, as it was in the Islamic Republic of Iran, it has been to the disapprobation and sometimes bewilderment of many. The documentary film *Divorce Iranian Style,* by legal anthropologist Ziba Mir-Hosseini and filmmaker Kim Longino, captures a telling moment. A girl married in her midteens argues to a judge that she was too young to get married and demands that he tell her the minimum age for marriage. His response of "nine" renders her speechless.

Like the marriage of minors, the framing of marriage in transactional terms sits uncomfortably with Muslims today. Commercial and slavery-related terminology rarely appears in discussions of marriage. One reason for the shift is the universal abolition of legal slavery. Another is the sidelining of analogy from the legal process. As legislated codes have replaced jurisprudence as the main way law is made, substantive rules have been adopted in isolation from the methodological and discursive frames in which they were originally embedded.

For the formative-period jurists, marriage was formed by consent—not necessarily the bride's and groom's—and invoked certain claims, especially dower, in the form of compensation, in ways that render it both like and unlike other transactions. The analogy between the contracting of a marriage and the purchase of a slave operated at several levels to render marriage intelligible. The analogy made possible the translation of legal rulings from one arena to the other. If a matter was clear for purchase, it was clear for marriage, and vice versa. Additionally, the transfer of control or ownership *(milk)* that occurred in both the sale of a slave and the contract of marriage made sex licit, when the object of the "purchase" is female and the "purchaser" male. When slavery is no longer part of the functioning legal framework, there are no relevant provisions to apply across categories.

For the formative-period jurists, on the other hand, slavery was essential. Ottoman historian Ehud Toledano has argued for understanding enslavement (a term he prefers to *slavery*) as "a form of patronage relationship, formed and often maintained by coercion, but requiring a measure of mutuality and exchange that posits a complex web of reciprocity."[139] Without discounting the necessary inequality—he refers to "an involuntary relationship of mutual dependence between two quite unequal partners"[140]—he situates enslavement and the "slaver-enslaved relationship" within existing social forms. The family and the household are both hierarchically constituted relationships based on unequal but reciprocal exchanges. Toledano's insights about the relationship between slaver and enslaved also apply to the marital relationship: wives were legally subordinate to a lesser extent than slaves, but they were constrained by, and yet still capable of responding within the constraints of, the unequal legal and human relationships they had with their husbands. These relationships and the claims and counterclaims that constitute their basic framework are the subject of the next two chapters.

2

Maintaining Relations

AḤMAD B. ʿUmar al-Khaṣṣāf (d. 261/874), an early Ḥanafī, devoted an entire treatise to the subject of maintenance.[1] His *Kitāb al-Nafaqāt* discusses a man's duty to support his wife alongside his obligation to maintain relatives and slaves, and also his obligation to feed animals. Most dependents' claim to support was contingent on need, and the obligation to pay support was conditional on financial capacity. This was the case for slaves, offspring, and parents and other relations. Not so with spouses: a husband owed his wife support regardless of her need or his ability to pay. Indeed, "a married woman does not claim maintenance from anyone other than her husband," even if her kin are wealthy and her husband is poor.[2] Her claim to support was not subject to the logic governing kin support because it arose from a different source. It was part of the marital bargain, due in exchange for her making herself available to him *(tamkīn)*.[3] Shāfiʿī explains the wife's claim to support in slightly expanded terms: "He maintains his wife whether she is rich or poor, for keeping her to himself in order to enjoy her *(bi-ḥabsihā ʿalā nafsihi li ʾl-istimtāʿi bihā)*."[4] Shāfiʿī's formulation neatly ties together the two elements constituting the wife's sexual availability: she provides enjoyment to the husband and acquiesces to the restriction of her mobility.[5] Although these aspects of the wife's duty were linked, they received varying emphasis. Abū Ḥanīfa and his followers generally stressed restrictions on the wife; Mālik and Shāfiʿī and their followers devoted more attention to the husband's right to take pleasure with her.[6]

The maintenance obligation—which broadly included food, clothing, and lodging—was part of a scheme of interdependent spousal claims. These included inheritance, dower, sex, and companionship. The marriage contract itself initiated mutual inheritance rights (save where either party was enslaved or the wife was non-Muslim), but both the full dower obligation and the commencement, suspension, and cessation of maintenance rights were tied to milestones in the couple's married life, consummation being the most notable. On an ongoing basis, maintenance was linked to other spousal rights and duties. Intimacy was at the center of these rules, though its regulations were strongly gendered. If a man had more than one wife, he was obliged to divide his time among them. A wife had to be sexually available. A husband could control his wife's movements and determine the marital domicile. Could these rights be modified by stipulations to the marriage contract? Although Ibn Ḥanbal (among others) thought so in keeping with his generally positive view of stipulations, the jurists studied here did not believe that spouses were free to set basic terms when it came to what husbands and wives owed one another.[7]

I begin with the case of an enslaved wife, whose situation—though in certain respects more complicated than that of a free wife—provides a lens through which to view the various dimensions of a wife's responsibilities and rights, as well as those of a husband (and, in the case of a slave, her master). In allocating rights, it made no difference whether the husband of an enslaved woman was free or himself enslaved. Next, I address the beginning of a wife's claim to maintenance, which generally arises when she becomes available for consummation. This raises a series of issues about female sexual maturity and its relation to majority. The third section discusses maintenance during an ongoing marriage, which hinges on whether her husband has continued sexual access to her; the jurists disagree, though, as to whether her willingness is required or only her physical presence. Here, the wife's *nushūz*—her disobedience, insubordination, or sexual refusal—is addressed. Minor differences in doctrine turn out to be predicated on diverging views of the source of the husband's obligation of maintenance: is it restrictions on mobility or sexual rights? This distinction is even more clearly visible in the case of divorcees. Mālik and Shāfiʿī link a divorced woman's maintenance rights to her sexual availability, while Abū Ḥanīfa and his disciples grant her support in recognition of the continuity of restrictions on her during her waiting period. Despite the basic agreement between Mālikī and Shāfiʿī jurists, they also have slightly different rationales governing postdivorce maintenance, as becomes clear from an investigation into the exceptional cases of divorced, pregnant slave women and invalid marriages resulting in pregnancy.

The quid pro quo logic of support for sexual access governs regulations surrounding maintenance in an ongoing marriage, but what if a husband cannot hold up his end of the bargain? The final section of this chapter considers the sharp disagreement between Abū Ḥanīfa and his disciples on the one hand, who refused to dissolve a marriage for nonsupport no matter how long it persisted, and Mālik, Shāfiʿī, and their students on the other, who were willing to do so, although they disagreed about the length of time required before dissolution was permissible. Divergent views on whether a woman could obtain divorce from a nonsupporting husband show different understandings of the link between ongoing spousal claims and the validity of the marriage contract itself: was the marriage still binding if ongoing duties were neglected? The variety of views on this point shows independent human reasoning. The extensive polemics over maintenance helped refine legal doctrines, as jurists honed their arguments in dispute with one another both within and across school lines. At the same time, they affirm the shared nature of the presumption that dissolving a marriage by a husband was a matter of individual choice, while a wife needed either her husband's agreement or a judge's intervention.

An Enslaved Wife

Juristic concerns over the wife's capacity and willingness for sex were inseparable from issues of physical access and control, as Shāfiʿī's definition makes clear. These dual elements of sexual availability are easier to separate for analytic purposes in the case of a married female slave. Her master had fewer rights over her than he would have had over an unmarried female slave; in particular, he lost his right of sexual access, though he would own any children born as a result of her marriage. (If she were his own concubine, her children would be free and legitimate; they would not be his property. I will say more about concubines in Chapter 5.) Her husband had less authority over her than he would have had over a free wife since her master controlled her living arrangements and determined when she could leave the premises. Control of a wife's domicile was an expected element of marriage to a free woman; contractual stipulations whereby a wife could determine her own domicile were roundly rejected. A husband could restrict himself only with his own oath attached to a divorce pronouncement or a financial penalty for violating an agreement not to relocate his wife. It is a notable abridgement of masculine privilege that an enslaved woman's husband cannot demand that she live with him. Yet insofar as these husbands were also enslaved—which was not necessarily the case, but texts often refer to such marriages—to even think of them as having masculine privilege already assumes things about masculinity that would not have been possible, for instance, in Roman society, where to be a male slave was to be in some essential sense emasculated. Where her husband was free (and in some views he could take an enslaved wife only if he were too poor to afford a free woman's dower),[8] this would merely be another inconvenience associated with having to share her time.

An enslaved wife combines aspects of the figures that are usually contrasted: the free wife and the enslaved concubine. Because she is married to a man other than her master, her situation poses a number of conceptual and logistical difficulties. Two men have claims over her that may conflict. Sexual exclusivity is the easiest to resolve, at least in theory: when her master gives consent for her marriage, he forfeits his own sexual access to her. Masters likely did not always restrain themselves. Some anecdotes suggest that owners sometimes failed to respect the husband's exclusive right to access; the jurists point out, in those cases, that the slave woman herself bore no blame for adulterous encounters.

More difficult are the ongoing questions of control over the female slave's time, her physical presence, and her performance of services. Moreover, these claims are attached to certain responsibilities, such as support. The *Mudawanna* devotes a long passage to assessing these conflicting claims.

> I said: What if a man marries a slave woman and the husband says, "Lodge her with me in my house and allow me to have privacy with her," and the master says, "I will not allow privacy between you and her and I will not lodge her with you in your house"; or if the husband comes [to her master] and says, "I want to have intercourse with her immediately," and her master says, "She is occupied *(mashghūla)* now

> with her work," may the husband keep *(manaʿa)* her from her work, or have privacy in order to have intercourse with her immediately, or is it lawful for her to forgo her work for her master to have intercourse with her husband? He said: I have not heard Mālik define this, except that Mālik said: Her master may not forbid her to her husband if he wants to have sex with her and her husband may not lodge her in his house except with the master's consent. The slave woman remains with her household *(ahlihā)* to serve them and [to do] what they need, but they may not harm [the husband by withholding] what he needs in terms of intercourse with her. I think that she remains with her household, and if her husband needs her, they grant privacy to him [in order to fulfill] his need for her. If the husband intends to harm them [by interfering excessively with her work], he is prevented from doing so.[9]

The use of *ahl,* which I have translated as "household," to describe the female slave's owners or employers is noteworthy. The term is semantically flexible. It means "family," or "people," though these English terms carry connotations of relationship by blood or marriage that do not apply here. But the Latin root of family is illuminating. The term *familia* in its classical Roman usage "had the primary meaning of a body of slaves (not wife and children)."[10] In fact, "the Romans rarely used it to mean family in the sense of kin."[11] The Arabic term *ahl* can encompass people connected only by a bond of servitude as well as those connected by "family ties." In this passage, it is used for the slave girl's superiors, rather than (as in the Roman case) subordinates. But *ahl* also frequently appears in Muslim texts euphemistically to refer to wives. The clearest example is the hadith where the Prophet declared, regarding the treatment of wives: "The best of you is he who is best to his *ahl.*" The *Mudawwana*'s use of a term with kinship connotations rather than ownership connotations reinforces the integration of the enslaved woman into a household economy of reciprocal, if unequal, obligations. As Ehud Toledano argues for the Ottoman period, slavers and enslaved had human relationships.[12] *Human* does not necessarily mean egalitarian; hierarchy even within the family was taken for granted, as discussions of consent in the previous chapter showed. Family is not necessarily a refuge from hierarchical society but a reflection of and model for it.

A legal text, of course, cannot account fully for the complexities of interpersonal relationships but this excerpt from the *Mudawwana* attempts to mediate competing demands on the enslaved woman. In doing so, it prioritizes male rights to sex. The wife's master may not prevent the husband from having sex with his wife, but the husband is not entitled to lodge her with him (as he would be able to do with a free wife) without her master's permission. A female slave's master retains much control over her mobility that would belong to her husband if she were free. The husband's only true claim on an enslaved wife, for the Mālikīs, was to have his desire—or rather, "his need"—for intercourse fulfilled.[13] In this attempt to ensure that neither husband nor master interferes with the other's legitimate claims, Ibn al-Qāsim treats the husband's need for a sexual outlet as urgent; it will brook no delay while the slave completes her duties.

In treating male desire as incapable of restraint once ignited, this anecdote echoes various hadith. In one, a woman whose husband calls her to bed even if she is at the oven cooking (or, in a variant version, mounted on a camel—that is, ready for an excursion) must go to him.[14] Another declares that a man who becomes attracted to a woman he sees while in public ought to go home and have sex with his wife.[15] Female desire makes no appearance in these reports, and if a wife's disinclination appears, it is quickly rendered irrelevant. In one example, discussed by Ze'ev Maghen in his study of sexuality and ritual purity in Islamic law, ʿUmar ibn al-Khaṭṭāb wakes his sleeping wife for sex one night during Ramadan. He then worries that he has violated a rule against having sex once one has fallen asleep during Ramadan.[16] ʿUmar expresses regret only for a possible violation of divine prohibition, not for running roughshod over his wife's objections. The report does not tell us whether she resisted his advances because she was sleepy or not in the mood, or whether she also feared violating God's command. Her feelings are irrelevant, both to the legal point at issue and also to the men involved, including ʿUmar, those who transmit the anecdote, and even Maghen, who glosses over the androcentric nature of this and similar accounts. Our authors assume that a wife would be available to satisfy her husband's urges and that male passion, once roused, must be satisfied. In its discussion of the sexual claims of a man married to a female slave, the *Mudawwana*'s accommodation of the husband's need affirms this view of the male libido.

Notably, for Mālik, a slave's husband had to support her, even if she lodged with her master; the right to have sex with her made him responsible for maintaining her. The link between lodging and support in the case of the married female slave must be understood within the basic framework for maintenance between free spouses. In marriage to a free woman, a husband controlled both the right of sexual enjoyment *(istimtāʿ)* and the right to restrict the wife's mobility (*ḥabs*, later *iḥtibās*), and determined her domicile. (He did not have an enforceable claim on her domestic service, though she might have some moral responsibility to perform those tasks that were customary for a woman of her class.) In the case of a slave woman, these claims were bifurcated: her husband had the right to sexual enjoyment, and her master had the right to restrict her movements and determine her domicile, as well as the right to her domestic labor. The relationship between restriction and enjoyment as sources of the obligation of support remains a subject of disagreement, separable in the case of a slave and but trickier to discern in the case of a free wife. A husband's ability to derive enjoyment from his wife and his control over her physical mobility were inextricably linked if she was free, but these rights were divided between a married slave's husband and her master. Rulings about the maintenance of enslaved wives help clarify the legal reasoning applicable to the marriages of free persons. The jurists place varying emphases on enjoyment and restriction as rationales for support: the Ḥanafīs, and to a lesser extent the Shāfiʿīs, stressed control over domicile and mobility, while the Mālikīs considered the enjoyment of sexual intimacy the overriding factor in obligating a husband to maintain his wife.

The *Mudawwana* stakes out two clear domains: "Her master may not forbid her to her husband if he wants to have sex with her and her husband may not lodge her in his house except with the master's consent."[17] Ḥanafī and Shāfiʿī texts concur.[18] But because rights to sex and to physical control over the slave were separated, the jurists disagreed over who was obligated to maintain her. Mālik held that it was the husband's duty, because of his access to sex. A master retains the right to use his slave's services at any time he needs them, even revoking previously granted permission to reside with her husband. Despite the master's clear control over the slave's mobility, the husband was always responsible for her support, regardless of where she lived: "She is a wife, and she is due dower and she must observe a waiting period [when the marriage ends] and she is due maintenance."[19] The husband's right to seek enjoyment, rather than any ancillary restrictions imposed on her, obligated him to support her, in Mālik's view.

Abū Ḥanīfa linked the duty to maintain with the right to have her dwell with and hence be continuously available to him.[20] Only a husband who controlled his wife's domicile and mobility was obliged to support her. The Ḥanafī jurists stressed a wife's physical presence with her husband; physical presence implied, as with a free wife, sexual access. Early Shāfiʿī texts were less categorical about the relationship between cohabitation and support. The *Umm* simply affirms that a husband must maintain his enslaved wife.[21] Al-Muzanī's *Mukhtaṣar* qualifies this general rule: the husband must maintain his enslaved wife only "if she is lodged with him in his house." Both affirm, though, that "if her master needs her service, he may [take her]." If he thereby impedes the husband's sexual access, "she is not due maintenance [from her husband]."[22] Of course, the master himself is then obliged, as in al-Khaṣṣaf's text, to provide her with sustenance.

Stipulations in Marriage Contracts

Discussions of lodging arise in jurists' treatments of maintenance. In the case of enslaved wives, lodging might be negotiable, in which case parties to the contract might stipulate terms. But apart from the case of enslavement, some elements of marriage—including male control of female mobility and male exemption from sexual exclusivity—were sacrosanct. Mālik, Abū Ḥanīfa, and Shāfiʿī concurred that spouses were not permitted to alter core marital rights through stipulations (*shurūṭ*, singular *sharṭ*). They uniformly rejected the most common stipulations— those preventing the husband from marrying additional wives, taking concubines, or moving his wife away from her town or domicile. The *Umm* addresses a contract that stipulates all three of these conditions:

> If he marries a virgin or a non-virgin with her approval *(bi amrihā)* for 1,000 on [the condition] that she may go out of his home whenever she wishes, and that he will not take her from her hometown, and that he will not marry [another wife] alongside her, and that he will not take a concubine alongside her . . . the marriage is binding, and the stipulation is void *(al-nikāḥ jāʾiz wa ʾl-sharṭ bāṭil)*.[23]

Shāfiʿī voids these stipulations because they interfere with a scripturally sanctioned division of marital rights and duties that cannot be modified to suit the whims of individuals. These stipulations, according to what the Prophet said, are not found in "the book of God." Thus, the *Umm* argued, "God, Exalted and Majestic, made it lawful for a man to marry four [wives] and [to take concubines from] what his right hand possesses. If she stipulates that he may not marry [additional wives] and may not take concubines she is restricting God's largesse to him."[24]

As with the husband's right to take additional sexual partners, his right to restrict his wife's mobility and unilaterally determine her domicile was not subject to limitation. The *Mudawwana* relates that "[A] man married a woman in the era of ʿUmar b. al-Khaṭṭāb and stipulated to her that he would not take her away from her hometown *(arḍihā)*. ʿUmar set aside that stipulation for him and said, A woman [goes] with her husband."[25] This report of ʿUmar's actions did not state whether the husband wished to take her away before or after consummation, nor did it suggest that there was a possibility of an annulment for this condition or a choice for the wife. The caliph simply affirmed that a woman must go where her husband goes, and disallowed the stipulation. The *Muwaṭṭaʾ* quotes the concurring opinion of Medinan authority Saʿīd b. al-Musayyab, voiding any stipulation that prohibits a husband from taking his wife out of her town: "He takes her away if he wishes."[26] Related to the husband's right to determine the marital domicile was his right to demand that his wife remain in the marital home. The *Umm* reports the Prophet's statement that "it is not lawful for a woman to voluntarily fast a day if her husband is present except with his permission."[27] Shāfiʿī argues that if a husband could prevent his wife from performing a voluntary act of devotion to God because it might interfere with part of his rights over her, then a fortiori he could restrict her in other ways, including removing her from her town or her domicile and prohibiting her from going out of the house.

Rejection of stipulations was not a strategy to impoverish or denigrate women, but rather to insist on a core minimum of marital rights. Less frequently discussed but equally void were stipulations that the husband need not maintain his wife, visit her regularly, or pay her any dower. Just as a woman had to remain in the marital domicile wherever her husband chose to establish it, and to accept that she had no claim to sexual exclusivity with her husband, men had to support their wives and allocate their time equally between them. Spouses were not free to eliminate the wife's claims against the husband for support, dower, or a portion of his time—though she might waive them later.[28]

They also could not be monetized: a wife could not give up her claim to a share of her husband's time for a larger dower, increased maintenance, or a one-time payment.

Ḥanafī and Shāfiʿī jurists held strictly to the principle that stipulations, no matter whether void themselves, never invalidated a marriage contract.[29] Illustrating both the significance of consummation in their thought and their greater concern for men's sensibilities, Mālikīs allow some void stipulations to result in dissolution of the marriage before consummation has taken place, but only at the behest of the spouse who would have benefited by the stipulation. For example, if a husband and wife had agreed that she would not receive maintenance but learned before consummation that this stipulation was unenforceable, the husband could choose either to remain married with the obligation to maintain her or to have the marriage annulled. If consummation had occurred, however, he had no option: the stipulation was void and the marriage endured. By contrast, Mālik and his followers allowed the wife no option to annul or dissolve an unconsummated marriage if she discovered the unenforceability of stipulations preventing polygyny, concubinage, or relocation. Even if the husband contravened the stipulation by contracting another marriage or taking a concubine before the original marriage was consummated, as one sample problem in the *Mudawwana* provides, that marriage would stand unaffected.[30] Gendered power differentials manifest themselves in doctrine here. Women have few options for marital dissolution if they find their husbands cannot be held to their agreements; husbands have greater latitude to withdraw without penalty from unions they find undesirable. Mālik's thought also provides a critical role for chronological priority: annulling certain marriages if unconsummated, but confirming them once consummation has occurred, shows that the social weight of consummation can supersede the validity of other considerations.

Though stipulations that altered basic marital rights and duties were unenforceable as contractual obligations, a man could bind himself to adhere to a promise by declaring a conditional divorce *(ṭalāq)*. For instance, he might state, "If I take another wife, you are divorced." A man's promise not to marry an additional wife "means nothing unless there is an oath of divorce or manumission attached to it." But if he does make such an oath, keeping his word "is obliged and required of him."[31] Should he breach the oath, divorce would result automatically.

A wife, then, could not force her husband to remain monogamous, but she could guarantee herself an exit from her marriage rather than tolerate a co-wife. Conditional divorce worked because pronouncements of *ṭalāq* were regulated by mechanisms that were not contractual stipulations.[32] The effectiveness of divorce oaths owed to the husband's absolute discretion over the power of divorce rather than to any actual change to the marital obligations of the spouses. In practical circumstances this distinction seems to have mattered little. Women in many times and places wrote such stipulations with enforcement provisions into their marriage contracts, as notarial formulae and court records attest.[33] Nonetheless, for these jurists the difference was vital.

The Duty to Maintain

Early Muslim jurists distinguished between the contracting of a marriage and its consummation. Some marriages were consummated immediately but others only after a delay. Months or even years could separate the marriage contract from *dukhūl* (literally, entrance; metaphorically, consummation), since one or both spouses could be married off during childhood, as in the case of Musayyab's son and Quray{ᶜ}a's daughter, whom we met at the beginning of Chapter 1. A marriage in which consummation was being postponed was nonetheless valid and fully binding, not merely a promise or betrothal. Certain effects came into force immediately: the bride could not be married off to another man, inheritance rights prevailed, and a full or partial dower payment became obligatory in most circumstances even if divorce or one spouse's death dissolved the marriage before consummation.[34] However, other spousal rights and duties remained in abeyance, including maintenance. The maintenance obligation could be triggered, once the wife attained sufficient maturity to consummate the marriage, by an invitation to consummate the marriage, the occurrence of valid privacy *(khalwa ṣaḥīḥa)* between the spouses, or consummation itself.

The bride's readiness for sex was a prerequisite, in the juristic imagination, for the support obligation. This makes sense, given that maintenance compensates the wife for her sexual availability rather than for household chores or any other duties. An extended discussion in the *Kitāb al-Nafaqāt* distinguishes a wife's duties from those of a servant *(khādim)*. A man is obligated to support his wife's servant, whether a female slave *(mamlūka)* that she herself owns, one lent by her father, or a free servant engaged by the husband. Even if she does not have a servant, her husband cannot compel her to bake bread or cook for herself if she refuses to do so. As al-Khaṣṣāf puts it, "his claim on her is her making herself available to her husband *(tamkīn al-nafs min al-zawj)* and not these tasks."[35] A servant who refused to perform these services could be denied maintenance and ejected from the house, but "[a wife's] maintenance is obliged because of her availability *(tamkīn)* not because of her service *(khidma)*."[36]

A husband need not support a wife too young for intercourse, but how young was too young? Readiness to consummate a marriage did not necessarily depend on a girl's attainment of *bulūgh*, majority. It was permissible to consummate a marriage with a minor if one has sex with those like her. The *Umm* discusses a case where "a man controlled *(malaka)* the [marriage] tie of a woman with the like of whom one may have intercourse, even if she is not in her majority *(bāligh)*," noting that he would be obligated to maintain her.[37] The *Kitāb al-Ḥujja* acknowledges the permissibility of sex with a minor when it refers to a man's "minor daughter who has matured so that one may have intercourse with her."[38] Al-Khaṣṣāf mentions a wife who "is an adolescent and is not in her majority *(kānat murāhiqa wa lam takun bāligha)* and her father delivers her to her husband and he goes in to her *(dakhala bihā)*."[39]

Rather than having a strict age-based limit, or one dependent on menarche, the determination of female readiness for sex (and thus cohabitation and support) hinged on physical sturdiness and appeal to men.[40] Age is occasionally mentioned, however. The age of nine appears sporadically as a minimum for consummation, majority, or both. This is presumably tied to the hadith, quoted by Shāfiʿī, that put ʿĀʾisha's age at nine when Muḥammad consummated their marriage. It is possible, though I think highly unlikely, that the causal link goes the other way— that is, that the hadith are an attempt to justify consummation from the age of nine.

Assuming that the wife was fit for intercourse, Mālik holds that expressed willingness on her behalf to consummate the marriage set in motion her husband's obligation to maintain her. In the *Mudawwana*, Saḥnūn asks Ibn al-Qāsim whether the maintenance obligation commences with the contracting of a marriage or with its consummation. His answer? Neither. According to Mālik, the wife's availability was the impetus for a husband's obligation to maintain her. The invitation might come from the wife herself or, as in many of the cited examples, from her family.[41] The texts treat as unremarkable, even usual, that the invitation to consummate the marriage would be issued by the bride's kin. Occasionally, we see that a bride's kinsmen are reluctant to hand her over to the groom, arguing that she is not yet ready for the rigors of conjugal life.

Our sources cannot tell us how frequent marriages of minor girls were as opposed to how frequent marriages of adult women were during the first centuries of Islam. We have little firm biographical data on which to base such attempted comparisons. One obvious sample would be the women in Muḥammad's household: he is reported to have had nine wives when he died. This number does not include his first wife, Khadīja, who is traditionally said to have been forty when he married her at the age of twenty-five. In addition to ʿĀʾisha, whom we have already discussed, Ṣafiyya (a captive turned bride) was probably in her late teens, as was Ḥafṣa, the daughter of ʿUmar ibn al-Khaṭṭāb.[42] Muḥammad's other wives, including Sawda and Umm Salama, were somewhat older. Apart from ʿĀʾisha (and probably Māriya, Muḥammad's concubine, a gift from the Christian governor of Egypt), all had been previously married, some twice; several were mothers. Although the reliability of these biographical sources has been contested, they tell us that marriage in one's teens was not unusual, perhaps even par for the course, and that remarriage after divorce or widowhood was common. As to whether Muḥammad's wives apart from ʿĀʾisha had been married to their first husbands as minors, there is no way to know.

Assuming that she is ready for the rigors of conjugal life, for Shāfiʿī, a private encounter between husband and wife (not hampered by Ramadan fasting or other impediments to intercourse) normally sets her claim to support in motion. However, should a man refuse an offer—likely from her family—to have a private encounter with his bride, he would still be required to commence his support of her. Formative-period Ḥanafī sources are silent on what is necessary for the commencement of the maintenance obligation, though one Shāfiʿī source attributes to them the view that the right to maintenance begins only after consummation except under exceptional circumstances.

Much rarer in the texts and presumably in the societies that gave rise to them was the case where the wife had reached majority while the husband remained a minor. In the *Mudawwana*'s discussion of this possibility—which presents the wife herself and not her kin issuing the invitation for consummation—Mālik's view is that "there is no maintenance due to her from him and she may not take possession of the dower until the youth *(ghulām)* is ready for intercourse."[43] This rule accords with the Mālikī stance that if any contract is made while its basic aim cannot not be fulfilled, then its provisions do not take effect until it can be; in the case of marriage, this basic aim was lawful intercourse.[44] Shāfiʿī and the Ḥanafī authorities argue instead that it is unfair to penalize the woman for the husband's incapacity due to his minority: "Her maintenance is due from him because the restriction is on his part."[45] In a similar vein, Shāfiʿī decides that if the husband is in his majority and the wife fit for intercourse, but the husband delays or refuses an offered consummation, then he must maintain her.[46]

If, despite both spouses' fitness for conjugal life, instead of inviting or acceding to consummation the wife or her family refuses to allow it, she loses her claim to maintenance, with one noteworthy exception. Any wife may refuse consummation and claim support as long as she has demanded, but not yet received, any portion of her dower that the parties agreed would be paid promptly.[47] The lack of payment constitutes an obstacle on the husband's part, as if he were refusing to consummate the marriage. Yet if the wife consents to consummation before receiving the dower, only Abū Ḥanīfa allows her to subsequently withhold herself without losing her right to maintenance.[48] Abū Ḥanīfa held that even after consummation the wife could refuse intercourse on the basis of her unpaid dower claim while still keeping her right to support. Shaybānī, Abū Yūsuf, Mālik, Shāfiʿī and their followers disagreed: she could continue to press her claim for dower but could not legitimately refuse further sexual encounters.

After the commencement of the maintenance obligation, support was predicated on the wife's continuing availability as a sexual partner. What mattered was her willingness, not whether sex actually transpired. If a man somehow made sex with her impossible or illicit—for instance, if he traveled, got imprisoned, or found himself required to abstain for any other reason—his wife retained her claim. Two thoroughly improbable scenarios illustrate the jurists' logic. If a man had sex with his wife's sister by mistake, she would be obliged to observe a waiting period to ascertain pregnancy. As a man could not have simultaneous access to two sisters, he would have to abstain from sex with his wife during the waiting period.[49] Or if a man with four wives divorced one of them absolutely, but did not know which (this is possible because oaths can be effective despite certain types of uncertainty), he would have to refrain from intercourse with all of them until he determined which one he had divorced; all, though, were due maintenance from him in the meantime.[50] Similar rules applied if he vowed to abstain from intercourse with his wife for a certain period (forswearing, *īlāʾ*) or swore an oath that made her forbidden to him *(ẓihār)* until he expiated it. These acts did not affect a wife's right to maintenance because she had kept her part of the bargain.[51] The same was true when the husband's physical separation from his wife made intercourse impossible. If a man got imprisoned, or fled from his wife, Abū Ḥanīfa and his followers argued that he had to continue to maintain her, asking rhetorically, "Is her [claim to] maintenance from him void when he is the one at fault, and he did it or it was done to him?"[52] The wife's availability meant that the husband's maintenance obligation continues.

On the other hand, when the wife's unavailability was her own fault (or more precisely, not her husband's fault), she forfeited maintenance. This forfeiture could occur either through her departure, with or without permission, from the conjugal domicile or her refusal *(imtināʿ)* to permit intercourse or other sexual intimacies. The formative-period authorities differed significantly in their treatment of these actions, some of which fell under the rubric of *nushūz*. *Nushūz* is often glossed as wifely disobedience, but jurists seldom discussed obedience per se. This is not because they found the notion of wifely obedience objectionable; to the contrary, they took it for granted. But the specific actions with which they were concerned related to the fulfillment of the marital obligations to which maintenance was linked: accepting restriction and making herself physically available. Even actions that did not constitute *nushūz*, such as travel with the husband's permission, could nonetheless lead to loss of maintenance.

Appearing twice in the Qurʾan, once (4:34) with reference to women and once (4:128) with reference to a husband, the term *nushūz* is central to contemporary debates over gender politics and spousal rights and roles. The first scriptural use of *nushūz* is generally taken to refer to wives, though the verse specifies only "women." My translation here reflects the usual understanding of the verse's meaning, to the extent that there is a shared perspective among exegetes and jurists.[53]

> Men stand over women *(al-rijāl qawwāmūn ʿala ʾl-nisāʾ),* with what God has favored some over others, and with what they expend *(bi mā anfaqū)* from their wealth. Righteous women are obedient (*qānitat,* "devout"), guarding [in the husband's] absence what God has [ordered to be] guarded. Those women whose *nushūz* you fear, appeal to them, and abandon them in bed *(wa ʾhjurūhunna fī ʾl-maḍājiʿ),* and strike them *(wa ʾḍribūhunna).* If they obey you, do not seek a way against them. Indeed God is Most High, Great. (4:34)

In its second appearance, the Qurʾan mentions rejection along with *nushūz:*

> If a wife fears *nushūz* or rejection *(iʿrāḍ)* from her husband *(baʿlihā),* there is no blame on them if they settle on a settlement, and such settlement is best, even though people's souls are swayed by greed. But if you do good and practice self-restraint, God is well-acquainted with all that you do. (4:128)

Drawing on these verses, but not circumscribed by them, the jurists understand *nushūz* in the context of marriage in varied ways.

Nushūz is a difficult term to pin down precisely. In the case of the wife, it may be used for one who refuses her husband sexually or disobeys him by leaving the home without his permission; in one case, it refers to her refusal to travel with him, or sometimes unspecified recalcitrance. In the case of the husband, it refers to a general dislike of, or rude behavior toward, the wife.[54] Although men can commit *nushūz,* only the wife who commits *nushūz* is designated by the term *nāshiz.* Though the husband's behavior can also constitute *nushūz,* the term *nāshiz,* despite being grammatically masculine, always refers to the wife. (*Nāshiza* sometimes appears, mostly in Ḥanafī texts, with no difference in meaning.) *Nushūz* may characterize the husband's behavior at times, but it cannot define him. *Nushūz* is used symmetrically in reference to either a wife's or husband's "antipathy" toward the other as a motive for divorce.[55]

Though the term *nushūz* rarely appears in these works, the concepts it encompasses are of vital importance to jurists' vision of spousal claims. While exegetes focus on the specific measures that the Qurʾan dictates for *nushūz* (admonition, abandonment, and striking, in the case of women's *nushūz;* settlement, in the case of a man's *nushūz*), when jurists discuss it they are more interested in other juridical consequences. Mālikī texts from the formative period do not discuss *nushūz* or its consequences extensively; indeed, the *Muwaṭṭaʾ* does not discuss it at all. The *Mudawwana,* broaching the subject in a discussion of divorce for compensation, records the view of Medinan authority Ibn Shihāb al-Zuhrī on attitudes and behaviors that make it lawful to accept compensation from a wife in exchange for divorce, including "attach[ing] no importance to her husband's right(s)," committing *nushūz* against him *(nashizat ʿalayhi),* going out without his permission, or permitting into his home someone that he dislikes, and "show[ing] repulsion toward him *(aẓharat lahu al-bughḍ).*"[56] Another declares that a woman's refusal to relocate with her husband qualifies as *nushūz:* "Bukayr said: [If] a woman refuses to move to one place from another *(ilā balad min al-buldān)* with her husband, I do not consider her anything but *nāshiz.*"[57] Neither Ibn al-Qāsim nor these authorities clarify the relationship between *nushūz* and the other types of misbehavior listed, nor do any of them define specific consequences for these actions, other than making it acceptable for the husband to take compensation in exchange for divorcing her. The *Muwaṭṭaʾ* and the *Mudawwana* are silent on the suspension of maintenance for *nushūz.* This omission might mean that it was not yet a widely shared view or, conversely, that it was taken for granted. Although suspension of support for *nushūz* becomes the authoritative school position, eleventh-century Mālikī authority Ibn ʿAbd al-Barr (d. 463/1071) states that Ibn al-Qāsim considered it obligatory to maintain a *nāshiz* wife.[58] David Santillana makes no mention of this purported view of Ibn al-Qāsim's in his classic study of Mālikī doctrine, where he summarizes as follows: "The woman may not refuse her conjugal duty without incurring the loss of maintenance."[59]

Shāfiʿī, concerned as always with hermeneutics—especially the possible contradictions between Qurʾan and sunna as sources of law—discusses the loss of maintenance for *nushūz* and other infractions at some length. He equates the wife's sexual refusal without cause *(imtināʿ)* to *nushūz;* a wife who rejected her husband's advances forfeited her claim to support. Absence from the conjugal home—including unauthorized departure and travel, with or without permission—also resulted in loss of maintenance. Otherwise, the husband's obligation to maintain his wife continued whether she was sick or well, even if menstruation, illness, or a defect prevented actual intercourse, so long as she allowed him other intimacies.[60] A wife who became ill or whose vagina became obstructed could still claim support, as "this is an unfortunate malady, not withholding by her."[61] In contrast, if she did not permit the sexual intimacies for which she was fit, then her refusal led to loss of maintenance.

Because the wife's accessibility was exchanged for her maintenance, her absence from her husband caused her to lose support.[62] Abū Ḥanīfa and his followers held to this rule stringently: a wife lost her maintenance if she were kidnapped or "imprisoned for a debt," or if she went on pilgrimage without her husband, even if she had his permission.[63] (Shāfiʿī authorities agreed about voluntary travel, except for pilgrimage. If a husband permitted his wife to go, she would keep her maintenance.)[64] Pilgrimage was an exceptional circumstance in any case, as once a person donned pilgrim garments *(iḥrām)*, he or she was not permitted to have intercourse. Nonetheless, for the Ḥanafīs, "if her husband goes [on pilgrimage] with her she is due maintenance."[65] According to al-Khaṣṣāf, he should go with her, in which case "he is obligated to maintain her, because it is possible for him to make use of (or benefit from) her."[66] Al-Khaṣṣāf does not further define "making use" *(al-intifāʿ bihā)*, though it cannot mean penetrative sex once she is in the state of pilgrim sanctity. Nevertheless, subsequent passages affirm a clear sexual component to "making use." Al-Khaṣṣāf declares that, outside the context of pilgrimage, the husband of a woman too ill for sex or with a vaginal obstruction preventing intercourse is obligated to maintain her "because of the lawfulness of making use of her." In the latter case, such use included "kissing and non-vaginal intercourse *(al-jimāʿ fīmā dūn al-farj)*."[67] In the former, it included looking at her.[68] In both cases, "intimacy" was established. When penetrative sex was impossible or forbidden due to illness or physical impediment, other forms of gratification constituted sufficient basis for maintenance.

Ḥanafī texts extend the ruling on loss of support for physical absence to also uphold its converse: physical presence in the marital home suffices for support. This leads them to treat a wife's disobedience or refusal differently from their counterparts in other juristic traditions. *Nushūz* becomes neither sexual refusal nor willful recalcitrance but rather the wife's unauthorized departure from the marital home: "I said: If a woman goes out of her husband's home to her family's home without his permission there is no maintenance due to her, because she is *nāshiza* . . . and the *nāshiza*, there is no maintenance due to her."[69] A wife who remained in her husband's home but refused him sexually retained her claim to maintenance. Sexual refusal did not constitute *nushūz*, because it did not, in this view, make her sexually unavailable; as long as she remained physically present, he could have sexual access to her even against her will.

Where the wife had legitimate grounds for sexual refusal, the situation was more complex. Abū Ḥanīfa and his disciples disagreed as to what constituted legitimate grounds and, moreover, what the line was between enforceable rules and ethical guidelines. When a wife refused sex in order to claim an unpaid dower, Abū Ḥanīfa supported her actions even after consummation.[70] In this case, he held that "it is not lawful and he sins [if he forces her]." According to Abū Yūsuf and Muḥammad al-Shaybānī, who did not grant her the right to withhold herself for nonpayment of dower after consummation, the husband's forcing her "is lawful and he does not sin." A variant manuscript reads, "It is lawful and he sins," making a distinction between the legality and morality of the husband's action.[71] Even where the two characterizations coincided—lawful / not sinful; not lawful / sinful—the attention to the ethical quality of a husband's forcing himself on his wife is noteworthy; the case is clearer still where there was a disjunction between the two: lawful *yet* sinful.[72] Still, while forcible intercourse might or might not be sinful if the wife had the moral high ground because of unpaid dower, if an unpaid dower was not at issue then the husband's right "to have sex with her against her will" went unquestioned. In this case, they agreed: "It is lawful, because she is a wrongdoer *(ẓālima)*."[73] The wife's reproachable behavior justifies the husband's action. Al-Khaṣṣāf, who reports these views, did not even raise the possibility that forced intercourse in these circumstances might be a sin.

Divorce

Like temporary impediments to sexual intercourse such as absence or refusal, divorce also suspended or ended the sexual relationship between two spouses. How divorce affected a woman's claim to maintenance depended on the type of divorce, whether she was pregnant, and whether the spouses were free or enslaved. Substantial differences between Ḥanafī doctrines, which granted all divorcees the right of support, and Mālikī and Shāfiʿī doctrines, which restricted support to pregnant women or those divorced revocably, illustrate again the importance of human interpretive choices in the development of legal rules. These differences involved varying interpretations of one Qurʾanic verse.

Apart from the death of one spouse, there were several ways of ending a marriage. Divorce could be unilateral or consensual, and unilateral divorce could be revocable or irrevocable. *Ṭalāq,* a repudiation of the wife by the husband, was the paradigmatic form of divorce. It was revocable at the husband's discretion if the marriage had been consummated, unless it was the third such repudiation or the husband had pronounced a formula tantamount to a triple repudiation. If the divorce was revocable, the husband was said to possess (or control, or own) the [right to] return *(yamliku al-rajʿa; lahu milk al-rajʿa),* meaning he could choose to take back his wife during the waiting period *(ʿidda),* usually three menstrual cycles, that followed the dissolution of any consummated marriage to determine whether the wife was pregnant and thus fix paternity.[74] *Khulʿ* occurred when a husband accepted his wife's offer of compensation in return for his divorce of her; he did not then have the right to return to her during her waiting period. *Firāq,* or judicial separation, was also generally irrevocable. Chapter 4 treats certain aspects of divorce more extensively; I outline the basics here because a husband's prerogative to resume his marital-sexual relationship with his wife affected her claim to maintenance.

The jurists also address the wife's right to lodging *(suknā)* in conjunction with their discussions of maintenance during the waiting period.[75] A free wife had a right to lodging while a marriage endured, in a domicile designated by her husband. If she had co-wives, she was legally entitled to separate lodging from them. She could claim a separate residence from her in-laws as well. It was when a marriage ended, though, that legal issues arose. If her husband had the right to take her back, all agreed, he had to support and lodge her, pregnant or not, during her waiting period, just as he had had to during the marriage. If the divorce was irrevocable, however, Mālik and Shāfiʿī held a husband responsible for maintaining a wife only if she was pregnant. Their basic agreement was predicated on competing rationales, though, which means that they differed on certain special cases involving slaves and invalid marriages.

The Ḥanafī rule on maintenance during the waiting period was, by contrast, exceedingly simple: "She is due lodging and maintenance until her waiting period is completed," whether the divorce is irrevocable or not and whether she is pregnant or not.[76] As certain restrictions related to the marriage persisted, so did the claim to support. Al-Khaṣṣāf opined that after an irrevocable divorce, the woman could continue to collect her regular maintenance during her waiting period, "because her maintenance is guaranteed while the marriage continues to last, and an aspect of marriage lasts *(al-nikāḥ bāqin min wajh)*."[77] After an irrevocable divorce, the husband no longer had any sexual rights to his wife. The marriage could be said to last only in its restrictions and prohibitions. The constraints on the divorcee's mobility were more severe than the constraints placed on a widow in mourning. A widow could go out during the day "for a legitimate reason that absolutely requires her to do so," so long as she returned to the marital home to sleep, but an irrevocably divorced wife was not to go out even during the daytime, "either with or without a legitimate reason."[78] A widow, it should be noted, was not entitled to maintenance during her waiting period; this lack of support correlated with the relatively lighter restrictions placed on her movements.

Women did not bear these lingering restrictions alone. Ḥanafī authorities also placed strictures on the divorcing husband—not on his mobility, which marriage never restricted in any case, but on his ability to remarry. They prohibited him from marrying anyone whom it would not be lawful for him to combine in marriage with the woman he had just divorced, such as her sister.[79] If a man with four wives divorced one irrevocably, he could not marry another until her waiting period expired.[80]

For Mālik and Shāfiʿī, irrevocable divorce ended all of these restrictions just as it ended the wife's claim to maintenance.[81] In contrast to the Ḥanafī view that the continuation of an aspect of marriage during the waiting period obliged continued maintenance, Mālikī and Shāfiʿī texts link a man's responsibility to maintain his wife during the waiting period to his ability to enjoy her sexually, as with a revocably divorced wife—if and when he took her back. For the Mālikīs, "she retains her status [as his wife] *(hiya ʿalā ḥalihā)* until her waiting period ends."[82] The *ṭalāq* introduced no real change before the end of the waiting period. It did not matter "whether his wife is pregnant or not" because she was due maintenance for the same reasons she had a claim to it before the divorce. When her waiting period ended, she ceased to be a wife, and her claim to support also ended.[83] For Shāfiʿī, a revocably divorced wife did not retain exactly the same status. However, because she was available to her husband if he chose to return to her, "her maintenance is due from him in the waiting period, because nothing prevents him from lawfully deriving enjoyment from her except his own [actions]."[84]

In the case of irrevocably divorced wives, Mālikī and Shāfiʿī authorities differentiated between one who was pregnant and one who was not; only the former could claim support.[85] The rationale in the case of a revocably divorced wife was (the possibility of) continued sexual access (with revocation of the divorce); there could be no lawful sexual access to an irrevocably divorced wife, so maintenance was due only if there was a pregnancy.

Though Mālikīs and Shāfiʿīs agreed on this basic rule, their rationales differed, as an exploration of the exceptional cases of enslaved spouses and invalid marriages shows. For Mālik, the father's duty to support his offspring necessitated support of the woman carrying his child, while Shāfiʿī attended to the Qurʾanic command in 65:6 to maintain pregnant divorcees until they gave birth, without reference to paternal obligations.

Source texts from Qurʾan and *sunna* figure prominently in these controversies, even as the use made of them is sometimes counterintuitive. Abū Ḥanīfa justified his view that all divorced women could claim support during their waiting periods (against his Kufan rival Ibn Abī Laylā's contrary view) by partially quoting Q. 65:6 ("God, Great and Majestic, said in his Book: "Expend on them until they deliver their burden") and by citing the precedent of ʿUmar ibn al-Khaṭṭāb, who "granted lodging and maintenance to the thrice-divorced woman."[86] Abū Ḥanīfa's choice of Qurʾanic reference is puzzling. Though the verse mentions lodging for all divorced women ("lodge them where you dwell"), it was interpreted by most to limit maintenance to pregnant women: *"and if they are pregnant,* expend upon them until they deliver their burden."[87] Further, ʿUmar's precedent as presented here opposes extremely well-known traditions about Fāṭima bint Qays, an irrevocably divorced woman to whom the Prophet reportedly denied both lodging and maintenance. In other versions of this report, including one recounted in Abū Yūsuf's *Kitāb al-Āthār,* ʿUmar explicitly discredits Fāṭima.[88]

The Mālikī jurists interpreted Q. 65:6 to apply to free spouses only, applying different rules when either spouse was enslaved. The maintenance of a pregnant, irrevocably divorced woman was based on the obligation to support minor children. Mālikī and Shāfiʿī doctrine on maintenance holds that slaves are not obligated to maintain their children, whether the children are free or enslaved.[89] Nor are free fathers obligated to maintain enslaved children. The support of relatives *(aqārib),* a category that includes children but excludes wives, takes means and necessity into account.

Two distinct cases presented in the *Mudawwana* exemplify this rule: that of a male slave who divorces his wife, who might be either free or a slave, and that of a free man who divorces his enslaved wife. (It is implicit in this passage that the divorces were irrevocable; otherwise, the general Mālikī rule that men must maintain their wives during their waiting periods would apply.) In the first case, Ibn al-Qāsim reported Mālik's view that when a slave divorced his pregnant wife, "there is no maintenance due from him unless he is manumitted while she is pregnant. Then, he maintains the free woman and does not maintain the slave woman unless the slave woman is manumitted after he is manumitted while she is pregnant. Then, he maintains her during her pregnancy because the child is his child."[90] The paternal obligation to maintain emerged only when all relevant parties became free. (This does not mean, as it does in Roman law, that slaves did not have recognized paternity, merely that filiation did not necessarily convey paternal rights and obligations.)[91]

When a slave man divorced a pregnant free (or freed) woman, the child in her womb would be free, because children born in marriage followed the mother's status. The husband did not have any obligation to maintain her during pregnancy so long as he remained enslaved, but his manumission while his free wife was pregnant obligated him to maintain her. The rationale behind his duty of support was his obligation to maintain his offspring (in this case, still in the mother's womb). If a slave man irrevocably divorced a slave woman, he did not become obligated to maintain her during her pregnancy when he was freed if she remained a slave, as the child was her master's slave.[92] However, if she was afterward manumitted while pregnant, the child in her womb also became free. The man then became the free father of a free (though not yet born) child and had to maintain the child—and by extension, the child's mother while she was carrying it. The same rationale applied to the free man who irrevocably divorced a slave woman, because "she and what is in her belly [belong] to her master and maintenance is due from the one to whom the child [belongs]."[93] The father became obligated to maintain her during pregnancy only if she was manumitted and the child in her womb also became free.

An additional comparison between the way Mālikī texts treat two types of pregnancies in free women confirms that maintenance of an irrevocably divorced pregnant woman was based on her ex-husband's obligation to support the child she was carrying. A woman absolutely separated from her husband through mutual imprecation *(liʿān)*—a presumably rare but Qurʾanically described ritual through which a man denies paternity of a child in his wife's womb—is not due maintenance during the pregnancy.[94] Mālik opined that he was not obligated to maintain her because the child was not "linked" to him. By contrast, where the pregnancy occurred in a marriage that had to be dissolved because of a previously unrecognized impediment to valid marriage between the spouses (a heretofore unknown relationship of milk fosterage, perhaps), paternity was legally established and maintenance therefore due during the pregnancy.[95]

Shāfiʿī considered pregnancy a necessary precondition but thought that the validity of the marital tie rather than the spouses' status determined whether maintenance is compulsory. In a departure from the Mālikī principle that the man to whom a child is attributed by paternity (if the child is free) or ownership (if enslaved) must support the irrevocably divorced woman carrying it, Shāfiʿī and his followers applied the provisions of Q. 65:6 to all spouses.[96] Further, the Shāfiʿīs hold that maintenance is not due when pregnancy results from an erroneous or invalid marriage. Though the child is attributed to the father, who must support it after birth, he bears no obligation to support its mother during her pregnancy because no valid marriage tie existed. An example clarifies the matter: if a woman married (unlawfully) during her waiting period from another husband, the later marriage was invalid and therefore dissolved. Pregnancy in this case might be attributed to either "husband." If the child was linked to the first husband,

Shāfiʿī ruled that he must maintain her throughout her pregnancy. However, if the child was attributed to the second, this man had no obligation to support her. Because no valid marriage tie ever existed, the second "marriage" did not oblige maintenance during the waiting period following its dissolution. The same rule applied to the wife of a missing man *(al-mafqūd)* if she remarried after he had been declared dead. If her first husband reappeared after she had become pregnant by her second husband, she had no claim to maintenance from the latter during the pregnancy. As al-Muzanī states, "none of the rules *(aḥkām)* for spouses apply between them except linking the child [to the father]."[97] In direct contrast, in the case of *liʿān,* Mālik points to precisely this link between father and child as the rationale for support.

Failure to Maintain

Just as the Ḥanafīs were distinctive in their insistence that all divorced women could claim support during their waiting periods, so too they differed from Shāfiʿī and Mālik on the question of a wife's right to be separated from a husband who could not maintain her, adhering steadfastly to the principle that nonsupport never justified judicial divorce. The Mālikī authorities gave her this out, but remained vague about specifics. Shāfiʿī and his followers, eschewing both of these alternatives, established a strict deadline of three days of nonsupport before giving the wife an option to be divorced. The ways in which the texts treat this issue clearly show the role of dispute and polemic in the evolution of legal thought and illustrate the significance of jurisprudential variation. To argue simply that the schools agreed on the husband's obligation to maintain his wife is insufficient; the disagreement on the wife's options if he failed to meet his obligations reveals the existence of crucial interpretive differences. The differences in eventual application were minimized, as later Ḥanafī judges consistently found ways out of the impasse through judicial maneuvering.[98] In legal logic, though, they are striking, illustrating the human factors that went in to making doctrinal determinations.

Mālikī texts treated the case of a woman whose husband was unable to support her with their usual pragmatism. The authority would be charged to investigate the matter and grant the husband an appropriate delay or delays, perhaps a month or two. The *Mudawwana*'s cited authorities were reluctant to proclaim a universal standard; every man's situation was different.[99] After the husband had been given ample opportunity to maintain his wife and failed to do so, judicial divorce was a valid solution. His marital rights persisted, though: "he has more right to return to her *(huwa amlaku bi rajʿatihā)* if his situation improves during the waiting period."[100] Taking her back despite unimproved financial circumstances would have no legal effect.[101] Here we see an attempt to balance the wife's right to support with consideration of extenuating circumstances that might affect a husband. They granted the husband as much leeway as possible, while ultimately ruling that prolonged nonsupport justified divorce.

Arguing vehemently against Mālik and the Medinan authorities, the Ḥanafī *Kitāb al-Ḥujja* declares that lack of maintenance was never grounds for divorce.[102] According to Shaybānī, no separation occurred when a man "does not find the means to support his wife."[103] He might have a legitimate reason, aside from incapacity, for being unable to maintain his wife. To allow her to seek divorce would breach his marital prerogatives. Shaybānī observes that the Medinans did not set a strict time limit after which a wife had the right to divorce, as various circumstances could temporarily interfere with a husband's fulfillment of his duty. Taking this logic further, Shaybānī constructs a scenario to illustrate that a man otherwise capable of supporting his wife might be prevented, through no fault of his own, from doing so. A wealthy man traveling on pilgrimage might be robbed. Because he would not know anyone to borrow from, he would temporarily be unable to maintain his wife, "though he is among the wealthiest in Iraq." "Are he and his wife separated?" Shaybānī demands.[104] It would not be fair to such a man to allow a wife who disliked or hated him *("takrahuhu imraʾatuhu")* to take advantage of his predicament to obtain a divorce. The possibility that her dislike of him might itself justify divorce was so far outside Shaybānī's frame of reference that he did not even entertain it.

He proceeds to argue, though, that a woman is not entitled to divorce from even a husband utterly incapable of maintaining her. To justify his view, he presents a famous account of the Prophet marrying a man to a woman for a dower of what the groom could teach her from the Qurʾan. This anecdote appears frequently in legal discussions of dower as an exception to standard rules. Here, Shaybānī ingeniously draws a different lesson: the Prophet married the couple knowing full well that the husband had nothing with which to support his wife. The Prophet would not have done this if poverty were grounds for divorce.[105] Here, as is often true when the *Ḥujja* draws on prophetic example, the tone shifts from legal hairsplitting to pious moralizing. Lack of support becomes an opportunity for the wife to exercise patience and piety.[106] The Companions of the Prophet were poor, and their families (i.e., wives), like those of the Prophet, suffered hunger. If lack of support entitled a woman to seek a divorce, then "each of these [men] would have been obligated to separate from his wife if she requested it of him."[107] Shaybānī counts on his audience's abhorrence of that notion. His rhetoriical strategy depends on their identification with these exemplary men of Islam's first generation. For the jurist, and presumably for his audience as well, it was inconceivable that these respected forbears could be challenged in this way.

Shāfiʿī rejects both approaches and allows a wife to opt for an irrevocable separation after only three days of nonsupport. The rapidity and ease with which she could gain divorce stands in contrast to both the vague Mālikī affirmation of her right and the intransigent Ḥanafī denial that any such right existed. It modifies and strengthens the Mālikī view, in the face of Ḥanafī critique, that divorce for nonsupport was permissible. In systematizing doctrines on this point, Shāfiʿī renders spousal claims interdependent in a way that they are not in either Mālikī or Ḥanafī texts: a husband's right to continue the marriage was tied inextricably to his control over his wife's movements and rendered contingent on his performance of his duty of support. Shāfiʿī argues that a husband could not fairly "detain" (or retain, or constrain) his wife while he failed to provide for her. So, "if he cannot find the means to maintain her that she should be given the option between staying with him or separating from him." During those days when he did not provide for her, he could not prevent her from leaving the dwelling to work or seek sustenance. His control over his wife's mobility depended on his provision of support. After three days of nonsupport, a wife could seek the authority to have her marriage judicially and irrevocably dissolved. Should she choose to remain with him, she was not bound to endure poverty forever but could have a new three-day deadline set whenever she wished. This rule contrasts sharply with two other cases where Shāfiʿī allowed her to seek judicial divorce: when the husband's impotence prevented consummation of the marriage and when the husband proved unable to pay dower in an unconsummated marriage. In these cases, the wife had a one-time right to choose separation. A more detailed exploration of dissolution for impotence will help in understanding the Shāfiʿī arguments on dissolution for nonsupport.

Sunni authorities were united in the view that a wife was entitled to dissolution of her marriage if her husband failed to consummate it.[108] In the absence of any explicit text of Qurʾan or sunna on the matter, they drew on a precedent from ʿUmar ibn al-Khaṭṭāb. When a wife complained to the authority of her husband's impotence, he was to set a deadline of one year during which the husband had to consummate the marriage. If he failed to consummate it, at the end of the year the marriage could be dissolved. Mālikī texts imply that the marriage would automatically dissolve when the term expired, whereas Ḥanafīs and Shāfiʿīs gave the wife an option, when the year was up, between separation and remaining married. Her choice was definitive. If she stayed, she had no further option to separate as a result of her husband's impotence, even if the marriage was never consummated. As the *Jāmiʿ al-Ṣaghīr* puts it, "If she chooses him, she has no option after that."[109]

This agreement on the proper way to handle claims of impotence becomes central to Shāfiʿī's argument against Abū Ḥanīfa's views on dissolution for nonsupport. In the *Umm*, Shāfiʿī reports a conversation with an interlocutor who expresses the view that nonsupport is not grounds for divorce. Shāfiʿī acknowledges that no scriptural text (for him, Qur'an or sunna) explicitly requires dissolution, but argues that the husband's obligation to maintain his wife is clear. It can be "inferred" from the sunna "that he may not, and God knows best, retain her for himself, deriving enjoyment from her and keeping others away from her, [compelling her] to make do with him alone, while he denies to her what is assigned to her from him, because he is incapable of fulfilling it, and the lack of maintenance and clothing ruins her so that she dies from hunger, thirst, and exposure."[110] Having dramatically outlined the harm that would befall women in such cases, he moves on to ʿUmar's precedent. At one point in his career, ʿUmar had ordered soldiers to either support their wives or divorce them. The citation of ʿUmar's view here serves a dual function. First, it serves as evidence, acceptable in instances for which there is no explicit scriptural text, for dissolving marriages in cases where husbands cannot support their wives. Second, and more important, it provides an opening for Shāfiʿī to attack the Ḥanafī position as inconsistent. Ḥanafī rejection of ʿUmar's precedent in the matter of nonsupport appears capricious in light of Ḥanafī acceptance of ʿUmar's precedent as authoritative on the impotent husband.

Shāfiʿī then proceeds to argue on the basis of the relative importance of the wife's rights in these two cases. His imaginary Ḥanafī mouthpiece had stated that "intercourse is one of the contractual claims" established by marriage *(al-jimāʿ min ḥuqūq al-ʿuqda)*. When pressed as to whether the wife's rights were to regular intercourse, as was customary *(kamā yujāmiʿ al-nās)*, or to one act of intercourse, he first states that she has an ongoing right to regular intercourse. However, Shāfiʿī forces the admission that she was not entitled to divorce for lack of sex after consummation. Shāfiʿī seizes on this concession to compare the wife's right to (one act of) intercourse to her right to food, and to argue that the former was far less important: "Loss of sexual intercourse is nothing more than loss of pleasure and offspring, and that does not destroy her self; but leaving off maintenance and clothing leads to the destruction of her self."[111] He notes that in extreme need God permits people to eat forbidden things; however, overpowering desire for sex never permits anything that God has forbidden. Thus, Shāfiʿī argues, to dissolve a marriage for failure to consummate it but not for something that threatens the wife's physical survival was to allow separation for the lesser of two harms and not the greater.

Two elements of Shāfiʿī's argument deserve emphasis. First, he appeals to an audience of educated legal thinkers who share his perspectives on textual evidence, precedent, and consistency. If his audience did not care if one was consistent in one's use of sources, there would be no point calling up the competing precedents from ʿUmar. We may assume that if this portion of the *Umm* reflects an actual encounter, the debate was more balanced than it might appear, and that it is only in Shāfiʿī's recollection that he so easily gets the better of his opponents. Nonetheless, the disputants share certain points of departure. Second, and deeply revealing of shared gendered assumptions, the success of this argument hinges on a view of wives' enforceable sexual rights being so restricted as to be essentially meaningless.

Conclusion

For the Muslim jurists, sex is a husband's right and support is a wife's right. Many things about marriage flow from this simple exchange. A brief comparison between Muslim and rabbinic treatments of maintenance in marriage reveals the Muslim configuration of expectations about sex, money, and domestic service to be distinctive. A Jewish husband maintained his wife in part because of the marriage portion that she brought with her into the marriage and that remained with him during the marriage, much as dowry did in Roman marriage.[112] Although Muslim women frequently brought wealth and household goods into marriage, the model of dower and *milk* shared by formative-period authorities neither requires such transfers nor is entirely capable of assimilating them; they do not fit into the formulation of marriage as or like a sale. Similarly, though most Muslim women presumably did a fair amount of housework in practice, the contrast between a wife's sexual duty and a servant's duty of service differs from rabbinic formulations, where a wife's work and that of her servant were aggregated: a wife who brought a certain number of servants to her husband's home was exempted from performing some (though not all) domestic duties.[113]

The most obvious difference between rabbinic and Muslim jurisprudential discussions of spousal rights is in regard to sex: who has the right to claim it and who has the duty to perform it. Though the rabbis occasionally discuss recalcitrant wives, and what a man whose wife repeatedly refuses him may do (generally, fine her), they frame marital sex in terms of the husband's obligation to have intercourse with his wife. The frequency of this duty (called *onah*) depended on his occupational status, but the notion that it was the husband's duty shifts the entire frame of reference.[114] For the rabbis, marriage still essentially consisted of gender-differentiated claims; the key differences were that the wife's duties were domestic rather than sexual and that her support was not exchanged for her sexual availability. This does not mean that the rabbis did not presume a patriarchal and androcentric framework for sexuality. "Male dominance," Judith Plaskow argues, "shapes every aspect of sexual relations, from the basic structures of marriage, to the expectations surrounding sexual relations within it, to the regulation of sexual interactions outside the marital bond."[115] My point in discussing "the marital debt rabbinic style"[116] is not to set it up as an ideal against which the Muslim model can be measured. I mention it to highlight the internal coherence of a legal model that contrasts sharply with that of the Muslim jurists. Sex, support, reproduction, and household labor are common concerns for the rabbis and their Muslim counterparts, but what they do with them differs considerably.

In the Muslim case, a wife's sexual availability was vital and the extent to which it was intertwined with support varies only when other legal-methodological principles are brought into the mix. The Shāfiʿī and Ḥanafī agreement that only the wife's availability to the husband matters in determining when she may claim maintenance highlights the one-sided nature of this right. The Mālikī position that a husband not yet capable of intercourse need not maintain a grown wife reflects a different legal principle that supersedes the standard rule about the wife's availability. It is not so much that the rules are incompatible as that the jurists draw on different principles in order to make their rulings.

For all, the commencement of maintenance payment clearly depends on the wife's sexual availability. Dower payment correlates to a woman becoming sexually lawful to her husband, but maintenance is linked to his ongoing right to exercise power over her movements and to enjoy her physically and sexually whenever he wishes. The wife's support was either premised on the husband's right to derive enjoyment from her or compensated her for the restrictions placed on her mobility and behavior. During a marriage, these were linked: to be sexually available to her husband, a wife had to remain at home and not rebuff her husband's advances or do anything that would prohibit intercourse, such as undertake a voluntary fast, without his permission. After an irrevocable divorce, only the restrictions on her mobility (and remarriage) persisted. The Ḥanafīs alone considered these sufficient reason to continue the wife's right to maintenance during her waiting period if she was not pregnant.

The wife's right to maintenance was contingent on her satisfactory performance of her duties, but a husband's right to derive enjoyment from his wife and to restrict her movements depended less on his performance of his financial obligations. And yet, though the formative-period jurists construed a Muslim husband's marital obligations as primarily financial (he paid dower and gained legitimate sexual access to a wife; he paid maintenance and could expect sexual availability in return), one of a man's marital duties concerned his behavior rather than his expenditures: he was required to apportion his time among his wives, if he had more than one. The wife's claim to regular visits from her husband shifted marriage from a commercial logic based on dominion toward an intimately personal one grounded in reciprocity. The next chapter will explore how the jurists' discussions of apportionment *(qasm)* mediated these two realms.[117]

3

Claiming Companionship

RĀFIʿ B. KHADĪJ had been married to one woman for many years when he "married a young lady and favored the young one over" his older longtime wife, whose name the *Mudawwana* does not report.[1] Complaining of favoritism toward her new co-wife, she requested divorce. Rāfiʿ complied, pronouncing a single, revocable divorce. Before her waiting period expired, she regretted her decision. At her request, he took her back. Yet the favoritism still bothered her and she asked for divorce once more. Again she regretted it; again, he took her back. The favoritism continued, however, so she sought divorce a third time. Rāfiʿ replied that only one divorce remained and gave her a choice: she could remain despite the favoritism or be irrevocably divorced. She chose to stay. According to the Mālikī authorities who recount this case in the *Mudawwana,* Rāfiʿ did nothing wrong. In fact, he seems to have done everything right. He did not divorce her until she requested it. He did not take her back except at her behest. Rāfiʿ's wife had options, even if she found them unpalatable. Her predicament reveals the irresolvable tensions between ideals about fairness and good treatment and the messy realities of human emotions and behaviors.

The *Mudawwana*'s section "Apportionment between wives" affirms both the wife's right to a share of her husband's time and the lawfulness of her giving up this right. In one scenario, a woman stipulates at the outset of her marriage that her husband may favor a previous wife, giving up her claim to an allotment of his time. Mālik declares this agreement invalid; a woman's portion of her husband's time is "one of the obligations of marriage" and she has a right to her turn.[2] But in another scenario, a woman is married to a man who "dislikes her and wants to divorce her." What if, Saḥnūn asks, she says to him, "'Don't divorce me, and I give all my days to my co-wife *(ṣāḥibatī);* don't allot anything to me' or she says to him 'Marry another in addition to me and I will give all my days to the one you marry in addition to me'?"[3] Ibn al-Qāsim responds with Mālik's matter-of-fact view that "there is no problem in that and he doesn't allot anything to her." The juxtaposition of these cases reveals a seeming contradiction at the heart of spousal intimacy. Providing for favoritism in a marriage contract vitiates an essential element of marriage, but allowing favoritism is acceptable later to avoid a divorce. This tension between the permissible and the desirable points to the limitations of law as a means to achieve fairness. On the one hand, an ideal of mutual companionship informs the jurists' work. On the other, as with Rāfiʿ's wife, the looming presence of unilateral divorce and the possibility of polygyny undercut the ideal.

Wives' sexual rights are an essential, if unstated, undercurrent to these discussions of polygyny. Just as the husband's sexual claims over his wife come to the fore in discussions of the support obligation, the dismissal of women's claims to regular sexual contact with their husbands emerges from discussions of a husband's allocation of his time among his wives. But to see this, we must read those passages with a squint: a wife's claim to sex does not emerge as a legitimate question within juristic rubrics, even as the differentiation between wives and concubines in this and other regards remains a significant concern of theirs. As Rachel Adler points out with regard to rabbinic texts, legal categories emerge from the priorities and interpretive preconceptions of the scholars who frame them.[4] These categories in turn structure the types of answers that can be given but also, more basically, the types of questions that are asked. Certain questions (for instance, how does the permissibility of polygyny affect wives' ability to negotiate equitable agreements with their husbands?) remain unaskable.

In the case of apportionment between women, differences in terminology among groups of jurists affect their rulings and also reveal a great deal about their visions of women's sexual rights. Their conceptual language both reflects and shapes their views of what constitutes fairness between wives. In regulating the minutiae of allocating time, making up for lost turns, and the effect of various behaviors by either spouse on the other's right or duty of apportionment, Shāfiʿī is concerned with ensuring justice *(ʿadl)*, while Mālik focuses on avoiding partiality *(mayl)*. Abū Ḥanīfa and his followers object to favoritism, but remain largely silent on questions of apportionment except for the question of the wedding nights due to a new bride, a topic that provides an important glimpse into the gendered division of spousal claims.

The second part of this chapter discusses what transpires during a woman's turn, focusing on how the right to ask for or decline sexual activity is gendered. Here, male sexual refusal leads to very different consequences from those of female refusal. Despite an underlying agreement about which obligations were enforceable (women's right to time and support, men's right to sex) and which were not (women's right to sex), the texts differ in the tone with which they address these points. Oaths of abstinence, discussed in the third section of this chapter, show that the jurists (though again varying in their approaches) ultimately agree that wives have few, if any, enforceable sexual claims after consummation. The final section of this chapter returns us to the case of Rāfiʿ's wife and those like her who try to ward off divorce by forgoing their allocated time. The wife's claim to her allotted turn, and her right to demand a resumption of her turns at any time after she had agreed to forgo them, existed within an asymmetrical spousal relationship.

I will argue that the jurists' attempts to ensure fairness in marriage were limited by their adoption of a strongly gendered model of interdependent spousal rights and duties. Taken cumulatively, the regulations surrounding apportionment and abstinence demonstrate that even when individual jurists wanted to enforce wives' rights to marital intimacy, their insistence on a gendered division of marital claims prevented them from doing so. Moreover, the culture of legal disputation in which pressing arguments to their fullest extension became necessary to formulate logically defensible, internally consistent positions led to the systematic discounting of women's claims. Even basic considerations that should have been uncontroversial, given the jurists' stated commitments to wives' rights, became indefensible under these rules of engagement. Reading these texts only for the rules that they can enforce is, at one level, necessary (there is a bottom line when it comes to women's rights), but at another level deeply misleading.

Taking Turns

Perhaps the best example of the extent to which jurists' categories shape their reasoning is found in their discussions of apportionment. The choice to discuss cohabitation and the intimate relations of spouses as a matter of allocating time between co-wives has profound ramifications, including the treatment of polygny as normative. Instead of orienting their discussions around the permissibility of polygyny or the rights of women to companionship from their husbands, the jurists' relevant category was apportionment. Though they did come to address issues such as women's claims to time and sex within the confines of the discussion of apportionment, the category itself was an androcentric one, concerned with male obligation.[5] Polygyny itself merited no special reflection. Texts addressed stipulations against polygyny—usually void unless attached to an oath of divorce, except under Ḥanbalī doctrine—and which women could not be combined in marriage, concurrently or sequentially, but never questioned the basic premise that a man could be married to more than one woman at a time. Discussions of apportionment went one step further: polygyny appeared not only as permissible but normative. By defining husbands' duty as dividing time among wives, rather than as spending time with wives, polygyny became the norm and monogamy the exception. Cohabitation, as a husband staying with each wife in turn, presumes that spouses do not share a single residence full time. Under the rubric of apportionment, a lone wife appeared as an exception. Even in this instance the jurists accounted for the "monogamous" husband's sexual access to one or more female slaves. Whatever the demographic reality concerning multiple, concurrent lawful sex partners, the idea of polygyny fundamentally shaped the regulation of marital intimacy for everyone.[6]

Muḥammad's personal precedent emerged frequently in discussions of apportionment. His behavior was the basis for the commonsense standard in allocation. Assuming all wives were free, a husband ought to spend one night in turn with each wife. (A man married to both a free woman and an enslaved woman owed two nights to the free woman for every night spent with the slave, except according to Mālik, who consistently differentiated less between enslaved and free people than his counterparts. He seems to have held that both free and slave wives were to receive the same number of nights. Other Medinan authorities, such as Saʿīd b. al-Musayyab, ruled that slaves received half the allocation of free wives.)[7]

Could a man modify the length of each turn without tampering with the overall proportion of nights granted to each wife? Abū Ḥanīfa does not state so directly, but in one report allows a man to choose even the length of turn granted to a new bride. Shāfiʿī thought it permissible. If a man with two wives "wants to allot his time two nights and two nights, or three and three, he may do so."[8] Mālik and the other Medinan authorities whom Ibn al-Qāsim cites disallow it. The *Mudawwana* focuses on the example of Muḥammad and his Companions:[9]

> I said: If two women are under (i.e., married to) [one] man, is he permitted to allot two days to this one and two days to that one, or a month to this one and a month to that one? He said: I have not heard Mālik say anything except "A day to this one and a day to that one." Ibn al-Qāsim said: What has been established from the Messenger of God, may God's blessings and peace be upon him, and his Companions suffices for you in this [matter]. It has not reached us that any of them allotted [his time] except a day for her and a day for her.[10]

Ibn al-Qāsim proceeds to report an incident on Mālik's authority that bolsters his view that a husband must alternate days. "ʿUmar b. ʿAbd al-ʿAzīz perhaps became angry with one of his wives, then he came to her on her day and slept in her room." Ibn al-Qāsim deduced that "if it were permissible for him to allot two days to this one and two days to that one, or more, he would have stayed with the one with whom he was pleased until he was pleased with the other and then made up her days to her."[11] The husband's feeling toward his wife was irrelevant. He was obligated to allot her turn to her, even if he would prefer to stay with another of his wives. The basic formula of one night each for a man's wives served to ensure fairness between them.

Implicitly, the minimum allocation of time for a free wife was one of every four nights—what she would get if married to a man with the legal maximum of four wives. This unofficial one-in-four standard recurs in various texts. Shāfiʿī's two-and-two or three-and-three allocation would give each wife *at least* one of every four nights, though this would no longer be the case if more than two wives were involved. Mālik applied the one-in-four standard when a man with only one wife spent time with his concubines. He could stay one day with his wife and then spend two or three days with one or more of his concubines. One

Medinan judge with a favorite *umm walad,* a slave who had borne him a child, was known to do so, and Mālik saw "no problem" with this behavior.[12] The issue was not parity between a man's wife and his concubine, as the latter, even if she were his *umm walad,* had no claim on his time.[13] At stake, rather, was the husband's freedom to spend his time as he chose as opposed to the wife's right to a portion of his time. Shāfiʿī stated that a man could refrain from visiting his wife or wives completely, so long as the proportion of time spent with each wife relative to any other or others did not change. "The slaves do not have an allotted portion along with his spouses. He may visit them *(fa yaʾtīhunna),* and have intercourse [with them], however he wishes, more or less than he goes to his wives, during the days and the nights." He must, though, abstain from all of his wives equally, "just as he may travel and be absent from his wives in [another] city." When he resumes taking turns, "he does justice between them."[14] A wife's allotted share was not a right to an absolute amount of time with her husband but only to fairness in relation to her co-wives.

In evaluating men's behavior in allocation, Shāfiʿī and his disciple al-Muzanī focused on doing justice, while Mālik and his followers stressed the avoidance of partiality. Divergent rules flowed from these starting points. We see this most clearly when circumstances such as travel or illness disrupted the normal apportionment of turns. Shāfiʿī justice demanded a strictly equal allocation of time, but the Mālikī focus on motivation meant that even spending unequal time, if done for a legitimate reason and not out of partiality, did not necessarily violate the obligation to be fair.

The *Mudawwana*'s discussion of a man's choice of travel partner shows the calculations:

> I said: What if he travels with one of them to his landed estate *(ḍayʿatihi)* and for a need of his, or he makes pilgrimage with one of them, or makes the lesser pilgrimage *(ʿumra)* with her or takes her on a military expedition *(ghazā bihā),* then he arrives [home] to the other one and she requests of him that he stay with her the same number of days that he traveled with her companion? He said: Mālik said: She is not due that. Instead he begins apportioning anew between them and the days that he was traveling with his [other] wife are ignored, except in the case of military expeditions.[15]

Ibn al-Qāsim here permits, in accordance with the teaching of Mālik, a major departure from the one-night rule that governed the division of time when a husband and his wives were together; a husband could choose the wife with whom he wished to travel: "He may take whichever one of them he wishes unless his taking one of them is due to partiality *('alā wajh al-mayl)* towards her and [inclination] away from his other wives."[16] Military expeditions merit special consideration because a relevant prophetic precedent exists. But though Ibn al-Qāsim recalls the Prophet's practice of drawing lots when he wished to travel with one or some of his wives, he does not consider it binding. Instead, he turns to his authoritative predecessors among the jurists: "I did not hear Mālik say anything about the case of military expeditions except that Mālik or someone else mentioned that the Messenger of God, may God's peace and blessings be upon him, used to draw lots between [his wives]. So, rather, in the case of military expeditions he has to draw lots between them. But my opinion is that all of this is the same, military expeditions and other [travel]."[17] Ibn al-Qāsim bases his own view on a legal similarity between the cases, ignoring prophetic precedent. This cavalier treatment of prophetic example contrasts with Ibn al-Qāsim's earlier insistence regarding the question of the length of each wife's turn, that "what has been established from the Messenger of God . . . suffices for you." Here, the husband may travel with "whichever one of them he wishes," without the duty to make up the lost turns of those who remained at home, provided only that his choice is not guided by partiality.

Besides favoritism, what would lead a man to choose one wife as travel companion rather than another? The *Mudawwana* poses a scenario in which one wife's admirable moral and administrative qualities lead to her indispensability at home: "If he goes out with her, and draws her lot, his wealth and children will be jeopardized and harm will come to him as a result." In this situation, he could legitimately choose her co-wife, "who does not have that capacity or that reliability, so instead he travels with her to lighten her burden and because of her uselessness *(li qillat manfa'atihā)* in what he might delegate to her from his estate and his affairs and in his [lack of] need for her to act on his behalf in his [affairs]."[18] The text recognizes women's varied capacities and the possibility that a wife could be a capable companion and helpmate for her husband. For her to act on his behalf in managing his estate and household exceeds what can be expected from her legally and goes beyond the quid pro quo logic of interdependent rights. Yet her performance of these tasks does not earn her compensatory time on his return. Her impressive skills and capabilities do nothing to alter the husband's prerogative to decide whom he takes with him on a journey.

The Mālikī focus on avoiding partiality, with only exceptional references to doing justice, drew implicitly on the Qur'anic assertion that doing justice is an impossible, and therefore inappropriate, standard. Q. 4:129 declares, "You are never able to do justice between wives even if you desire to; but do not incline completely away *(lā tamīlū kulla al-mayl)* from a woman." The *Mudawwana* only alludes to the Qur'an, but the *Umm*'s hermeneutical approach on the same subject is explicitly scriptural, quoting the Qur'an and referring to its provisions. Lest his insistence on a husband's duty to do justice between wives seem to contradict the Qur'anic declaration that justice is impossible, Shāfiʿī interprets the verse through the lens of a prophetic hadith that narrows the scope of justice in conjugal matters. The Prophet acknowledges that he allocates equally that which he controls *("mā amliku")*, which Shāfiʿī understands to be his actions, while God is responsible for what he cannot control—in Shāfiʿī's interpretation, his emotions.[19] Although justice might be impossible in matters of the heart, feelings are irrelevant; God judges on the basis of one's actions and statements. Justice required avoiding any inequity in word or deed (though it did not extend to equality in sexual matters), specifically in the measurable dimension of time spent. Such inequity constituted the "inclining completely away" that the Qur'an forbade. Shāfiʿī's restrictive exegesis argues for justice as a positive and objective standard in apportionment in contrast to the Mālikī focus on avoiding partiality, a negative and subjective measure.[20]

The divergent effects of using "avoiding partiality" or "ensuring justice" as organizing rubrics become clearer when travel or illness disrupts the normal order of rotation. Mālik forgives an imbalance of time as long as a man avoids favoritism. As with travel, where "he may take whichever one of them he wishes unless his taking one of them is due to partiality towards her and [inclination] away from his other wives,"[21] a husband might have a valid reason, such as illness, for departing from an equal division while at home. If capable of continuing his visitations, he had to do so. However, according to Mālik, if his illness was so grave that he could not do so, "then I see no problem with him staying wherever he wishes, unless it is out of partiality."[22] No makeup of missed turns was due. Even if a man simply shirked his responsibility to one wife by staying with another for a month, Mālik condemned his actions but did not require him to make up the time, only noting that if he persisted in his unfair treatment he could be punished.[23]

Shāfiʿī, by contrast, defined justice as precisely equal allocation of time. But justice could involve a substitute mechanism of lot drawing, as with travel. If a husband intent on a journey drew lots to determine which wife would accompany him, he thereby exempted himself from the need to make up the time to those who remained behind. Should he fail to draw lots, he was obliged to make up the time.[24] Drawing lots to choose whom to take on a journey demonstrated a concern for strict fairness to individual wives.[25] Random selection made the process acceptable: each wife had an equal chance of being selected. (However, if after drawing lots the husband decided that he would rather travel alone than with the wife whose lot was drawn, he could leave her at home without penalty as long as he did not take another in her place—humiliating for the woman, perhaps, but legally acceptable, as a man could not be forced to spend time with his wives.) The *Umm*'s discussion under "Juristic Disagreement on Apportionment during Travel" offers a rationale in the context of rebutting a putative Ḥanafī position. According to the *Umm*, Ḥanafīs held that a man had to make up travel days to those who remained behind, whether he selected his travel partner himself or chose her by lot. This Ḥanafī position—as far as I can tell not corroborated in formative-period Ḥanafī sources—rectifies the perceived deficiency of the Mālikī view, which is overgenerous toward the husband, by positing the need to make up days. Shāfiʿī substitutes the equal chance of each wife in the selection process for the equality of time.

Apart from travel, though, strict equality of time governed Shāfiʿī regulation. If a husband missed or shortened a visit with one of his wives because of illness or some other pressing necessity, Shāfiʿī insisted on his making up the time scrupulously.[26] If a wife fell seriously ill, her husband could remain with her until she recovered or died; if she died, he could remain until her corpse was buried. Nonetheless, even in this admittedly extreme case, he was still obliged to make up the lost nights to his other wife or wives. A husband who sickened had to continue his rounds unless he was too weak to do so. Then he might remain where he took ill (not, as in the Mālikī view, "wherever he wishes") until capable of resuming his visitations. Then he had to make up to his neglected wife or wives the same amount of time he spent, in his grave illness, with one wife.

The choice of organizing concepts resulted in real differences in doctrine with regard to calculating wives' rights to a portion of their husbands' time under the exceptional circumstances of travel, illness, or a man's shirking of his duty. Yet despite these differences, there was important common ground among the formative-period jurists. The presumption of multiple wives indelibly stamped jurists' thinking about cohabitation. Their rules sprang from the notion that a wife had no enforceable claim to an absolute proportion of her husband's time, though Mālik does suggest that even if he visits his concubines, she should get one of four nights. However, she may not object to his travel; it goes without saying that a man's wives have no right to restrict his movements in order to have their regular turns with him. Even to consider the question makes no sense: no jurist asks whether a man's wife may prohibit him from traveling to ensure her share of his time. Juristic differences regarding the selection process for travel are slight in comparison to their agreement on the husband's right to take some or all of his wives with him if he wished and the wives' obligation to accompany him if chosen.[27] At the same time, no wife has a right to go with him. As Shāfiʿī puts it, "he is not obligated to take [all of] them or any of them." A wife claims a portion of her husband's time, but the overarching context is still that of her availability to him, not the reverse. Finally, and only alluded to briefly thus far, the jurists agree that whatever standard of fairness governs apportionment, equality in sexual matters is neither obligatory nor expected. Later sections of this chapter will address this question of sexual rights more directly. First, however, I turn to the wedding nights.

Wedding Nights

When a man marries a woman, how many nights may or must he stay with her? Does this change depending on whether she is a virgin? And if he already has a wife or wives, what about her or their share of his time? When an already married man takes a new wife, the requisite wedding nights may interfere with his duty to his other wife or wives. Jurists' various approaches to these questions illustrate their common dependence on a view of gender-differentiated spousal claims, their diverse ways of drawing on scriptural texts to render rules, and the refinement of doctrines through debate and disputation.

Mālik's view can be summed up as follows: a virgin bride is due seven nights with her groom; a non-virgin, three. These are her right and are not counted against her in calculating each wife's turn; the husband begins apportionment with a clean slate after the wedding nights: "If the man has another wife, he divides his time equally between them after the wedding nights. He does not count the wedding nights against the one he has just married."[28] The *Muwaṭṭaʾ* invokes prophetic precedent for its distinction between virgin and non-virgin brides. When the Prophet married Umm Salama, a widow, he gave her a choice: "If you wish, I will spend seven [nights] with you and then spend seven with them. If you wish, I will spend three with you and then visit them in turn."[29] She replied, "Spend three." The text goes on to report Anas b. Mālik's maxim: "Seven for the virgin, and three for the non-virgin." Umm Salama's choice between three and seven nights raises the tricky issue of whether the wedding nights are the wife's right. This issue is absent from the *Muwaṭṭaʾ* but present in the *Mudawwana*, where the treatment of the topic implicitly responds to Ḥanafī critique. Mālikī authorities understand the Prophet's granting Umm Salama a choice between three and seven nights to mean that as a non-virgin she was entitled to three nights with her new husband that would not need to be made up to his other wives. However, if she were to take the full week offered to her, it would need to be made up in its entirety to the others. In the *Mudawwana*, Ibn al-Qāsim affirms that the wedding nights are the bride's right and the husband cannot choose to forgo them.[30] Both the virgin and the non-virgin have a claim to the wedding nights: "Seven for *(li)* the virgin and three for *(li)* the non-virgin." The preposition *li*, "for" or "due to," stands opposed to *ʿalā*, "upon" or "due from": "And you are told in the hadith of Anas b. Mālik that these are *for* the woman and not *for* the man." Three elements thus constitute the Mālikī doctrine on wedding nights: they are the bride's right, they need not be made up to any additional wives, and their number depends on whether she has been previously married.

Both the *Muwaṭṭaʾ Shaybānī* and the *Kitāb al-Ḥujja* argue, on the authority of Abū Ḥanīfa, against two of these points: the differentiation between virgin and non-virgin brides and the exemption of the wedding nights from the rules of apportionment. Instead, al-Shaybānī states that all brides receive the same number of nights and that those nights must be made up to each of a husband's previous wives. (The *Kitāb al-Ḥujja* further attributes to Abū Ḥanīfa the view that the husband could determine how many wedding nights were to be spent with the bride.) This view that the wedding nights had to be made up to a man's other wives responded to a perceived flaw in the Mālikī position, which ignored the conflict between the bride's right to wedding nights and the other wives' rights to their allotted turns. Shaybānī criticizes Mālikī doctrine for giving a new bride wedding nights at the expense of the turns of her co-wife or co-wives. Abū Ḥanīfa resolves the problem by making the wedding nights simply a regular part of a man's apportionment to his wives.

These Ḥanafī texts treat hadith strategically, addressing them where necessary to bolster their arguments. They do not, however, serve as the starting point for Ḥanafī doctrines in the way that they do for the Mālikīs. Behnam Sadeki, in treating the topic of prayer, argues that Ḥanafī jurisprudence is "nearly maximally hermeneutically flexible," meaning that the contents of hadith do not determine Ḥanafī doctrines.[31] In the case of legal works specifically addressing Mālikī doctrines, however, the hadith that serve as proof for their positions must be addressed. Both the *Muwaṭṭaʾ Shaybānī* and the *Kitāb al-Ḥujja* address the hadith, either by interpreting the same hadith in a different way or by offering an alternate rendering.

Ḥanafī authorities dissolve the distinction between wedding nights and normal apportionment, and between new bride and an existing wife or wives, using variants of the Umm Salama hadith. The *Muwaṭṭaʾ Shaybānī* presents substantially the same text as the *Muwaṭṭaʾ* but proffers an alternate interpretation as authoritative: "If he spends seven with her, he must spend seven with them, he does not add anything for her and against them. And if he spends three with her, he spends three with them."[32] Mālik holds that after the three nights that are due to the new wife alone, the husband begins his regular rounds, taking equal turns with each. According to Shaybānī, however, if he spends three nights with his new wife, he must also spend three nights with each of the others, lest he impermissibly favor the new wife.

The *Kitāb al-Ḥujja* expands on this need for equality, drawing explicitly on prophetic precedent:

> Muḥammad said: Abū Ḥanīfa, may God be pleased with him, said about the man who marries a woman and [already] has another wife, whether the one he just married is [either] a virgin or a non-virgin: He does not stay with the one he just married except the same amount he stays with the other. If he wishes, he spends seven [days] with the one he married and spends seven with the other, and if he wishes, three [days] with the one he married and three with the other, and if he wishes a night and a day with the one he married and with the other, and so forth. He does not spend with the one he married [any time] except what he spends with the other [also].[33]

This passage reiterates the irrelevance of virginity to the number of wedding nights and asserts the need for spending equal time with the new wife and any other wife or wives. It also makes another point worth digressing briefly to address: Shaybānī reports Abū Ḥanīfa's statement that the husband had the prerogative to decide how many wedding nights a bride received: "If he wishes, he stays seven . . . and if he wishes, three . . . and if he wishes, a night and a day." If the wedding nights were nights like any other, the length of time spent with the bride became the husband's choice, provided the condition of equality was met. Nonetheless, the *Kitāb al-Ḥujja* remains uncharacteristically reticent on this point, acknowledging it in passing but marshaling no evidence to contest the opposing view. Perhaps because the reports about Umm Salama, even in the preferred Ḥanafī version, suggest that it is the bride who determines how many wedding nights she gets, Shaybānī skates over this issue even as he challenges other components of the Medinan reading of the hadith.

The *Ḥujja* further contests the Mālikī position by giving a version of the Umm Salama hadith that differs from that in the *Muwaṭṭa'* and the *Muwaṭṭa' Shaybānī*. Shaybānī introduces the text in a way that makes clear it is intended to rebut Mālik's position: "How can they say that [all seven nights would need to be made up] when the hadith has come about the Messenger of God, may God's blessings and peace be upon him and his family, when he married Umm Salama, may Exalted God be pleased with her, that he, may God's blessings and peace be upon him, said to her: "If you wish I will spend seven with you and spend seven with them; if you wish I will visit you and them in turn *(durtu ʿalayki wa ʿalayhinna)?*"[34] The key difference in the Prophet's words appears in the last phrase: "I will visit you and them in turn." (The other version has "I will spend three with you then visit them in turn.") The parallelism between the bride and any previous wives avoids room for the misinterpretation (in Shaybānī's opinion) that leads to the Mālikī view.[35] Nonetheless, Shaybānī condescends to argue in the *Ḥujja* against the Mālikī position utilizing their preferred version of the tradition as well, as in the *Muwaṭṭaʾ Shaybānī*.[36] Here he appeals to logic. It makes no sense to accept that the non-virgin bride has three nights that are hers by right and that need not be made up to co-wives, then state that if she takes the option of having seven nights, all seven would need to be made up. Instead, if three are her right, exempt from the regular apportionment, then only four would need to be made up to the other wives if she were to choose seven.[37] His phrasing "obligatory *to* her and *upon* them (i.e., the other wives)" depicts the Mālikī position as giving a bride rights against her co-wives. Taking the wedding nights from the allotted portions of co-wives is logically untenable.

Shaybānī follows his logical argument with an appeal to prophetic example. He elicits from the sunna a principle of nonfavoritism that explains both the Ḥanafī allocation and also the nondifferentiation between virgin and non-virgin brides. The *Ḥujja* explicitly links the two: "It is not the right of the bride and the other [i.e., a previous wife] to [his] privacy with her except [with] equality, and we do not think that the Messenger of God, may God's blessings and peace be upon him and his [family,] favored the bride over those beside her and he did not favor the virgin over the non-virgin and he did not stay alone with them or have privacy with them except equally." In addition to being illogical, the Mālikī interpretation of the Umm Salama hadith violates this principle of nonfavoritism. It ought to be clear, says Shaybānī, that the "the first part of the hadith enters upon the last"; that is, "it does not favor her against them in its first part when it says 'If you wish, I will spend seven with you and seven with them.' Likewise, in the last part indeed its meaning is: 'I will take turns with them like what I did for you.'"[38]

In contrast to the Ḥanafīs, who treat the wedding nights as simply part of an ongoing allocation of time to a man's wives and who granted a newly married woman no special consideration, Shāfiʿī and al-Muzanī upheld both key elements of Mālik's stance: that a husband spent a different number of nights with virgin and non-virgin brides, and that these nights need not be made up to any co-wives.[39] As they grappled with the challenge posed by the Ḥanafīs to Mālik's reasoning—one cannot simply ignore the question of how the wedding nights affect existing wives—the *Umm* and the *Mukhtaṣar* of al-Muzanī differ in how strictly they separate male and female claims. The question of whether the nights are the wife's right or the husband's right turns out to be key.

To sidestep the logical problem of favoritism of one wife over another, the *Umm* argues that a new bride is not really yet a wife and so the rules about apportionment do not apply to her. The husband has the right to depart from his normal apportionment of time in order to spend wedding nights with his bride: "Shāfiʿī, may God be merciful to him, said: If a man marries a woman and consummates [the marriage] with her, then her situation is not the situation of [those wives] who are [already] with him. If she is a virgin, he may stay seven days and nights with her, and if she is a non-virgin, then he may spend three days and nights. Then he begins the division *(al-qisma)* between his wives."[40] Until her wedding nights have passed, "her situation is not the situation" of his existing wives. By framing the issue this way, Shāfiʿī sidesteps the grounds on which the Mālikī position was attacked by the Ḥanafīs, that is, that one wife was being given time at the expense of her co-wives. In the *Umm*'s formulation, the time spent with the new wife is simply an exemption of the husband from his regular duty, analogous (though this is not stated explicitly) to his right to travel without his wives or to abstain from visiting his wives in order to be with his concubines. However, unlike his unrestricted right to stay away from his wives in these cases, the wedding night exemption is limited. After seven nights (if a virgin), or three (if a non-virgin), the bride becomes a wife and may not receive preferential treatment: "She is one of them after her days have ended, and he may not favor her over them."[41] (The shift from bride to wife is no doubt momentous in other ways as well, but the point at issue is the honeymoon period.)

Shāfiʿī justifies the husband's departure from his normal visitations of his previous wives, but by making the right to the wedding nights the husband's, Shāfiʿī leaves open the possibility that the husband might not spend the requisite number of wedding nights with his new bride. Shāfiʿī's compulsive separation of men's and women's claims precludes arguing that the bride has the "right" to wedding nights or that the husband has them as his duty, which would effectively be the same thing. (Claims that are "for" [*li*] one spouse are "due from" [*ʿala*] the other.) Shāfiʿī must maneuver delicately to ensure the bride gets her wedding nights without suggesting that a husband and wife have reciprocal, mutual claims. First, he speaks of the husband's right to spend wedding nights with his new bride and apart from this other wives: "If a man marries a virgin he may *(kāna lahu)* stay seven nights with her and if a non-virgin, three. These nights are not counted against him and to his wives who were with him before her. He begins the apportionment from after the seven [or] from after the three [wedding nights]." If he fails to spend this time with his new bride, he must make it up to her: "And if he does not do this and he allots time to his wives, omitting [the wedding nights], he makes up that amount to either [bride, the virgin or the non-virgin] as if he left her rights in the apportionment and he makes it up to both of them."[42] He meticulously avoids any declaration that the wedding nights are the bride's right: "And it is not his right with regard to the virgin or the non-virgin except to stay with them [i.e., the brides] this number, unless they permit it."[43] It makes no sense to require the wife's permission to forgo the wedding nights if they were not her right. The husband had to make up any shortfall in the wedding nights to his bride, just as if he were to shortchange her in his allocation of time; functionally, the wedding nights were, as in Mālikī doctrine, the bride's right, exempt from the usual rules of apportionment of time. The *Umm* goes to extraordinary lengths to avoid acknowledging this because this position was vulnerable to the same critique leveled by the Ḥanafīs at the Mālikī position: one wife was being favored at the expense of the other or others.

The subtlety of the *Umm*'s argument stands out when juxtaposed to al-Muzanī's matter-of-fact treatment of the wedding nights in his *Mukhtaṣar*.[44] Al-Muzanī simply says outright, without pussyfooting around, that the wedding nights are the husband's duty. At the same time, he declares that they are not to be counted against him by his previous wives, implying that they are his right with regard to his other wives. Like Shāfiʿī, al-Muzanī treads a fine line. The Prophet's words to Umm Salama were "an indication that if a man marries a virgin he must *(ʿalayhi an)* stay seven nights with her, and three with the non-virgin, and it is not counted against him by his wives who were already with him before her"[45] The wedding nights were the husband's right insofar as they could not be counted *against him* by his other wives and he was exempt from making the time up to them; in this, the *Mukhtaṣar* agrees with the *Umm*. The texts diverge, though, where al-Muzanī claims that Shāfiʿī holds that the wedding nights are a man's duty to his bride that he "must" fulfill. The *Umm* continually resists stating that the husband has the wedding nights as a duty upon him *(ʿalayhi)* as well as being a right that he possesses *(lahu)*, relying instead on circumlocutions such as Shāfiʿī's declaration that "he *may* stay *(lahu an)* . . . And it is not his right . . . except to stay with them this number [of nights]." In contrast to the *Umm*'s painstaking separation, al-Muzanī summarizes Shāfiʿī's rules commonsensically: the wedding nights were the husband's right with regard to his previous wives but his duty with regard to his new wife.

The wedding nights have limited significance for the ongoing relationship between spouses—at most, in Shāfiʿī's formulation, the bride has a week before she becomes a wife—but they reveal a great deal about the jurists' visions of fairness regarding co-wives. As with other aspects of apportionment, fairness was necessary. But what precisely did it entail? The Mālikīs did not question how a new wife's claim to wedding nights interfered with any existing wives' rights. The Ḥanafīs worried about favoritism toward the bride at the expense of her co-wives and insisted that any time spent with the bride be made up to the others. The Shāfiʿīs made the point that the husband had a right to wedding nights with his new wife; for this reason, brides were temporarily exempt from the apportionment among his other wives. Did virginity merit special treatment? The Ḥanafīs downplayed it, but others gave a virgin bride more time with her groom, or her groom more time with her. Why? The answer could be as simple as the presence of the three-vs.-seven distinction in the hadith account of the Prophet's wedding nights: it cried out for explanation. There are also hadith that recommend that men marry virgins, stressing their greater playfulness.[46] This perspective suggests the husband's right to enjoy his virginal bride, but the emphasis on considering the wedding nights the wife's right suggests instead her need for greater time to become acclimated to her new husband.[47] One could speculate about the slow introduction of a virgin to the delights of the marital bed, but this would be pure invention.

Did a wife have an enforceable claim to wedding nights with her new husband? The Mālikīs straightforwardly view the nights as the wife's right. The Ḥanafīs hold—though Shaybānī in the *Kitāb al-Ḥujja* does not defend this point with his usual vehemence—that the husband decided how many nights the bride received; she had no say. These views jibed with stances on whether wedding nights were exempt from apportionment. However, both the *Umm* and the *Mukhtaṣar al-Muzanī* betray the Shāfiʿī jurists' struggle to find a formulation that preserves the husband's right to wedding nights while holding him accountable for fulfilling these nights to his new bride—a task made difficult by the vision of strictly separated rights and duties for husbands and wives.

Lose a Turn

Sex is another crucial claim that ideally was mutual, but in legal thought ultimately one-sided. In contrast to Jewish law, which defined conjugal obligations primarily as the wife's claim on the husband, in Muslim marriage sex was the husband's claim on his wife. Paul Powers sets "mutual sexual access and fidelity" among the contractual rights and duties of marriage. This is accurate insofar as one understands both access and fidelity to mean quite different things for husbands and wives.[48] This is not to suggest that Muslim source texts or jurists ignored women's sexual needs entirely, much less that in practice men regularly withheld sex from women because they were legally entitled to do so. Occasional references to women collecting a "bed fee" from husbands in exchange for conjugal favors suggest the operation of a rather different model of sexual access.[49] Moreover, classical Muslim medical and other literature reflects a more balanced notion of conjugal sexuality.[50] As jurists drew on this repertoire of ideas about male and female desire, they selected those elements that fit their scheme, ignored those that did not, and fit them into a mostly coherent set of rules.[51] Containing the sexual drive, which both men and women possessed, was one key function of marriage. These rules privilege male sexual needs and desires, discounting without ever directly denying women's claim to fulfillment.

Though wives had an obligation to fulfill male sexual needs in exchange for their claim to support, marriage was also a way of "fortressing" women's sexuality.[52] Early jurists were deeply ambivalent about wives' sexual claims.[53] They repeatedly alluded to women's claim to sex, and yet in nearly every instance where a wife pressed a specific claim, they renounced coercive measures to compel a husband to intercourse. Again and again they declined to impose consequences on neglectful husbands. They were caught between competing agendas: promoting social chastity, envisioning marriage as a bastion of mutual satisfaction and repose, and constructing a legal framework for marriage with strictly separate male and female claims. The gap between obligation and recommendation became a chasm.

The discourse of apportionment stemmed from an unwillingness to see women's conjugal claims as sexual. It emphasized cohabitation and companionship. The purpose of the husband's allocation of time to each wife was "dwelling [together] and intimacy *(ilfan).*"[54] Terminology for taking turns emphasized physical presence: *mabīt,* "residing," or *qāma bi,* "staying with." Defining turn taking asexually meant that impediments to sex on either party's part were irrelevant. So was the husband's willingness to have sex. A wife's refusal, though, made her liable to losing her turn, her right to support, or both. The legal treatment of these three cases—impediments to intercourse on the part of either spouse, the husband's refusal, and the wife's refusal—show how dependent the logic of marital rights was on a strict division of claims by gender.

A wife was due companionship from her husband. A husband might want and perhaps enjoy companionship with his wife. What the jurists focused on, though, was his right to enjoy her sexually. This could and presumably would involve penetration but could also include other sexual activities. When intercourse was temporarily forbidden or even permanently ruled out, a wife retained her claim to a turn and her husband remained obligated to stay with her. Illness was a common reason that intercourse might be contraindicated, as was menstruation, which precluded penetration but permitted other intimacies. Provided she did not refuse her husband those activities for which she was fit, a wife with a physical impediment to intercourse such as a disease *(dāʾ)* or vaginal obstruction nonetheless retained her right to her allotted time.[55] Ibn al-Qāsim justified his opinion that the husband of a woman with such an obstruction "apportions to her and does not set aside her day" by analogy to Mālik's ruling that both "the menstruant and the ill woman with whom he cannot have intercourse" were due their turns despite the fact that it was not permissible to have intercourse with them.[56] The texts presume that nonpenetrative sexual activities were allowed, and the gratification thus obtained meant that the wife was fulfilling her end of the bargain.

A husband's physical defects likewise did not affect apportionment, though the wife's satisfaction in such a case was little discussed. A husband who "is impotent, or a eunuch, or has had his penis severed, or who is incapable with women" must still, Shāfiʿī says, allocate his time appropriately, just like the "healthy, potent man" *(al-ṣaḥīḥ al-qawī)*.[57] Eunuchs were persistent figures in legal texts concerning marriage. Their appearance in legal treatises, clearly disproportionate to their presence in the population, can be explained as the result of jurists' attempts to sort out what precisely defined individuals as capable of exerting the rights and prerogatives of husbands.[58] (In similar fashion, jurists debate whether and how a mute or deaf-mute man can contract a marriage or divorce a wife.) Eunuchs consistently figure as men, with the rights and prerogatives of husbands. Sometimes rules distinguish between those men whose testicles had been removed and those who had undergone complete castration, including removal of the penis. Though either defect was usually grounds for dissolving a marriage if it prevented consummation, once consummation had taken place or a woman had waived her right to it by remaining with a husband whom she knew could not perform sexually, his sexual inability was not grounds for divorce. Nor, Shāfiʿī insists, did it affect his duty to take turns among his wives, since "apportionment is for dwelling *(sukn)*, not for intercourse."[59]

More revealing of legal assumptions was a man who was capable of intercourse with his wife but simply unwilling or uninterested. He had to spend the night with his wife when it was her turn, and this turn "count[ed] against her" even if he did not have sex with her.

Intersecting nonlegal discourses about marriage posit a parallel between husbands and wives with regard to sex. Marriage makes a wife licit for her husband, and it also makes him licit for her. In that sense, it is reciprocal. Female desire appears, from time to time, as a consideration, as does care for female satisfaction in the carnal act. The hadith take note of women's sexual needs, though most of the focus is on men's sexual claims on their wives, and a Qurʾanic passage (Q. 2:223) suggests to men how to conduct themselves amorously. Commentators drew on prophetic statements about proper treatment (a man should not fall upon his wife like a beast, but approach her with kisses and caresses). Despite the availability of these texts, the jurists apparently found them extraneous. Desirous women were largely absent from these texts' discussions of sex in marriage: marriage conveyed reciprocal sexual licitness but lopsided or even one-sided sexual rights. On the one hand, marriage made a man lawful to his wife as a sexual partner, just as it made her lawful to him. On the other hand, the structuring of rights and duties by gender rendered women's availability to their husbands a condition of their support. A husband's satisfaction of his wife's desires was at once necessary and incompatible with the quid pro quo logic of marital transactions. Apportionment partially bridged this gap even as it construed wives' claims in nonsexual terms. The jurists wrestled with a wife's human needs within the confines of their gender-differentiated parameters for enforcing marital rights.

Mālikī authorities engaged this ambiguity most directly, considering both a man's wants and his wife's desires. They affirmed a wife's right to satisfaction but vacillated about consequences for a neglectful husband. Treating wives unequally in sexual matters was permissible, provided it was not done out of partiality. An exchange between Saḥnūn and Ibn al-Qāsim focused on this point. Asked about whether a man with two wives who was "in the mood for sex" on one wife's day but not on the other's day *(yanshaṭu fī yawm hādhihi li 'l-jimāʿ wa lā yanshaṭu fī yawm hādhihi li 'l-jimāʿ)* was obligated to the latter wife in any way, Ibn al-Qāsim replied that "whenever he abandons sex with one of them and has sex with the other by way of cruelty *(ḍarar)* and partiality, keeping away from this one because of finding his pleasure with the other one, then it is not appropriate for him and it is not lawful." However, "there is no problem" if he abstains because of lack of desire since, in Mālik's view, "the man is not compelled to do justice between the two of them with regard to sex."[60] The passage that follows provides a clue about how this ruling fits into the broader framework of conjugal rights. It asks whether free and slave women are due equal portions of their husband's time, presenting Mālik's insistence—not shared by the other Medinan authorities—on equal division of time between wives of various statuses. The *Mudawwana* then turns to the subject of a wife whose monogamous husband fails to have intercourse with her regularly. Placing the issue of whether co-wives' turns must be alike before a further discussion of the neglectful husband reaffirms the difference between a woman's claim to an equal share of her husband's time and her lack of claim to equality in sexual matters. Her allotment of time with her husband is not subject to the vagaries of his mood, but her access to intercourse depends on his desire.

Nonetheless, the Mālikī authorities ultimately conclude that depriving a wife of sex entirely could harm her. A wife whose husband's daytime fasting and nighttime prayer kept him from having sex with her complained to Saḥnūn. Saḥnūn asks Ibn al-Qāsim whether "there is anything due her or not." Ibn al-Qāsim replies that the husband "is harming [her] *(muḍārrun)*". The wife's claim to intercourse "became incumbent on him when he married her." In accordance with Mālik's view, the husband should be told, "You may not leave your wife without intercourse, so either have intercourse with her or we will separate you and her."[61] Ibn al-Qāsim omits mention of any specific frequency of intercourse, but his threat of intervention by the public authority assumes that lack of sex harms the wife—her complaint constitutes evidence of this harm—and gives grounds for separation.

This affirmation of a wife's claim to marital intercourse conflicts, though, with other elements of Mālikī rulings on allotting time and sexual favors between wives. Although lack of sex could harm a wife, elsewhere the husband's desire and motives alone determined the frequency of intercourse with a particular wife. Broad assertions, like Ibn al-Qāsim's, of a wife's sexual claims warred with the denial of a wife's regular rights to intercourse during her allotted turns as well as with the refusal to fix a specific allocation of sex. Additionally, the husband's freedom to spend time with his concubines rather than his wives and to travel whenever he wished, with whomever he wished, provided his actions were not motivated by partiality, further limited the wife's claim to time with him. The wife's right to divorce for continual deprivation of intercourse reflected a concern with the husband's harm of one wife, parallel to a concern with partiality in matters of apportionment. In both cases, the harm he inflicts rather than the lack of sex per se justifies intervention by the authorities.

Shāfiʿī was less conflicted about wives' sexual rights and more staunchly defended their rights to apportionment. He took a more restricted view of the husband's sexual obligations, denying harm or cruelty any relevance. A husband had no obligation to have intercourse with his wife during her turn, even in the absence of any impediments. Inequality between or among wives in sexual intimacy was inherently permissible, as it was a matter only of the husband's desire. However, a wife's allocated time had to be carefully protected. A man could visit his other wives in their quarters out of necessity during the daytime, but not for social or sexual purposes *(lā li ya'wī)*. If he wished to receive one of his wives in his own dwelling, it had to be the one whose turn it was; there was no getting around the restriction on visiting the other wives by bringing them to his lodgings rather than going to theirs. If he had sex with a wife out of turn, he became obliged to make up the time spent having sex to the wife whom he had shortchanged; this remedy reflected the view that it was *time* that the husband owed his wife, not sex.[62] By asserting that a man should receive only the wife whose turn it was, Shāfiʿī aimed to increase each woman's chance to find her husband in the mood without blurring the rigid demarcation between sex (the husband's right and the wife's duty) and apportionment of time (the wife's right and the husband's duty).

Again, we see Shāfiʿī's logic at play more clearly in the exceptional case of a woman who has no co-wives and thus has sole claim on her husband's attention (exceptional in that the texts treat polygyny as normative). Where there was no question of justice to co-wives, Shāfiʿī explicitly denies the wife's claim to a specific amount of intercourse:

> He said: And so if she is alone with him [i.e., he has no other wives], or with a slavegirl he has that he has sex with, he is ordered [to fulfill his obligations] in reverence to God the Exalted, and not to do her harm with regard to intercourse, and he is not obligated to any specific amount of it *(wa lam yufraḍ ʿalayhi minhu shay' bi ʿaynihi)*. Rather, he is only [obligated] to provide what she absolutely cannot do without, maintenance and lodging and clothing, and also to visit her *(ya'wī)*. However, intercourse is a matter of pleasure and no one is compelled to it.[63]

Shāfiʿī is unaware of his blinders. He obviously refers only to men when he declares that "intercourse is a matter of pleasure and no one is compelled to it." Women's sexual availability is, for him, a condition of their support and a prerequisite for their rights to visitation: "if any of them [his wives] refuses to have sex with him, she has disobeyed and abandoned her claim."[64]

We turn, now, from the husband's capacity and willingness for sex to the wife's. Unlike the case of a wife who was menstruating, ill, or prevented from intercourse by a physical defect, a wife who was absent from the marital home was unavailable. She would lose her allotted turn, even if she had a legitimate reason for her absence. If she traveled, even with permission and for a lawful purpose such as pilgrimage or the management of her financial affairs, she was not entitled to any compensatory time on her return.[65] (This Shāfiʿī ruling on her lack of compensatory time when she travels for pilgrimage stood in contrast to the rule that she retained her right to maintenance in the same circumstances, despite the usual linkage of rights to apportionment and maintenance.) If she was a slave whose master demanded her services, her husband need not make up the time to her later.

Only the Shāfiʿī texts explicitly address how a wife's sexual refusal affects her claim to time with her husband. The early Mālikī texts do not address this issue, for reasons that are unclear. The silence of the Ḥanafīs can be explained easily: a wife's sexual refusal is irrelevant if not accompanied by her departure from the conjugal home, because her husband is permitted to have sex with her without her consent. Non-Ḥanafīs do not penalize a husband for forcing sex on his wife, but neither do they explicitly authorize it in the way that al-Khaṣṣāf does. For all, marital rape is an oxymoron; rape *(ightiṣāb)* is a property crime that by definition cannot be committed by the husband. Still, they do make a distinction between forced and consensual sex within marriage.

Shāfiʿī, however, explicitly declares that a wife who thwarts her husband's advances forfeits her claim on his companionship. This loss of her allotted turn directly parallels her loss of maintenance for the same infraction. To justify his view, Shāfiʿī alludes to Q. 4:34, one of the two verses that mention *nushūz:* "Shāfiʿī, may Exalted God be merciful to him, said: And so we say: Do not allot [time] to the woman who refuses her husband, the one who is absent from him, because of God's permission for her husband to abandon her in bed."[66] In equating "the woman who refuses her husband" and "the one who is absent," Shāfiʿī gave the husband the right to "abandon" both. Of course, one cannot "abandon" someone who is not present—as already noted, she will not get a makeup turn—so the scriptural support here is for the husband's right to leave a wife who will not accommodate him and seek the company of one who will.

Oaths of Abstention

The disparity between a husband's sexual claims on his wife and hers on him also manifests itself in two types of oaths or vows that impose sexual abstention: forswearing *(īlāʾ)* and *ẓihār*. Both were pre-Islamic forms of divorce whose parameters were adjusted by the Qurʾan. Legal texts typically discussed both under the heading of divorce. They are discussed here because they reveal legal authorities' attitudes toward women's sexual claims in marriage and highlight the tension between exhortation and adjudication.[67] In discussing *ẓihār* and forswearing, Ḥanafī and Shāfiʿī jurists focused on discerning the letter of the law, whereas Mālikīs tended to attend to the oaths' effects, sometimes expressing concern with harm that might be inflicted on a wife by an abstaining husband. Nonetheless, taken cumulatively, these regulations safeguarded a wife's claim to her apportioned time but rendered her right to intercourse largely illusory.

Ẓihār and forswearing differed in important ways but shared an element of sexual abstention. In *ẓihār*, a husband swore that his wife[68] was to him like the back *(ẓahr)* of his mother, with "back" standing as a euphemism for sexual organ. This taboo forbade intercourse with her until he expiated his oath; the Qurʾan prescribes freeing a slave, feeding a number of poor people, or fasting (during daytime) for two consecutive months.[69] *Ẓihār* did not necessarily affect the ongoing rights and obligations of marriage; Shāfiʿī held that in addition to continuing to support her, a man remained obligated to continue apportioning time to a wife from whom he had sworn *ẓihār*.[70] *Ẓihār* neither resulted automatically in divorce nor entitled a woman to seek judicial intervention, though Mālikī authorities sometimes made an exception in cases of harm.

Forswearing had potentially more significant effects on the marital relationship. The Qurʾan establishes a four-month waiting period for men who forswear their wives. It declares that "if they return *(fāʾū)*, indeed God is Forgiving, Merciful. If they are resolved on divorce, indeed God is Hearing, Knowing."[71] The four-month period was critical, though a vow could be for significantly longer. A husband who broke his vow by having sex with his wife before the term expired had to expiate his broken oath. If four months expired and he had not had sex with her, Abū Ḥanīfa and his disciples, along with the Medinan authority Saʿīd b. al-Musayyab, held that forswearing automatically resulted in an irrevocable divorce.[72] They interpreted "return" in the Qur'anic text to mean having intercourse before the four-month period was up. Failing to have intercourse within that time was evidence of being "resolved on divorce."

Mālik and his followers, as well as Shāfiʿī, disagreed: the four-month period was not definitive. For them, rather, when this time had passed the wife could complain to the authority, who would impose a suspension in which normal marital claims continued. The husband would be asked to choose between the alternatives provided in the Qur'an: either "returning" to his wife, demonstrated by having intercourse with her, or pronouncing a divorce. However, as with cases of impotence, this ultimatum depended on the wife's appeal to the authority. If she did not press a claim before the time specified in his oath expired, the marriage continued.[73]

For the formative-period legal authorities, four months was not a legal maximum. Simple abstention without a vow of forswearing, no matter what the duration, did not automatically grant a woman the right to divorce. Moreover, a husband who forswore his wife and then, when four months had passed, had a valid excuse for not having intercourse with her could retain her by verbally expressing his intent to keep her as his wife.[74] These cases presupposed a wife's lack of a right to sex; the jurists' concern was only to demonstrate that none of these situations entitled her to claim divorce on grounds of forswearing.

Hypothetical cases, which all of the jurists discussed here were willing to entertain, explored the vow's logical limits. Forswearing occurred only when a husband vowed to abstain entirely from intercourse with his wife for more than four months. If he swore to abstain for a day or a month, then continued to abstain until more than four months had passed, the wife had no legal recourse.[75] The same was true if the husband left a loophole allowing him to have intercourse with his wife without breaking his vow.[76] Abū Ḥanīfa, Shāfiʿī, and Mālik agreed on the logical requirements for a valid vow, but diverged sharply in the tone with which they addressed logical slips in forswearing. Take the Ḥanafī discussion of an oath where "a man swears that he will not approach his wife in that house for four months and he leaves her for four months and doesn't approach her in it or elsewhere." Abū Ḥanīfa held that the man had not forsworn his wife because he could still have intercourse outside the house without violating his vow. His sole concern was to determine whether or not the husband's vow met the strict criteria of forswearing, which it did not.[77] A Shāfiʿī example is similar, except that instead of a house it is a town where the husband has sworn not to have sex with his wife: "If he says, 'By God, I will not approach you until I take you out of this town *(balad)*,' he has not forsworn her. This is because he can take her out before four months are up." Again, simply the possibility that he *could* have intercourse with his wife without breaking his oath sufficed to exempt him from the consequences of forswearing; he was not actually required to do so.[78]

A parallel passage from the *Mudawwana* gives a quite different overall effect. The Mālikīs attempted to balance an assessment of the vow's validity with concern over the wife's welfare:

> [Saḥnūn] said: What if he says to his wife, "By God, I will not have sex with you in this house of mine for a year," and he is dwelling in it with his wife, then when four months have passed, she seeks clarification of [her situation]. She says, "He has forsworn me." The husband says, "I have not forsworn [her], rather, I am a man who has sworn not to have intercourse in this house of mine. If I wished, I could have intercourse with her elsewhere without expiation." [Ibn al-Qāsim] said, I do not consider him to have forsworn her but I think that the authority orders him to take her out and have intercourse with her because I fear that he is harming [her], unless the wife forgoes it and doesn't want that.[79]

Like the the Ḥanafī and Shāfiʿī scenarios that begin by considering the husband's oath ("And if a man swears . . ." or "If a man says . . ."), the *Mudawwana* commences with the husband's words. However, unlike the other texts, it proceeds to the wife's complaint to the authorities: "He has forsworn me." Abū Ḥanīfa and Shāfiʿī only point to the logical flaw in the vow: "There is no forswearing upon him from that; can you not see that he may approach her somewhere beside that house and no expiation will be obligatory for him?" In the *Mudawwana*, the husband rather than the jurist defended his position on these grounds. Ibn al-Qāsim, though agreeing with the husband's logic (reluctantly?), exploits this loophole to address the wife's concern. The husband could have sex with her elsewhere and still keep his vow, so the authority should order him to do so.[80] None of the Ḥanafī authorities requires or even encourages the husband to take this step, and the Shāfiʿī text explicitly absolves him from doing so: "He is not compelled to take her out."[81] Equally absent from the Ḥanafī and Shāfiʿī texts was any consideration of the wife's wishes. The *Mudawwana*, by contrast, takes the wife's sentiments as the starting point for determining how the authority ought to proceed. Not only does Ibn al-Qāsim express his concern for the vow's effect on the wife, but his order that the husband take her elsewhere in order to have sex is subject to her desire that it take place.[82]

The unique Mālikī concern with harm to the wife in cases of forswearing carries over into their regulation of *ẓihār*. In some instances they apply forswearing's four-month period to cases where they perceive *ẓihār* to be harming women.[83] Mālik affirms that *ẓihār* and forswearing are normally separate but if a husband does not want to resume sexual relations with his wife, and has no intention of expiating his oath of *ẓihār*, the issue of harm *(ḍarar)* enters in.[84] The determination of whether harm is involved relies on the discretion of the authorities, whose intervention must be sought here just as in cases of forswearing.

Mālikī discussions of harm are practical and case specific. This subjective criterion, to be assessed by a judge or the public authority, determines how and when certain legal regulations are to be applied. Mālik and his followers avoid prescribing universal rules. Rather, they favor individual juristic flexibility to provide an equitable solution to a particular problem. In several areas—such as vows of *ẓihār* made with the intent to harm the wife, considerations of partiality in a husband's allocation of time among his wives, or the wife's deprivation of sex by a husband who is continually engaged in worship—the *Mudawwana*'s authorities attempt to coax husbands to behave thoughtfully. They do not draw the bright line between lawful and unlawful or between valid and void that characterizes the doctrines of the other schools.

In contrast, Ḥanafīs and Shāfiʿīs strictly separate *ẓihār* and forswearing, never evincing any willingness to impose a deadline for the husband to take any action in *ẓihār*.[85] The Shāfiʿī texts put it most directly: forswearing and *ẓihār* are separate, and God revealed different rules for each.[86] This is true even "if he makes *ẓihār* from her then he leaves her (*tarakahā* [i.e., does not have sex with her]) for more than four months."[87] Yet while insisting that there could be no legal assimilation of *ẓihār* to forswearing, Shāfiʿī authorities also acknowledge the possibility of harm to the wife, which these Ḥanafī sources ignore. Unlike for the Mālikīs, such harm is a question of the husband's sin before God; there are no legal remedies for his cruel behavior.[88] The Shāfiʿī jurists do aver that if a man who has made an oath of *ẓihār* decides not to divorce his wife, he must expiate his oath.[89] However, there is no legal requirement that he have intercourse with his wife, even if he decides to remain married to her.

To return briefly to forswearing and sexual abstention, it is worth noting that even Mālik, who was the most concerned with the effects of sexual abstention on a wife, makes exceptions to the rules requiring a husband to have intercourse with a wife whom he has forsworn. When the husband has a legal excuse, he need not actually have intercourse with his wife to cancel the vow and prevent a divorce. For example, if a man forswears his wife and then travels, making it impossible for him to rescind his oath by having intercourse with her, he may expiate his oath in another way. He is not obligated to return from his journey or bring his wife to join him, a fact that assumes his freedom of movement and her lack of claim to a specific portion of his time. Likewise, if he is ill, he can rescind his vow verbally and perform expiation if able to do so.[90] In other circumstances where intercourse is physically impossible, as with an elderly husband or one who has a defect of his sexual organs, even one that occurred after he made the vow, the wife has no right to seek judicial intervention after four months; the oath simply becomes ineffective.[91] Despite the concern expressed in other passages for the wife's experience of harm, Mālik and his followers here take no account of it. Their only concern with the wife's right to intercourse is to note that "whether she is a virgin or a non-virgin" he must have "had sex with her once." If, after that, "by the order of God, [he is afflicted with] something that renders him unable to have intercourse with her . . . he and she are never separated [for his sexual incapacity]."[92] There is no discussion here of her complaining to the authorities or of her willingness to forgo sexual intercourse. Harm or cruelty, so often mentioned in other contexts, is absent, suggesting that their real concern was not with the woman's experience of harm so much as with the husband's willful infliction of it. This is in keeping with the

Mālikī concern with the husband's motivations in all questions of apportionment.

Abandoning All Claim

A contradiction lurks at the heart of these jurists' treatment of sex and companionship in marriage. On the one hand, they—especially the Mālikīs—stress intimacy between spouses and acknowledge women's needs for sexual gratification as well as companionship. On the other hand, they insist on men's rights to withdraw from visitation or abstain from intercourse, provided certain limits on behavior or motivation are observed. The most important of these limits is the requirement of fairness between or among wives in the apportionment of time. Yet even this requirement, it turns out, is not absolute: a woman may give up her rights to all or a portion of her due visitation. Why would a woman do such a thing? Rāfiʿ's wife, with whom this chapter began, shows us: to forestall an unwanted divorce. A woman who forgoes her allotted turns might, the jurists maintain, rescind her consent at any time and reclaim her turn. But ultimately, men's unilateral divorce prerogatives constrained wives' ability to do so; insisting on their allotted time might result in the divorce they were attempting to avoid by giving up their turns in the first place.

Abandoning her core marital rights to time and support was one of the few tools at a wife's disposal in negotiating the continuation of her marriage. The jurists who so adamantly reject stipulations to this effect at the outset of marriage deem such compromises acceptable later, viewing them as both Qur'anically sanctioned and, in the case of a wife surrendering her allotted time, grounded in prophetic precedent. According to Medinan authorities cited in the *Mudawwana,* Q. 4:128, the second verse discussing *nushūz,* permits a wife whose husband feels disinclination toward her to give up some of her marital rights in order to remain with him, though they also hold that he "had the duty to offer to divorce her." As with Rāfiʿ and his longtime wife, "If she agreed to remain with him with that [favoritism] and she disliked that he should divorce her, there is no blame on him for what he favors [another] over her."[93] The *Muwaṭṭaʾ Shaybānī* concurs that Rāfiʿ acted appropriately when he allowed his wife to choose whether she would rather be divorced or remain with him despite his favoritism of his new young wife. In this view, "there is no sin upon him since she consented to remain despite the favoritism."[94]

Shāfiʿī describes the case of Rāfiʿ and his wife as the occasion of revelation for Q. 4:128.[95] Drawing explicitly from scripture to support his position, he interprets the Qurʾanic passage as favoring a settlement where the wife forgoes her claims to remain with a husband who dislikes her:

> It is clear that if a woman fears the *nushūz* of her husband *(baʿl)*, there is no problem for them if they reach a settlement. The husband's *nushūz* toward her is his dislike of her. God has permitted him to retain her despite disliking her, and they may reach a settlement. And that is an indication that her settlement with him is by forgoing part of her claims on him.[96]

Another example in the *Mudawwana* involves an anonymous woman who does not wish to be separated from her husband. As with the *Umm*'s discussion of Rāfiʿ and his wife, this husband "dislikes" his wife. Both texts use derivations of the root *k-r-h*, a term from Q. 4:19, which declares that there might be "much good" in a woman whom a man dislikes. Shāfiʿī's quotation of the first and last portions of this verse fits the standard pattern of Qurʾanic quotation in the *Umm*. It also manages to leave out the term *dislikes*, drawing attention instead to two other aspects of the verse: the husband's obligation to "relate to them [i.e., wives] equitably" and the "much good" that could be in these women. Shāfiʿī subtly criticizes men who treat their wives badly because they dislike them. But, when Rāfiʿ's wife surrenders complete control of the allocation to him, stating "allot to me what seems good to you," Shāfiʿī concludes that there is "no problem" with her giving up her turns. Similarly, in the *Mudawwana* the wife offers to give her turns to a co-wife, either extant or to be married in addition to her. Mālik's reply is similar to that of Shāfiʿī: "There is no problem in that, and he doesn't allot anything to her."

Another case has special precedential value. Appearing in both the *Kitāb al-Āthār* of Abū Yūsuf and the *Umm*, it concerns the Prophet and his wife Sawda. The Prophet, according to the jurists, modeled justice in his marital behavior. As befits his special status, he was exempted from some of the obligations governing other husbands and was subject to rules that did not apply to ordinary believers. The Qur'an excuses him from the requirement of apportioning his time among his wives, allowing him to "defer the turn of any" he wished. The fact that he was exceptional in this regard makes the jurists' frequent references to him as a paragon of fairness in turn taking even more noteworthy. For the most part, his example is cited, as earlier in this chapter, as evidence for equality in division. Here, his behavior with Sawda is likewise taken to apply to other husbands. At issue is Muḥammad's agreement to retain Sawda in exchange for her giving up her right to a portion of his time. According to the account presented in the *Kitāb al-Āthār,* the Prophet divorced Sawda by ordering her to begin observing a waiting period ("Count."). Her offer to give her turn to ʿĀ'isha was the key to getting taken back. Sawda's expressed motive to remain one of the Prophet's wives was looking toward a privileged heavenly status.[97] In a similar account from the *Umm,* the Prophet was only contemplating divorce when Sawda declared, "I give my day and my night to my sister ʿĀ'isha."[98]

These hadith avoid any suggestion of the Prophet's dislike of or *nushūz* toward Sawda, which would constitute unthinkable censure of Muḥammad. Though male *nushūz* was not a legal offense, it was distasteful and incompatible with Muḥammad's exemplary persona. That said, the precariousness of Sawda's situation parallels that of the anonymous woman in the *Mudawwana* and Rāfiʿ's first wife. "The Messenger of God wanted to divorce one of his wives" echoes both "what if a man is married to a woman and he dislikes her and wants to divorce her?" and "Rāfiʿ b. Khadīj . . . disliked something about her . . . and wanted to divorce her." The women's statements resemble each other even more clearly: "And she said: Don't divorce me . . . ; I give my day and my night to my sister ʿĀ'isha"; "and she says: "Don't divorce me, and I give all my days to my companion, don't allot anything to me"; "and she said: "Don't divorce me; retain me and allot to me what seems good to you."

Sawda's strategy worked. She remained among the "Mothers of the Believers" and her "settlement" (though the *Umm* does not use the term here) remained in effect for the rest of Muḥammad's life: "The Prophet died having nine wives, and he apportioned to eight."[99] One cannot know whether other husbands retained their wives on the basis of them giving up their turns, or whether the wives later found the terms of the settlement intolerable. All agreed that a wife who relinquished her allotted time was not forever bound by that decision. "She may change her mind" and reclaim her turns at any time.[100] For Ibn al-Qāsim, if she rescinded her agreement her husband was obliged to either "apportion to her or separate from her if he has no need for her."[101] Similarly, in Shāfiʿī's words, "If she changes her mind about it, [no course of action] is lawful for him except justice towards her or separating from her."[102] Yet these references to divorce, and to the husband's privilege to choose it, insistently recall the rationale for the wife's original choice to forgo her right.

Asked about a husband who refused to either allot a wife her fair share of time or divorce her, Shāfiʿī confronts the limits and possibilities of the jurisprudential enterprise. He answers that "he is compelled to apportion to her, and he is not compelled to divorce her." "He is not," Shāfiʿī adds, "compelled to apportion sex *(al-iṣāba)* to her, and he should (or 'must,' *yanbaghī lahu*) strive to do justice toward her regarding it."[103] Shāfiʿī insists that a husband could be forced to apportion time to his wife if he was unwilling to divorce her, but proffers no mechanism for doing so; the compulsion is purely hypothetical. He also makes no pretense at ensuring equal treatment in sexual matters; the basic framework of gender-differentiated rights holds. The role of advocate for ethical comportment remains, though: the husband "ought to" or even "must" attempt to do justice to the wife.

At this point it is helpful to compare directly the formative-period authorities' perspectives on male and female *nushūz*. Their stance toward men's *nushūz* might be best characterized as disapproving, in stark contrast to their condemnatory stance on women's *nushūz*. A wife's *nushūz*—at least insofar as it encompassed sexual refusal, abandonment of the marital home, or both—clearly violated the husband's rights. It justified him suspending her maintenance (for the Ḥanafīs and Shāfiʿīs) and ceasing to allocate a turn to her (according to the Shāfiʿīs). Later Mālikīs concur, and though the *Muwaṭṭa'* and the *Mudawwana* are silent on the subject, it is probable that the formative-period authorities did so as well. When a husband committed *nushūz*, by contrast, the jurists presumed that he no longer desired a particular wife and wished to avoid her—unfortunate, perhaps, but understandable. His *nushūz* did not violate any of her rights. It was his prerogative to allocate his sexual favors as he wished or to divorce her if he no longer liked her. The jurists thus did not impose any consequences on him. Instead, his *nushūz* became the impetus for his wife to forgo some or all of her claims—above all, her allotted turn with him.

The jurists partially anchored their treatments of male and female *nushūz* in the two verses from the Qurʾan where they are discussed in strikingly different ways. Leila Ahmed has pointed out that the jurists tended to render male duties as recommended while treating female duties as obligatory.[104] For the interrelated marital claims of support, companionship, sex, and physical availability, her analysis certainly resonates. Though there were glimmers of disapproval for husbands whose favoritism or partiality led a wife to forgo her rights, the juristic consensus held that there was ultimately "no problem" with such agreements. Still, the jurists' discussions of negotiated divorce for compensation *(khulʿ)*, discussed in the next chapter, treat male and female *nushūz* in more directly parallel ways, suggesting a more balanced assessment of human behavior.

Conclusion

With few exceptions, a double standard surrounding male and female sexual exclusivity is a pervasive feature of most premodern legal systems and social practices. The widespread normalization of legal polygyny by Muslims, however, was historically unusual in the Near East and Mediterranean. Neither Greek nor Roman law allowed polygyny. Certain strands of Christianity barely tolerated remarriage after the death of a spouse, much less after divorce; to have more than one wife at a time would be entirely beyond the pale. Jewish law permitted concurrent marriage of a man to more than one wife but treated such marriages as exceptional. The rabbis' treatment of *onah*, the husband's sexual obligations to his wife, began from the assumption that a man had one wife to keep appropriately sated. The Muslim framework of apportionment diverges not only in assigning the sexual duties primarily to the wife rather than the husband, but also in starting from the assumption that a man will have more than one wife at a time.

Even with presumptive polygyny, though, husbands' responsibilities to their wives included an affective or intimate component. Though it was not precisely sexual, it relied on closeness and companionship. Their insistence on this right serves to compensate, in a small way, for the sexual claims they would like to give women—or so repeated gestures in that direction attest—but cannot because of their insistence on differentiating rights by gender.

Several considerations mitigate a man's prerogatives to spend his time entirely as he chooses, but concern for a wife's marital experience is not primary among them. A woman cannot permanently forfeit her share of her husband's time. However, the guiding principle in regulating apportionment was not the husband's absolute duty to spend time with any wife, but rather his responsibility to be fair between or among his wives. Each wife's claim to a portion of his time was relative, not absolute, hence a man's freedom to travel without his wives or remain apart from all of them while visiting his concubines. Apart from complaining to the judge, a woman had no juridical means to ensure that her husband spent time with her, while he had at his disposal a range of consequences to mete out if she made herself unavailable to him.

Even when a husband dutifully took turns among his wives, he had no obligation to treat them equally when it came to sex. A wife had a right to a share of her husband's time but no claim to sex during her turn. The Mālikī jurists pointed out that a man's having sex with one wife more than another because of partiality was "not lawful." Yet only the husband's desire mattered: if he felt frisky with one wife and not the other, his abstention was acceptable. The wife's desire was irrelevant. For Shāfiʿī, the matter was even simpler: sex was the husband's right and not his duty; he could not be "compelled to do it." There was a substantial difference between the Mālikī approach to marital sex, however, and that of the others. A wife whose husband neglected her completely in favor of supererogatory acts of worship could seek judicial relief on the basis of harm, as in certain cases of *ẓihār*. The practical effects of this recognition of a wifely right to intercourse were still limited by the larger framework of gender-differentiated spousal rights. This gender division of marital rights governed the husband's *nushūz*, which was reinterpreted not as rebellion or recalcitrance but as dislike or antipathy. Rather than censuring the husband, the jurists presented the wife's waiving of her marital rights as the solution. Though a wife had the right to her share of his time, the jurists uniformly permitted her to relinquish this claim. Though explicitly concerned only with the legalities of women's giving up their rights to their allotted portion of time, the situations the jurists presented, where women bargained with husbands to avoid being divorced against their will, attested to a fundamental imbalance of legal power in the marital relationship. The husband's unilateral prerogative to terminate the marriage inescapably affected the whole fabric of spousal claims.

4

Untying the Knot

A MAN, the *Kitāb al-Ḥujja* informs us, divorces his wife in absentia. She learns of the divorce and, after observing a waiting period to ensure that she is not pregnant, marries someone else. However, before the expiry of her waiting period, her original husband takes her back, not bothering to inform her.[1] Sometime thereafter, he returns and expects to resume their conjugal life, her new "husband" notwithstanding. Abū Ḥanīfa thinks he may do so:

> Muḥammad [al-Shaybānī] said: Abū Ḥanīfa, may God be pleased with him, said about the man who divorces his wife then takes her back, and [news of] her divorce reaches her but [news of] his taking her back does not reach her until she has become lawful and married [another man]: Her first husband has more right to her, whether the second man has consummated [the marriage] with her or not. She and the second man are separated. If he has not consummated [the marriage] with her, she is not due anything from him, and if he has consummated it, she has either what he fixed [as dower] for her or her fair dower, whichever is less. She is returned to her first husband, and he does not approach her until her waiting period from the second man is completed.[2]

As is usual with legal texts, this passage presents the least information necessary to resolve the specific matter at stake. It states neither how long the husband was away before the divorce (even that he was traveling remains implicit) nor how much time elapsed before he returned and found his wife remarried; juridically, it was immaterial whether weeks, months, or years had passed. Questions of sentiment were likewise irrelevant. The husband's reason for divorce? Unimportant. The wife's wishes with regard to the divorce? Ditto. Her feelings on learning that her (original) husband had chosen to take her back? Utterly beside the point.

Other information is omitted not because it is irrelevant but because it is taken for granted. Abū Ḥanīfa, his Medinan interlocutors, and the Sunni legal tradition more generally agreed that the husband's right to take his wife back was, like his right to divorce her, not dependent on her presence, consent, or even awareness. It went without saying, then, that the wife's not knowing of the husband's taking her back did not affect the validity of his act. Shaybānī could simply assume that the husband's declaration took immediate effect without any action or knowledge on the wife's part. Only the points in dispute receive dedicated attention.

In this case, the *Kitāb al-Ḥujja* has the dual aim of explaining Abū Ḥanīfa's position on the invalidity of one irregular marriage and justifying it against a competing doctrine of the "people of Medina." In doing so, the *Ḥujja* attends carefully to the subtleties of the positions it argues against. The *Ḥujja*'s scrupulous attention to the picayune details of competing Medinan views shows that early legal thinkers paid close attention to their opponents' views. This attests to significant communication across the lines of incipient legal schools. It also demonstrates that that legal disputation, at least at its best, was not merely an excuse for caricatured presentation (or even slanderous misrepresentation) of others' ideas, but a real contributing factor to the refinement of jurisprudential views. The world of early legal discourse was both contentious and vibrant.

In the disputed divorce, the *Ḥujja* declares Abū Ḥanīfa's view that the second marriage was never valid. How could it be, when the woman's husband had taken her back before the completion of her waiting period? At the time she attempted to remarry, she was another man's wife. When this man, her original husband, returned, therefore, the woman and her putative second husband had to be immediately separated so that, after the appropriate waiting period to ensure proper attribution of paternity, she could be reunited with him. Shaybānī subtly reinforces the first marriage's legitimacy through his choice of terms for the two men: the divorcing man is *her first husband.* Although the use of "first" implies that there is another husband from whom this one must be distinguished, in referring to the other man Shaybānī avoids the term *husband* and refers to him as *al-ākhir,* literally "the later one."

In recounting the opposing Medinan view that the second marriage is valid, Shaybānī accurately describes Mālik and certain other Medinan authorities as holding that "her second husband" *(zawjuhā al-ākhir)* had more right to the woman in question, while "the first one" *(al-awwal)* had no access to her.[3] The use of "husband" in reference to the second man emphasizes Mālik's view that he had legitimate claim to the woman. Mālik's view, and that of some other Medinan authorities, was that the second marriage was valid only if consummated. The *Ḥujja* also notes a minority Medinan position that the second marriage was valid even if unconsummated. This latter view accords with Mālik's in validating the second marriage but, like Ḥanafī and Shāfiʿī doctrine, places no weight on consummation.

This dispute over certain exceptional elements masks underlying similarities in the jurists' conceptions of divorce. The most basic of these, of course, was the husband's right to end marriage by unilateral pronouncement. Another was his prerogative to "revoke" certain divorces during the waiting period. The major complication in the *Ḥujja* arises from the conjunction of two elements: (1) the husband resuming his marriage during the waiting period, and (2) the wife's remarriage. Had he not taken her back during the waiting period, her second marriage, consummated or not, would be valid according to everyone. Likewise, had she not remarried, there would be no disagreement: his return to her would be valid.

Like the formation of marriage, its dissolution reveals a great deal about marriage as a contract. The first section of this chapter briefly surveys divorce regulations, highlighting the practical and symbolic parallels between unilateral divorce by pronouncement *(ṭalāq)* and manumission *(ʿitq)*. The two sections that follow explore divorce for compensation *(khulʿ)*, including who may contract it and what compensation can be involved, and the divorce rights of slaves. The former illustrates the commercial framework of marriage and the usefulness of transaction analogies, and discusses mutual antipathy as a motive for divorce. In the latter case, the consensus arrived at by formative-period jurists that enslaved husbands or men married to enslaved women were the ones vested with powers of divorce shows the limitations of ownership language to describe marriage and divorce, even as it reinforces the centrality of unrestricted unilateral male divorce to the jurists' conception of marriage.

Divorcing a Wife, Freeing a Slave

In *ṭalāq*—literally, "release"—a man ends his marriage by pronouncement. As the *Ḥujja*'s example of the absent man who pronounces divorce illustrates, the presence of the wife was unnecessary. (Shiʿi jurists required witnesses, but Sunnis did not.)[4] A husband might pronounce the formula once or make multiple pronouncements, either at one sitting or spread over time. Multiple repudiations could also—in the view of most Sunnis, though not Shiʿis—be combined into one statement ("You are triply divorced") or implied by the formula chosen ("You are absolutely [*al-batta*] divorced").[5] Divorce pronouncements could be conditional ("If I take another wife, you are divorced") or delegated ("Choose" or "Your affair is in your hand" or "You are divorced if you wish"). In some cases, delegated divorce could be conditional ("If I take another wife, your affair is in your hand"). The jurists expended a great deal of effort to sort out the effects of various types of formulae.

The impact of the words uttered sometimes depended on the husband's intention, particularly if the formula was allusive (*kināya*, e.g., "You are free," *Anti ḥurra*) rather than clear (*ṣarīḥ*, e.g., "You are divorced," *Anti ṭāliq*). Paul Powers sums up the role of intent: "In terms of basic sincerity and effectiveness, explicit statements are valid and binding regardless of intent, allusive statements are valid and binding if so intended, and some statements are too ambiguous to count regardless of intent."[6] It was important to know the effect of the chosen statement because a man's right to return to his wife during her waiting period, or to remarry her after it ended, depended on the nature of the divorce.[7]

The husband's divorce prerogatives can best be understood through jurists' frequent analogies between divorce and manumission. A husband, like the master of a slave, controlled the tie joining the parties. This right was basic to marriage: the husband acquired limited *milk* (ownership, control) over his wife at the time of contract through payment of a dower, just as an owner acquired *milk* through the purchase of a slave. Either could relinquish it unilaterally whenever he chose. As Norman Calder writes, "Divorcing wives and freeing slaves are peculiar problems because these are, in Islamic law, performative utterances: simply uttering the correct words in the correct form can produce a change in the status of others."[8] In contrast to marriage, which was a bilateral contract *(ʿaqd)* that required consent of the wife, someone acting on her behalf, or both, divorce by *ṭalāq* was a unilateral act.

Gail Labovitz has noted the significance of the parallel between divorce and manumission in rabbinic discourse which like Muslim jurisprudence maintains "a model in which the dissolution of a marriage is understood by comparisons to the end of slavery. Both are understood as acts in which a male free agent relinquishes his rights over a female and/or enslaved object."[9] Though the rabbis' mode of release was document rather than declaration, the ease with which they moved from divorce of a wife to manumission of slave mirrors the practice of Muslim jurists: "The fact that one form of (metaphorical) human property—the wife—is released from ownership by a particular means becomes evidence that another—the slave—may also be released in the same way."[10]

Although the legal analogy between repudiating a wife and freeing a slave rests on the proprietary or quasi-proprietary nature of each bond, Yossef Rapoport notes that both had a broader symbolic significance, arising from their capacity to destabilize a basic unit of social organization. He writes, "Divorce and manumission were an extreme manifestation of patriarchal authority, as well as its symbols, precisely because they severed the ties that held a household together."[11] Again, we have a salutary reminder that slaves were members of households, even if they were not precisely kin. Rapoport also points out "the inextricable link between the patriarchal order of the domestic sphere and the patriarchal values at the heart of the political and social order."[12]

There was, though, a predominant legal rationale: the analogy between *ṭalāq* and manumission provided descriptive efficiency much like that achieved by treating marriage and commercial sales together. Ḥanafī, Shāfiʿī, and—less frequently—Mālikī texts drew from rulings in one area to clarify rulings in another, just as with marriage and purchase. The Ḥanafī *Jāmiʿ al-Kabīr* takes for granted the utility of such analogies: "[If] a man says to his wife, you are released with every wife I have, or to his slave *(ʿabd)*, you are free[d] along with every slave I have, his wives are released and his slaves are manumitted."[13] By referring to "a man" who "says to his wife . . . or to his slave," Shaybānī sets up a close parallel between a wife and a (male) slave, contrasting both to the free man with power to sever the legal ties binding them to him by pronouncing the correct formula.[14] Sometimes the distinction might be elided. Accepting the phrase "you are free" as an allusive form of divorce implies that a woman is in some sense unfree while married, as *ḥurr(a)* is used to identify a free person in contrast to a slave, one who is *"mamlūk(a),"* owned.[15] For Shāfiʿī's disciple al-Muzanī, the rule works both ways: "And if he says to [his wife], "You are free," intending divorce, and to his female slave, "You are released *(ṭāliq),*" intending manumission, [the release] is binding on him."[16] For Shaybānī, *ḥurra* can divorce a wife but *ṭāliq* does not suffice to manumit a slave.[17]

Certain oaths highlight the sexual elements of *milk* in marriage and in ownership of a female slave by linking sexual agency to legal agency. A man might hinge a conditional divorce or manumission on his own sexual act: "A man says to his wife, 'If I have intercourse with you, you are triply divorced'. . . . Likewise if he says to his female slave, 'If I have intercourse with you, you are free.' "[18] Wife and slave appear here in the same position relative to the husband/master: subject to his sexual act and his decision to terminate their tie. The two acts are conjoined by his oath, which assumes and affirms the essential penetrability of female bodies, free or enslaved. Penetration activates the oath, releasing either woman from his dominion. Of course, this creates a problem. At its commencement, intercourse was licit precisely because of his *milk*. Penetration instantaneously ended this *milk*, rendering sex forbidden. Shaybānī, alert to this danger in his discussion of the wife in this case, notes that the man could continue the sexual act to completion without consequences so long as he did not withdraw his penis completely. If he withdrew fully and then penetrated her again, it would count as a new act of intercourse—with a woman who was no longer licit to him. (This "erroneous" sex would oblige a compensatory payment in addition to whatever dower was due from the marriage.)[19] This hypothetical reflection is as interesting for what it does not discuss as for what it does. The entire encounter occurs at the man's discretion. There is no exploration, for instance, of the possibility that the woman in question might want him to stop the sexual act once she is no longer his wife or his slave, let alone that she might have objected at the outset.

Parallels between marriage and slavery as cases to which the same remedies can be applied slide at times into an erasure of dividing lines. Al-Muzanī's *Mukhtaṣar* begins its discussion of future oaths by considering wives and slaves separately but ends up treating both with the same terminology of ownership:

> Shāfiʿī, may God be merciful to him, said: If he says, "Every woman that I marry is divorced" or [if he names] a specific woman or, [says] to

> a [male] slave, "If I own you [you are] free," and he marries [a woman] or owns [a slave], nothing is compulsory for him. [That is] because when he made the relevant statement, he was not an owner *(mālik)*, so it is void. Al-Muzanī, may God be merciful to him, said: If he says to a woman whom he does not own *(lā yamlikuhā)*, "You are divorced now," she is not divorced. . . . Al-Muzanī, may God be merciful to him, said: there is consensus that there is no path *(sabīl)* to divorce for the one who does not own *(yamliku)*.[20]

The legal issue at stake was not the parallel between wife and slave, which is assumed, but rather the time at which a particular oath could be validly made. Shāfiʿī held that pronouncements of divorce or manumission made before a legal tie existed between the parties could never be valid. The power to relinquish *milk* resulted only once the bond was established, therefore "there is no divorce before marriage" and "there is no divorce before ownership." (Alternately, "there is no release before control.")[21] The line between analogy and identity blurs here. Shāfiʿī refers to releasing a wife by *ṭalāq* or freeing a slave, treating the two actions as analogous but distinct. The next sentence collapses the statuses of husband and master into the category of *mālik*, owner, implying a similar if unarticulated merging of wives and slaves into the category of "owned" individuals. Al-Muzanī then applies the terminology of *milk* solely to marriage and *ṭalāq*, with no further mention of slavery or manumission. Instead of using terms such as *husband, wife*, or *marriage*, Muzanī refers to the man who cannot pronounce divorce as "one who does not own" and to the woman in question as the one "whom he does not own." In a few lines, enslavement shifts from an institution parallel to marriage—to which an analogous legal decision applies—to being the primary conceptual language through which marriage is itself described. Mālikī and Ḥanafī authorities disagree with the Shāfiʿīs on certain future oaths, but they also apply the same criteria to divorce as to manumission.[22] In any case, differences on a comparatively minor point (the divorce of women not yet married and the manumission of slaves not yet owned) should not distract from consensus on the main issue: a man's unhampered freedom to divorce any woman to whom he was married or manumit any slave whom he owned.

There was one vital distinction between *ṭalāq* and manumission, though, that accounts for the specification of triple divorce in oaths such as the one linking intercourse to *ṭalāq*. Manumission of a slave was always final and irrevocable, but as noted earlier *ṭalāq* could be either revocable *(rajʿī)* or irrevocable *(bāʾin)*.[23] If revocable, as in the case of the absent husband with which this chapter begins, the husband would "control (or own) the [right to] return" *(yamliku al-rajʿa; lahu milk al-rajʿa)* or have "more right to take her back" *(aḥaqqu bi rajʿatihā)* so long as the wife was in her waiting period.[24] These expressions use the terminology of control, dominion, or rights over the return, rather than directly over the wife; this is perhaps indicative of the liminal state of the marriage pending the husband's decision on whether to resume conjugal life. In comparison, the terms used for consent to marriage express the wife's control over her affair *(milk amrihā)* or over herself *(aḥaqqu bi nafsihā)*. Still, divorce placed the husband's dominion in abeyance but it endured: if he decided to take her back, no new marriage contract was necessary, nor was her consent needed. Shāfiʿī, adopting his customary strategy of culling proof from scripture, alludes to Q. 2:228 as he argues, "When God, Exalted and Majestic, granted the husband more right to take back his wife during the waiting period, it was proof that she may not prohibit him from taking her back."[25] Further, since what resulted from his taking her back was a continuation of the original marriage, the wife had no claim to an additional dower.[26]

Like *ṭalāq* itself, the resumption of marital relations following a revocable *ṭalāq* was a unilateral procedure, effected by the husband without any intervention from the public authority or a judge. However, the jurists differed as to exactly how the husband might take back his wife. Formative-period Ḥanafī texts do not discuss the subject, but the Shāfiʿī authorities hold that a verbal declaration—preferably witnessed—is absolutely necessary for any return to take effect.[27] Without this declaration, sex between the parties is illicit. It constitutes "mistaken intercourse," for which a compensatory dower would be owed.[28] The need for compensatory dower in this case highlights the fact that divorce is, above all, a severing of the tie that makes sex lawful. Though preferring a witnessed declaration, in keeping with their commonsensical approach the Mālikīs held that in some cases action combined with intent was sufficient for a husband to take back a wife.

When it comes to both divorce and return, Mālikī discussions take for granted both that actions and intent matter and that only the husband's actions and intent matter; the wife's participation and consent do not figure at all. Again, we have the confluence of legal and sexual agency. When Saḥnūn inquires of Ibn al-Qāsim about what actions could bring about a "return," he depicts the husband as actor and the wife as object. If "he kisses her lustfully during her waiting period," he asks, "or caresses her lustfully, or has vaginal or non-vaginal intercourse with her *(jāma'ahā fī 'l-farj aw fīmā dūn al-farj)*, or undresses her and looks at her and at her sexual organ *(farj)*, is this a return in Mālik's opinion or not?"[29] Ibn al-Qāsim replies that actions alone are insufficient to determine this, as the husband's intent cannot be inferred from his actions, even if these include significant physical intimacy. According to Mālik, "If he has sex with her during her waiting period and he intends by that to return and he is ignorant of [the need for] witnessing, then it is a return; otherwise, it is not a return."[30]

The husband's caresses, kisses, or other acts are performed upon his wife's body, as one-sided as the divorce or the return. In Arabic, the unidirectional nature of these actions appears even more clearly. In English, those verbs for sex that take direct objects tend to be more forceful.[31] In Arabic, the standard neutral verb for "to have intercourse" *(j-m-ʿ)* takes a direct object, not a prepositional phrase: not "he has sex with her" but "he sexes her." Even if women appear occasionally as sexual agents, female sexual agency is not linked to legal agency in the same way: women's intent is disregarded. For men, it is not just the acts that matter, but both desire and intent. Ibn al-Qāsim and Mālik attend to the husband's desire as he performs the acts they discuss: his kissing or caressing nonlustfully will not lead to a return, but if his desire motivates the act, it can. When copulation is involved, desire is presumed. But desire matters only if the husband intends to take his wife back. This attention to the husband's intent sharply contrasts with Ibn al-Qāsim's view that if the husband has given his wife the right to decide about whether to remain married to him and she kisses him, this voids her right to opt for divorce.[32] In the case of the wife, then, any action on her part that is perceived as a sexual overture automatically signifies her wish to remain married to her husband. There is no assessment of the relative lustfulness of her kiss or whether her intent was to remain married; her intent is simply inferred from her action.[33]

Though *ṭalāq rajī'* is generally translated as "revocable divorce," the husband taking back the wife did not actually revoke the *ṭalāq*. Rather, its effects were suspended and the couple returned to a normal married state. Despite the resumption of standard rights and obligations, the pronouncement counted toward the limit of three *ṭalāq*s that a husband could pronounce before he lost the right to take back his wife. In an irrevocable *ṭalāq*—as with other forms of irrevocable divorce, such as divorce for compensation *(khulʿ)* or judicial divorce[34]—the husband had no right of return.

Irrevocable *ṭalāq* occurred in two situations. First, *ṭalāq* in an unconsummated marriage was irrevocable because the wife, exempt from a waiting period, was free to remarry immediately. Second, three *ṭalāq*s pronounced on successive occasions or at the same time made divorce both irrevocable and absolute. In an absolute divorce, the spouses could remarry only after the wife's marriage to a different husband.[35] Once this intervening marriage ended, and the wife's waiting period expired, the original spouses could remarry. This remarriage required a new contract, the wife's consent, and a new dower. To reunite after an irrevocable (but not absolute) *ṭalāq* or another form of irrevocable divorce, a new marriage between the former spouses was necessary, but not an intervening marriage of the wife to another man.

In regulating divorce, the jurists oscillated between concern for the specific requirements of the husband's pronouncement and the broader ethical question of whether divorce ought to be pronounced at all and, if so, what form it ought to take. The notion of "model divorce," or *ṭalāq al-sunna,* gives a normative structure that, among other things, discourages multiple divorces, provides ample opportunity for reconciliation, and renders calculation of the waiting period simpler. In *sunna* divorce, the husband pronounces a single *ṭalāq* when his wife is not menstruating and before he has had intercourse with her during that cycle.[36] He then avoids sexual contact with her for two more menstrual cycles. During this waiting period, the *ṭalāq* is revocable. Her third menstrual period makes the divorce definitive.[37] Because he has pronounced only one *ṭalāq,* though, they could remarry (with her consent and a new dower) without her having to conclude and consummate an intervening marriage.

Divorcing husbands frequently strayed from these guidelines, and early Sunni authorities regularly conceded the effectiveness of *ṭalāq* declarations that deviated from the model. Though it receives barely any attention in contemporary discussions of *ṭalāq,* which tend to center on so-called triple divorce, the question of whether divorce pronounced to a menstruating woman was valid preoccupied the jurists extensively.

Its importance was in large part due to the hermeneutical questions it raised about prophetic precedent. Reflections centered on a case where Muḥammad ordered a man who divorced his menstruating wife to take her back and then divorce her again when her period had ended. Was the Prophet's order a command to be obeyed or a recommendation using an imperative verb? If he did take her back, did one count a divorce as having taken place? That is, did the phrase "take back" constitute recognition that the divorce pronouncement was effective, even if reprehensible? Jurists depending on the same foundational texts arrived at divergent verdicts because of their decisions about how to interpret specific legal language.

There was less debate over triple divorce: the thinkers studied here considered it offensive but effective. On the question of three simultaneous divorces or so-called "absolute" pronouncements, early authorities express varying degrees of reservation about its use, particularly when the women were not at fault. But men's unilateral and unrestricted exercise of *ṭalāq* was entirely valid, legally speaking. Shāfiʿī opposes triple divorces less strongly than Mālik, reasoning that the Prophet knew of cases where men triply divorced their wives by *ṭalāq*. His failure to reproach them for doing so or to forbid it outright meant that he tacitly accepted it. Yet, for Shāfiʿī, revocable *ṭalāq* is always preferable because it allows the husband to preserve his control over the marriage tie for as long as possible.

A husband's power of *ṭalāq* extended to a right to transfer his power to another individual, including his wife. Delegated divorce temporarily granted the recipient the husband's power of *ṭalāq*, though the scope and duration of the power varied with the particular formulae used and, in some cases, the husband's intention.[38] In most cases (for the Shāfiʿīs, the Ḥanafīs, and Ibn al-Qāsim, though not in Mālik's later view), the delegation of power to the wife was limited to the session *(majlis)* in which the husband delegated it—as with a bargain struck in the marketplace, the wife could accept or refuse the offer at that time only. Demonstrating the flexibility of the jurists' use of analogy—based in part on its explanatory power, not a simple equation of wife with slave—an implicit parallel with sales rather than with manumission structured the rules as well as the terminology for delegated divorce. The husband's granting of his power of divorce to another (male) individual constituted a relationship of agency; the agent, in such a case, could divorce the wife on the husband's behalf so long as the husband had not withdrawn the agency. Mālik's view that the wife retained the right to divorce after the session in which it was granted can also be understood as a type of agency.

The *Muwaṭṭaʾ* reports three cases where a man puts his wife's affair into her hands, transferring control over the marriage tie to her. In each, she divorces herself. Regretting his actions, the husband seeks guidance. In the first case presented, the authority, Ibn ʿUmar, states that the woman's decision is final:

> Yaḥyā related to me, on the authority of Mālik, that it reached him that a man came to ʿAbd Allāh b. ʿUmar and said: "Oh Abū ʿAbd al-Raḥmān, I placed my wife's affair in her hand and she divorced herself; what is your view?" ʿAbd Allāh b. ʿUmar said: "I think it is as she said." The man said: "Don't do this, Oh Abū ʿAbd al-Raḥmān." Ibn ʿUmar said: "Me do it? You did it."[39]

The husband protests Ibn ʿUmar's opinion that "it is as she said," blaming him for the separation. Ibn ʿUmar replies that he has done nothing; it is the husband's actions that have led to this unwanted result. Rather than being a case for adjudication or interpretation, the husband's transfer of control over divorce to his wife was entirely valid. He may not, therefore, revoke her actions. The man here is not asked about his intentions, the number of divorces, or their revocability. In the absence of any limiting information, Ibn ʿUmar assumes that the power over the wife's affair that the husband places "in her hand" is the same as that which he possesses.

The report that immediately follows, however, reinterprets Ibn ʿUmar's position in a way that suggests he espoused a more limited model of transfer of control:

> He related to me from Mālik, from Nāfiʿ, that ʿAbd Allāh b. ʿUmar used to say: When a man transfers control to *(mallaka)* his wife over her affair, then the decision is whatever she decides on, unless he denies it *(an yunkira ʿalayhā)* and says: I only meant one. And he swears to that, and has more control over her *(yakūnu amlaka bihā)* while she is in her waiting period.[40]

Ibn ʿUmar's previous decision did not allow the husband to deny that he intended to give his wife full control but rather upheld the wife's action ("I think it is as she said"). This report suggests that though there is a presumption in favor of the woman being entirely able to decide the number (and thus the revocability) of divorces when she is granted control, this presumption is rebuttable by the husband's sworn claim that he delegated only a single divorce.

In the report that follows these, the opposite presumption seems to operate; it is assumed that the woman's control is only over a single divorce. Muḥammad b. Abī ʿAtīq comes, teary-eyed, to Zayd b. Thābit, who inquires as to the reason. He informs Zayd, "I gave my wife control of her affair and she divorced me *(fāraqatnī)*." Zayd replies, "Take her back *(irtajiʿhā)* if you wish. Indeed it is [only] one and you have more control over her *(anta amlaku bihā)*."[41] Zayd makes no inquiry into the husband's intentions and does not make him swear as to his intent.

Ultimately, the opinion endorsed by Mālik falls between the two extremes. Mālik rejects Ibn ʿUmar's stated decision that the woman's word is final ("I think it is as she said") and also Zayd's blanket assumption that a wife's control is only over a single divorce ("You have more control over her"). Mālik declares a final report to be "the best of what I have heard" about the subject. A man grants his wife control over herself but protests when she repudiates herself more than once. The spouses appeal together to Marwān b. al-Ḥakam, who makes the husband swear that he "only gave her control of one [divorce]" and then returns the wife *("raddahā")* to him.

This case agrees with Ibn ʿUmar's view that the husband is to be believed if he swears that he intended to give his wife power only over a single divorce. The critical distinguishing factor is that the husband objects at the time his wife pronounces multiple divorces, rather than complaining subsequently. This makes the husband's claim that he intended to grant control of only a single repudiation more credible to Mālik. Subsequent applications of Mālik's view, however, do not require the husband to demonstrate that he objected at the time the wife was exercising her delegated right of divorce. The *Mudawwana* simply states that if the husband swears he intended to grant control of only a single divorce, he is believed and allowed to return to his wife during her waiting period.[42]

Though differing on the extent of the power over the marriage tie granted to the wife by various formulae used delegation, all agreed that it was never any expression of a wife's power over whether she remained married or obtained divorce. Rather, in these forms of divorce the husband temporarily permitted his wife to exercise a prerogative that belonged exclusively to him.[43] Delegated divorce, despite the fact that it could involve the wife in its operation, was not a bilateral agreement. The wife, bound by the marriage tie, did not share the power of unilateral divorce. Instead, her opportunities to dissolve the marriage were limited to judicial divorce for cause, grounds for which varied greatly depending on the school; delegated divorce, if authorized by her husband; and *khulʿ*, divorce for compensation, the main form of female-initiated divorce.

"Sell Me My Repudiation": Khulʿ and Marital Dissolution

In crucial respects, *khulʿ* is the mirror image of marriage. Like marriage, *khulʿ* is a bilateral contract.[44] *Khulʿ* and the compensation required for it illustrate the conceptual centrality of control of the wife's sexuality to marriage, as well as the ways in which that control was analogous to property transactions; *khulʿ* frequently was discussed in the language of sales. In marriage, the dower was exchanged for *milk* over the wife or, more particularly, over her sexual organ *(buḍʿ)*. This *milk* legitimized sex and established for the husband control over the end of marriage. In *ṭalāq,* the husband unilaterally relinquished this control, either revocably or irrevocably, without financial consideration. In *khulʿ*, the wife bought back *milk* over herself by compensating the husband in return for a divorce. *Khulʿ* might or might not require that the husband pronounce *ṭalāq;* some texts associated this term with their discussions of *khulʿ* and others used terms such as *ṭaṭlīqa* or *firāq* (single divorce, separation).[45] Regardless of which term was employed, *khulʿ* differed from *ṭalāq* in two important ways. First, it required the wife's assent (if she was free and in her majority—i.e., if she had control over the compensation). Second, it was always, except in one dissenting opinion, irrevocable. Following *khulʿ*, if the husband wished to resume marital relations with his ex-wife, a new marriage contract was necessary, along with a new dower and her consent. However, *khulʿ* could count as more than a single divorce, either by agreement between the divorcing spouses or the husband's intent.[46]

If *ṭalāq* is analogous to manumission, *khulʿ* parallels *kitāba,* a transaction in which a slave contracts to pay for his or her emancipation.[47] Both *khulʿ* and *kitāba* require the husband or master's consent and the payment of a sum from the wife or slave for her or his release. *Ṭalāq* and manumission were both accomplished by the husband or master's utterance of a few words; *khulʿ* and *kitāba* required the participation and agreement of the wife or slave, both in principle and as to the specific financial terms. The *Jāmiʿ al-Ṣaghīr* demonstrates these parallels in its discussion of the effect of particular formulae in both divorce for compensation and manumission for compensation. The Ḥanafī authorities disagreed as to whether a particular phrase was (1) a unilateral pronouncement of *ṭalāq* or manumission, or (2) an offer of *khulʿ* or *kitāba* that required acceptance from the wife or slave in order to take effect.

> [If] a man says to his wife: "You are divorced [in exchange] for one thousand [dirhams] *(ʿalā alf)*" and she accepts, then she is divorced and she owes [him] one thousand *(ʿalayhā al-alf)*. This is like his saying "You are divorced for one thousand *(bi alf)*." If he says to her, "You are divorced and you owe [me] one thousand *(wa ʿalayki alf)*, and she accepts, or he says to his slave, "You are free and you owe [me] one thousand" and [the slave] accepts, [then according to Abū Ḥanīfa] the slave is manumitted and the wife is revocably divorced, and neither of them owes [him] anything. Abū Yūsuf and Muḥammad, may God be pleased with them, said: Each of them owes [him] one thousand dirhams. If they do not accept, the wife is divorced and the slave is manumitted according to Abū Ḥanīfa, may God be pleased with him. Abū Yūsuf and Muḥammad, may God be merciful to them, said: If they do not accept, the wife is not divorced nor is the slave manumitted.[48]

The first two formulas mentioned, linking the *ṭalāq* to the compensation (divorced "*ʿalā* one thousand" or "*bi* one thousand"), unanimously required the wife's acceptance of the terms for the divorce to occur; she was then liable for the thousand. No one mentioned manumission, as there was no need to clarify the matter; all agreed that the two statements were equivalent and constituted offers of *khulʿ*, which took effect only with the wife's acquiescence.

The next formula, though, provoked disagreement, so *kitāba* was brought in to clarify the issues at stake. "You are divorced [or free] *and* you owe [me] one thousand" was understood by Abū Ḥanīfa as a unilateral pronouncement and by his two disciples as an offer, like the others, that took effect only with both parties' agreement. Whether the formula constituted a unilateral pronouncement or a bilateral agreement determined whether it would be an irrevocable *khulʿ* divorce or a revocable *ṭalāq*. Abū Ḥanīfa understood this third formula as two separate statements: first a divorce (or manumission), which was automatically effective, followed by a declaration that the wife (or slave) owed the husband (or master) one thousand dirhams. In Abū Ḥanīfa's view, the statement that the wife (or slave) owes this sum has no effect, irrespective of whether she (or he) agreed: the release had already taken effect. However, the *ṭalāq* was revocable because the wife did not compensate the husband in exchange for divorce. (In the case of manumission, the pronouncement was effective, the slave owed no money in exchange for it, and it was irrevocable since there is no such thing as a revocable manumission.) Abū Yūsuf and Muḥammad, in contrast, understood the statement "You are divorced and you owe [me] one thousand" to be, like the previous formulas, an offer rather than a declaration. In this context, "and" meant "if." It did not count as a pronouncement of *ṭalāq* or manumission if the offer to pay for freedom was not accepted.

Compensation made *khulʿ* irrevocable. Despite the Ḥanafī authorities' disagreement about the phrasing of one formula, they agreed on both the consensual nature of *khulʿ* and the link between compensation and irrevocability. For Mālik and Shāfiʿī, likewise, both spouses' consent was necessary for a *khulʿ* divorce, which was irrevocable even in the presence of a stipulation to the contrary.[49] The view of early Medinan authority Saʿīd b. al-Musayyab—that, by returning the compensation, a husband who had agreed to *khulʿ* had the right to return to his wife—remained isolated.[50] However, it also linked compensation and the severing of the husband's marital *milk*.

The jurists' preoccupations with issues of consent, compensation, and revocability in *khulʿ* must be understood in light of their presumption that *khulʿ* was to be used when a woman desired to dissolve her marriage for no fault of the husband's. *Ṭalāq* allowed dissolution of the marriage at the husband's whim, though an astute wife might be able to use it for an exit strategy in case of polygyny or relocation through suspended, conditional, or conditional delegated divorce. *Khulʿ* was assumed to apply when a wife disliked her husband and wanted out of a marriage: if it were revocable, the husband could simply take her back during the waiting period, defeating the purpose. Because *khulʿ* severed the husband's marital authority at the wife's behest, irrevocability was an integral component. But this irrevocability had to be fit into a legal framework of mutual claims.

Much as marriage with the wife's fair dower fixed in advance exemplified the norm for marriage, in the paradigmatic *khulʿ* the husband bore no fault and the compensation was the exact dower given at marriage. However, *khulʿ* could take many additional forms. Where the wife sought dissolution for no fault of the husband's, she could offer any amount necessary to secure his agreement, even more than the original dower.[51] If the husband was partially or fully to blame for the marital discord, the jurists disagreed on whether he could or should take any compensation whatsoever.

Both the *Muwaṭṭaʾ* and the *Mudawwana* distinguish between the situations where the husband was blameworthy and those where he was not. Referring to the conduct of the at-fault spouse as *nushūz*, Mālik declared it "lawful for her husband to take from her what she gives him for the *khulʿ*" when she was the one at fault and "she consents to that and there is no harm of her by him."[52] Among the behaviors that justified taking compensation, Medinan authority Ibn Shihāb al-Zuhrī included "demonstrating repulsion toward him," "attach[ing] no importance to her husband's rights," going out without permission, and allowing into the home someone that the husband disliked.[53] Even with wifely *nushūz*, the text warns that there had to be "no harm of her by him." If the wife was not guilty of any offense, the at-fault husband could divorce her at will by *ṭalāq* but was not allowed to extort compensation in exchange.

Mālikī texts make a legal distinction between taking compensation for marital dissolution in the case of the wife's *nushūz* as opposed to the *nushūz* of the husband, but Ḥanafī texts distinguish between the two as a matter of ethics. Mālik's stance that a wife who had obtained *khulʿ* from a husband who harmed her was entitled to have her compensation refunded is logical, given his willingness to grant the wife judicial divorce because of that harm. The Ḥanafī position is equally in keeping with the contrary view that virtually never permitted judicial divorce. Because a woman could not get a divorce from a husband who harmed her by any means except his divorce of her, it was legally permissible for her to pay exorbitantly for *khulʿ*; she had no other recourse. In discussing a woman who pays all her wealth to get a divorce, the *Muwaṭṭaʾ Shaybānī* concludes, "Whatever a woman ransoms herself from her husband for is legally permissible *(jāʾiz fī ʾl qaḍāʾ)*." Where the wife is at fault and the husband blameless, "we do not like him to take from her more than he gave her [as dower], even if the *nushūz* is on her part." In the opposite case, when the fault was the husband's, the *Muwaṭṭaʾ Shaybānī* condemns his taking anything at all for agreeing to the *khulʿ*: "If the *nushūz* is on his part, we do not like him to take [anything] from her, whether little or much." Ultimately, "if he does take [something] from her it is legally permissible, but it is reprehensible *(makrūh)* for him as to what is between him and his Lord. This is the opinion of Abū Ḥanīfa."[54] Two authorities on whom Abū Ḥanīfa often draws differ on this question, with Ḥammād b. Abī Sulaymān holding that "it is reprehensible for him to take more than he has given her" (not, it should be noted, anything at all) and Ibrāhīm al-Nakhaʿī holding that "it is perfectly acceptable for him to do this."[55]

The *Jāmiʿ al-Ṣaghīr* presents a slightly different stance on the legitimacy of various amounts of compensation in case of either spouse's *nushūz*: "[If] woman gets *khulʿ* for more than her dower while the *nushūz* is from her, the excess is appropriate for her husband [to take]." If, however, "the *nushūz* is from him, it is reprehensible for him [to take] the excess, [but] it is legally permissible." This passage treats only the "excess" compensation, the amount that exceeded the woman's actual dower; it is acceptable—unlike in the *Muwaṭṭaʾ Shaybānī*—for him to take the original dower amount, even if he is at fault. These two Ḥanafī texts concur, though, that regardless of how reprehensible it might be for the husband to take a particular amount of compensation in exchange for repudiating his wife, it is "legally permissible."[56]

In discussing compensation and consent in *khulʿ* divorces, the jurists frequently compare *khulʿ* to sales, *kitāba*, marriage,[57] and *ṭalāq* in ways that assimilate *khulʿ* to and distinguish it from these other transactions. As commerce provided the standard vocabulary for most transactions, it is not a surprise to find it used for *khulʿ*. What is interesting is the type of transaction discussed: *khulʿ*, like marriage, is usually compared to sales, but *ṭalāq*, when not for compensation, is compared to manumission. Mālikī jurists matter-of-factly accepted the language of sales for *khulʿ*, considering its use to create binding contracts: "I said: If she says, 'Sell me my *ṭalāq* for one thousand dirhams,' and he does so, is that permissible in Mālik's opinion? He said: Yes."[58] Likewise, for Shāfiʿī, *khulʿ* was either *like* a sale or it *was* a sale. The *Mukhtaṣar* of al-Muzanī gives the following case: "A wife saying 'If you divorce me triply, I will [give] you one hundred [dirhams]' is like a man saying 'Sell me this robe of yours for one hundred.' "[59] Here, a woman transacts business just like a man, unlike in divorce by *ṭalāq,* where she is an object rather than a participant. The *Umm* alternates between treating *khulʿ* as *like* a sale—"*khulʿ* is allowed during illness and health, just as sale is allowed during sickness and health"[60]—and *as* a sale. By likening *khulʿ* to a sale, Shāfiʿī differentiated it from *ṭalāq,* particularly with regard to revocability. *Khulʿ*'s nature as a sale rendered it irrevocable: "*Khulʿ* is a divorce [where] he does not possess the right to return [to her], because it is a sale among sales. It is not permissible for him to own her property and [at the same time] to have more control over her *(wa yakūn amlaka bihā).*"[61] When the husband claimed the property that the wife gave as compensation, the wife became, in exchange, "more the owner" of herself. In turn, the husband did not "control the right to return to her." As in the Ḥanafī authorities' discussion of particular formulae, compensation made the difference between the husband possessing the unilateral right to return and the wife having control over herself. *Khulʿ* was structured as a sale and was therefore a bilateral contract. Like marriage but unlike most (other) sales the transfer of *milk* was irrevocable once agreed on. Shāfiʿī explained that when the husband took the compensation from the wife ("the property"), he could not continue to own "the right to return." It was this right that "left him and for which he took property [in exchange]."[62]

In addition to their statements that *khulʿ* was the wife's purchase of a *ṭalāq* or the husband's sale of his right to take her back, the jurists also described the transaction as an exchange for the wife's *buḍʿ*. (Though *buḍʿ* is most easily translated as "vulva," it also implies the initiation of marriage.) According to the *Mudawwana,* she "give[s] him something from her property *(mālihā)* [in exchange] for taking her *buḍʿ* from him."[63] And in the *Umm, khulʿ* was described as payment in consideration for transferring control of the wife's *buḍʿ (al-khulʿ huwa ʿiwaḍ min al-buḍʿ).*[64] That both marriage and *khulʿ* were transactions that involved payment for the transfer of control over the wife's sexual organ could not be clearer; discussing compensation in *khulʿ,* Shāfiʿī noted that "the fair value of the *buḍʿ* is her fair dower" *(qīmat mithl al-buḍʿ mahr mithlihā).*[65] In marriage, the husband paid fair dower to acquire control over the wife's *buḍʿ* (the *Umm* refers to the wife's fair dower, in the contracting of marriage, as the "price for [her] *buḍʿ*");[66] in *khulʿ,* the wife paid her fair dower to reclaim it.

Rather than contradicting each other, these rationales express facets of one overarching explanation: in *khulʿ* the wife irrevocably purchases back the sexual rights over herself that her husband gained through the marriage contract, rights that were bound up with his *milk* over the marriage tie. *Khulʿ* essentially reversed the transaction of marriage, in which he became obligated to pay her a dower to make her sexually lawful for himself; this lawfulness was conveyed through his control over the marriage tie. This ceding of control *(milk)* by the wife to the husband at the time of marriage was associated with a payment from husband to wife: the dower. In *khulʿ*, this relinquishment of control by the husband back to the wife likewise was associated with payment.

The specifics of the payment, however, varied from that required in the regulation of dower. Mālikī authority Ibn al-Qāsim approved a *khulʿ* where a wife gave her husband one thousand dirhams and received both a divorce and a slave worth approximately that amount. He reasoned that if the slave was worth less than that, she had paid for the *khulʿ*. On the other hand, "if it is equivalent, then it is divorce by mutual agreement," a lawful arrangement where both spouses "mutually relinquish [their claims], with him not giving her anything and her not giving him anything."[67] Such a transaction would not be permissible in marriage because a woman could not transfer sexual rights over herself without the creation of an obligation to pay dower, while the husband could relinquish his rights gratis in divorce *(ṭalāq)*.[68]

Much like dower, whatever compensation the parties agreed on for *khulʿ* was valid unless it broke regulations for the commercial transfer of property. Even if the compensation was invalid, *khulʿ*, like marriage, was not invalidated or annulled, as would be the case with commercial sales; rather, as with dower, a substitute compensation was arranged.[69] In the Shāfiʿī view, fair dower was the almost universal remedy for *khulʿ* when the specified compensation was problematic, as well as in situations where no compensation was specified.[70] In neither case did the irregularities with the compensation for *khulʿ* lead to the dissolution being rescinded.[71]

Capacity to contract *khulʿ* centered on axes of sex, age, and legal status. *Khulʿ* involved both relinquishment of marital authority and financial remuneration, each of which could be wielded or not according to gender, majority, and freedom. To consent to *khulʿ*, a wife had to have financial control and, for Shāfiʿī, a husband had to have the ability to wield *ṭalāq*. Shāfiʿī is always keenly attuned to these elements of legal personhood. The *Umm* insists that a woman had to be capable of controlling her own assets: "We permit anyone who controls her[72] own assets to make *khulʿ*." She could not be a minor or have lost her reason *(maghlūba ʿalā ʿaqlihā)* or be subject to interdiction *(ḥajr)*, or any *khulʿ* she contracted would be canceled and her compensation returned to her. The wife had to be, at a minimum, free and in her majority to enjoy this legal capacity. If she were not, her part of the exchange would be void. Voiding the compensation did not, however, invalidate the *ṭalāq* for Shāfiʿī: "His divorce of her [in exchange] for [the compensation] he took from her is effective *(wāqiʿ ʿalayhā)*, but he possesses the right to return." Signaling again the link between compensation and irrevocability, the *Umm* notes, "If [the compensation] he has taken is void, he possesses the right to return in the divorce that took effect for it."[73]

Though for the wife to contract *khulʿ* she had to have control over her financial affairs, a husband had only to be capable of validly pronouncing *ṭalāq*. According to the *Umm*, "A husband's *khulʿ* is not permissible until his *ṭalāq* is permissible. For this, he [must be] in his majority *(bāligh)* and [must] not have lost his reason *(maghlūb ʿalā ʿaqlihi)*. If he has not lost his reason, then his *khulʿ* is valid . . . because [of the fact that] his *ṭalāq* is valid."[74]

The way *khulʿ* regulations applied to the case of slaves illustrate these gendered considerations at the same time that they affirm male slaves' rights in divorce. A female slave could not contract *khulʿ* without the consent of her master, since she possessed no property rights. It was irrelevant, according to Shāfiʿī, whether she was intellectually mature *(rashīda)* or foolish *(safīha)*; she had no ownership over any assets and thus no right to dispose of them. In fact, her master could contract *khulʿ* for her without her involvement or consent. By contrast, a male slave could validly grant *khulʿ* despite his equal lack of property rights, since he possessed the capacity to pronounce a valid divorce. However, "whatever the slave receives for *khulʿ* belongs to his master." Thus, a female slave has no role in *khulʿ* because she controls neither the property used for compensation nor the divorce rights exercised by her husband. In sharp distinction, "if a [male] slave's master makes *khulʿ* on behalf of his [male] slave without his permission, the *khulʿ* is invalid, because no one can divorce on behalf of another, [not] a father, nor a master, nor a *walī,* nor a *sulṭān*. Rather, a male *(marʾ)* divorces on his own behalf or the *sulṭān* divorces for him" for cause.[75] *Khulʿ* could not be compelled for a slave husband, just as a divorce could not be compelled for him: despite his enslavement he was male and a husband.

Divorce Rights of Slaves

Slave marriage had legal and social ramifications, and Muslim jurists attempted to balance the marital rights of slaves with the ownership rights of masters. Slave marriages could be validly contracted only with the owners' permission. Some seventh- and eighth-century authorities held that slave unions were subject to owners' whims for both formation and dissolution. A male slave's master could divorce the slave's wife, or a master could wrench his female slave away from her husband, and the sale of a female slave automatically resulted in divorce because the master's proprietary interest trumped her marital bond. From the ninth century onward, however, Sunni authorities held that once a slave's marriage was validly established, its dissolution was subject to the same rules as marriages in which both spouses were free. Enslaved husbands, and the husbands of female slaves, were fully vested with marital authority in matters of divorce. How and why did the jurists arrive at consensus on this point, when they continued to disagree over other matters involving the marriage of slaves? At stake in these controversies are the definition of a husband's role and the emerging unanimity on the central place of the right to divorce in the jurisprudential understanding of marriage.

The *Muṣannaf*s of ʿAbd al-Razzāq al-Ṣanʿānī and Ibn Abī Shayba contain numerous anecdotes and opinions traced back to the Companions of the Prophet and successive generations expressing the view that "the male slave's divorce is in his master's hand."[76] Some authorities, including the Companion Ibn ʿAbbās, declare that a male slave's master may pronounce divorce of the slave's wife if he wishes. Further, some hold that the slave himself has no power to effect the divorce, except with his master's permission. In the case where both the husband and the wife are slaves belonging to the same owner, according to Jābir b. ʿAbd Allāh, "their master joins them and separates [them]."[77] Others disagree, holding that the slave himself wields divorce. Confronted with the view of Jābir b. Zayd that "[the slave's] divorce is in his master's hand," Saʿīd b. Jubayr replies that "Jābir is wrong; rather, the divorce is in the hand of the one who has sex with the woman."[78] ʿUmar ibn al-Khaṭṭāb likewise reportedly declares, "If he marries with his masters' permission, then the divorce is in the hand of the one for whom the sexual organ is lawful"[79]—that is, the slave himself. Saʿīd b. al-Musayyab, cited frequently by later Mālikīs, also held that "if the master marries off his male slave, he may not separate them (i.e., the slave and his wife)." All agreed that the slave could marry only with his master's permission; the second group merely held that once permission was granted, the master had no power to dissolve the slave's marriage.[80]

The jurists of the nascent legal schools were, by contrast, united on the subject of the male slave's control over divorce.[81] The *Muwaṭṭa'* and the *Kitāb al-Ḥujja* betray the previous existence of dispute only by their vehemence in defending the enslaved husband's sole control over the dissolution of his marriage. "The divorce is in the hand of the slave. Nobody else has any power over his divorce."[82] In the *Umm*, Shāfiʿī acknowledges the existence of the alternate position, introducing it as archaic: "Some of those in the past said, 'The male slave may not divorce, rather the divorce is in the master's hand.' "[83] Archaism notwithstanding, Shāfiʿī went on to argue against it. If someone argued that by divorcing his wife, the slave was "destroying assets"—presumably because of the dower involved—then the appropriate reply was that the husband had no share in his wife's assets that could be destroyed, nor did she herself constitute an asset. The power to divorce has nothing to do with property, which a slave cannot own, but rather with obligatory, lawful, and prohibited acts. Here, Shāfiʿī's view recalls those of earlier authorities who linked the right to have lawful sex with a woman to the right to divorce her: "The [male] slave is among those to whom the [categories] of forbidden and lawful apply. He makes [her] forbidden to him by divorce. The master is not the one to whom the woman is lawful"—that is, sexually—"and who [therefore] can make her forbidden" by divorcing her.[84]

Like a male slave's control over divorce, whether a female slave's master could dissolve her marriage was the subject of disagreement among seventh- and eighth-century legal authorities. It was also resolved in favor of the husband's exclusive right to divorce. Texts often assume that a master had permitted two of his own slaves to marry each other. Though the same rule applied as in cases where both spouses belonged to different owners, here the female slave would originally have been licit to her master. The marriage made her sexually lawful to her husband and forbidden to their joint master. Debating the dissolution of the male slave's marriage was often a roundabout way of considering whether and how the master could reinstate his own sexual access to the woman in question if he owned her as well.

May a master who has permitted his female slave to marry dissolve her marriage? If so, how? Most held that he could not do anything of the sort, which became the consensus view by the formative era. Isolated early authorities, however, held that a master who owned both spouses could unilaterally "wrench" the wife away from her husband; having done so, she would again be lawful to him. Implicit in the Companion Ibn Abbās's opinion to this effect is the view that the marriage of a slave woman merits less respect than a marriage bond between free persons. In his view, the Qur'anic passage prohibiting access to married women "except what your right hands own" (Q. 4:24) applies not only to married non-Muslim women captured in battle, but even to slave women married to Muslims. Thus, he argued, "A man may wrench away a female slave *(walīda)*, the wife of his slave, and have sex with her if he wishes."[85] Though seldom explicitly attributed to any authority, the vociferousness with which this doctrine was denounced by other authorities attests to it having been well known. It represents one end of the spectrum concerning how binding the marriage ties of a female slave are compared to the strength of her master's ownership rights.

Nearer the middle of the spectrum, there were numerous proponents on both sides of a related issue: if a female slave was sold, did her marriage tie persist despite the transfer of ownership? Many of those who held that an owner could not unilaterally rescind his female slave's marriage nonetheless thought that this marriage did not survive a sale. Al-Ḥasan explicitly contrasted the two situations: "Her sale is her divorce . . . but if he marries her off, he may not separate them."[86] It seems that it was all right to relinquish one's own claim to sexual access, but that when the transfer of ownership took place, the right to sexual relations with the female slave transferred alongside it. Disagreement on this point was eventually replaced by consensus that sale did not lead to the dissolution of marriage, but it is noteworthy that everyone agreed that a new master could not have sexual access if the marriage tie persisted, because two men could not both have lawful sexual access to the same woman.

The *Muṣannaf* of ʿAbd al-Razzāq presents a roster of authorities who, like al-Ḥasan, held that the sale of a married female slave automatically dissolved her marriage, making her sexually lawful for her new owner. Eight entries assert, "A female slave's sale is her divorce," or simply, "Her sale is her divorce."[87] Among those who held that the sale of a female slave was her divorce, there was disagreement about whether the sale of her husband, assuming he belonged to the same master, also dissolved the union. Some held, "Whichever of the two of them is sold, it is a divorce." Others, though, saw only the sale of the wife as breaking up the marriage. Saʿīd b. al-Musayyab and Mujāhid declare, "Her sale is her divorce, but if the male slave is sold, she is not thereby divorced."[88] These verdicts treat the marital tie with an enslaved woman as less secure than one with a free woman because of the scope of her master's claims over her.

These casual views with regard to the dissolution of slave marriages were disputed from the first generations, however. Numerous Companions and Successors objected to the idea that a female slave's marriage dissolved when she changed hands. Their views usually appear in anecdotes telling of men who purchased, or were given, female slaves whom they subsequently learned were married. These men's reactions demonstrated that they believed the slave's marriages continued in force despite the transfer of ownership. As a result, they either bought the right to sexual access to these women from their husbands or, if the husband refused, returned the female slaves to their previous owners. In one example from the *Muṣannaf* of ʿAbd al-Razzāq, a man "sent ʿAlī a slavegirl" as a gift. ʿAlī—the Prophet's cousin and son-in-law, the fourth Sunni caliph and the first Imam of the Shiʿa—"said to her: Are you available or unavailable *(mashgūla)*?" When she replied that she was unavailable, meaning that she had a husband, ʿAlī returned her to the man who had sent her. The man, in turn, "bought her *buḍʿ* [from her husband] for 1,500 dirhams, and sent her [back] to ʿAlī," who "accepted her."[89] ʿAlī's principled stance in refusing to have sex with a married slave supported the view that a transfer of ownership did not dissolve a slave's marriage. Notably, no actual divorce pronouncement was mentioned. As Isḥāq b. Rāhawayh, a slightly younger contemporary of Shāfiʿī, sums up the views he deems authoritative, a female slave who had a husband did not become lawful to a new owner "until he divorces her or her body is bought from the husband."[90] This language strongly parallels that used for *khulʿ* divorce. In the case of a slave, the act of buying (rights to) the woman's sexual organ from the husband served as an equivalent to, or a substitute for, divorce. Marriage of a female slave transferred a type of partial ownership over her: to make her fully available to her new master, that ownership had to be reintegrated with the rest of the control over her.

Though ostensibly concerned with the sale of a married female slave, these anecdotes ultimately revolve around the marital prerogatives of her husband. In another case, ʿAlī affirms that "he is her husband, until he divorces her or dies."[91] Another notes that even though a female slave might be sold away, "a slave has more right to his wife wherever she is found unless he divorces her irrevocably."[92] The inviolability of the marriage tie even when the parties to it were enslaved was as critical to the evolving jurisprudence on marriage as the sexual exclusivity of marriage (as far as the wife was concerned). The once-contested view that only the husband of a female slave controlled her divorce came to be settled.[93] For Mālik, Abū Ḥanīfa, Shāfiʿī, and their followers, it was inconceivable that the sale of a female slave could trigger the dissolution of her marriage—this power rested with her husband, regardless of his status.[94]

A look at the way al-Khaṣṣāf's ninth-century treatise on maintenance handles the sale of a female slave of ambiguous marital status shows how entrenched these assumptions had become. In a discussion of how much one can or must rely on others' representations of given situations, a slavegirl tells a man who has just purchased her that she has a husband. Al-Khaṣṣāf sums up the relevant legal ruling: "If a man buys a slavegirl and she claims that she is a married woman *(annahā dhāt zawj)* and the seller says 'She had a husband but he divorced her,' the buyer cannot return her."[95] Al-Khaṣṣāf assumes that her marital status would affect the buyer's decision: it is universally accepted not only that a female slave with a husband is sexually off-limits but also that her sale has no effect on any existing marriage. If she is in fact married, al-Khaṣṣāf presumes that the buyer would wish to void the transaction, since he would be barred from sexual access to her. (The use of the term *jāriyya,* "slave girl," rather than *ama* or *mamlūka* hints at a primarily sexual purpose for the slave.) One must also explain the difference between the enslaved woman's response and the seller's response; presumably, one of the two is lying. The slave might lie to scotch the sale entirely or to avoid sex with her new owner. The seller might lie to preserve the sale. In either case, no one suggests that the sale itself would dissolve any extant marriage of hers; the debate has shifted.

These decisions about the enslaved husband's exclusive right to decide on divorce and the persistence of a slave woman's marriage through a transfer of ownership both reflected the strengthening of the husband's marital authority. As marriage law became increasingly systematized, certain property rights of owners were weakened when these conflicted with a husband's prerogatives. These shifts reflect a larger process of consolidation of male marital authority as well as the centrality of divorce to the structure of rights regulating Muslim marriage.

Doctrinal disagreements on a variety of issues, including some relating to the rights and obligations of a male slave, persisted. A male slave's consent to marriage continued to provoke disagreement, as did questions about maintenance of a married female slave. The husband's sole authority to dissolve his marriage unilaterally, however, was not something on which formative-period Sunni jurists could agree to disagree: the husband's right to unilateral divorce was a crucial defining element of Muslim marriage. Slave husbands' power to exercise divorce rights without possessing or controlling assets clearly distinguished marriage from property transactions. Likewise, the fact that the husband of a female slave retained his control of the marriage tie even while another owned her as commercial property means that one cannot define their marital relationship unproblematically as "ownership." Yet the centrality of the husband's right to divorce was parallel to the slave owner's control over manumission. Ironically, because the jurists defined marriage for enslaved persons as being immune (once established) from the interference of property owners, they vested analogous power in the husband who—whether himself enslaved or married to a slave—found himself with the right to unilaterally sever the legal tie joining his wife to him.

A male slave's diminished legal capacity as compared to that of a free man meant less autonomy and control over his own marital destiny. Yet once validly married, a male slave became, in relation to his wife, simply a husband. His continued enslavement did not weaken his marital authority. He alone could divorce his wife by *ṭalāq;* his consent was needed for *khulʿ* divorce. Once married, a male slave gained all of the rights as well as (most of the) duties associated with the role of husband. Though he was *mamlūk,* "owned," by his master, a slave was still *mālik,* "owner," of the marriage tie. In the case of slave and free, or male and female, whatever equality or inequality existed between the two types of persons before or outside of marriage was irrelevant inside marriage.

Becoming husbands allowed male slaves to act autonomously in the sexual realm. Jennifer Glancy has asserted that for ancient Mediterranean slavery "the male slave endured the permanent status of a boy, excluded from maturing into the category of manhood."[96] For the Muslim jurists, by contrast, becoming a husband made a slave a man. Though debarred from marrying without permission, once married he could freely wield a husband's powers. His manly status, though, pertained only with regard to his wife. It did not change his relationship to his master, who retained rights over his labor and his domicile, or to his offspring, if any. Nor did it affect his ability to engage in property transactions. Control over divorce translated to control over sexual licitness; it was available to married men without regard to their legal status.

Conclusion

The centrality of unilateral divorce to legal constructions of manhood was probably less significant in practice than in theory. Rapoport, studying Mamluk society, concludes that "in spite of the value of repudiation as a unilateral and patriarchal privilege actual divorce tended to be a much more balanced event."[97] Numerous historical studies bear him out. Judges often worked around doctrinal restrictions to grant women divorces outside the parameters of the expected. And increasing women's access to divorce as a matter of statute was one of the most significant objectives of twentieth-century legal reformers. But restricting men's exercise of *ṭalāq* has proved more difficult; its place as a marker of authentic Islamic law remains. As this chapter has shown, in the extension of divorce prerogatives to male slaves, the formative-period jurists cemented a model of marriage with male-initiated divorce as a nonnegotiable element.

As much as any imbalance of practical power, perceived inequities in divorce rules have also led reformist thinkers to tackle divorce as a way of approaching the larger question of Islamic law and women's rights. Western Muslim feminists, themselves not subject to state-defined and enforced Islamic law, have grappled with the relationship between law and scripture on matters of divorce. Some have defended Islamic marriage and divorce laws as generally fair toward women, excusing inequalities that manifest in jurisprudence as deviations from equitable scriptural provisions. In this view, the law that elite men in the early and medieval periods formulated reflected their socially conditioned views: "problematic jurisprudence was often the result of a misunderstanding or misapplication of the Qur'anic text resulting from cultural distortions or patriarchal bias," Azizah al-Hibri asserts.[98] Maysam al-Faruqi concurs: "The limitations that ended up in Islamic law around women did not come from the Qur'anic text."[99]

Al-Faruqi's argument merits more detailed consideration because it highlights a common failure to see the interconnected nature of jurisprudential concepts. She acknowledges some inequities in existing divorce law. However, she attributes them solely to bad interpretations of scripture, in particular of two verses (Q. 4:34 and 2:228). Al-Faruqi views Qur'anic pronouncements as the main substance of jurisprudential doctrine. This is necessary to her argument that Islamic law is required for Muslim self-identity. If Islamic law is necessary, it must be legitimately Islamic. If it is to be legitimately Islamic, it must come from the Qur'an.[100] In her view, shared by most if not all Muslim feminists, only the Qur'an is above reproach as a source of "true" Islam. Given al-Faruqi's approximation of the authority of the Qur'an to the authority of the law, problematic legal rules, such as the unequal rights to divorce granted to men and women, must be treated as minor problems, not systemic issues, if the legitimacy of Islamic law is not to be undermined. She writes that

> most of the problems of women arise from custom rather than Islamic law. There still are some problems, however, whether stemming from tradition or from the understanding of the jurists, that can be found in Islamic law in contradiction with the actual rulings of the Qur'an. An obvious example is that of divorce. A man is allowed to get a divorce without waiting for the period mandated by the Qur'an. The jurists

> disapprove of it, but, as a matter of fact, allow it. By contrast, they limit the access by women to divorce by having them go through a court although the Qur'an does not have any such provision. . . . Hence, the law, in actuality, helped provide unwarranted privileges to men and restrict the rights granted to women by the Qur'an itself. . . . One must say, however, that these limitations are all a matter of juristic opinion rather than central tenets of the law. . . . Nor is there a problem with most parts of Islamic law—except those interpretations that clearly contradict the rights granted absolutely by the Qur'an itself.[101]

Al-Faruqi here offers a defense of law. Where it errs, it is not with regard to "central tenets of the law" but only isolated provisions, the results of "juristic opinion." In her model, jurist's assumptions about "the instability, ignorance, and fickleness of women" lead them to disregard scripture, which otherwise they apply clearly and faithfully.[102] Al-Faruqi perceives this as a problem of specific provisions rather than of the overall legal structure of marriage. She views the restrictions placed on women's access to divorce, and the restraints lifted from men's access to it, as isolated instances of faulty scriptural interpretation.

There are, though, two main problems with Faruqi's critique, which fails to account for the complex process of juridical reasoning. First, who is to judge when something "clearly contradict[s]" the Qur'an? Traditional jurists would no doubt claim that their doctrines about divorce reflect fairly the relevant scriptural provisions. Second, and more significant, the juristic regulations on divorce are central to the jurists' overall understanding of the marital contract as conveying to the husband a type of ownership or control *(milk)* over the wife and the marriage tie. Divorce is inseparable from the rest of the legal regulations surrounding marriage and its dissolution. It forms part of a system of interlocking spousal rights and duties.

The questions raised by al-Faruqi about the overall nature of marriage and divorce resurface in modern discussions of national legal reform. Discussing the inclusion of a right to *ʿiṣma*—which, in Egyptian marriage contracts, is the wife's "right to divorce herself before the marriage registrar without recourse to the court"[103]—Mona Zulficar likewise assumes a model of divorce that diverges in a very basic way from that of the formative and classical legal texts. The right of *ʿiṣma* has been exercised since late Ottoman Egypt, though its origins in Ḥanafī doctrine remain murky and deserve a full study. Zulficar concludes that "a wife's right to delegated divorce *(ʿiṣma)* is a legitimate right under the principles of Shariʿa." In her estimation, it makes perfect sense to include such a condition in Egyptian marriage contracts, because "the legal effect of this condition is to confirm equal rights of termination for both the husband and the wife. This is a natural reflection of the contractual nature of the marriage contract. If a contract is concluded based on mutual consent, it is natural to require termination by mutual consent or provide for a unilateral right of termination by either party."[104] Zulficar's comments emphasize the notions of naturalness, contract, and consent. In her view, it is "natural" to assume that because marriage is a bilateral contract, then divorce ought to be bilateral as well, or at least equally available to each spouse. Yet nothing could be further from the understanding of the early Muslim jurists, for whom marriage was a bilateral contract conveying unilateral control *(milk)*. The next and final chapter explores the gendered nature of this *milk*.

5

Marriage and Dominion

> If a man is married to a female slave [belonging to someone else], then he purchases her, his purchase of her cancels the marriage, and he has sex with her by his [right of] ownership *(bi milkihi)*.
>
> —MUDAWWANA

THE TERMINOLOGY of *milk* saturates jurists' writings. Phrases such as *milk amrihā* ("control of her affair") appear in the contracting of a marriage, and *tamlīk* ("delegation of authority") and *milk al-rajʿa* ("possession of [the right to] return") in its dissolution. In these instances, *milk* signifies "control" or "authority"—or even "prerogative"—rather than "ownership," as of commodity property *(māl)*. Elsewhere, *milk* denotes ownership, especially of slaves. *Milk al-yamīn*, or "ownership by the right hand," refers to slave ownership, and a man's *milk* over his female slave allows him, except when she is married to someone else, sexual access to her. The wide semantic range of terms derived from the root *m-l-k* creates an inherently ambiguous relationship between "control" in a marital relationship and "ownership" in a master-slave relationship, especially where sex is at stake. A man *yamliku* (exercises *milk* over) both his wife and his slave, and "it is the sense of possession or ownership *(milk)*, implied both in the relationship between a man and his female slave and a man and his wife, that makes cohabitation between the two lawful."[1] The linguistic parallels facilitate, though they cannot entirely account for, a conceptual slippage between these modes of dominion.

What linguistic overlap initiates, analogy completes. Analogy occupies the center of developing juridical discourse on marriage and slavery. Previous chapters have shown how analogies between the institutions of marriage and slavery create parallel legal categories of wives and slaves. Marriage and purchase (of a female slave) operate with payment of dower or price to legalize intercourse; release of a wife through *ṭalāq* parallels the release of a slave of either sex through manumission: both terminate *milk* and thereby, in the case of the divorcee and the freed concubine, render sex illicit. Yet marriage remains in some essential way distinctive and irreducible to matters of property. This chapter explores three example cases that force attention to the intersection of gender, sex, and property relations.

The first case concerns a person who comes to own his or her spouse. Chapter 4 explored the situation of a married female slave who was sold to another owner. There, marriage trumped property rights: the marriage remained intact, her husband retained his power of divorce, and her new owner did not gain sexual rights. But a husband coming to own his enslaved wife pitted marriage and enslavement against one another with a different outcome: the marriage was dissolved and the commercial ownership tie persisted. If the parties' genders were reversed, and a woman came to own her enslaved husband, the situation would shift dramatically, as the male prerogative to make his ex-wife his concubine did not apply in the other direction.

The next section analyzes the dispute over whether a male slave could take a concubine. Licit sexual relationships depended on the interaction of three variables: the sex of the parties, their legal status as free or enslaved, and whether the tie between them was marriage or concubinage. Jurists agreed on most possible configurations. A free male could marry a free female; a free male could take a female slave as a concubine; a male slave could—in certain circumstances—be married to a free woman; a free male could—in certain circumstances—be married to a female slave. A free female, it was taken for granted, could never be anyone's concubine. But could a male slave take a female slave as a concubine? Mālik permitted it but Abū Ḥanīfa and Shāfiʿī forbade it.[2] For them, a licit sexual relationship based on ownership depended not only on the woman's status as property but also on the man's capacity to own property. Because a slave could not own property, he could not own a concubine. Without the (commercial) ownership tie, there could be no licit sex outside of marriage.

The third section returns to the topic of female owners taking male concubines. Unlike the situation with the male slave, there is no dispute here; the authorities roundly forbid it. Yet the rationale necessarily differs from the preceding case. Despite universal agreement that a free woman had untrammeled rights to commercial property, the lack of which prevented a male slave from exercising concubinage in Ḥanafī and Shāfiʿī thought, she could not wield sexual access to her male slave. The unusual passages that treat this issue in the *Umm* bring to the fore essential assumptions about men, women, and sex that undergird the entire structure of Islamic jurisprudence on marriage.

Milk al-nikāḥ and Milk al-yamīn

Despite the parallels between the ownership of a female slave and marriage to a (free or enslaved) woman, there is a significant difference between the legal status of a concubine and that of a wife.[3] In the liminal moments of establishing or dissolving the tie between husband and wife or owner and slave, the jurists often invoke the analogy between marriage and slavery and draw upon their repertoire of common ownership terms. While a marriage endures, though, they do not routinely equate matrimony with slavery.[4] When they do compare the two, it is often to express a cautionary sentiment: fathers should be careful about whom they marry their daughters off to, because their daughters will be like captives or slaves to their husbands. Husbands are exhorted to treat their wives kindly, with the vulnerability of the wives expressed in the notion that they are like slaves. This vulnerability is assumed even when the treatment due to a wife and to a slave is sharply distinguished. A prophetic hadith commands that one should not strike a wife as one would a (male) slave and then have sex with her that night. That a wife is subject to her husband's authority, even to the point of physical discipline, goes without saying; the lesson conveyed is that he should not abuse that authority by treating her like a slave. At the very least, it will not be conducive to intimacy.

Beyond the ethics of customary good treatment, wives had rights that were both greater than and qualitatively different from those of slaves in general and concubines more particularly. These included the claim to a portion of their husbands' time, to non-need-based support, and in most views to the right to withhold consent to contraception.[5] Because of the crucial differences between marriage and slave ownership, the two types of *milk* could not be combined. A man could not simultaneously own and be married to the same woman.[6] Unlike free women, to whom sexual access was lawful only within marriage, unmarried slave women were sexually lawful to their male masters as a result of *milk al-yamīn*. They were also lawful *only* to their own masters. Early authorities occasionally discuss a man permitting others (e.g., guests) to have sex with his female slaves. At the very least, this is reprehensible; at most, it may be punishable as illicit sex.[7] Particularly forbidden were a man's wife's slaves.[8] The care taken to make this point suggests that in practice men were not as cautious with this distinction as one might have wanted them to be. It also affirms the separateness of property owned by wives and the inability of husbands to assume command of it.

Although a man could have sex with his own female slave, he could not marry her so long as he owned her. To marry her, he had to manumit her first. In that case, she went from being a slave concubine to a free wife.[9] The Prophet set a precedent for this by manumitting and marrying Ṣafiyya, a war captive whom he purchased from the soldier to whom she had been allotted as part of the booty. His action prompted substantial later debate about whether manumission alone sufficed as dower or whether the husband was required to give his newly freed wife an additional *mahr*.

An enslaved woman could also make the transition in the opposite direction, from wife to concubine. A man's enslaved wife (who belonged by necessity to another owner) could become his own slave if he came to own her through purchase, inheritance, or gift. She went from being a wife to being a concubine while remaining enslaved. The *Jāmiʿ al-Ṣaghīr* assumes that a husband coming to own his wife automatically dissolves their marriage: "[If] a man buys his wife, then divorces her, nothing takes effect."[10] The husband's power of *ṭalāq* has vanished because the marriage tie has disappeared, replaced by ownership.[11] A similar verdict in the *Mudawwana* points out the continued permissibility of intercourse when a husband purchases his wife: "If a man is married to a female slave, then he purchases her, his purchase of her cancels the marriage, and he has sex with her because of his ownership *(bi milkihi)*."[12] In using *milk* to refer to concubinage, the text implicitly defines marriage as "not-*milk*."[13]

This continued permissibility of sex assumes his full ownership of her. If anyone else holds partial ownership, he should not have intercourse with her. Shāfiʿī quotes Ibn ʿUmar on the topic: "A man does not have sex with a slave woman except one who if he wished, he could sell her, and if he wished, he could give her away, and if he wished, he could do with her whatever he wished."[14] Though Shāfiʿī and others cite this report, it should be noted that none of these formative-period jurists entirely follows Ibn ʿUmar's view. In the most obvious exception, the owner of a slave who has borne him a child (an *umm walad*) is forbidden to sell her even though he may continue to have intercourse with her. The early development of rules about the *umm walad* has not yet been adequately studied, but it is clear that the protections granted to her by formative-period jurists were not unanimously upheld by earlier authorities, some of whom allowed her to be sold.[15] Formative-period jurists dispute whether she can or should be forced to marry. For example, Rabīʿ held that the *umm walad* could be married off against her will. Mālik and his followers strongly object, but the Shāfiʿīs permit the master of an *umm walad* to marry her off without her consent.[16]

A situation may result where a man's ownership of the slave woman who was previously his wife is sufficient to invalidate the marriage but not sufficient to make her sexually licit to him. A certain Abū Zinād says about such a case, "She is not lawful for him by marriage or in concubinage."[17] The reason, which takes center stage in some arguments against slave men's ability to own concubines, is that exclusivity of sexual access cannot be guaranteed. Ownership of a slave, like ownership of other property, can be shared between more than one owner. But if two men each held a half-share of a particular female slave, which of them would have rights to sex with her? Certainly it could not be both. As there are no grounds for preferring one fractional owner's claim to that of the other, neither can have access to her. Like marriage, concubinage requires one man's exclusive dominion.

As already shown, marriage constitutes a form of ownership or dominion: a husband wields exclusive control over his wife's sexual (and when she is free, reproductive) capacity; controls her mobility; pays her dower, as if he were paying a purchase price; and gains the unilateral right to dissolve the marriage, a right similar to a slaveholder's power of manumission. Yet a husband is not free to do what an owner can (usually) do with his slave: sell her.[18] If her status changes from wife to concubine, she becomes subject to sale by the man who used to be her husband and is now her owner. A man can purchase his enslaved wife. Once she is his slave and not his wife, he gains the right to sell her, which he was barred from doing when she was his wife. The *Mudawwana* quotes several authorities on the extent of an owner's powers as compared to a husband's. Ibn Wahb quotes the declaration of Makhrama, on the authority of his father and Ibn Qasīṭ, that now that she is his slave, the owner may sell her if he wishes or give her away. ʿAbd Allāh ibn Abī Salama concurs, but insists that he should wait until he knows whether she is pregnant.[19] Her pregnancy would not prevent the sale if she had become pregnant during their marriage; it would, however, if she had become pregnant as his slave, since she would gain the protections of *umm walad* status. For others, if he owned her during the pregnancy, even if she had become impregnated as his wife, she would become an *umm walad*.

Before we can consider the reverse case—a woman coming to own her enslaved husband—we must first address the issue of marriage between free women and male slaves. We cannot know how prevalent such unions were. Texts often presume certain configurations, such as slaves marrying other slaves belonging to the same owner. This may reflect the most common practice. Other discussions may reflect the complexity and intrinsic interest of the legal issues raised by particular situations. For instance, discussions of the permissibility of free men marrying female slaves, addressed in Qurʾan 4:24, served to illuminate exegetical rationales. The verse sets forth certain conditions for such marriages, and jurists debated whether the conditions outlined in scripture were meant to be advisory or absolutely necessary.[20] The extent to which jurists discussed this topic does not necessarily tell us anything about the frequency of free men's marriages to enslaved women.

There is no corresponding direct consideration of the marriage of male slaves to free women, except occasionally as it pertains to social equality. That marriage between a free woman and a male slave could in various circumstances be valid is indicated by offhand references to its occurrence. In articulating one regulation, Shāfiʿī notes that it applies "to every husband and wife, the free man who has a female slave under him and the male slave who has a free woman or a female slave under him, all of these are the same."[21] (The absence of a free man married to a free woman from this list testifies only to the assumption that such a marriage is the norm, intended unless otherwise specified.) Some such matches might have occurred originally while both parties were enslaved, then become mixed marriages when the wife was freed.[22] Even as various texts refer in passing to male slaves married to free women,[23] these unions raised qualms, as attested to by the unanimous agreement that a manumitted female slave could have her marriage to a male slave dissolved. Such a marriage would originally have been one of slave and slave, and hence unproblematic. Manumission would create a status differential where none initially existed. Dissolution was allowed because marriage between a free female and a male slave was unbefitting. At the same time, it was not inherently impermissible for such a marriage to continue. As to the rationale, there was disagreement over whether the right to dissolve the marriage was because she had had no choice in the first place or was simply due to the new disparity in the spouses' status. Thus, there was dispute over whether the same privilege extended to her if she were married to a free man.

A free woman marrying a male slave was not a priori forbidden, but the jurists certainly looked askance at such unions. In questioning the extent of a father's power over the marriages of his minor children, for instance, the Ḥanafī authorities disagree over whether a father can marry his minor son or daughter to one of the father's slaves. At issue is not the desirability of marrying free children to slaves but rather the scope of paternal authority: can a father act in a manner so clearly detrimental to his children's interests? Nonetheless, condemning marriages between free females and enslaved males was not a major preoccupation.[24] The texts leave the clear impression that it was not frequent, though this may be an artifact of their discomfort with the notion of high-status women married to low-status men. We have seen one example of this concern in the notion of parity *(kafā'a)*. Under Ḥanafī rules, as discussed in Chapter 1, *kafā'a* gave a father the prerogative to reject his daughter's marriage if her groom was not her social equal. This tendency to frown on unions where women hold superior rank is by no means limited to Muslim contexts. Roman legislation, for instance, treated a man manumitting and marrying his own female slave as normal and salutary (though it was usually preferable to take a freedwoman as a concubine) but evinced horror at a woman doing the same, even where it was legal.[25] Judith Evans-Grubbs links this disapproval "of unions in which the wife had significantly more wealth or higher rank than her husband" to the status of the man as "acknowledged head of the household *(paterfamilias)*" whose "superior authority had to be unquestioned."[26]

A mismatch, then, would have existed in cases where a free woman married a slave. We have seen that a woman's shift from wife to concubine left lawful sexual relations unaffected, but if a free woman came to own her enslaved husband there was no such continuity. As with a free husband who purchases his enslaved slave wife from her owner, "the marriage between the two of them is invalidated if one of them owns any [portion], small or large, of his [or her] companion."[27] There, however, the similarity between men and women in this situation ends. The *Mudawwana* considers only what the woman's ownership means for the validity of the marriage, never raising the question of whether her ownership of her (former) husband renders him sexually licit to her. The presumption that it never could means that the question of a continued sexual relationship is settled by the point that she cannot be married to her own slave. A sexual relationship between a free woman and a male slave could only be licit (even if still disapproved of) within the framework of male marital *milk*. If she comes to own him, the dissolution of the marriage severs the possibility of a legitimate sexual relationship, unless and until they remarry after he is no longer her property, according to the *Umm*.[28] The *Muwaṭṭaʾ* makes clear Mālik's own view that only remarriage can reestablish the husband's *milk* over the marriage tie, necessary once his authority has been severed by the wife's *milk* over him.[29] This view is repeated in the *Mudawwana*, where the wife's manumission of her husband cannot salvage the marriage tie: "she has become forbidden to him." But the *Mudawwana* also presents Ibn Wahb's slightly softer stance in cases where the wife immediately manumits a husband she has come to own; he "prefers that they remarry."[30] This earlier Medinan authority means only that the marriage can survive the momentary interval in which she owns her husband, not that there can be any possibility of a lawful relationship outside of marriage.

The divergent scenarios when it is a wife who comes to own her husband rather than a husband who comes to own his wife reveal the starkly gendered nature of sexual licitness. Lawful sex requires male control or *milk*, in both marriage and concubinage. Baber Johansen refers to the "social-symbolic good" that the husband obtains in exchange for the dower with the phrase used by later jurists, *milk al-nikāḥ*. "The medieval jurists look at marriage as a legal bond which can only be dissolved by the husband. Therefore, he has the right to dissolve it unilaterally and to demand a countervalue *(ʿiwaḍ)* from his wife should she want to end the marital relationship."[31] *Milk al-nikāḥ* is a special type of property and maleness is a requisite for exercising it. "A woman—according to the medieval lawyers—can never acquire this 'property.' Thus her capacity to acquire rights and duties, i.e., her status as a legal person, is inferior to that of the free male person."[32]

The preceding chapter's analysis of unilateral repudiation and divorce for compensation confirms this view. But the distinction between men's legal capacities and women's goes further than divorce prerogatives. For Johansen, as discussed in Chapter 1 with regard to dower, the central distinction is between commercial and social exchange. In commercial exchange, men and women are equal, but in social exchange—the area where Johansen places marriage—they are differentiated. Johansen points to the disjunction between the equality of (free) men and women in commercial transactions and their inequality in transactions associated with marriage. Men and women may be equally fit to be property holders, but husbands and wives are not equal with regard to the "property of marriage."

Slaves Owning Slaves

Johansen's distinction between commercial and social exchange also helps explain enslaved men's marital prerogatives. Although slave men and free men are unequal in terms of ability to possess commercially valuable assets (least so in Mālikī doctrine, where slaves exercise de facto property rights), as husbands slave men have essentially the same rights over their wives as free men, including rights to divorce. Where there are restrictions on their rights over wives, such as with regard to domicile or mobility, these relate to the wife's status as slave and pertain even if her husband is free. Johansen's model explains why male slaves can exercise *milk al-nikāḥ* despite their defective property rights. The case of slave husbands shows intricate connections but also vital disjunctions between marital authority and property rights.

Married male slaves were both owner and owned. Which characteristic predominated depended on which aspect of their legal personality was under scrutiny. Despite disagreement about whether he could be compelled to marry, once married with his master's consent, the slave himself wielded the power of divorce and became, in Johansen's term, a "proprietor of marriage." Although how many wives a man could have might depend on his status (Mālik allows him four, but the others limit him to two, following a logic that halves certain rights as well as consequences for slaves), the basic capacity to be a husband did not hinge on property rights. On the other hand, the exercise of *milk al-yamīn* did. Abū Ḥanīfa, his disciples, and Shāfiʿī and his followers categorically denied slaves the capacity to own assets—especially slaves and, most particularly, slave concubines. At stake was the relationship between property ownership and sexual dominion. Mālik and his followers, on the other hand, allowed a male slave to exercise ownership of the right hand. Mālik's insistence on the right of male slaves to take concubines presupposed that slaves could "own" property. This ownership was attenuated—the master could expropriate the slave's property at any time—but nonetheless sufficient for ownership not only of goods but also of slaves. The *Mudawwana* considers, for example, a case where a free man swore that all his slaves *(mamālīk)* were manumitted "and he [the free man] has slaves and his slaves have slaves." In such a case, according to Mālik "only his [i.e., the free man's] slaves are manumitted and his slaves' slaves are left in the possession of those of his slaves whom he had manumitted, [remaining] enslaved to them."[33] Given that slaves could own other slaves, Mālik granted a male slave licit sexual access to his female slaves, subject to the same restrictions as a free owner.[34]

The relative weakness of the slave's property rights in contrast to his undiminished marital rights accounts for Mālik's view that the slave could purchase a concubine from his own funds even without his owner's permission, despite needing that permission to marry.[35] There was little risk, after all, in allowing a slave to exercise property rights because all of his "assets," including any concubines, were subject to expropriation by his owner. A master could lawfully appropriate his male slave's slave concubine and have sexual access to her himself: "Nothing is held against a man who takes the female slave of his male slave or the female slave of his female slave."[36] The ability of a master to take his male slave's slave woman contrasted sharply with his inability to pronounce divorce on behalf of his male slave, even when that slave's wife was also the master's own property. Indeed, Mālik's permission to wrench away a slave's slave follows directly on the heels of reaffirmation of the enslaved husband's sole control over divorce: "The divorce is in the hand of the slave. Nobody else has any power over his divorce."[37]

The confluence of Mālik's doctrines on slave marriage and slave concubinage created a loophole. In an end run around the enslaved husband's prerogative, a master could dissolve the marriage of a female slave whom he owned if her husband was also his own slave by giving her to her husband. This gift would transform her into her enslaved (former) husband's property and automatically end their marriage, just as though a free man married to a female slave purchased her. Her change in status did not pose an immediate problem for a continued sexual relationship between the previously married couple, as under Mālikī doctrine her former husband could have access to her by *milk al-yamīn* just as a free man might. But as she was now his slave concubine rather than his wife, she was subject to expropriation by his (and her former) master. This creates, the *Mudawwana* acknowledges, a potential way around the prohibition of dissolving her marriage. Medinan authorities affirmed that if it were known that the master's intention was to render the female slave lawful for himself, his gift would be invalid; he would retain ownership and the slaves' marriage would continue in force. However, unless this was known to be the master's motive, the gift would be valid and the female slave would go from being a wife to being owned by the slave's right hand. (This willingness to grant legal weight to the subjective intention of an actor is a distinctive feature of Mālikī jurisprudence.)[38]

Abū Ḥanīfa and Shāfiʿī objected forcefully to the possibility of such a gift, deeming any attempt by a master to give his female slave to her enslaved husband void. They appealed to logical consistency. Either marriage or *milk al-yamīn* was necessary for making sexual intercourse lawful; a slave's intercourse with a concubine would not be lawful because he would not own her. Shāfiʿī stresses that divine regulation of lawful sexual relations is at stake, so the master's permission is irrelevant. "It is not lawful, and Exalted God knows best, for a slave to take a concubine whether his master permits him or not," Shāfiʿī declares, "because Exalted God has only permitted taking concubines to owners *(mālikīn)*, and the slave is not an owner."[39] Al-Muzanī elaborates on the connection between freedom, property rights, and concubinage: "Ownership of the right hand is only for those who are free, who [can] own property. Slaves do not own property."[40]

Ḥanafī authorities concur. The *Kitāb al-Ḥujja* directly attacks the Medinan example of a master who gives his male slave the slave's enslaved wife to use as a concubine. Abū Ḥanīfa holds that "the gift does not invalidate the marriage because the slave does not exercise ownership *(lā milk lahu)*."[41] (*Milk* is again here implicitly defined as *not* including marriage.) The *Kitāb al-Ḥujja* asks rhetorically, in objecting to the Mālikī position, "How can the slave own his [former] wife while he does not even own himself?"[42] Slaves might exercise de facto control over property, but any property a slave held was actually owned by his master—a fact that was implicit, the Ḥanafī authorities note, in the Mālikī acceptance of the master's appropriation of his slave's concubine.

Abū Ḥanīfa contrasts the slave's inability to have sex licitly with an owned slave woman with his ability to engage in licit marital intercourse: "It is not lawful for a [male] slave to take a concubine because he has no [ownership over] property *(māl)*. He must not have sex [with a woman] *(laysa yanbaghī lahu an yaṭa' farjan)* except in marriage."[43] (We might better read his statement as "should not" or "ought not" or "it is not fitting for him to. . . .") Abū Ḥanīfa distinguishes clearly between marital authority, which does not depend on the ability to own assets, and ownership of a concubine, which does. A slave can therefore exercise only the former. One thing this makes clear is that a wife was not a commercially valuable asset. A slave could not have access to her if licit sex required him to own her in this fashion, because he was not capable of owning anything this way. Rather, his sexual access to her hinged on a transaction that was, in Johansen's terms, social and not commercial.

Despite his disagreement with his counterparts on the question of male slaves taking concubines, Mālik agrees with them that licitness is contingent on sexual exclusivity in both marriage and concubinage. The *Ḥujja*'s rebuttal of the Medinan position focuses on this weak point. It evokes horror at the possibility of confusion over who has sexual rights to the woman in question. Discussing the scenario in which a master appropriates his male slave's female slave, Shaybānī frequently refers to the question of exclusivity of access. Because the female slave was not the male slave's property—"anything his right hand owns belongs to his master"[44]—the slave could not prevent others, specifically his master, from having sexual access to her. In a dialogue with an imaginary Medinan interlocutor, Shaybānī asks, "What is your view if [a male slave] has a slavegirl and he has not had sex with her, is it lawful for his master to take her and have sex with her?" The Medinan replies that in such circumstances "there is no problem with him [i.e., the slave's master] having sex with her." Though he prefers that the master formally "take her away" from the slave first, his having intercourse with her is not forbidden even if he fails to do so. The Medinan then accepts that "if he [the master] does not have sex with her" then the slave could do so. He concedes, "Whichever one does so earliest, it is lawful for him to have sex with her and she is forbidden to the other." As with the discussion of remarriage at the beginning of Chapter 4, Shaybānī vigorously contests the notion that chronological priority matters to sexual lawfulness.[45]

Shaybānī aims to unmask the illogic of the Medinan doctrine. "What is your view," he asks, "if the slave kisses her and the master is present: is it lawful for the master to kiss her after that while the slave is present?" Since it is generally agreed that only copulation obliges a waiting period, the Medinan could not object to this. Shaybānī continues: "So, in your view, there is no problem if this one kisses her once, then that one kisses her once, and this one fondles her once, and that one once, and this one has non-vaginal intercourse with her once, and that one once *(wa yujāmiʿuhā hādhā marra fīmā dūn al-farj wa hādhā marra)*?" His escalating rhetoric underscores the point that the Mālikī position is untenable if the object is to ensure exclusive sexual access to a particular woman. Having arrived at his narrative climax, Shaybānī concludes without any pretense at a Medinan reply. After all, what reply could there be? It is unanimous: any woman, no matter her legal status, could have only one licit sexual partner at any given time.

Freedom, Gender, and Ownership

Just as any woman could have only one lawful sexual partner, any man could have more than one concurrent licit partner. The extent of his prerogative varied with his legal status. Shāfiʿī and Ḥanafī doctrine forbade concubines to a male slave and limited him to two wives on the basis of a logic that halved slaves' privileges and liabilities. A free man was universally permitted four wives, and Mālik extended this rule, as well as the permission for however many concubines he could afford, to a male slave.[46] The lack of limit on concubines (for free men) becomes, in the *Umm,* the occasion for an intriguing discussion of lawful partners. In a section entitled "Regarding the number of free women and slave women who are lawful and what makes sexual organs lawful," Shāfiʿī notes that God limited a man to four wives but placed no limit on the number of female slaves he could own and have sex with. In what seems a digression from his main topic, Shāfiʿī broaches the subject of women taking male slaves as concubines. This discussion of women taking male slaves as concubines is not as disconnected as it might appear, since it reveals fundamental jurisprudential assumptions about sex, gender, and ownership—in other words, "what makes sexual organs lawful."

Joseph Schact, in his famous *Introduction to Islamic Law,* notes, "The unmarried female slave is at the disposal of her male owner as a concubine, but no similar provision applies between a male slave and his female owner."[47] Jonathan Brockopp admits the possibility for a disconnect between Qurʾanic rules and reality: "Sexual intercourse was allowed by virtue of a master's ownership of the slave's body and right to deal with his property as he saw fit. . . . These rules are for male masters and their female slaves; no mention is explicitly made of female masters having intercourse with their male slaves in the Qurʾan, nor is there any mention of homosexual relations with slaves, but it is quite likely that such relations existed."[48] It is unclear whether Brockopp means to suggest that both "female masters" and male masters might have sex with their male slaves, or, as I think more likely, only the latter. Johansen simply asserts the obviousness of the point: "It goes without saying that the female slave owner is not entitled to have sexual intercourse with her male slaves because only female slaves may be sexually appropriated and only by male owners."[49]

It does indeed go without saying for most Muslim scholars. The vast majority of texts assume free men's right to take slave concubines and never raise the issue of female owners taking male concubines, even to reject it as impermissible. A similar silence obtains on the question of a Muslim woman marrying a *kitābī* (roughly, Christian or Jewish) man. Although more or less universally forbidden, this prohibition on Muslim women's intermarriage was taken for granted; most do not bother to explain it.[50] Because Muslim jurists regularly, heatedly, and in excruciatingly minute detail debate the legal consequences of various wildly improbable scenarios, these gaps are notable. They also make Shāfiʿī's discussion of male concubines and female owners remarkable. It remains an open question why Shāfiʿī believed it necessary to address the subject at all. His mode of doing so, by means of an "anonymous objector,"[51] is similar to the way in which he frames discussion of positions that were held by identifiable authorities of his time. I have not, however, come across other discussions that seriously posit the permissibility of a woman using her male slave sexually.

Shāfiʿī introduces his discussion of male concubinage using a questioner who "holds the view that a woman has *milk al-yamīn,* and says: Why does she not take her male slave as a concubine as a man takes his female slave as a concubine?" Shāfiʿī answers categorically: "The man is the one who marries, the one who takes a concubine, and the woman is the one who is married, who is taken as a concubine. It is not permissible to make analogies between things that are different."[52] As proof, he refers to fundamental difference between men and women, explicitly linking gendered rights to concubinage with male and female roles in marriage.

By using a circular argument, Shāfiʿī rebuts the notion that a woman could take her male slave as a concubine: a woman cannot take a concubine because she is the one who is taken as a concubine, and a man cannot be taken as a concubine because he is the one who takes a concubine. This answer, however, ignores the variable of slavery and reduces the problem to one of gender. The hypothetical query "Why does she not take her male slave as a concubine?" refers to a free, slave-owning woman and a male slave whom she owns. The male slave in the original query could not take a concubine, according to Shāfiʿī's doctrine,[53] though this is the defined "male" role; nor can the woman, who had to be free in order to own a slave, be taken as a concubine, even though that is the "female" role he sets forth. Shāfiʿī's response frees the man and enslaves the woman. His sweeping pronouncement—unusual, given jurists' predilection for narrow, specific rulings—about male and female roles reveals the extent to which gender governs, or underlies, his conceptions of human social roles: he temporarily overlooks even the rules about enslavement and property ownership that preoccupy him elsewhere.

Shāfiʿī posits a fundamental dissimilarity between men and women that prevents meaningful comparison, as well as a fundamental similarity between marriage and concubinage that allows for it. Anticipating a challenge to his assertion of male and female difference, Shāfiʿī shores it up by reference to male marital prerogatives:

> If the man divorces the woman and makes her forbidden to him—and she may not divorce him—and he divorces her once, then [the fact]

> that he may take her back during the waiting period even against her will indicates that he may make her prohibited, and he stands over her, and she does not stand over him, and she is different from him *(mukhālifa lahu)*.[54]

Concubinage drops out entirely from this account of gender difference, replaced by a focus on marriage—or rather, divorce. A man could unilaterally divorce his wife, but "she may not divorce him." Further, "he may take her back during the waiting period even against her will." Men's exclusive control over the marital tie is the key. It indicates to Shāfiʿī that the man "stands over" the woman, not the reverse.

Shāfiʿī states that the man "is *al-qayyim* in relation to her, and she is not *al-qayyima* in relation to him." The concept of men being *qayyim* in relation to women presumably relates to Qurʾanic verse 4:34, which begins by stating, "Men stand over *(qawwāmūn ʿalā)* women." Though Shāfiʿī and the other jurists are aware of this verse, and of the ways that exegetes have interpreted it to refer to marital relationships, legal texts devote little attention to discussing male *qiwāma* over women in general or wives in particular. There are a few scattered references to this verse's treatment of *qiwāma* in the *Umm*, but no comprehensive attempt to define *qiwāma* or relate it to other spousal rights and duties. Generally, jurists were far more concerned with the elaboration and adjudication of issues relating to specific rights than with broad statements about the spousal relationship. *Qiwāma* appears in this passage because the issue of women taking male concubines cuts directly to the heart of maleness and femaleness and the roles played by each gender within sexual relationships.[55]

Having thus established the vital element differentiating male and female roles in marriage, the *Umm* returns to concubinage to draw a firmly gendered distinction between active and passive that ties marriage and concubinage together. Grammatical active and passive translate into socially and legally active and passive. A woman does not take a concubine but rather *is taken* as one; she does not marry but rather *is married.* The transitive verb *nakaḥa* in both of its senses—to marry and to have intercourse with—carries the expectation of female passivity. As with other transitive verbs used for sex, here the woman is "done to" in much the same way that she "is married."[56] As with Chapter 4's discussion of a husband taking back his wife by having sex with her, or having a divorce oath take effect with penetration, male legal and sexual agency are directly conjoined. Women do not generally exercise either.

Shāfiʿī repeatedly emphasizes women's passivity. He declares, "So it is not permitted to say to her that she may take her male slave as a concubine, because she is the one who is taken as a concubine and the one who is married, not the one who takes a concubine or the one who marries." This statement reprises his earlier parallel between marriage and concubinage, which identifies women with passivity and men with activity. In this passage, though, he mentions only the woman's role, first in positive terms ("she is the one" who is legally passive in both marriage and concubinage) and then in negative terms (she is "not the one" who is active in marriage or concubinage).

The *Umm*'s other brief mention of women taking (male) concubines is situated within a discussion of permitted and prohibited sexual activity, including male masturbation *(istimnāʿ)*. It relies even more strongly on the semantic ambiguity of the verb *nakaḥa* and the conceptual link between control over marriage and the active role in intercourse. According to Shāfiʿī, "it is not lawful for a woman to take a concubine from what her right hand possesses, because she is taken as a concubine or married." Even if one refers to her as "one who marries" *(nākiḥa)*, this merely "means that she is married *(mankūḥa)*."[57] Shāfiʿī states that masturbation runs afoul of the Qurʾanic proclamation that "those who protect their sexual organs except from their spouses *(azwājihim)* or what their right hands own" will not be blamed, but that those who exceed those bounds will. Masturbation by a man's own hand, although not manual stimulation to orgasm by his wife or female slave, breaches the Qurʾanic bounds of permissibility (as does sex with livestock, *ityān al-bahāʾim*). The *Umm* then turns to why women cannot take men in concubinage. In his explanation, Shāfiʿī uses the phrase "what her right hand owns" to describe a woman's ownership of a slave. He denies that this conveys sexual rights, though he has just quoted a Qurʾanic verse that affirms licit sexual access to "what their right hands own." Shāfiʿī is unusual in even entertaining the hypothetical question about women taking male slaves as concubines, but he does not truly allow the question to disturb his basic sense of what is possible.

Shāfiʿī's insistence on relating a woman's incapacity to take a male concubine to her status as "the one who is married, not the one who marries" suggests a deeper parallel between marriage and concubinage than simply the Qurʾanic joining of the two as licit sexual partners in verses like the one he quotes. Shāfiʿī declares that one should not draw analogies between different things. His decision to treat marriage and concubinage together implies an essential similarity between the man's role as "the one who marries" and as "the one who takes a concubine." This active, controlling role is the critical difference between men and women, allowing men to take concubines and prohibiting women from doing the same. A woman licitly can be only the object and never the subject of the marriage contract and the sexual act.[58]

The active and passive gendering of terminology about marriage and sex is also found in some of the *Muṣannaf* anecdotes discussing the "marriage" of a male slave and his female owner, in the section titled "The slave [who] marries his mistress" *("Bāb al-ʿabd yankiḥu sayyidatahu")*. The semantic ambiguity of the verb *nakaḥa* means it could also be read "the slave who has sex with his mistress." This section, after all, includes anecdotes in which a woman takes or attempts to take her slave as her concubine. Those where the woman's actions are condemned have the woman marrying or having sex with her slave: it is an inversion of the correct order of things. But in the title of the section, all is put to rights; the man, even if he is a slave, is the active party.

Both marriage and slave concubinage required the husband or master to have unilateral control over the termination or continuation of the relationship. Was a woman, then, unable to take a slave concubine because she could not exercise this control? Rather, this control was an integral part of both *milk al-nikāḥ,* ownership in marriage, and *milk al-yamīn,* ownership by the right hand—although this phrase could also, as just noted, be understood only to encompass proprietorship without sexual rights. A woman could not exercise control over a sexual relationship because *as a woman* she was incapable of being an owner in marriage or concubinage. The *Umm*'s discussion of a free woman's (in)capacity to exercise sexual ownership rights over her male slave explicitly present doctrines implicit in formative-period Mālikī and Ḥanafī texts. Though Mālik and his followers differed from the other authorities on whether a male slave could exercise *milk al-yamīn,* they agreed that a man needed exclusive *milk* over a woman—whether as his wife or as his slave—in order for sex to be lawful between them.

Just as women were unlike men, men were unlike women. Only men could exercise *milk* in marriage and concubinage and only women were subject to these types of ownership. Shāfiʿī affirmed that a man—even an enslaved one—could not be taken as a concubine. Ownership of a male slave did not permit his owner control over his sexual organ *(farj)*. Indeed, some later jurists held that saying to a female slave, "Your sexual organ is free," served to manumit her, while the same formula said to a male slave did not free him.[59] Despite his enslavement, his sexuality was not subject to his master's control. Although he could, for some, be married off without his consent, his control over the dissolution of his own marriage made clear that a male slave remained in some vital way his own man.

These texts on concubinage address only sexual relations with slaves of the opposite sex, forbearing mention of men's sexual use of male slaves, even to forbid it, or women's sexual use of female slaves.[60] Shāfiʿī's emphatic denial that a male could be anything but "one who marries" and "one who takes a concubine" occurs in discussion of male and female relations. Other legal texts occasionally address the sexual use of male slaves by their male owners, usually in the context of criminal offenses, when discussing the appropriate punishment to be meted out. Some later Mālikī jurists are said to have held that access to male slaves by male owners was permitted because of *milk al-yamīn*.[61] The Mālikī authorities, not surprisingly, deny this—the accusation that someone held anal sex to be permissible, even between husband and wife, was considered particularly scurrilous.

There is an important distinction between declaring something forbidden—pretty much all agreed that sex with male slaves was—and insisting that it requires a *ḥadd* punishment, which almost no one believed.[62] A man's anal intercourse with his own male slaves would not be subject to *ḥadd* punishment because of the "semblance" of these relations to lawful relations predicated on the ownership of female slaves. (A similar analogy between male-male anal intercourse and illicit [vaginal] intercourse between a man and a woman led to a majority view that the former should be punished like the latter.) A similar distinction is at work in the anecdotal cases from ʿAbd al-Razzāq's *Muṣannaf* in which women admitted to sexual relationships with their male slaves. Even though *ḥadd* punishments were avoided, the women's sexual encounters with their male slaves were not considered lawful. Rather, the authorities were willing to accept even tenuous claims to acting on the mistaken belief that a prohibited action was, in fact, permissible if it meant averting *ḥadd* punishments.

The exercise of "ownership" over another person, as property or as a spouse, was dependent on variables of both freedom and gender. The free adult male was the paradigmatic example of an owner, and others were measured against this standard. An enslaved female of any age stood at the opposite extreme. In between, the jurists had varying views on what type of rights enslaved males and free females could exercise. However, when it came to the crucial question of sexual lawfulness, male *milk* over a woman's sexual organ was a legal requirement for lawful intercourse, regardless of either the man's or the woman's status. Women's inability to take concubines, though they were not restricted as owners of slaves or other commodity property, shows that *milk al-yamīn* was not merely a matter of property ownership, though this was a prerequisite, but was also dependent on maleness.

A woman could not exercise control over a sexual relationship because *as a woman* she was incapable of being an owner in marriage or concubinage. The *Muṣannaf* texts, which preserve a rare query questioning the gendered division of rights and obligations, illustrate this point. ʿAbd al-Razzāq's *Muṣannaf* presents a report of a woman who married a man, giving him a dower and stipulating that she would control divorce and sex.[63] One authority opines that this marriage is not lawful, and therefore it is rescinded. A contrary view holds that the marriage is valid, but that she will receive the dower and that rights over divorce and sex will be in the man's hand. The same issue arises in the slightly later *Muṣannaf* of Ibn Abī Shayba; there, the responding authority declares that such an arrangement does not constitute a valid marriage because it is not the tradition, *sunna*, of marriage. It is noteworthy that not only the responding authorities but also the couple who contracted this unconventional marriage shared the view that paying dower entitled the payer to have control over both sex and marital dissolution. And, despite their different perspectives on the legal status of the marriage (whether it is valid, void, or to be annulled), these authorities unanimously forbade switching male and female roles within marriage. Gender alone does not determine social or legal status for early Muslim jurists but interacts with other components of legal personhood, including age and freedom. Nonetheless, within the context of sexual relationships, maleness or femaleness was the most significant distinction between human beings.

Conclusion

For many years, scholars addressing the subject of women and Islam vigorously debated whether Islam improved or diminished women's "status." In the search for the origins of female subordination in Muslim societies, marriage and family structure were crucial topics, as they were for scholars researching the origins of patriarchy elsewhere. In *Kinship and Marriage in Early Arabia*, published near the close of the nineteenth century, W. Robertson Smith argued that both matrilineal and patrilineal forms of marriage existed in pre-Islamic Arabia. According to him, the latter could be initiated either by purchase or by capture; in both cases, the husband wielded significant control over the wife and her offspring, who were counted as part of his tribe. Further, the husband had sole control over the wife's domicile and over the continuation or termination of the marriage. Robertson Smith termed these arrangements "*baʿal* marriage," from the Semitic term meaning *lord* or *master*.[64] As an English translation for this phrase, he selected "marriage of dominion." Though Robertson Smith's conclusions about matrilineality are now largely discredited, his phrase "marriage of dominion" is suggestive. Dominion is one of the words associated with the root complex *m-l-k* and the term *milk*. It could be argued that the husband's dominion over his wife, or rather over her sexuality, is the crucial defining characteristic of Islamic marriage as regulated by formative-period jurists.

If dominion over a free woman's sexuality characterized marriage, ownership of a slave did not necessarily involve sexual dominion. In *Slavery in Early Christianity*, Jennifer Glancy notes, "Sexual access to slave bodies was a pervasive dimension of ancient systems of slavery. Both female and male slaves were available for their owners' pleasure."[65] In practice, this was sometimes true in the Muslim world. But legally, this could never be the case. Male slaves could not licitly be sexual objects; rather, they could only be sexual agents.

The clearest statement of the gendered nature of both sexuality and personhood emerges from the Shāfiʿī treatment of male and female legal capacity in all its gradations. Shāfiʿī categorizes and classifies, drawing boundaries between men and women, majors and minors, free and slave, virgins and non-virgins. He clearly delineates the legal rights and duties of each type of person. Shāfiʿī texts insist on certain logical rules and show no juristic acceptance of pragmatic accommodations. But some individuals seem to require two things at once. Sometimes one aspect of a person's status requires legal treatment that is incompatible with what is required by another aspect. In some cases, these needs can be reconciled, but not always. When attempts to reconcile the legal roles attributable to slave and free, male and female, fail, it is gender that proves definitive when sexuality is at stake.

Consider Shāfiʿī's view on the marriage of a male slave. Because of the man's enslavement, his master's consent is necessary for the validity of the marriage. By itself, this rule is not noteworthy. Ḥanafīs and Mālikīs likewise require the master's consent. However, both of these schools allow the master to authorize his male slave's marriage after the fact. For Shāfiʿī, however, the master's consent must be given before the marriage. Any marriage contracted without the master's permission is legally void, not merely remediably invalid.[66] Shāfiʿī places importance as well on the fact that the slave is male. As a male, his own consent is necessary for any marriage contracted for him to be valid. And, as with his master's consent, it must be given before the marriage takes place. The slave's maleness and his enslavement can be accommodated by requiring *both* the slave and the master to consent beforehand. If either refuses, the marriage cannot occur.

In other cases, though, it proves impossible to reconcile the two dimensions of identity; something has to give way and one categorization must dominate. A male slave again provides the best example. Here, it is his exemption from being taken as a concubine by his (female) owner that illustrates the vital role his gender plays. Just as a free female slave owner's gender limits the extent of her power over the sexuality of her male slave, his maleness makes him invulnerable to sexual use. As a woman, his owner is not legally capable of exercising the sexual prerogatives of ownership, nor is he, despite his enslavement, subject to them.

These unstated assumptions about gender and ownership are most fully illuminated in Shāfiʿī's response to the query about concubinage between a female owner and her male slave but they undergird the entire shared jurisprudential structure of marriage. No matter what the understanding of women and their legal capacities in other contexts, when a woman becomes a wife, she inherits a remarkably consistent legal status. The specifics of her rights and duties can differ, sometimes significantly, from school to school, but the basic control over her sexuality and physical mobility that the husband gains by the marriage contract—with due modifications in the case of enslaved wives whose owners' claims must be considered—is the same. Along with his sole prerogative to end the marriage unilaterally, this control is the most basic element of marriage as regulated by the jurists.

The jurists worked hard to thwart rare attempts to transgress the gender boundaries they were working so diligently to establish. Yet how transgressive these acts really were is an open question. Even in those reported cases where women sought to take on the privileges of men, they did so in a context that presumed hierarchical sexual relationships. The case of the marriage where the woman paid a dower and stipulated control over sex and divorce does not reflect an egalitarian marriage, merely a role reversal. Likewise, the unnamed woman who established a sexual relationship with her male slave justified her action by affirming her rights as an owner, which, in her view, transcended any limitations of gender. Muslim marriage as formulated by the early jurists had gendered spousal rights and roles, but these were also intricately bound up with the scriptural and legal sanction of the ownership of one human being over another.

Conclusion

FOR MANY centuries, Islam was an imperial force to be reckoned with. Its scholarly class was confident of the imperative to preserve and expand Muslim rule and, by extension, its law. Premodern advocates of Islamic government presumed that Muslim rule was the surest path to justice, because the sovereign was bound to uphold the *sharīʿa*. Since Islam was the natural religion of humanity, extending its reach was the optimal means of achieving the greatest good.[1]

Since the eighteenth century, European and North American pressures have placed Muslim-majority societies on the defensive politically, economically, and militarily. Governments no longer operate from a place of confidence, assured in the correctness of Islam and the benevolence of Muslim rule. Today, the phrase *Islamic state* conjures in Western minds images of fanatics bent on conquering territory and subjecting its inhabitants, especially its women, to draconian laws in the name of a tyrannical, repressive God. Part of the reason the idea of an Islamic state is so unpleasant—at worst, terrifying and brutal; at best, ethically sterile—is that militant ideologues offer little of the richness and depth of the premodern tradition. The *sharīʿa* they envision is about authenticity, not justice; about communal identity, not community welfare. Yet many ordinary Muslims continue to hold that the purpose of *sharīʿa* is to defend the inherent dignity of all human beings and to safeguard the rights of the weaker members of society. A Gallup poll of Muslims worldwide found that in many countries a majority of women as well as men advocate religious law as a source, or even the sole source, of national law.[2]

These Muslim hopes repose in an ideal *sharīʿa*, not the actual legal systems that govern contemporary nation-states or the hybrid systems that operated in the precolonial era. Among the massive transformations wrought by modernity has been civil law's primacy over "Islamic law" in almost all areas of law except those regulating "personal status" (marriage, divorce, custody, inheritance) and (sometimes) certain high-profile criminal offenses. Adherence to Islamic law has become a defining criterion of individual and collective Muslim-ness; personal status codes are central to identity politics not only in countries with Muslim majorities but also—sometimes especially—where substantial Muslim minorities exist.

Palpable injustices are too often meted out to women in these contemporary legal systems, whether the personal law applies to nearly everyone or only to a minority. India, for example, applies its civil code to Hindus, but the default for Muslims is a partially codified religious law based on Ḥanafī jurisprudence. The raw deal granted to divorcee Shah Bano provoked a national controversy over Muslim law in the 1980s. The eventual compromise legislation resolved none of the problems inherent in selectively upholding certain provisions of Ḥanafī divorce and maintenance law while ignoring others.[3] Historian Amira Sonbol's anecdotal comparison between a nineteenth-century Egyptian woman's easy access to divorce from a court and the obstacles her twentieth-century counterpart confronted in trying to obtain the same result illustrates that modernizing reforms did not always increase female rights and could sometimes diminish them.[4]

"Muslim women," Wael Hallaq observes, surveying the history of legal practice, "were full participants in the life of the law."[5] This participation does not mean that there was gender equality. Still, something perceived as substantive justice was consistently delivered by legal institutions. To what extent were the courts adjudicating a vision of fairness founded in legal texts? The society envisioned by premodern jurists was undoubtedly hierarchical, from the relationship between ruler and ruled to the relationship between spouses. Muslims were to be dominant over non-Muslims; men were to "stand over" women. Yet the subordinate parties enjoyed rights and protections, and the dominant parties had not only privileges but also obligations. Writing about Roman laws on slavery, Suzanne Dixon notes, "The law is not consistent in its viewpoint. At times it clearly takes the part of the ruling class, and at other times it is amenable to common-sense and humane considerations."[6] The same could be said of Islamic jurisprudence and would hold true if one replaced *the ruling class* with *free men*. There is often no direct link between the writings of the jurists and the verdicts of the judges, but the consistent sense that vulnerable people would get a fair hearing from the courts has contributed to a lingering view of *sharīʿa* as guarantor of justice.

Judith Tucker puzzles over this in *Women, Family, and Gender in Islamic Law*. How can women, she wonders, view the discriminatory *sharīʿa* as a source of justice?[7] One element of their support is undeniably a vagueness about what precisely constitutes the religious law they advocate. "Islamic" serves as a code word for "just" and "fair." These women's ideas about what marriage is and how men and women should relate to one another in family and society differ dramatically from those of the jurists whose intellectual labor forms the law's doctrinal foundation. The same can be said for many contemporary religious thinkers, from Muslim feminists who advocate for legal reform using terms like *justice* and *dignity* to neotraditionalists who peddle patriarchy in terms of complementarity rather than hierarchy. On matters of gender and sex, the assumptions of early scholars about male dominance are at once most at evidence in their doctrines and most in conflict with contemporary sensibilities. Formative-period jurists shared presuppositions about marriage, kinship, and slavery despite their sometimes heated disagreements on specific points of law. Their views about what kinds of legal capacity males and females could exercise, especially when sex was at stake, shaped their doctrines on core matters such as divorce and dower. Even though a great social and intellectual distance separates early Muslim societies from their present-day counterparts, key components of their established rules on marriage remain influential.

It is worth revisiting two vital elements of jurisprudence on marriage as it solidified in the formative period. First is the understanding of marriage as a relationship of control, dominion, or ownership conveying sexual lawfulness—a control which was linked to the increasingly sacrosanct nature of unilateral male divorce. Second is the gender differentiation of the marital claims of husband and wife, with strict separation of men's claims to sex and control over mobility from women's claims to support and companionship. The logical imperatives of marriage-as-dominion, above all the strict gender differentiation of spousal claims, stifled impulses toward reciprocity for certain claims—for instance, to conjugal intimacy. Women's sexuality was licit only within the confines of a man's control, and a man's sexual activity was licit only with women over whom he had exclusive dominion.

This vision of social relations structured by hierarchies of gender and freedom was undercut at numerous points by the recognition of female personhood, of women's needs, of slaves' humanity. Scattered through the texts, there are points at which the discourse of male prerogative rubs up against a stubborn recognition of women's selfhood. Glimpses of a yearning for mutuality (though not equality or sameness) are discernable. The jurists' exhortative discourse and their verdicts jostle one another uneasily. Admonishment and enforcement conflict and diverge.

This is not merely a conflict between ethical and legal elements of jurists' writings, with a triumph of the latter over the former. Today, when we speak of the ethical with regard to gender in Islamic law, we often mean egalitarianism. It is vital to recall that these jurists did not idealize an egalitarian order. Instead, they believed that some people were, though not inferior as believers, properly subordinate to others in the life of this world. The jurists' attempts to mold ideal believers, who treated others as they should be treated and with all due care for their interests, were emphatically not guided by the expectation—or even the hope—that this would result in a society free of hierarchy.

To read the texts as the victory of the doctrinal over the ethical, enforcement over exhortation, pragmatism over the ideal, is to impose an inappropriate categorization on them: these texts always present an ideal, even if it is one that notices and attempts to account for the human propensity to flout divine guidance and worldly authority. Jurisprudence is irreducible to law plus ethics; the two cannot be disentangled. Persistent tensions between an ideal and what is necessary for a systematized law may be inevitable. Though some rulings were eventually implemented by judges, the texts discussed here were neither guides to adjudicatory practice nor themselves enforceable. Instead, they present an ideal, or rather a series of interlinked ideals, sometimes in tension when not in outright conflict with one another. This discourse had implications for the practice of law in a system of justice but also sought to guide believers as to *ought,* not just *must.* And, of course, they were part of a specialized scholarly discourse concerned with internal methodological consistency and with winning arguments with advocates of opposing doctrines. Throughout this book, I have argued that many legal pronouncements about marriage and women emerged less from unremitting chauvinism than from a broader set of prior methodological commitments that had little to do, intrinsically, with gender.

These competing objectives and constraints of legal reasoning help us understand better how Shāfiʿī can simultaneously insist on a father's right to compel his virgin daughter's marriage and recommend strongly that he consult her and take her preferences into account. "Consulting her," he declares, "is better as a precaution, and more wholesome for her well-being, and a more beautiful manner of conduct."[8] And yet, despite his association of consultation with beauty and goodness, Shāfiʿī refuses to budge on the permissibility of marriage performed without consultation when the daughter is a virgin.

There were specific legal-technical reasons, as well, that the wife-slave analogy garnered so much usage, even though wives were not slaves (or at least, if enslaved, were not their own husband's property). This analogy, I have argued, had broad implications for how law developed and how jurists treated female legal capacity and sexuality. For the most part, I have drawn attention over the course of this book to the ways in which wives and slaves, and marriage and ownership, were brought closer through juristic reasoning. A brief consideration of one vital way in which they were distinguished can help explain what some have perceived as inexplicable: the widespread and intransigent insistence of Muslim jurists and judges on respecting female rights to property, whether inherited, dowered, or earned.

According to Baber Johansen, a woman's "capacity to acquire rights and duties, i.e., her status as a legal person, is inferior to that of the free male person."[9] A woman has the capacity to own property but not to be a "proprietor of marriage." Tucker also notes the "whiff of disability"[10] that attaches to women's legal capacity, the persistent sense that women are less fully legal subjects than men. At the same time, she notes the consistency with which scholars and judges have defended women's property rights, even when social discrimination would seem to indicate women's relatively weaker social position. Instead of seeing these tensions as paradoxical, I want to suggest that they are deeply interlinked.

They owe to the "pervasive process" of treating women and slaves similarly and distinguishing them, here to establish boundaries between types of legal subjects.[11]

Legal restrictions on women typically relate to women's sexuality and bodily presence. Women cannot, in most views, contract marriages for themselves or others; women cannot take concubines. Women's sexuality can only be licit when under the exclusive dominion of a particular man. Paternal guardianship over daughters, the ability to compel them into marriage, persists (in Mālikī and Shāfiʿī though not Ḥanafī doctrine) longer than that over sons. A husband's right to control his wife's movements and restrict her visitors might interfere with her ability to exercise otherwise unobjectionable rights and prerogatives, including the right to manage her property. In these ways, a wife is in some sense like a slave: she is not entirely mistress of herself.

By contrast, the vitality of (free) women's property rights, the vigor with which they are asserted by jurists and, as archival research shows, consistently defended by judges—even as they are the rights most frequently flouted in practice—owes to the vital role that the ability to own property played in distinguishing free from slave. The gender boundary was ultimately less fluid than the status boundary, because manumission enabled individuals to cross the latter. The insistence on free women's ability to own and transact property, and the inability of anyone to waive those rights on her behalf (except the father when contracting marriage for his minor virgin daughter in some but not all views), stands as a critical instance of boundary affirmation. Free women are free precisely in the ways that they are unlike slaves. (And the corollary: enslaved men are men and thus free—masters of themselves—in precisely the ways they are unlike women.)

An examination of Mālikī rules for property ownership by women and slaves lends credence to this suggestion that female property rights were sacrosanct to the extent they served to differentiate *free* females from *enslaved* persons. Mālik was freest in allowing paternal control over a daughter's dower: in setting it, waiving it, and receiving it. Later Mālikī jurisprudence and court practice delayed (free) females' control over their property not merely until majority but at least until consummation of their marriages, when they were established in other households.[12] Moreover, Mālik's followers permitted a husband to exert some control over his wife's property: he could prevent her from alienating more than a third of it. Though this still does not approach the powers theoretically wielded by Roman, Jewish, or, later, European husbands over their wives' property, it remains decidedly unusual within Muslim jurisprudence. The fact that the Mālikī school is least keen in some respects on female property rights perhaps, speculatively, we might owe to Mālik's making a smaller distinction between slave and free than the other legal schools: slaves could exercise de facto control over property; male slaves could marry four women, not only two; and enslaved wives were due the same number of allotted nights from their husbands as free women. That is to say, (free) female property rights were less important because the rigid line separating free from slave did not here rest as fully on control of property. The impact of these twin imperatives—to distinguish free people from slaves, and to distinguish women from men—led to an essential if rarely explicitly stated model of the distinctions and interrelations between marriage, licit sex, and property rights that structured early legal thinking.

The collective work of these jurists still exerts an indirect influence on the world. In a study of "Arabo-Islamic" literature, Fedwa Malti-Douglas suggests "that in the centuries old Arabic textual tradition, a dialectic operates between mental structures involving women and sexuality in the modern age and their antecedents in the classical period, that modern literature must also been seen against its classical background."[13] The same is vitally the case for law. Certain elements of premodern law—the place of slavery, the central use of commercial terminology—have quietly slipped into the past, and others—such as female consent to marriage—have been publicly subject to reform. Marital sexuality and divorce remain contentious.

Recognizing the centrality of the legal tradition but disturbed by the methodological incoherence as well as the repugnant results of various contemporary legal thinkers, some have advocated a revival of traditional forms of expertise applied to the modern situation. Khaled Abou El Fadl writes about the failings of contemporary legal thought to carry out the legacy of the past. He proffers a devastating critique of "puritan" legal opinions as they pertain to women, dispassionately unveiling their intellectual and moral bankruptcy.[14] But in doing so, he lumps newfangled rules together with doctrines firmly rooted in the classical legal tradition itself, illustrating Malti-Douglas's point.

To illustrate these "limitations on women that can only be described as suffocating," Abou El Fadl reproduces "misogynist" selections from the writings of one "purported scholar" from the late twentieth century. Two items are especially worthy of note. He begins his list with: "A Muslim wife may not worship God by fasting without the permission of her husband because her husband may want to have sex with her during the day." Another, which appears roughly halfway through, is that "a woman may not refuse her husband sex, except if she is ill. Refusing a husband sex without compelling justification is a grave sin *(kabira)*. On the other hand, a husband may refuse his wife sex for any reason or no reason at all."[15] By including these rulings alongside others clearly meant to strike readers as absurd ("Women may not chew gum because it is seductive"), Abou El Fadl suggests that they are emblematic of the "unprecedented level of deterioration" of once sophisticated Muslim legal culture.[16] But both statements are deeply embedded in the traditional juristic legacy that he so prizes.

The notions about marital sexuality and the widely divergent obligations of husbands and wives that Abou El Fadl finds so repulsive are, this book has shown, entirely consonant with core ideas about marriage widely shared among premodern jurists. Shāfiʿī articulates precisely the position regarding fasting that perturbs Abou El Fadl. Shāfiʿī cites a prophetic hadith: "It is not lawful for a woman to voluntarily fast a day if her husband is present except with his permission."[17] Though Shāfiʿī does not directly state his rationale for the ruling, it is obvious from the context that it is the wife's sexual availability that is at issue. Moreover, there is no reason to think that the other jurists demurred from it, since they agreed that the husband supports his wife in exchange for her sexual availability to him. Abou El Fadl's second example—in which a husband has no obligation for sex, but a wife, barring a legitimate excuse, does—is again central to the jurists' common vision of spousal rights. Though they disagreed on the exact consequences of a wife's sexual refusal, they concurred that she had no legitimate right to turn her husband down. They expended little energy defining whether her behavior was sinful, gravely or otherwise. Instead, they outlined specific legal repercussions of her act, especially suspension of maintenance rights and loss of her turn with her husband. (Physical discipline, which loomed large in exegetical discussions of wifely recalcitrance, or *nushūz*, made few appearances in the jurists' books.) As for the corollary that "a husband may refuse his wife sex for any reason or no reason at all," this is equally obvious to the jurists discussed here, as Chapter 3 showed. The gender differentiation of spousal rights is basic to the understanding of marriage as a relationship of exclusive control. What goes on inside a marriage cannot help but be affected by its basic structure.

I firmly believe that the jurists were, on the whole, genuinely interested in doing the right thing by women. Their aim was often to create justice and kindness. However, as a Jewish feminist critic has put it:

> Insofar as the rabbis do attempt to 'protect' women—by trying to find ways to get a husband to divorce his wife if she so desires, for example—they indicate some awareness of the limits and injustices of the system they have created and, in this sense, offer some resources for criticism. But insofar as they are willing to address these injustices only within the framework of the system that gives rise to them, they close off any possibility of women entering as subjects and reframing the issues in genuinely new terms.[18]

Inequality makes fully meaningful consent difficult when not impossible. A model of autonomous individuals with full power to negotiate contracts does not account for the ways that female agency is constrained, not only with regard to giving or withholding assent to the formation of marriage but also to acting once the contract exists. Women fundamentally have lesser rights both while a marriage endures and when it is ending. All spousal negotiations are affected by imbalances of power. Gail Labovitz points out, for the rabbinic sources, that "the lack of 'equal footing' between man and woman brings us back to the ownership metaphor. . . . [W]e might ask just how many details of her marital relationship such a woman was really in a position to negotiate."[19] In the Muslim sources, the male privilege of declaring or withholding divorce constrains married women's actions. There can be no level playing field.

Rachel Adler has argued that the rabbinic model of marriage suffers from a systemic contradiction. It combines certain features derived from covenant and partnership, wherein women are fully human participants in marriage, with other elements derived from a model of patriarchal ownership and control, where women are objects acted upon by others. This fundamental divergence creates tension and legal difficulty. In the Muslim system, this "unresolved tension between woman as possession and woman as partner"[20] appears most clearly in the discussion of apportionment and sex. On the one hand, not only does marriage make a wife licit for her husband, it also makes him licit for her. On the other hand, the gendered division of marital rights militates against reciprocity.

Additionally, the adversarial style adopted in juristic disputations leads to a lowest-common-denominator view of female rights in marriage. When conjoined with the near-total exclusion (even if incidental rather than deliberate) of women from the processes whereby law was formulated, this means that women's basic rights are often sacrificed when dominant modes of argument press claims into their extreme form. The prominence of disputation and polemic leads to the increased slippage of categories and pushes jurists into logically defensible but otherwise absurd positions. How else do a group of scholars who agree in principle that a wife has the right to sex conclude that women never have the right to divorce for impotence once a marriage has been consummated? The extent to which such rules were benignly neglected, or work-arounds found, attests to the imperative of justice as well as the creativity of the courts.

That said, law functions in myriad ways to constitute the individuals who are its subjects. As Tucker writes, "The law is productive of gender difference and is part of a society's gendering practices alongside other forms of knowledge."[21] Social practices shape laws, which in turn affect both collective actions and individual moral, social, and psychic formation. Actors deploy legal doctrines, then, to achieve concrete effects in real life situations. But these effects are not necessarily predominantly legal ones. In modernity, legal texts and the doctrines they contain (or sometimes, are assumed to contain) retain an aura of authenticity even when their application by nation states is mediated through legislative and judicial processes.

Thinking of oneself as a subject of Islamic law, or as subject to the law, facilitates a certain kind of identity formation as a Muslim, male or female. In closing, I proffer a decidedly unscientific and preliminary attempt to link the textual and the real. As I began this book by recounting a casual conversation, let me close with another. About five years ago, at a barbecue hosted by friends, I met a divorced Egyptian woman. She was a professional, educated woman in her late thirties living in the United States. When someone told her that I wrote about

Islamic law, the conversation came around to the failed attempt by a group of female reformers to get a checklist of stipulations placed on the standard Egyptian marriage contract. One would have granted wives the uncontested right to divorce, provided they compensated their husbands. My new acquaintance insisted that she would never marry a man who would forfeit his right to unilateral repudiation nor one who would accept her having it. Such a man would not be a real man.

What, if anything, can we make of her assertion? It is probably only partially representative of her views. Anthropologist Gabriele Marranci reports being told by an Egyptian immigrant to Ireland that she intended to divorce her husband, who was not living up to her idea of what a real man should do and how a real man should act. She lamented his lost masculine prerogatives. Of course, under the system that constituted them, including through unilateral divorce, she would not have been able to obtain such marital dissolution. Her nostalgia was for a patriarchal masculinity that would deny her the release she sought.[22] I suspect that if my acquaintance were to remarry and be unhappy in her marriage, she would want the ability to exit it regardless of her husband's consent. That thousands of Egyptian women immediately filed for judicial *khulʿ* when a reform in 2000 allowed them to do so suggests that, in practice, women do seek to get out of unhappy marriages, whatever qualms they may have about the challenge to an ideal masculinity that their right to do so presents. So what are we to understand from this woman's statement? Anecdotal evidence can be only suggestive, not probative. One woman's perspective cannot be taken as representative of even a class or generation, much less a country, and certainly not a region or a vast religion. We cannot directly connect her view to legal doctrine, much less a specific text. And yet, it cannot be entirely coincidental that it is a legal standard that determines authentic gender roles, nor that it is precisely the right of divorce—so central to the norms of masculine authority formulated by the jurists whose works I have discussed—that stands at the center of her vision of what it means to be a man, a husband, or that it is the absence of that right that makes one a woman, a wife.

Notes

Introduction

1. For a recent survey, see Judith E. Tucker, *Women, Family, and Gender in Islamic Law* (Cambridge: Cambridge University Press, 2008). To the works she cites on p. 32, n. 48, I would add, for the Mamluk era, Yossef Rapoport, *Marriage, Money, and Divorce in Medieval Islamic Society* (Cambridge: Cambridge University Press, 2005); and, for Andalusia, Amalia Zomeño, *Dote y matrimonio en al-Andalus y el norte de África: Estudios sobre la jurisprudencia islámica medieval* (Madrid: Consejo Superior de Investigaciones Científicas, 2000), and Maya Shatzmiller, *Her Day in Court: Women's Property Rights in Fifteenth-Century Granada,* Harvard Series in Islamic Law (Cambridge, MA: Harvard University Press 2007). Another recent noteworthy source is Asifa Quraishi and Frank E. Vogel, eds., *The Islamic Marriage Contract: Case Studies in Islamic Family Law,* Harvard Series in Islamic Law (Cambridge, MA: Islamic Legal Studies Program, Harvard Law School, 2008).

2. Ziba Mir-Hosseini, *Marriage on Trial: Islamic Family Law in Iran and Morocco,* rev. ed. (London: I. B. Tauris, 2000); Susan F. Hirsch, *Pronouncing and Persevering: Gender and the Discourses of Disputing in an African Islamic Court* (Chicago: University of Chicago Press, 1998).

3. Courts could also be better for women than customary patterns. See, e.g., Leslie P. Peirce, *Morality Tales: Law and Gender in the Ottoman Court of Aintab* (Berkeley: University of California Press, 2003), 365, writing about those who confessed sexual infractions to the court: "By allying themselves to its legal structure and culture, they might hope to escape a harsher local legal culture."

4. For a recent example, see Elyse Semerdjian, *"Off the Straight Path": Illicit Sex, Law, and Community in Ottoman Aleppo,* Gender, Culture, and Politics in the Middle East (Syracuse, NY: Syracuse University Press, 2008), xix; see also viii, xxiii.

5. Amira El Azhary Sonbol, "Introduction," in Amira El Azhary Sonbol, ed., *Women, the Family, and Divorce Laws in Islamic History* (Syracuse, NY: Syracuse University Press, 1996), 5.

6. Semerdjian, *"Off the Straight Path,"* 159

7. Abdullahi An-Na'im, "Shari'a and Islamic Family Law: Transition and Transformation," in Abdullahi An-Na'im, ed., *Islamic Family Law in a Changing World* (London: Zed Books, 2002), 4.

8. Dror Ze'evi, *Producing Desire: Changing Sexual Discourse in the Ottoman Middle East, 1500–1900* (Berkeley: University of California Press, 2006), 50. Ze'evi provides a close study of late Ottoman regulation of illicit sex (pp. 48–76). See also Tucker, *Women, Family, and Gender,* 8–9.

9. Tucker, *Women, Family, and Gender,* 15.

10. For the implications of this, see An-Na'im, "Shari'a and Islamic Family Law," and the case studies in An-Na'im, *Islamic Family Law.*

11. Tucker, *Women, Family, and Gender,* 196–200, 204–206, 216; Semerdjian, *"Off the Straight Path,"* xxi.

12. Tucker, *Women, Family, and Gender,* 23.

13. Ibid., 36.

14. Cristina de la Puente, "Juridical Sources for the Study of Women: Limitations of the Female's Capacity to Act According to Mālikī Law," in Manuela Marin and Randi Delguilhem, eds., *Writing the Feminine: Women in Arab Sources* (London and New York: I. B. Tauris, 2002), 100.

15. Norman F. Cantor, *Antiquity: From the Birth of Sumerian Civilization to the Fall of the Roman Empire* (New York: Harper Perennial, 2003), 225.

16. See, e.g., the treatment of *kitāba* and the *umm walad* in Jonathan Brockopp, *Early Mālikī Law: Ibn ʿAbd al-Ḥakam and His Major Compendium of Jurisprudence* (Leiden, Netherlands: Brill, 2000).

17. Jere L. Bacharach, "African Military Slaves in the Medieval Middle East: The Cases of Iraq (869–955) and Egypt (868–1171)," *International Journal of Middle East Studies* 13:4 (November 1981): 471–495; see also Matthew S. Gordon, "The Khāqānid Families of the Early ʿAbbasid Period," *Journal of the American Oriental Society* 121:2 (April–June 2001): 236–255, and the literature cited on p. 236, n. 2.

18. E. Savage, "Berbers and Blacks: Ibadi Slave Traffic in Eighth-Century North Africa," *Journal of African History* 33:3 (1992): 351–368.

19. Bernard Lewis, *Race and Slavery in the Middle East* (Oxford: Oxford University Press, 1990), 56.

20. Muslim concubinage has been romanticized in some of the scholarly literature, perhaps because of its association with the Ottoman imperial harem (on which see Leslie P. Peirce, *The Imperial Harem: Women and Sovereignty in the Ottoman Empire* [New York: Oxford University Press, 1993]). Occasional asides in legal texts suggest that men did not always acknowledge and sometimes specifically rejected paternity of children borne by their female slaves. Early

discussions of the *umm walad*, the slave who has borne her master's child, refer to a Companion who rejects paternity of his slave's child; the caliph ʿUmar affirms that whenever a man admits having sex with his slave girl, he always attributes paternity to him. On the post-facto attribution of this ruling to ʿUmar, see Khalil ʿAthamina, "How Did Islam Contribute to Change the Legal Status of Women? The Case of the *Jawārī*, or the *Female Slaves*," *Al-Qantara* 28:2 (July–December 2007): 386–387. Concubines, one must note, were not automatically exempt from housework. For a much later discussion of this topic, see Ehud R. Toledano, *As if Silent and Absent: Bonds of Enslavement in the Islamic Middle East* (New Haven: Yale University Press, 2007), 19.

21. Wael B. Hallaq, "Review: The Use and Abuse of Evidence: The Question of Provincial and Roman Influences on Early Islamic Law," *Journal of the American Oriental Society* 110:1 (January–March 1990): 90.

22. Ibid.

23. One comparative article does exist: Judith Romney Wegner, "The Status of Women in Jewish and Islamic Marriage and Divorce Law," *Harvard Women's Law Journal* 5:1 (1982): 1–33.

24. For patriarchy and history, see Judith Bennett, *History Matters: Patriarchy and the Challenge of Feminism* (Philadelphia: University of Pennsylvania Press, 2007). For attempts to theorize patriarchy within specific Muslim societies or regions, see Selma Botman, *Engendering Citizenship in Egypt* (New York: Columbia University Press, 1999), 107–115, and Deniz Kandiyoti, "Islam and Patriarchy: A Comparative Perspective," in Nikki R. Keddie and Beth Baron, eds., *Women in Middle Eastern History: Shifting Boundaries in Sex and Gender* (New Haven: Yale University Press, 1991), 23–42. Ghada Karmi, "Women, Islam, and Patriarchalism," in Mai Yamani with Andrew Allen, eds., *Feminism in Islam: Legal and Literary Perspectives* (New York: New York University Press, 1996), 69–83, attempts to reconcile Arab practice with Islamic norms. See also Scott Kugle, *Sufis and Saints' Bodies: Mysticism, Corporeality, and Sacred Power in Islam* (Chapel Hill: University of North Carolina Press, 2007), 84–87. On shifting patterns of households and the rise of the nuclear family in modernity and its pluses and minuses for women, see, among others, Ze'evi, *Producing Desire*, 75; Deniz Kandiyoti, "Bargaining with Patriarchy," *Gender and Society* 2 (1988): 274–290; and Soraya Altorki, *Women in Saudi Arabia: Ideology and Behavior among the Elite* (New York: Columbia University Press, 1988).

25. Suzanne Dixon, *The Roman Family* (Baltimore: Johns Hopkins University Press, 1992), 53–54 and passim.

26. The text describes her action as follows: "Tasarrat imra'atun ghulāman lahā." (One manuscript used by the editor of this text reads *sharaqa* in place of *tasarrat*, which makes little sense.) ʿAbd al-Razzaq al-Ṣanʿānī, *Muṣannaf* (Beirut: Dār al-Kutub al-ʿIlmiyya, 2000), "Bāb al-ʿabd yankiḥu sayyidatahu," 7:164, no. 12873. The immediately preceding entry discusses a woman marrying her own male slave. ʿUmar does not punish her with *ḥadd*, though it is

mentioned, but rather forbids her from ever marrying a free man. Al-Ṣanʿānī, *Muṣannaf,* "Bāb al-ʿabd yankiḥu sayyidatahu," 7:164, no. 12872.

27. For uses of this Qurʾanic euphemism for slavery, "what your/their right hands own" *(mā malakat aymānukum/aymānuhum),* see 4:3, 24–25, 36; 16:71; 23:6; 24:31, 33, 58; 30:28; 33:50, 52, 55; 70:30.

28. On ʿUmar, see Linda Kern, "The Riddle of ʿUmar ibn al-Khaṭṭāb in Bukhārī's *Kitāb al-Jāmiʿ aṣ-Ṣaḥīḥ* (and the Question of the Routinization of Prophetic Charisma)" (doctoral dissertation, Harvard University, 1996). Fatima Mernissi, *The Veil and the Male Elite: A Feminist Interpretation of Women's Rights in Islam,* trans. Mary Jo Lakeland (Reading, MA: Addison-Wesley, 1991), is among those who have made ʿUmar a scapegoat for patriarchal survivals.

29. On the *Muṣannaf,* see Harald Motzki, "The Muṣannaf of ʿAbd al-Razzāq al-Ṣanʿānī as a Source of Authentic Aḥādīth of the First Century A. H." *Journal of Near Eastern Studies* 50:1 (January 1991): 1–21, as well as Motzki's *The Origins of Islamic Jurisprudence: Meccan Fiqh before the Classical Schools,* trans. Marion Katz (Leiden, Netherlands: Brill, 2002), which argues for the authenticity of its transmitted material. Motzki utilizes the books of Marriage and Divorce from the *Muṣannaf* as his source material (as one discovers for the first time on p. 74), but does not undertake any analysis of the content and significance of the material.

30. *"Anā bi manzilat al-rajul."* Marion Katz, *Body of Text: The Emergence of the Sunni Law of Ritual Purity* (Albany: State University of New York Press, 2002), 249, n. 17, cites the *Mudawwana,* where Saḥnūn likewise pronounces a woman *bi manzilat* (which Katz translates as "equivalent to") a man with regard to ablutions necessitated by touching the opposite sex.

31. According to Fatima Mernissi's analysis, "Islam banished all practices in which the sexual self-determination of women was asserted." Fatima Mernissi, *Beyond the Veil: Male-Female Dynamics in Modern Muslim Society,* rev. ed. (Bloomington and Indianapolis: Indiana University Press, 1987), 66–67; see also 53, 61, 62. For her discussion of a hadith in which four types of marriage practiced in the pre-Islamic period are discussed, see *Beyond the Veil,* 75–77, and Mernissi, *The Veil and the Male Elite,* 83–84.

32. These reports appear in a section of the *Muṣannaf* bearing the title "The male slave who marries (or, has sex with) his female owner" ("Bāb al-ʿabd yankiḥu sayyidatahu"). This title ascribes agency to the slave. He is the actor, and his owner is grammatically the direct object of his action. Still, several reports under this heading present the owner as the initiator of a relationship, including both cases where not marriage but a nonmarital relationship is in question. See Chapter 5 in this book.

33. Muḥammad b. Idrīs al-Shāfiʿī, *Al-Umm* (Beirut: Dār al-Kutub al-ʿIlmiyya, 1993) (hereafter *Al-Umm*).

34. Scholarly debates over the precise chronology and textual history of the *Umm* and other works attributed to Shāfiʿī are ongoing and will undoubtedly reveal much about the post-Shāfiʿī development of jurisprudence. None-

theless, the *Umm* clearly reflects Shāfiʿī's doctrines and his own jurisprudential sensibilities. For the most recent assessment of the situation and citations of relevant literature, see Ahmed El Shamsy, "From Tradition to Law: The Origins and Early Development of the Shāfiʿī School of Law in Ninth-Century Egypt" (doctoral dissertation, Harvard University, 2009).

35. *Al-Umm*, K. al-Nafaqāt, "Mā jāʾa fī ʿadad ma yaḥillu min al-ḥarāʾir wa ʾl-immāʾ wa mā taḥillu bihi al-furūj," 5:215.

36. For a brief survey of twentieth-century European and North American scholarship on the early history of the legal schools, see Christopher Melchert, *The Formation of the Sunni Schools of Law, 9th–10th Centuries CE* (Leiden, Netherlands: Brill, 1997), xx–xxv.

37. Jonathan Brockopp, "Competing Theories of Authority in Early Mālikī Texts," in Bernard G. Weiss, ed., *Studies in Islamic Law and Legal Theory* (Leiden, Netherlands: Brill, 2002), 3–22; and Brockopp, "Early Islamic Jurisprudence in Egypt: Two Scholars and Their *Mukhtaṣars*," *International Journal of Middle East Studies* 30 (1998): 167–182.

38. See, e.g., Aḥmad b. ʿUmar al-Khaṣṣāf, *Kitāb al-Nafaqāt*, "Bāb nafaqat al-marʾa ʿalā ʾl-zawj wa mā yajib lahā min dhālika," 32, where he notes a difference in views among the early Ḥanafī authorities and explains that one arrived at his view using *qiyās* while another used juristic preference *(istiḥsān)*. The latter provides the preferred school position *(wa ʿalayhi al-fatwā)*.

39. Christopher Melchert, "The Adversaries of Aḥmad Ibn Ḥanbal," *Arabica* 44:2 (April 1997): 235–236.

40. Susan A. Spectorsky, ed. and trans., *Chapters on Marriage and Divorce: Responses of Ibn Ḥanbal and Ibn Rāhwayh* (Austin: University of Texas Press, 1993). Spectorsky's *Women in Classical Islamic Law: A Survey of the Sources* (Leiden, Netherlands: Brill, 2010), treating a broader range of formative period sources, appeared just as this book was going to press.

41. Mālik ibn Anas, *Al-Muwaṭṭaʾ li ʾl-Imām Mālik b. Anas, bi riwāyat Yaḥyā b. Yaḥyā b. Kathīr al-Laythī al-Andalusī* (Beirut: Dār al-Fikr, 1989) (hereafter *Muwaṭṭaʾ*) and [Saḥnūn b. Saʿīd al-Tanūkhī] Mālik b. Anas, *Al-Mudawwana al-Kubrā* (Beirut: Dār Ṣādir, 1323 AH [1905 or 1906]) (hereafter *Mudawwana*).

42. The *Muwaṭṭaʾ* is known in several recensions apart from the common one used here, the recension of Yaḥyā b. Yaḥyā al-Laythī (d. 234/849). Norman Calder's controversial suggestion that the *Muwaṭṭaʾ* is later than the *Mudawwana* and should be redated to Cordoba, ca. 270 A.H., has been convincingly refuted. See Calder, *Studies in Early Muslim Jurisprudence* (Oxford: Clarendon, 1993), 24, 37; Harald Motzki, "The Prophet and the Cat: On Dating Mālik's *Muwaṭṭaʾ* and Legal Traditions," in *Jerusalem Studies in Arabic and Islam* 22 (1998): 18–83; and Yasin Dutton, review of Calder's *Studies in Early Muslim Jurisprudence*, *Journal of Islamic Studies* 5 (1994): 102–108. Brockopp suggests a distinction between canonization and compilation which, taking account of other

recensions of the *Muwaṭṭaʾ*, may help explain some of the dissension. Brockopp, *Early Mālikī Law*, xvi. On other recensions, see Brockopp, *Early Mālikī Law*, 74–77, and Yasin Dutton, *The Origins of Islamic Law: The Qur'an, the* Muwaṭṭaʾ *and Madinan ʿAmal* (Surrey: Curzon Press, 1999), 22–26. On the style of the *Muwaṭṭaʾ*, see Wael B. Hallaq, *Authority, Continuity, and Change in Islamic Law* (Cambridge: Cambridge University Press, 2001), 31–34.

43. The dating of the *Mudawwana*, in at least some form, is likely to become more secure: Brockopp reports having been shown a manuscript fragment dated 235 A.H. Brockopp, "Competing Theories of Authority," 5, n. 8.

44. Muḥammad b. al-Ḥasan al-Shaybānī, *Al-Jāmiʿ al-Ṣaghīr* (ʿĀlam al-Kutub, Beirut, n.d.), and Muḥammad b. al-Ḥasan al-Shaybānī, *Al-Jāmiʿ al-Kabīr* (Lahore, Pakistan: Dār al-Maʿārif al-Nuʿmāniyya, 1967).

45. Muḥammad b. al-Ḥasan al-Shaybānī, *Muwaṭṭaʾ al-Imām Mālik, riwāyat Muḥammad b. al-Ḥasan al-Shaybānī* (Beirut: Al-Maṭbaʿa al-ʿIlmiyya, 1997) (hereafter *Muwaṭṭaʾ Shaybānī*), and Muḥammad b. al-Ḥasan al-Shaybānī, *Kitāb al-Ḥujja ʿalā Ahl al-Madīna* (Hyderabad, India: Lajnat Iḥyā al-Maʿārif al-Nuʿmāniyya, 1965). On these texts, see Melchert, "The Early History of Islamic Law," in Herbert Berg, ed., *Method and Theory in the Study of Islamic Origins* (Leiden, Netherlands: Brill, 2003), 311–324, where he uses material on recitation behind an imam and prostration to compare these texts with those they critique. On p. 312, Melchert states, "Certainly, the *Ḥujjah* as we know it cannot be entirely Shaybānī's work[.]" For the *Muwaṭṭaʾ Shaybānī* as well as Shaybānī's *Kitāb al-Āthār*, see Behnam Sadeki, "The Structure of Reasoning in Post-Formative Islamic Jurisprudence (Case Studies in Ḥanafī Laws on Women and Prayer)" (doctoral disertation, Princeton University, 2006), 164–186. Sadeki argues (p. 186) that both are "authentic works of al-Shaybānī."

46. Abū Yūsuf Yaʿqūb b. Ibrāhīm al-Anṣārī, *Ikhtilāf Abī Ḥanīfa wa Ibn Abī Laylā, li ʾl-imām Abī Yūsuf Yaʿqūb b. Ibrāhīm al-Anṣārī* (Cairo: Maṭbaʿat al-Wafāʾ, 1938) and Abū Yūsuf Yaʿqūb b. Ibrāhīm al-Anṣārī, *Kitāb al-Āthār*, ed. Abūʾl-Wafāʾ (Hyderabad, India: Lajnat Iḥyāʾ al-Maʿārif al-Nuʿmāniyya 1355 AH [1936 or 1937]).

47. Noel Coulson, *A History of Islamic Law* (Edinburgh: Edinburgh University Press, 1964), 53.

48. In a few places, its solution of particularly thorny problems differs from that of the *Umm*, suggesting that al-Muzanī's compendium derives from a somewhat different corpus of material than that constituting the present-day *Umm*. See, in this book, Chapter 3 on wedding nights, and also Calder, *Studies in Early Muslim Jurisprudence*, 89–90. Calder has also suggested (p. 96) that, like *Al-Umm*, al-Muzanī's *Mukhtaṣar* was a composite rather than an authored text. This seems a more difficult case to make on the basis of the available evidence.

49. On Muzanī's importance and possible equivocal place within the Shāfiʿī school, see Melchert, *Formation of the Sunni Schools;* Jonathan Brockopp,

"Competing Theories of Authority," and, especially, "Early Islamic Jurisprudence in Egypt." On the *Mukhtaṣar* compiled by a more tradition-minded student, see Ahmed El Shamsy, "The First Shāfiʿī: The Traditionalist Legal Thought of Abū Yaʿqūb al-Buwayṭī," *Islamic Law and Society* 14:3 (2007): 301–341.

50. Nurit Tsafrir, "Semi-Ḥanafīs and Ḥanafī Biographical Sources," *Studia Islamica* (November 1996/2): 84, 71–72.

51. Steven C. Judd, "Al-Awzāʿī and Sufyān al-Thawrī: The Umayyad Madhhab?" in Peri Bearman, Rudolph Peters, and Frank E. Vogel, eds., *The Islamic School of Law: Evolution, Devolution, and Progress* (Cambridge, MA: Islamic Legal Studies Program, Harvard Law School, 2005), 10–25.

52. Brockopp, *Early Mālikī Law,* xvi.

53. Peter Hennigan, *The Birth of a Legal Institution: The Formation of the Waqf in Third-Century AH Ḥanafī Legal Discourse* (Leiden, Netherlands: Brill, 2004), 2.

54. Alasdair MacIntyre, *Whose Justice? Which Rationality?* (Notre Dame, IN: University of Notre Dame Press, 1988).

55. MacIntyre, *Whose Justice?,* 12.

56. Leila Ahmed, *Women and Gender in Islam: Historical Roots of a Modern Debate* (New Haven: Yale University Press, 1992), chapter 5, "Elaboration of the Founding Discourses," 79–101. On the Abbasid era, see Hugh Kennedy's narrative political history, *When Baghdad Ruled the Muslim World: The Rise and Fall of Islam's Greatest Dynasty* (Cambridge, MA: Da Capo Press, 2005).

57. Ahmed, *Women and Gender,* 85; see also 67.

58. Ibid., 83.

59. Nadia Maria El Cheikh, "The *Qahramâna* in the Abbasid Court: Position and Functions," *Studia Islamica* 97 (2003): 42. But for the view that all were concubines, see ʿAthamina, "How Did Islam Contribute," 389.

60. Christopher Melchert, *Ahmad ibn Hanbal* (Oxford: Oneworld Publications, 2006), 5; Kecia Ali, *Al-Shafiʿi* (Oxford: Oneworld Publications, forthcoming).

61. ʿAthamina, "How Did Islam Contribute," 389.

62. Rapoport, *Marriage, Money, and Divorce,* 114.

63. Huda Lutfi, "Manners and Customs of Fourteenth-Century Cairene Women: Female Anarchy versus Male Sharʾi Order in Muslim Prescriptive Treatises," in Keddie and Baron, *Women in Middle Eastern History,* 99–121.

64. Amira El Azhary Sonbol, "Introduction," in Sonbol, *Women, the Family, and Divorce Laws in Islamic History,* 5.

65. On the usefulness of legal texts for social history, see Leor Halevi, *Muḥammad's Grave: Death Rites and the Making of Islamic Society* (New York: Columbia University Press, 2007); Zeʾevi, *Producing Desire,* 48; and Dror Zeʾevi, "The Use of Ottoman Sharīʿa Court Records as a Source for Middle Eastern Social History: A Reappraisal," *Islamic Law and Society* 5:1 (1998): 35–56.

66. Shatzmiller, *Her Day in Court,* 8–9. The importance of muftis and their fatwas in the largely Mālikī Muslim West is not necessarily characteristic,

though. On fatwas more generally, see Muhammad Khalid Masud, Brinkley Messick, and David S. Powers, "Muftis, Fatwas, and Islamic Legal Interpretation," in Muhammad Khalid Masud, Brinkley Messick, and David S. Powers, eds., *Islamic Law and Legal Interpretation: Muftis and Their Fatwas* (Cambridge, MA: Harvard University Press, 1998), 3–32.

67. For instance, see the material on marriage in two *adab* texts in Nadia Maria El Cheikh, "In Search for the Ideal Spouse," *Journal of the Economic and Social History of the Orient* 45:2 (2002): 179–196. For a related point with regard to rabbinic texts, see Gail Labovitz, *Marriage and Metaphor: Constructions of Gender in Rabbinic Literature* (Lanham, MD: Lexington Books, 2009), 14.

68. For this insight with regard to a later period, see Khaled Al-Rouayheb, *Before Homosexuality in the Arab-Islamic World, 1500–1800* (Chicago: University of Chicago Press, 2005), 11.

69. Labovitz, *Marriage and Metaphor.*

70. Joan Wallach Scott, *Gender and the Politics of History,* rev. ed. (New York: Columbia University Press, 1999), 41.

71. Hayden White, *The Content of the Form: Narrative Discourse and Historical Representation* (Baltimore: Johns Hopkins University Press, 1987), 193.

72. I owe the phrase *descriptive efficiency* to Behnam Sadeki, personal communication.

73. One might use the treatment of certain topics in marriage and divorce to track the chronology of legal texts, but the endeavor would be fraught with difficulties. See Katz's criticism of Norman Calder's attempted dating, using doctrines on an issue of ritual purity, of two of the Ḥanafī texts explored here, the *Kitāb al-Ḥujja* and the *Muwaṭṭaʾ Shaybānī* (Katz, *Body of Text,* 130–135).

1. Transacting Marriage

1. On marriage proposals made in jest, see ʿAbd al-Razzāq al-Ṣanʿānī, *Muṣannaf* (Beirut: Dār al-Kutub al-ʿIlmiyya, 2000), 6: 107–108, no. 10281–10291; Yaʿakov Meron, "The Moslem Marriage between Status and Contract," *Studia Islamica* 92 (2001): 197–203; and Paul Powers, *Intent in Islamic Law: Motive and Meaning in Medieval Sunni Fiqh* (Leiden, Netherlands: Brill, 2005), 127, 136.

2. Muḥammad al-Shaybānī, *Kitāb al-Ḥujja* (Hyderabad, India: Lajnat Iḥyāʾ al-Maʿārif al-Nuʿmāniyya, 1965)(hereafter *Kitāb al-Ḥujja*), K. al-Nikāḥ, "Bāb al-marʾa tuzawwiju amatahā aw ʿabdahā aw taʿqidu ʿuqdat al-nikāḥ," 3: 116–117. Note that this reading of her name is speculative; the *Ḥujja*'s editor discusses his difficulties in ibid., n. 2.

3. Kecia Ali, "Marriage in Classical Islamic Jurisprudence: A Survey of Doctrines," in Asifa Quraishi and Frank E. Vogel, eds., *The Islamic Marriage Contract: Case Studies in Islamic Family Law* (Cambridge, MA: Harvard University Press, 2008), 11–45, 11–12; Powers, *Intent in Islamic Law,* 123.

4. Nabia Abbot, *Aishah, The Beloved of Mohammed* (Chicago: University of Chicago Press, 1942), 3–4.

5. See, e.g., Muḥammad b. Idrīs al-Shāfiʿī, *Kitāb Ikhtilāf al-ʿIrāqiyayn*, in Muḥammad b. Idrīs al-Shāfiʿī, *Al-Umm* (Beirut: Dār al-Kutub al-ʿIlmiyya, 1993) (hereafter *Al-Umm*), vol. 7, "Bāb al-ḥudūd," 7:250; Susan Spectorsky, ed. and trans., *Chapters on Marriage and Divorce: Responses of Ibn Ḥanbal and Ibn Rāhwayh* (Austin: University of Texas Press, 1993), 117. In the case of a male, *bikr* would refer to his never having contracted and consummated a marriage.

6. [Saḥnūn b. Saʿīd al-Tanūkhī] Mālik b. Anas. *Al-Mudawwana al-Kubrā* (Beirut: Dār Ṣādir, 1323 AH [1905 or 1906]) (hereafter *Mudawwana*), K. al-Nikāḥ I, "Fī waḍʿ al-ab baʿḍ al-ṣadāq wa dafʿ al-ṣadāq ilā ʾl-ab," 2:160.

7. *Mudawwana*, K. al-Nikāḥ, I, "Fī inkāḥ al-ab ibnatahu bi ghayri riḍāhā," 2:155.

8. If she remains with her husband for an extended period, even if intercourse has not actually occurred, she is due a full dower and obliged to observe a waiting period on divorce; she is no longer subject to her father's power of compulsion. *Mudawwana*, K. al-Nikāḥ, I, "Fī inkāḥ al-ab ibnatahu bi ghayri riḍāhā," 2:156. By contrast, illicit intercourse does not create a change in her status. Shāfiʿī disagrees. Any intercourse, in or outside of marriage, results in a change to her status. Nothing other than intercourse does so. *Al-Umm*, K. al-Nikāḥ, "Mā jāʾa fī nikāḥ al-abāʾ," 5:29.

9. Mudawwana, K. al-Nikāḥ I, "Fī waḍʿ al-ab baʿḍ al-ṣadāq wa dafʿ al-ṣadāq ilā ʾl-ab," 2:160.

10. Muḥammad Amīn ibn ʿUmar ibn ʿĀbidīn, *Radd al-Muḥtār ʿalā ʾl-Durr al-Mukhtār Sharḥ Tanwīr al-Abṣār* (Beirut: Dār al-Kutub al-ʿIlmiyya, 1994), 4:154; Burhān al-Dīn al-Farghānī al-Marghīnānī, *Al-Hidāya: The Guidance*, vol. 1, trans. Imran Ahsan Khan Nyazee (Bristol, England: Amal Press, 2006), 495. But for a case in the Ottoman Empire in which a minor non-virgin contested a remarriage on the basis that she was a *thayyib*, see Dror Ze'evi, "The Use of Ottoman Sharīʿa Court Records as a Source for Middle Eastern Social History: A Reappraisal," *Islamic Law and Society* 5:1 (1998): 41–42.

11. *Al-Umm*, K. al-Nikāḥ, "Mā jāʾa fī nikāḥ al-ābāʾ," 5:30; Ismāʿīl b. Yaḥyā al-Muzanī, *Mukhtaṣar al-Muzanī* (*Al-Umm*), "Bāb mā ʿalā ʾl-awliyāʾ wa inkāḥ al-ab al-bikr bi ghayri idhnihā . . . ," 9:176–177.

12. *Muṣannaf ʿAbd al-Razzāq*, K. al-Nikāḥ, "Bāb mā yukrah ʿalayhi min al-nikāḥ fa lā yajūz," 6:116–122.

13. Ibid., 6:117, 10340 (2848), refers instructively to a "virgin woman" *(imraʾa bikr)*.

14. Mālik ibn Anas, *Al-Muwaṭṭaʾ li ʾl-Imām Mālik b. Anas, bi riwāyat Yaḥyā b. Yaḥyā b. Kathīr al-Laythī al-Andalusī* (Beirut: Dār al-Fikr, 1989) (hereafter *Muwaṭṭaʾ*), K. al-Nikāḥ, "Bāb istiʾdhān al-bikr wa ʾl-ayyim fī anfusihimā," 331. For this rendering of "wa huwa al-amr ʿindanā," see Hiroyuki Yanagihashi, *A*

History of the Early Islamic Law of Property: Reconstructing the Legal Development, 7th–9th Centuries (Leiden, Netherlands: Brill, 2004), 68.

15. See Yasin Dutton, *The Origins of Islamic Law: The Qurʾan, the* Muwaṭṭaʾ, *and Medinan ʿAmal* (Surrey, UK: Curzon Press, 2000).

16. *Mudawwana,* K. al-Nikāḥ I, "Fī riḍā al-bikr wa ʾl-thayyib," 2:158.

17. On the marriage of minors, see *Mudawwana,* K. Irkhāʾ al-Sutūr, "Khulʿ al-ab ʿalā ibnihi wa ibnatihi," 2:350; K. al-Nikāḥ I, "Fī inkāḥ al-rajul ibnahu al-kabīr wa ʾl-ṣaghīr wa fī inkāḥ al-rajul al-ḥāḍir al-rajul al-ghāʾib," 2:173–174.

18. *Mudawwana,* K. al-Nikāḥ I, "Fī riḍā al-bikr wa ʾl-thayyib," 2:157. For reports that the Prophet consulted his daughters about their marriages, see Abū Bakr ʿAbd Allāh b. Muḥammad ibn Abī Shayba, *Al-Kitāb al-Muṣannaf fī ʾl-Ahādith wa ʾl-Āthār,* 9 vols. (Beirut: Dār al-Kutub al-ʿIlmiyya, 1995), 4:136 (hereafter *Muṣannaf Ibn Abī Shayba*), and ʿAbd al-Razzāq al-Ṣanʿānī (Bāb mā yukrah ʿalayhi min al-nikāḥ fa lā yajūz, *Muṣannaf ʿAbd al-Razzāq* 6:115, no. 10327/2842). See also Kecia Ali, " 'A Beautiful Example': The Prophet Muḥammad as a Model for Muslim Husbands," *Islamic Studies* 43:2 (Summer 2004): 273–291.

19. On Shāfiʿī's concern for noncontradiction between the Qurʾan and sunna, see Joseph E. Lowry, *Early Islamic Legal Theory: The* Risāla *of Muḥammad ibn Idrīs al-Shāfiʿī* (Leiden, Netherlands: Brill, 2007).

20. *Al-Umm,* K. al-Nikāḥ, "Mā jāʾa fī nikāḥ al-ābāʾ," 5:28–29.

21. Shāfiʿī states outright that ʿĀʾisha was still a minor at consummation (*Al-Umm, Kitāb Ikhtilāf al-ʿIrāqiyayn,* Bāb al-Nikāḥ, 7:237). Ibn Ḥanbal, on the other hand, may assume that though she was a minor when the marriage took place, she had attained majority before it was consummated (Spectorsky, *Chapters on Marriage and Divorce,* 96.) He insists that girls of age nine or older must be consulted, even by their fathers, though he does not explicitly discuss majority. Note that while Spectorsky's Introduction connects the age of nine with menarche (p. 10), Ibn Ḥanbal refers only to physical desirability (p. 183) as a criterion for consummation.

22. *Al-Umm,* K. al-Nikāḥ, "Mā jāʾa fī nikāḥ al-ābāʾ," 5:28–29.

23. Ibid., 5:29; *Mukhtaṣar al-Muzanī,* "Bāb mā ʿalā ʾl-awliyāʾ wa inkāḥ al-ab al-bikr bi ghayri idhnihā," 176–177.

24. *Al-Umm,* K. al-Nikāḥ, "Mā jāʾa fī nikāḥ al-ābāʾ," 5:29.

25. *Al-Umm,* K. Ikhtilāf al-ʿIrāqiyayn, "Bāb al-Nikāḥ," 7:238, 240.

26. *Al-Umm,* K. al-Nikāḥ, "Mā jāʾa fī nikāḥ al-ābāʾ," 5:29.

27. Al-Marghīnānī, *Al-Hidāya,* 491: "The *walī* is asked to undertake her marriage so that she is not characterized as being immodest." On twentieth-century Egyptian practice, see Ron Shaham, *Family and the Courts in Modern Egypt: A Study Based on Decisions by the Sharīʿa Courts, 1900–1955* (Leiden, Netherlands: Brill, 1997), 47

28. On the right of other guardians to marry off minors and the latter's possible option *(khiyār)* to reject the marriage on arriving at maturity, see *Kitāb al-Ḥujja,* K. al-Nikāḥ, "Bāb nikāḥ al-ṣaghīr wa 'l-ṣaghīra wa mā yajūzu ʿalayhimā idhā adrakā wa mā lā yajūzu," 3:140–141.

29. Abū Yūsuf Yaʿqūb, *Ikhtilāf Abī Ḥanīfa wa Ibn Abī Laylā, li 'l-imām Abī Yūsuf Yaʿqūb b. Ibrāhīm al-Anṣārī* (Cairo: Maṭbaʿat al-Wafā', 1938) (hereafter *Ikhtilāf*), Bāb al-Nikāḥ, 178–179. See also *Kitāb al-Ḥujja,* K. al-Nikāḥ, "Bāb awliyā' al-nikāḥ ʿalā 'l-kabīra al-bāligha mā yajūz wa mā lā yajūz," 3:126–139.

30. Gail Labovitz, *Marriage and Metaphor: Constructions of Gender in Rabbinic Literature* (Lanham, MD: Lexington Books, 2009), 52.

31. *Kitāb al-Ḥujja,* K. al-Nikāḥ, "Bāb awliyā' al-nikāḥ ʿalā 'l-bāligha, mā yajūz wa mā lā yajūz," 3:135–136.

32. *Mudawwana,* K. al-Nikāḥ I, "Fī inkāḥ al-ab ibnatahu bi ghayri riḍāhā," 2:155. See also *Al-Umm,* K. al-Nikāḥ, "Mā jā'a fī nikāḥ al-ābā'," 5:29.

33. *Al-Umm,* K. al-Nikāḥ, "Mā jā'a fī nikāḥ al-ābā'," 5:29.

34. Ehud R. Toledano, *As if Silent and Absent: Bonds of Enslavement in the Islamic Middle East* (New Haven: Yale University Press, 2007), 23, argues for using this concept instead of the "master-slave dyad."

35. Paul G. Forand, "The Relation of the Slave and the Client to the Master or Patron in Medieval Islam," *International Journal of Middle East Studies* 2:1 (January 1971): 61.

36. For instance, Roman law allowed only "a quasi marital relationship" called *contubernium,* in which at least one of the partners was enslaved. Susan Treggiari, "'Contubernales' in 'Cil' 6," *Phoenix* 35:1 (Spring 1981): 42–69.

37. Suzanne Dixon, *The Roman Family* (Baltimore: Johns Hopkins University Press, 1992), 67.

38. Ibid., 71.

39. Social practice consistently allowed more leeway than the jurists did. A man could claim an erroneous presumption of ownership that averted *ḥadd.* For the Ottoman case, see Dror Ze'evi, *Producing Desire: Changing Sexual Discourse in the Ottoman Middle East, 1500–1900* (Berkeley: University of California Press, 2006), 54. Ze'evi sees this as evidence of "distinctions in punishment for male and female," but it seems to me that the mitigation of punishment is of a piece with attempts to avert *ḥadd* punishments generally.

40. *Mudawwana,* K. al-Nikāḥ I, "Fī inkāḥ al-ab ibnatahu bi ghayri riḍāhā," 2:155.

41. The fifth-/eleventh-century Ḥanafī al-Sarakhsī explains why coercion of female slaves is permitted, but provides no rationale for forced marriage of male slaves, simply declaring, "A master may force his female slave or his male slave into marriage." Al-Sarakhsī, *Kitāb al-Mabsūṭ* (Beirut: Dār al-Kutub al-ʿIlmiyya, 2001), K. al-Nikāḥ, "Bāb nikāḥ al-imā' wa 'l-ʿabīd," 5:107. The much later *Fatawa-i-Kazee-Khan* attributes both contradictory positions to Abū Ḥanīfa.

Fatawa-i-Kazee Khan: Relating to Mahomedan Law of Marriage, Dower, Divorce, Legitimacy, and Guardianship of Minors, According to the Soonnees (Lahore, Pakistan: Law Publishing, 1977), sect. 4, "On the Marriage of Slaves," 1:57–58.

42. *Kitāb al-Ḥujja* (K. al-Nikāḥ, "Bāb al-ʿabd yatazawwaju bi ghayri idhn sayyidihi," 3:509–512); Abū Yūsuf, Abū Yūsuf Yaʿqūb b. Ibrāhīm al-Anṣārī, *Kitāb al-Āthār,* ed. Abū'l-Wafāʾ (Hyderabad, India: Lajnat Iḥyāʾ al-Maʿārif al-Nuʿmāniyah, 1355 AH [1936 or 1937]), "Abwāb al-Ṭalāq," 130, no. 600; *Mudawwana,* K. al-Nikāḥ II, "Bāb al-ḥurma," 2:187–188, and "Fī ʾl-nikāḥ alladhī yufsakhu bi ṭalāq wa ghayri ṭalāq," 2:183.

43. *Al-Umm,* K. al-Nikāḥ, "Nikāḥ al-ʿadad wa nikāḥ al-ʿabīd," 5:68.

44. One motive for marrying her off might have been the desire to increase his household population of slaves: a master owned children born to his female slaves from marriage, whether the husbands were free or enslaved and, if the latter, his own slaves or those of others. Jennifer Glancy suggests that for ancient Romans, one finds "the pervasive use of female slaves for breeding the next generation of human chattel." Jennifer Glancy, *Slavery in Early Christianity* (Minneapolis: Fortress Press, 2006), 10.

45. Muḥammad al-Shaybānī, *Al-Jāmiʿ al-Ṣaghīr* (Beirut: ʿĀlam al-Kutub, n.d) (hereafter *Al-Jāmiʿ al-Ṣaghīr*), K. al-Nikāḥ, "Fī tazwīj al-ʿabd wa ʾl-ama," 189. Subsequent authorization is not sufficient to validate the marriage for the Mālikīs and Shāfiʿīs; it is void ab initio, just as any such marriage contracted by a free woman would be void. *Mudawwana,* K. al-Nikāḥ, "Fī ʾl-tazwīj bi ghayri walī," 2:180.

46. *Al-Umm,* K. al-Nikāḥ, "Nikāh al-ʿadad wa nikāh al-ʿabīd," 5:68.

47. This does not mean, as Paul Powers suggests, that "a non-virgin is generally allowed to contract her own marriage" (*Intent in Islamic Law,* 127), but only that she must consent verbally. For the silent assent of the virgin in her majority, see n. 48 below.

48. Muḥammad al-Shaybānī, *Muwaṭṭaʾ al-Imām Mālik, bi riwāyat Muḥammad b. al-Ḥasan al-Shaybānī* (Beirut: Al-Maṭbaʿa al-ʿIlmiyya, 1997) (hereafter *Muwaṭṭaʾ Shaybānī*), K. al-Nikāḥ, "Bāb al-thayyib aḥaqqu bi nafsihā min waliyyihā," 177.

49. *Mudawwana,* K. al-Nikāḥ I, "Fī riḍā al-bikr wa ʾl-thayyib," 2:157. For the consent of the *thayyib,* see also Majid Khadduri, ed. and trans., *Islamic Jurisprudence: Shafiʾi's* Risala (Baltimore: Johns Hopkins University Press, 1961), 174.

50. *Muwaṭṭaʾ,* K. al-Nikāḥ, "Bāb Jāmiʿ mā lā yajūz min al-nikāḥ," 338. See also *Al-Umm,* K. al-Nikāḥ, "Mā jāʾa fī nikāḥ al-ābāʾ," 5:29.

51. *Muwaṭṭaʾ Shaybānī,* K. al-Nikāḥ, "Bāb al-thayyib aḥaqqu bi nafsihā min waliyyihā," 177.

52. *Kitāb al-Ḥujja,* K. al-Nikāḥ, "Bāb awliyāʾ al-nikāḥ ʿalā ʾl-bāligha, mā yajūz wa mā lā yajūz," 3:131–132.

53. Ibid., 3:135–136.

54. *Kitāb al-Ḥujja,* K. al-Nikāḥ, "Al-mar'a tuzawwiju amatahā aw ʿabdahā aw taʿqidu ʿuqdat al-nikāḥ," 3:99–100; see also 3:103–1044 and 3:105–1088. These terms (*inkiḥī, tazawwajī*) appear in accounts in the *Muṣannaf ʿAbd al-Razzāq* (6:118, 10342/2850 and 10341/2849).

55. Ahmad Atif Ahmad, *Structural Interrelations of Theory and Practice in Islamic Law: A Study of Six Works of Medieval Islamic Jurisprudence* (Leiden, Netherlands: Brill, 2006), xvi–xvii.

56. *Al-Jāmiʿ al-Ṣaghīr,* K. al-Nikāḥ, "Bāb al-ikfā'," 173–174. See also *Kitāb al-Ḥujja,* K. al-Nikāḥ, "Bāb al-mar'a tankiḥu bi ghayri idhn waliyyihā ghayr kuf'," 3:512–515. For Shāfiʿī views, see *Al-Umm,* K. al-Nikāḥ, "Lā nikāḥ illā bi walī," 5:23, and especially "Al-ikfā'," 5:25–26.

57. *Muwaṭṭa' Shaybānī,* K. al-Nikāḥ, "Bāb al-nikāḥ bi ghayri walī," 182.

58. *Muwaṭṭa' Shaybānī,* K. al-Nikāḥ, "Bāb al-nikāḥ bi ghayri walī," 182. See also *Muwaṭṭa',* K. al-Nikāḥ, "Bāb isti'dhān al-bikr wa 'l-ayyim fī anfusihimā," 331; *Mudawwana,* K. al-Nikāḥ I, "Fī annahu lā yaḥillu nikāḥ bi ghayri walī wa anna wilāyat al-ajnabī lā tajūz illā an takūn waḍīʿa," 2:166. *Al-Umm,* K. Ikhtilāf Mālik wa 'l-Shāfiʿī, 7:375–376. I borrow the translation of *sulṭān* as "constituted authority" from Michael Bonner, *Jihad in Islamic History: Doctrines and Practice* (Princeton: Princeton University Press, 2008), 107, n. 19. He notes that "the formal office or function of sultan did not come about until much later," and in the time period here it both refers to "authority" in a general sense and "is also applied, by metonymy, to caliphs and other representatives of the government."

59. See *Kitāb al-Ḥujja,* K. al-Nikāḥ, "Bāb al-mar'a tankiḥu bi ghayri idhn waliyyihā ghayr kuf'," 3:512. Abū Ḥanīfa's reliance on ʿUmar's opinion here is noteworthy.

60. Mona Siddiqui, "Law and the Desire for Social Control: An Insight into the Hanafi Concept of *Kafa'a* with Reference to the Fatawa ʿAlamgiri (1664–1672)," in Mai Yamani, ed., *Feminism and Islam: Legal and Literary Perspectives* (New York: New York University Press, 1996), 49–68. See also Farhat Ziadeh, "Equality *(Kafā'ah)* in the Muslim Law of Marriage," *American Journal of Comparative Law* 4 (1957): 503–517.

61. The lack of importance of suitability in Jaʿfarī jurisprudence, however, militates against placing too much importance on this point.

62. *Muwaṭṭa' Shaybānī,* K. al-Nikāḥ, "Bāb al-nikāḥ bi ghayri walī," 182.

63. See, e.g., *Mudawwana,* K. al-Nikāḥ I, "Fī annahu lā yaḥillu nikāḥ bi ghayri walī wa anna wilāyat al-ajnabī lā tajūz illā an takūn waḍīʿa," 2:166.

64. *Mudawwana,* K. al-Nikāḥ I, "Fī riḍā al-bikr wa 'l-thayyib," 2:157.

65. *Mudawwana,* K. al-Nikāḥ I, "Fī tazwīj al-waṣī wa waṣī al-waṣī," 2:166–167.

66. *Mudawwana,* K. al-Nikāḥ I, "Fī annahu lā yaḥillu nikāḥ bi ghayri walī wa anna wilāyat al-ajnabī lā tajūz illā an takūn waḍīʿa," 2:166 and "Fī nikāḥ al-daniyya," 2:170.

67. *Al-Umm,* K. Ikhtilāf Mālik wa ʾl-Shāfiʿī, 7:376.

68. *Al-Umm,* Kitāb al-Nikāḥ, "Al-marʾa lā yakūn lahā al-walī," 5:31. See also "Lā nikāḥ illā bi walī," 5:21–23. See similar opinions cited in the *Muṣannaf* of Ibn Abī Shayba, in the section "Man qāla: Laysa li ʾl-marʾa an tuzawwija al-marʾa wa innamā al-ʿaqd bi yad al-rijāl," 4:134–135. For a contrary precedent, see the account of ʿĀʾisha marrying off her brother's daughter ("Man ajāzahu bi ghayri walī wa lam yufarriq," 4:134), which is also reported in *al-Umm* and other early texts.

69. Cristina de la Puente, "Juridical Sources for the Study of Women: Limitations of the Female's Capacity to Act according to Mālikī Law," in Manuela Marin and Randi Delguilhem, eds., *Writing the Feminine: Women in Arab Sources* (London and New York: I. B. Tauris, 2002), 100–101.

70. De la Puente, "Juridical Sources for the Study of Women," 100–101.

71. *Al-Umm,* Kitāb al-Nikāḥ, "Al-marʾa lā yakūn lahā al-walī," 5:32. *Mudawwana,* K. al-Nikāḥ III, "Al-ṣadāq bi ʾl-ʿabd yūjadu bihi ʿayb," 2:220, reports that being married decreases a female slave's value because "the slave woman if she has a husband, then that is a defect *(ʿayb min al-ʿuyūb).*" See also *Al-Jāmiʿ al-Ṣaghīr,* K. al-Nikāḥ, "Fī tazwīj al-ʿabd wa ʾl-ama," 189.

72. *Kitāb al-Ḥujja,* K. al-Nikāḥ, "Bāb al-marʾa tuzawwiju amatahā aw ʿabdahā aw taʿqidu ʿuqdat al-nikāḥ," 3:99. Compare this against the view, attributed to al-Ḥasan, that "a woman marries off her female slave *(amatahā)* but if she is manumitted (alternately: if she manumits her), she does not marry her off." (*Muṣannaf Ibn Abī Shayba,* 4:135) The text does not mention a male slave.

73. *Al-Umm,* Kitāb al-Nikāḥ, "Al-marʾa lā yakūn lahā al-walī," 5:32.

74. Ibid.

75. Glancy, *Slavery in Early Christianity,* 10–15.

76. Oussama Arabi defines interdiction *(ḥajr)* as "the judicial denial of the ability to dispose freely of one's wealth." Oussama Arabi, "The Interdiction of the Spendthrift *(al-Safīh):* A Human Rights Debate in Classical *Fiqh,*" *Islamic Law and Society* 7:3 (2000): 300.

77. *Al-Umm,* Kitāb al-Nikāḥ, "Al-marʾa lā yakūn lahā al-walī," 5:32.

78. On restrictions of legal capacity in Mālikī jurisprudence, see de la Puente, "Juridical Sources for the Study of Women," 96–101.

79. Scott C. Lucas, "Justifying Gender Inequality in the Shāfiʿī Law School: Two Case Studies of Muslim Legal Reasoning," *Journal of the American Oriental Society* 129:2 (2009), surveys material on witnessing. See also the brief discussion by Mohammed Fadel in "Reinterpreting the Guardian's Role in the Islamic Contract of Marriage: The Case of the Mālikī School," *Journal of Islamic Law and Culture* 3:1 (1998): 1–26.

80. *Mukhtaṣar al-Muzanī,* "Al-kalām alladhī yanʿaqidu bihi al-nikāḥ . . . ," 179. Elsewhere, al-Muzanī notes, citing a prophetic hadith, that "women are sexually forbidden *(al-nisāʾ muḥarramāt al-furūj),* and are not made lawful except"

with, in addition to the marriage guardian, proper witnesses and either the agreement of the non-virgin bride or the silence of the virgin. *Mukhtaṣar al-Muzanī,* "Bāb mā ʿalā ʾl-awliyāʾ wa inkāḥ al-ab al-bikra bi ghayri idhnihā . . . ," 176.

81. *Mudawwana,* K. al-Nikāḥ I, "Fī tazwīj al-waṣī wa waṣī al-waṣī," 2:167.

82. *Al-Umm,* K. al-Shighār, "Al-khiyār min qibal al-nasab," 5:121; see also *Mukhtaṣar al-Muzanī,* "Bāb mā ʿalā ʾl-awliyāʾ wa inkāḥ al-ab al-bikra bi ghayri idhnihā . . . ," 175.

83. Judith E. Tucker, *Women, Family, and Gender in Islamic Law* (Cambridge: Cambridge University Press, 2008), 222.

84. Labovitz, *Marriage and Metaphor,* 181.

85. Ibid.

86. Glancy, *Slavery in Early Christianity,* 35.

87. Ibid.

88. For this reason, Shāfiʿī and Abū Ḥanīfa hold that if he marries two of his own slaves to one another, a master need not allocate a dower: his male slave has no wealth to give, and his female slave has no capacity to own it in any case. The *Mudawwana* presents a dissenting view it attributes to Mālik: there must be a dower, though whether the master is expected to provide it or to claim it remains unclear. "Ibn Wahb from Muḥammad b. ʿAmr from Ibn Jurayj from ʿAṭāʾ b. Abī Rabāḥ that he said: 'A man does not marry his male slave to his female slave without a dower.' Ibn Wahb said: Mālik said that." (*Mudawwana,* K. al-Nikāḥ II, "Fī inkāḥ al-rajul ʿabdahu amatahu," 2:204.) The opposing opinion holds this stance illogical: "Muḥammad said: Abū Ḥanīfa may God be pleased with him, said: A man must not *(lā yanbaghī)* marry his female slave to his male slave without witnesses, but there is no problem with him marrying his female slave to his male slave without a dower. This is because the dower, if he fixed one, would be the master's. The master is not due a dower from his male slave. [But] if he marries his female slave to another man or to someone else's slave, there is no marriage without a dower." (*Kitāb al-Ḥujja,* "Bāb al-rajul yuzawwiju ʿabdahu amatahu bi ghayri mahr," 3:417–418.)

89. Yossef Rapoport, "Matrimonial Gifts in Early Islamic Egypt," *Islamic Law and Society* 7:1 (2000): 1–36; Yossef Rapoport, *Marriage, Money and Divorce in Medieval Islamic Society* (Cambridge: Cambridge University Press, 2005); and Amalia Zomeño, *Dote y matrimonio en al-Andalus y el norte de África: Estudio sobre la jurisprudencia islámica medieval* (Madrid: Consejo Superior de Investigaciones Científicas, 2000).

90. Rapoport, "Matrimonial Gifts in Early Islamic Egypt," 5–9.

91. Charles Torrey, *The Commercial-Theological Terms in the Koran* (Leiden, Netherlands: Brill, 1892), 1.

92. John Ralph Willis, "The Ideology of Enslavement in Islam," *Slaves and Slavery in Muslim Africa,* vol. 1, *Islam and the Ideology of Enslavement* (London: Cass, 1985), 1.

93. Shaun E. Marmon, "Domestic Slavery in the Mamluk Empire: A Preliminary Sketch," in Shaun E. Marmon, ed., *Slavery in the Islamic Middle East* (Princeton: Markus Wiener, 1999), 18–19; Willis, "Ideology of Enslavement in Islam," 1; Rapoport, *Marriage, Money, and Divorce.*

94. John Ralph Willis, "Ideology of Enslavement in Islam," 1.

95. Baber Johansen, "Commercial Exchange and Social Order in Hanafite Law," in Christopher Toll and Jakob Skovgaard-Petersen, eds., *Law and the Islamic World: Past and Present,* Royal Danish Academy of Sciences and Letters monograph series Historisk-filosofiske Meddelser, vol. 68 (Copenhagen: Munksgaard, 1995), 82. Baber Johansen, "The Valorization of the Body in Muslim Sunni Law," in Devin J. Stewart, Baber Johansen, and Amy Singer, eds., *Law and Society in Islam* (Princeton: Markus Wiener, 1996).

96. Johansen, "Commercial Exchange and Social Order," 84.

97. Labovitz, *Marriage and Metaphor,* 32.

98. Ibid., 1.

99. Ibid., 16. The Roman form of marriage known as *manus* also brings the language of control to marriage.

100. Sandra R. Joshel and Sheila Murnaghan, "Introduction: Differential Equations," in Joshel and Murnaghan, eds., *Women and Slaves in Greco-Roman Culture: Differential Equations* (London: Routledge, 2001), 3.

101. *Al-Jāmiʿ al-Ṣaghīr,* K. al-Ṭalāq, "Bāb al-kināyāt," 207–209.

102. *Mudawwana,* K. al-Nikāḥ I, "Fī man wakkala rajulan ʿalā tazwījihi," 2:174–176.

103. *Mudawwana,* K. al-Nikāḥ I, "Fī man wakkala rajulan ʿalā tazwījihi," 2:175. The terms *wakīl* and *maʾmūr* are used interchangeably.

104. *Mukhtaṣar al-Muzanī,* K. al-Nikāḥ, "Al-ʿayb fī ʾl-mankūḥa," 9:189.

105. See Abū Yūsuf, *Kitāb al-Āthār,* "Abwāb al-Ṭalāq," 135, no. 618. A range of other stipulations about dower, or the specification of an item the husband did not yet possess, led to additional disagreements. See, e.g., *Mudawwana,* K. al-Nikāḥ III, "Al-nikāḥ alladhī lā yajūz wa ṣadāquhu wa ṭalāquhu wa mīrāthuhu," 2:241; K. al-Nikāḥ III, "Fī ʾl-tafwīḍ," 2:238; and K. al-Nikāḥ II, "Fī nikāḥ bi ghayri bayyina," 2:192–193; *Al-Umm,* K. al-Ṣadāq 5:88 (at the beginning of the Kitāb al-Ṣadāq, before the first titled section); *Mukhtaṣar al-Muzanī,* K. al-Wadīʿa, "Bāb al-tafwīḍ," 9:194; and *Kitāb al-Ḥujja,* K. al-Nikāḥ, "Bāb al-rajul yatazawwaju al-ama wa yashtariṭu anna kulla waladin taliduhu ḥurr," 3:215.

106. Basic provisions for such cases can be found in summary form in Qurʾan 2:236–237. The verses are cited in passing in the *Mudawwana,* and in the *Umm* they constitute the basis for an exegetical argument as to why a marriage is valid without a specified dower. On the *mutʿa,* see Rapoport, "Matrimonial Gifts in Early Islamic Egypt."

107. *Al-Umm,* K. al-Ṣadāq, "Al-mahr al-fāsid," 5:105. Yves Linant de Bellefonds, *Traité de Droit Musulman Comparé,* vol. 2 (Paris: Mouton, 1965), 23–26. See also K. al-Ṣadāq, 5:88.

108. *Kitāb al-Ḥujja*, K. al-Nikāḥ, "Bāb al-rajul yatazawwaju al-ama wa yashtariṭu anna kulla waladin taliduhu ḥurr," 3:215.

109. *Al-Umm*, K. al-Ṣadāq, "Al-mahr al-fāsid," 5:105.

110. *Mudawwana*, K. al-Nikāḥ III, "Al-nikāḥ bi ṣadāq aqallu min rubʿ dīnār," 2:223; *Kitāb al-Ḥujja*, K. al-Nikāḥ, "Al-rajul yatazawwaju al-ama wa yashtariṭu anna kulla waladin taliduhu ḥurr," 3:218; *Muwaṭṭaʾ Shaybānī*, K. al-Nikāḥ, "Bāb adnā mā yatazawwaj ʿalayhi al-marʾa, 176.

111. The jurists acknowledge that an intact hymen is not proof of virginity, and yet treat a ruptured hymen as a defect requiring compensation.

112. *Al-Umm*, K. Ikhtilāf Mālik wa ʾl-Shāfiʿī, K. al-ʿItq, "Bāb mā jāʾa fī ʾl-ṣadāq," 7:376. For a similar use of the term *mutabāʾiʿān*, see Q. 2:282. On strict and metaphorical interpretations of this term, see Ahmad, *Structural Interrelations*, 119–120.

113. Body: literally, neck *(raqaba)*, but metonymically, ownership of her entire body. See *Al-Umm, K. Ikhtilāf al-ʿIrāqiyayn*. As for the extent to which one can see this language as conscious reliance on physicality, vs. the extent to which it has lost the ability to immediately bring those connotations to mind for its users, see Glancy's discussion of *soma* (body) in *Slavery in Early Christianity*, 11.

114. *Mudawwana*, K. al-Nikāḥ I, "Mā jāʾa fī nikāḥ al-shighār," 2:153; *Muwaṭṭaʾ Shaybānī*, K. al-Nikāḥ, "Bāb nikāḥ al-shighār," 179. *Shighār* differs from other situations where a specified dower is invalid; it also differs from situations where the dower is left unspecified.

115. Richard Antoun mentions "sister-exchange marriages" briefly in a useful discussion of "the accommodation of tradition" in the Jordanian Islamic court system, where he primarily focuses on brides' claims to dower. Richard T. Antoun, "The Islamic Court, the Islamic Judge, and the Accommodation of Traditions: A Jordanian Case Study," *International Journal of Middle East Studies* 12:4 (1980): 457. Such marriages are mentioned in passing in anthropological literature. For a suggestion of the complexities of the social (as opposed to the legal) view of exchange marriage, see Zeʾevi, "The Usefulness of Ottoman Sharīʿa Court Records." For similar ambiguities with regard to virginity and abductions, see Judith E. Tucker, *In the House of the Law: Gender and Islamic Law in Ottoman Syria and Palestine* (Berkeley: University of California Press, 1998); Aharon Layish, *Women and Islamic Law in a Non-Muslim State: A Study Based on Decisions of the Shariʿa Courts in Israel* (New Brunswick, NJ: Transaction Publishers, 2006), 100–101; also p. 21. Pinar Ilkkaracan notes that in "semi-feudal" Eastern Turkey in the 1990s, such *berdel* marriages account for one out of every twenty marriages among 599 survey respondents. Pinar Ilkkaracan, "Islam and Women's Sexuality: A Research Report from Turkey," in Radhika Balakrishnan, Patricia Beattie Jung, and Mary E. Hunt, eds., *Good Sex: Feminist Perspectives from the World's Religions* (Piscataway, NJ: Rutgers University Press, 2000), 69.

116. *Muwaṭṭa' Shaybānī,* K. al-Nikāḥ, "Bāb nikāḥ al-shighār," 179.

117. *Mudawwana,* K. al-Nikāḥ V, "Fī 'l-iḥlāl," 2:292.

118. Ibn Wahb, quoted in *Mudawwana,* K. al-Nikāḥ I, "Mā jā'a fī nikāḥ al-shighār," 2:153. See the statement that the Prophet forbade *shighār,* defining it thus: "*Shighār* is that a man marries his daughter to a man on the condition that the other man marries his daughter to him and there is no dower between them."

119. *Al-Umm,* K. al-Shighār, 5:113 (at the beginning of the Kitāb al-Shighār, before the first titled section). See also *Mukhtaṣar al-Muzanī,* K. al-Wadī'a, "Bāb al-shighār wa mā dakhala fīhi . . . ," 9:187–188.

120. *Mudawwana,* K. al-Nikāḥ I, "Mā jā'a fī nikāḥ al-shighār," 2:154.

121. *Al-Umm,* K. al-Ṣadāq, 5:91; *Mudawwana,* K. al-Nikāḥ III, "Niṣf al-ṣadāq," 2:227. As discussed, when a woman was contracting a marriage for herself without a marriage guardian under Ḥanafī doctrine, her dower had to be her full fair dower or the marriage could be challenged.

122. *Mudawwana,* K. al-Nikāḥ I, "Fī inkāḥ al-ab ibnatahu al-bikr wa 'l-thayyib," 2:155. On the corollary issue of whether the father of a minor boy could commit his son to pay more than fair dower, again Abū Ḥanīfa allowed it and Muḥammad al-Shaybānī and Abū Yūsuf disallowed it. *Al-Jāmi' al-Ṣaghīr,* K. al-Nikāḥ, "Bāb fī tazwīj al-bikr wa 'l-ṣaghīrīn," 171–172.

123. *Al-Umm,* K. al-Ṣadāq, "Al-tafwīḍ," 5:103–104.

124. *Mudawwana,* K. al-Nikāḥ II, "Fi 'l-nikāḥ bi 'l-khiyār," 2:195.

125. Abdullah Hasan, *Sales and Contracts in Early Islamic Commercial Law* (Islamabad: Islamic Research Institute, 1994), 21. Hence the problematic cases where goods such as pork or wine had been specified as dowers in marriages of non-Muslims who subsequently converted to Islam.

126. On the categories of fungible and unique, see Frank E. Vogel and Samuel L. Hayes III, *Islamic Law and Finance: Religion, Risk, and Return* (The Hague, London, Boston: Kluwer Law International, 1998), especially chapter 4, 94–95.

127. *Al-Jāmi' al-Ṣaghīr,* K. al-Nikāḥ, "Bāb fī 'l-muhūr," 184–185.

128. Ibid.; *Mudawwana,* K. al-Nikāḥ III, "Fī 'l-ṣadāq yūjadu bihi 'ayb aw yūjadu bihi rahn fa yahlik," 2:218.

129. *Al-Umm,* K. al-Ṣadāq, "Ṣadāq al-shay' bi 'aynihi fa yūjad ma'īban," 5:111.

130. *Mukhtaṣar al-Muzanī,* K. al-Wadī'a, "Ṣadāq mā yazīd bi budnihi wa yanquṣu," 9:194 (where the slave is free, not defective). On al-Muzanī's use of *ghalaṭ* with regard to Shāfi'ī's positions, see Jonathan Brockopp, "Early Islamic Jurisprudence in Egypt: Two Scholars and their *Mukhtaṣars,*" *International Journal of Middle East Studies* 30 (1998): 173.

131. *Mukhtaṣar al-Muzanī,* K. al-Wadī'a, "Ṣadāq mā yazīd bi badanihi wa yanquṣu," 9:194.

132. *Al-Umm*, K. al-Ṣadāq, "Ṣadāq al-shay' bi ʿaynihi fa yūjad maʿīban," 5:111. See also *Mukhtaṣar al-Muzanī*, K. al-Wadīʿa, "Ṣadāq mā yazīd bi badanihi wa yanquṣu," 9:194. "Likewise, she claims [the consideration] for what she gave [him], and [what she gave him] is her *buḍʿ*. [Its price is] her fair dower, and this is Shāfiʿī's final position." *Al-Umm*, K. al-Ṣadāq, "Fī 'l-ṣadāq bi ʿaynihi yatlafu qabla dafʿihi," 5:92.

133. On disagreements over dower and unpaid or unpayable dower in an unconsummated marriage, see *Mudawwana*, K. al-Nikāḥ IV, "Alladhī lā yaqdiru ʿalā mahr imra'atihi," 2:253, and *Al-Umm*, K. al-Nafaqa, "Bāb al-rajul lā yajidu mā yunfiqu ʿalā imra'atihi," 5:132–133.

134. *Al-Umm*, K. al-Nikāḥ, "Al-ikfā'," 5:26. See also *Kitāb Ikhtilāf al-ʿIrāqiyayn*, 7:240. For somewhat different analogies between marriage and sales, see *Al-Umm*, K. al-Shighār, "Bāb mā yakūn khiyār qabla al-ṣadāq," 5:120–121.

135. Assuming both were not only free but also Muslim. *Mudawwana*, K. al-Nikāḥ III, "Al-ṣadāq bi 'l-ʿabd yūjadu bi ʿayb," 2:220.

136. See, e.g., Azizah al-Hibri, "Muslim Women's Rights in the Global Village: Challenges and Opportunities," *Journal of Law and Religion* 15:1/2 (2000–2001): 43. For debates among twentieth-century North African scholars over compulsion, see Tucker, *Women, Family, and Gender*, 67.

137. Ali S. Asani, "The Experience of the Nizari Ismaili Community," in Quraishi and Vogel, *The Islamic Marriage Contract*, 289.

138. See Woodrow Wilson Center, Middle East Program, "'Best Practices': Progressive Family Laws in Muslim Countries," August 2005, http://www.wilsoncenter.org/topics/pubs/English.pdf, last consulted 04.03.09, 8–11; Pieternella van Doorn-Harder, *Women Shaping Islam: Reading the Qu'ran in Indonesia* (Urbana and Chicago: University of Illinois Press, 2006), 248.

139. Toledano, *As if Silent and Absent*, 8.

140. Ibid., 33; italicized in original.

2. Maintaining Relations

1. Aḥmad b. ʿUmar al-Khaṣṣāf, *Kitāb al-Nafaqāt* (Beirut: Dār al-Kitāb al-ʿArabī, 1984). On al-Khaṣṣāf, see the brief biographical notice in Peter C. Hennigan, *The Birth of a Legal Institution: The Formation of the Waqf in Third century A. H. Ḥanafī Legal Discourse* (Leiden, Netherlands: Brill, 2004), 4–7.

2. Al-Khaṣṣāf, *Kitāb al-Nafaqāt*, "Bāb nafaqat al-mar'a ʿalā 'l-zawj wa mā yajib lahā min dhālika," 29, where the woman's wealthy brother must provide the support but can claim it as a debt from her indigent husband. For a similar example with regard to her son (by a previous husband), see al-Khaṣṣāf, *Kitāb al-Nafaqāt*, "Bāb al-nafaqa ʿalā dhawī al-raḥm al-muḥarram," 73.

3. Al-Khaṣṣāf, *Kitāb al-Nafaqāt,* "Bāb nafaqat al-mar'a ʿalā 'l-zawj wa mā yajibu lahā min dhālika," 42.

4. Muḥammad b. Idrīs al-Shāfiʿī, *Al-Umm* (Beirut: Dār al-Kutub al-ʿIlmiyya, 1993) (hereafter *Al-Umm*), K. al-Nafaqāt, "Wujūb nafaqat al-mar'a," 5:128.

5. *Ḥabs* appears in early legal texts also with regard to "detention" as a species of imprisonment. For this use of *ḥabs,* see Irene Schneider, "Imprisonment in Pre-Classical and Classical Islamic Law," *Islamic Law and Society* 2:2 (1995): 157–173. Schneider argues that imprisonment was generally not punitive but rather a species of administrative detention, usually for debt collection. My extension of the term to a husband's right to restrict his wife is imperfect. A recalcitrant debtor is detained to encourage him to pay his debt and thereby obtain freedom; a wife is detained because her debt cannot be paid: she owes precisely the acquiescence to detention. Hennigan translates *ḥabs* as "sequestration."

6. On the maintenance obligation in Ḥanafī law, see Yaʿakov Meron, "The Development of Legal Thought in Ḥanafī Texts," *Studia Islamica* 30 (1969): 73–118, and Yaʿakov Meron, *L'Obligation Alimentaire entre Époux en Droit Musulman Hanéfite* (Paris: Librairie Generale de Droit e de Jurisprudence, 1971).

7. See Susan Spectorsky, ed. and trans., *Chapters on Marriage and Divorce: Responses of Ibn Ḥanbal and Ibn Rāhwayh* (Austin: University of Texas Press, 1993).

8. See Mohammed Hocine Benkheira, "Un libre peut-il épouser une esclave? Esquisse d'histoire d'un debat, des origins à al-Shāfiʿī (m. 204/820)," *Der Islam* 84 (2008): 246–355.

9. [Saḥnūn b. Saʿīd al-Tanūkhī] Mālik b. Anas, *Al-Mudawwana al-Kubrā* (Beirut: Dār Ṣādir, 1323 AH [1905 or 1906]) (hereafter *Mudawwana*), K. al-Nikāḥ IV, "Al-ama yankiḥuhā al-rajul fa yurīdu an yubawwi'ahā sayyiduhā maʿahu . . . ," 2:248. Christina de la Puente, "Esclavitud y matrimonio en la *Mudawwana al-kubra* de Sahnun," *Al-Qanṭara* 16 (1995): 328, summarizes this discussion.

10. Richard P. Saller, "Pater Familias, Mater Familias, and the Gendered Semantics of the Roman Household," *Classical Philology* 94:2 (1999): 191; also see Richard P. Saller, "'Familia, Domus,' and the Roman Conception of the Family," *Phoenix* 38:4 (Winter 1984): 336–355.

11. Suzanne Dixon, *The Roman Family* (Baltimore: Johns Hopkins University Press, 1992), 2. However, "they did sometimes use *familia* to mean family of kin, but in technical discussions rather than common parlance."

12. Ehud R. Toledano, *As if Silent and Absent: Bonds of Enslavement in the Islamic Middle East* (New Haven: Yale University Press, 2007).

13. For "need" in a sexual context, see also Ze'ev Maghen, *Virtues of the Flesh: Passion and Purity in Early Islamic Jurisprudence* (Leiden, Netherlands: Brill, 2004), 35–36, n. 101; the hadith quoted there also uses *ahl* for wife.

14. Ibid., 27–28; Kecia Ali, *Sexual Ethics and Islam: Feminist Reflections on Qur'an, Hadith, and Jurisprudence* (Oxford: Oneworld Publications, 2006), 10–13.

15. Ali, *Sexual Ethics and Islam*, 60.

16. Quoted in Maghen, *Virtues of the Flesh*, 22–23.

17. *Mudawwana*, K. al-Nikāḥ IV, "Al-ama yankiḥuhā al-rajul fa yurīdu an yubawwi'ahā sayyiduhā ma'ahu . . . ," 2:248. For one opinion that the husband might stipulate the right to lodge his slave wife with him in the marriage contract, see 2:248–249.

18. Ismā'īl b. Yaḥyā al-Muzanī, *Mukhtaṣar al-Muzanī* (*Al-Umm*), K. al-Wadī'a, "Mā yaḥillu min al-ḥarā'ir wa lā yatasarrā al-'abd wa ghayr dhālika," 9:180.

19. *Mudawwana*, K. al-Nikāḥ IV, "Fī nafaqat al-rajul 'alā imra'atihi," 2:255.

20. Muḥammad al-Shaybānī, *Al-Jāmi' al-Ṣaghīr* (Beirut: 'Ālam al-Kutub, n.d.), K. al-Nikāḥ, "Fī tazwīj al-'abd wa 'l-ama," 190. See also Muḥammad al-Shaybānī, *Kitāb al-Ḥujja* (Hyderabad, India: Lajnat Iḥyā' al-Ma'ārif al-Nu'māniyya, 1965) (hereafter *Kitāb al-Ḥujja*), "Al-rajul yatazawwaj al-mar'a wa lā yajid mā yunfiq 'alayhā," 3:452, and ibid., *Al-Jāmi' al-Kabīr* (Lahore, Pakistan: Dār al-Ma'ārif al-Nu'māniyya, 1967), K. al-Qaḍā', "Bāb min al-nafaqa ayḍan," 193.

21. *Al-Umm*, K. al-Nafaqāt, "Bāb nafaqat al-'abd 'alā imra'atihi," 5:131.

22. *Mukhtaṣar al-Muzanī*, K. al-'Idad, "Al-ḥāl allatī yajibu fīhā al-nafaqa wa mā lā yajib," 9:246. Though the passage refers to a slave husband, the rule applies to free men married to slave women as well. See also *Al-Umm*, K. al-Nafaqāt, "Bāb fī 'l-ḥāl allatī tajib fīhā al-nafaqa wa lā tajib," 5:131.

23. *Al-Umm*, K. al-Ṣadāq, "Al-sharṭ fī 'l-nikāḥ," 5:107.

24. Literally, "she is narrowing what God made wide for him." *Al-Umm*, K. al-Ṣaḍāq, "Al-sharṭ fī 'l-nikāḥ," 5:108.

25. *Mudawwana*, K. al-Nikāḥ II, "Fī shurūṭ al-nikāḥ," 2:197. Statements ascribed to 'Umar in other texts espouse the opposite view.

26. Mālik ibn Anas, *Al-Muwaṭṭa' li 'l-Imām Mālik b. Anas, bi riwāyat Yaḥyā b. Yaḥyā b. Kathīr al-Laythī al-Andalusī* (Beirut: Dār al-Fikr, 1989) (hereafter *Muwaṭṭa'*), K. al-Nikāḥ, "Bāb mā lā yajūz min al-shurūṭ fī 'l-nikāḥ," 335. In other sections, a man's right to relocate his wife is simply assumed; see, for example, *Mudawwana*, K. Irkhā' al-Sutūr, "Nafaqāt al-wālid 'alā wildihi al-aṣāghir wa laysat al-umm 'indahu," 2:365–366

27. *Al-Umm*, K. al-Ṣadāq, "Al-sharṭ fī 'l-nikāḥ," 5:108.

28. Ibid.; *Mudawwana*, K. al-Nikāḥ IV, "Al-qasm bayna al-zawjāt," 2:270–271.

29. *Kitāb al-Ḥujja*, K. al-Nikāḥ, "Al-rajul yatazawwaj al-ama wa yashtaraṭ inna kulla waladin taliduhu ḥurr, 3:214–221; see also "Al-rajul yatazawwaj 'alā shay' ba'ḍuhu naqd wa ba'ḍuhu ilā ajal," 3:211–212.

30. *Mudawwana*, K. al-Nikāḥ II, "Fī shurūṭ al-nikāḥ," 2:197.

31. *Muwaṭṭa'*, K. al-Nikāḥ, "Bāb mā lā yajūz min al-shurūṭ fī 'l-nikāḥ," 335. This conflation of the validity of stipulations with the validity of conditional divorce oaths gives rise to a great deal of confusion in contemporary discussions of Islamic law, which often refer to women's ability to stipulate monogamy or other conditions. For Mālik, Abū Ḥanīfa, and Shāfiʿī, such stipulations are unenforceable as contractual conditions.

32. The *Kitāb al-Ḥujja* cites early authority Ibrāhīm al-Nakhāʿī's view that any stipulation made at marriage is "wiped out" by the marriage itself, with only stipulations attached to repudiations surviving. *Kitāb al-Ḥujja,* K. al-Nikāḥ, "Al-rajul yatazawwaj ʿalā shay' baʿḍuhu naqd wa baʿḍuhu ilā ajal," 3:210–211.

33. Thus, for instance, one scholar uses fourth-/eleventh-, fifth-/eleventh-, and eighth-/fourteenth-century Mālikī notarial formulae to show that "wives possess rights whose basic conditions may be included in the marriage contract." Among "these rights," she finds those preventing the husband from taking a concubine without the wife's consent, limiting his right to travel for extended periods, protecting her from major relocation, and securing her right to visit and be visited by close relatives. Christina de la Puente, "Juridical Sources for the Study of Women: Limitations of the Female's Capacity to Act According to Mālikī Law," in Manuela Marin and Randi Delguilhem, eds., *Writing the Feminine: Women in Arab Sources* (London and New York: I. B. Tauris, 2002),101–102.

34. If the wife died, her dower would be paid to her heirs.

35. Al-Khaṣṣāf, *Kitāb al-Nafaqāt,* 33.

36. Ibid., 34.

37. *Al-Umm,* K. al-Nafaqāt, "Wujūb nafaqat al-mar'a," 5:128.

38. *Kitāb al-Ḥujja,* K. al-Nikāḥ, "Al-rajul yaghīb wa lahu ibna ṣaghīra amara akhāhu an yuzawwijahā," 3:172.

39. Al-Khaṣṣāf, *Kitāb al-Nafaqāt,* "Bāb nafaqat al-mar'a ʿalā 'l-zawj wa mā yajibu lahā min dhālika," 36

40. *Al-Umm,* K. al-Nafaqāt, "Bāb fī 'l-ḥāl allatī tajib fīhā al-nafaqa wa lā tajib," 5:131. The legal discussions on this point remained similar until the Ottoman period. For judicial determinations about female readiness, see Judith E. Tucker, *In the House of the Law: Gender and Islamic Law in Ottoman Syria and Palestine* (Berkeley: University of California Press, 1998), 148, 155–156; Mahmoud Yazback, "Minor Marriages and *Khiyār al-Bulūgh* in Ottoman Palestine: A Note on Women's Strategies in a Patriarchal Society," *Islamic Law and Society* 9:3 (2002): 391–392 and passim. On child marriages in the Ottoman period more generally, see Harald Motzki, "Child Marriage in Seventeenth-Century Palestine," in Muḥammad Khalid Masud, Brinkley Messick, and David Powers, eds., *Islamic Law and Legal Interpretation: Muftis and Their Fatwas* (Cambridge, MA: Harvard University Press, 1998), 129–140; and Amira El Azhary Sonbol,

"Adults and Minors in Ottoman Sharīʿa Courts and Modern Law, in Sonbol, ed., *Women, the Family, and Divorce Laws in Islamic History* (Syracuse, NY: Syracuse University Press, 1996), 326–357. Discussing the Ottoman provincial town of Aintab, Leslie Peirce (*Morality Tales: Law and Gender in the Ottoman Court of Aintab* [Berkeley: University of California Press, 2003], 136–139) suggests that social norms might diverge considerably from legal doctrine and that laypeople were not always shy about expressing their views when they considered girls too young. Peirce suggests that laypeople's view of how old was old enough may have differed from the jurists' legal determination. As part of a broader discussion of virginity, sex, and property rights, Maya Shatzmiller (*Her Day in Court: Women's Property Rights in Fifteenth-Century Granada*, Harvard Series in Islamic Law [Cambridge, MA: Islamic Legal Studies Program, Harvard Law School, 2007], 97) affirms that "Jurists of all schools save that of the Hanafis agreed on the law's insistence that puberty was required before sexual intercourse was permissible." However, she also notes that "the legal status of sexual maturity for intercourse was neither clearly established nor forcefully stated in the law books; however, the common practice of child marriage put it to the test."

41. *Mudawwana*, K. al-Nikāḥ IV, "Fī nafaqat al-rajul ʿalā imraʾatihi," 2:254.

42. Ronen Yitzhak points to evidence that Ṣafiyya was seventeen at marriage and had already been married twice—divorced once, and then widowed at the battle where she was taken captive. See "Muhammad's Jewish Wives: Rayhana bint Zayd and Safiya bint Huyayy in the Classic Islamic Tradition," *Journal of Religion and Society* 9 (2007): 6. We must be wary of any attempt to treat the biographical literature on Muḥammad or his household as a straightforward repository of factual data.

43. *Mudawwana*, K. al-Nikāḥ IV, "Fī nafaqat al-rajul ʿalā imraʾatihi," 2:254.

44. Ibid., 2:255–256.

45. *Al-Umm*, K. al-Nafaqāt, "Bāb fī ʾl-ḥāl allatī tajib fīhā al-nafaqa wa lā tajib," 5:131. As in the preceding passage, the masculine form *bāligh* is used to refer to a woman; see also *Kitāb al-Nafaqāt*, "Bāb nafaqat al-marʾa ʿalā al-zawj wa mā yajib lahā min dhālika," 47; *Kitāb al-Ḥujja*, K. al-Nikāḥ, "Bāb al-marʾa al-kabīra yatazawwajuhā al-ṣaghīr fa tuṭālibu al-nafaqa," 3:483–486.

46. *Al-Umm*, K. al-Nafaqāt, "Bāb fī ʾl-ḥāl allatī tajibu fīhā al-nafaqa wa lā tajibu," 5:131; see also "Wujūb nafaqat al-marʾa," 5:128.

47. *Mudawwana*, K. al-Nikāḥ IV, "Alladhī lā yaqdiru ʿalā mahr imraʾatihi," 2:253; *Al-Umm*, K. al-Nafaqa, "Bāb al-rajul lā yajid mā yunfiq ʿalā imraʾatihi," 5:132–133; *Al-Jāmiʿ al-Ṣaghīr*, K. al-Nikāḥ, "Bāb fī ʾl-muhūr," 183.

48. *Al-Jāmiʿ al-Ṣaghīr*, K. al-Nikāḥ, "Bāb fī ʾl-muhūr," 183. See also *Kitāb al-Nafaqāt*, "Bāb nafaqat al-marʾa ʿalā al-zawj wa mā yajib lahā min dhālika," 35–36. Extant texts from the formative period shed no further light on the

logic behind Abū Ḥanīfa's view. Mona Siddiqui ("*Mahr:* Legal Obligation or Rightful Demand?" *Journal of Islamic Studies* 6 [1995]) argues that Abū Ḥanīfa holds that the dower obligation becomes more important after consummation and therefore the wife is justified in using various means to claim it. However, she does not cite specific textual evidence in support of this argument. If the father of a minor wife delivers her for consummation before she reaches majority, he may take her back even after consummation in order to promote full payment of the dower, because she did not originally consent to consummation. *Kitāb al-Nafaqāt,* "Bāb nafaqat al-mar'a ʿalā 'l-zawj wa mā yajib lahā min dhālika," 36.

49. *Kitāb al-Nafaqāt,* "Bāb nafaqat al-mar'a ʿalā 'l-zawj wa mā yajib lahā min dhālika," 48.

50. *Al-Umm,* K. al-Nafaqāt, "Bāb fī 'l-ḥāl allatī tajibu fīhā al-nafaqa wa lā tajib," 5:131. For instance, he might specify "whichever of my wives has given the most in charity." Proper information would have to be obtained to make a determination. Until then, he would have to abstain from sex with all of his wives. Here, *imtināʿ* describes the obstacle to intercourse that is the husband's fault. (Note that this particular scenario is my invention.)

51. *Kitāb al-Nafaqāt,* "Bāb nafaqat al-mar'a ʿalā 'l-zawj wa mā yajibu lahā min dhālika," 41.

52. *Kitāb al-Ḥujja,* K. al-Nikāḥ, "Bāb al-mar'a al-kabīra yatazawwajuhā al-ṣaghīr fa taṭlub al-nafaqa," 3:484–486.

53. *Qawwāmūn,* a notoriously contested concept, has been translated as "protectors and maintainers," "guardians," and "breadwinners." Some state that "men are in charge of women." (In addition to this verse, the term *qawwāmūn* also appears in Q. 4:135 and 5:8, where the context is not male *qiwāma* over women.) There are numerous reinterpretations of this verse, including some that suggest less patriarchal readings. See Karen Bauer, "Room for Interpretation: Qur'ānic Exegesis and Gender" (doctoral dissertation, Princeton University, 2008). See also the essays in the special issue of *Comparative Islamic Studies,* 4:3 (2006), as well as Ali, *Sexual Ethics and Islam,* chapter 7.

54. See Vardit Rispler-Chaim, "*Nušūz* between Medieval and Contemporary Islamic Law: The Human Rights Aspect," *Arabica* 39 (1992): 315–327; Sa'diyya Shaikh, "Exegetical Violence: Nushūz in Qur'anic Gender Ideology," *Journal of Islamic Studies* 17 (1997): 49–73.

55. I borrow the translation of *nushūz* as antipathy from Susan Spectorsky.

56. *Mudawwana,* K. Irkhā' al-Sutūr, "Mā jā'a fī khulʿ ghayr al-madkhūl bihā," 2:341–342.

57. Ibid.

58. Ibn ʿAbd al-Barr, *Al-Kāfī fī Fiqh Ahl al-Madīna* (Beirut, Dār al-Kutub al-ʿIlmiyya, 1987), K. al-Nikāḥ, "Bāb fī 'l-nafaqāt ʿalā 'l-zawjāt wa ḥukm al-

īʿsār bi ʾl-mahr wa ʾl-nafaqāt," 255; in this, Ibn al-Qāsim is said to differ from the other school authorities. This view was, though, held by Andalusian Ẓāhirī Ibn Ḥazm, who reasoned that neither Qurʾanic nor prophetic directives provided any basis for suspending the wife's support in cases of *nushūz*. Ibn Ḥazm, *Al-Muḥallā bi ʾl-Āthār*, ed. Aḥmad Muḥammad Shākir (Beirut: Dār al-Fikr, 1988), 7:88–89. It is possible that a different Andalusian Ibn Qāsim, who was connected to Ẓāhirism, might account for the confusion; see Christopher Melchert, *The Formation of the Sunni Schools of Law, 9th–10th Centuries* ce (Leiden, Netherlands: Brill, 1997), 186, n. 55.

59. David Santillana, *Instituzioni di Dirrito Musulmano Malichitta* (Rome: Istituto per L'Oriente, 1925), 1:230.

60. *Al-Umm*, K. al-Nafaqāt, "Wujūb nafaqat al-marʾa," 5:128; "Bāb ityān al-nisāʾ ḥayḍan," 5:132; *Mukhtaṣar al-Muzanī*, "Bāb ityān al-ḥāʾiḍ wa waṭʾ ithnatayn qabla al-ghusl," 9:187. See also A. Kevin Reinhart, "Impurity/No Danger," *History of Religions* 30 (1990): 1–24.

61. The *Mukhtaṣar al-Muzanī* discusses both illness and defects that arise after consummation in this passage, worth quoting: "Shāfiʿī, may God be merciful to him, said: If she is ill he is compelled [to provide] her maintenance; she is not like a minor. And if having intercourse with her will cause her grave harm, he is prohibited [from doing so] and she takes her maintenance. And if, after he has had intercourse with her, her vagina becomes obstructed *(wa law irtataqat)* and he cannot have intercourse with her, then this is an unfortunate malady, not withholding *(manʿun bihi)* by her." *Mukhtaṣar al-Muzanī*, K. al-ʿIdad, "Al-ḥāl allatī yajibu fīhā al-nafaqa wa mā lā yajib . . . ," 9:246; see also *Al-Umm*, K. al-Nafaqāt, "Bāb fī ʾl-ḥāl allatī tajib fīhā al-nafaqa wa lā tajib," 5:131. Worth investigation: a possible correlation between obstruction and infibulation, hinging on terms from the root *r-t-q*.

62. An exception to this rule is when he "dispatches" her on some type of journey; her undertaking that trip does not cancel her rights. *Mukhtaṣar al-Muzanī*, K. al-Wadīʿa, "Mukhtaṣar al-qism wa nushūz al-rajul ʿalā al-marʾa," 9:198. The *Jāmiʿ al-Kabīr* presents several scenarios together, including the wife's abduction, her imprisonment as a debtor, and her making pilgrimage without her husband. *Al-Jāmiʿ al-Kabīr*, K. al-Qaḍāʾ, "Bāb mā yanbaghī li ʾl-qāḍī an yaḍaʿahu ʿalā yaday ʿadlin idhā qaḍā bihi," 193. On the wife's abduction, see also *Kitāb al-Nafaqāt*, "Bāb nafaqat al-marʾa ʿalā ʾl-zawj wa mā yajib lahā min dhālika," 39.

63. *Al-Jāmiʿ al-Kabīr*, K. al-Qaḍāʾ, "Bāb mā yanbaghī li ʾl-qāḍī an yaḍaʿahu ʿalā yaday ʿadlin idhā qaḍā bihi," 193

64. *Al-Umm*, K. al-Nafaqāt, "Bāb fī ʾl-ḥāl allatī tajib fīhā al-nafaqa wa lā tajib," 5:131; *Mukhtaṣar al-Muzanī*, K. al-ʿIdad, "Al-ḥāl allatī yajibu fīhā al-nafaqa wa mā lā yajib . . . ," 9:246. Likewise, he does not suspend her maintenance for withdrawal to a mosque for spiritual retreat *(iʿtikāf)* during Ramadan if she

undertakes it with the husband's permission. Intercourse becomes forbidden for the wife during the retreat.

65. *Al-Jāmiʿ al-Kabīr,* K. al-Qaḍāʾ, "Bāb mā yanbaghī li ʾl-qāḍī an yaḍaʿahu ʿalā yaday ʿadlin idhā qaḍā bihi," 193

66. Al-Khaṣṣāf, *Kitāb al-Nafaqāt,* "Bāb nafaqat al-marʾa ʿalā ʾl-zawj wa mā yajib lahā min dhālika," 40.

67. Ibid., 41. Al-Khaṣṣāf does not specify what nonvaginal intercourse comprises. Other texts firmly prohibit anal sex but allow rubbing the penis between the buttocks or thighs. On distinctions between penetrative and intercrural intercourse in juridical definitions of male-male sex, see Khaled Al-Rouayheb, *Before Homosexuality in the Arab-Islamic World, 1500–1800* (Chicago: University of Chicago Press, 2005), 136–138.

68. On looking as a sexual act, see Shaybānī's discussion of expiatory consequences when a man in pilgrim sanctity ejaculates as a result of looking at his wife. Muḥammad al-Shaybānī, *Kitāb al-Aṣl, al-maʿrūf bi ʾl-Mabsūṭ* (Beirut: ʿĀlam al-Kutub, 1990), K. al-Manāsik, Bāb al-Jimāʿ, 2:395. The intersections of the scopic and the sexual merit substantial further investigation.

69. Al-Khaṣṣāf, *Kitāb al-Nafaqāt,* "Bāb nafaqat al-marʾa ʿalā ʾl-zawj wa mā yajib lahā min dhālika," 35–36. See also p. 39, on the parallel case of a woman who forbids her husband entry to the house where she is living, either with or without justification.

70. Likewise, for Abū Ḥanīfa she could leave the marital home and retain her right to support if she was doing so in order to claim her dower, even after consummation: "However, if her departure is to claim the dower, if he has gone in to her one time, Abū Ḥanīfa, may God be pleased with him, said she may do that and they [Abū Yūsuf and Muḥammad al-Shaybānī] said she may not. . . . That is if she goes out of his house." Ibid., 35–36,

71. Ibid., 36, n. 2.

72. The Ḥanafī jurists did not define nonconsensual sex in marriage as rape, but they distinguished between consensual and forced intercourse within marriage. (The Ḥanafīs make a point of ethical vs. legal distinctions in other cases as well.) The early jurists usually treated rape as *ghaṣb* or *ightiṣāb* (usurpation), a property crime that by definition could not be committed by the husband. On the issue of rape and sexual violence in Islamic law, see Hina Azam, "Sexual Violence in Maliki Legal Ideology: From Discursive Foundations to Classical Articulation" (doctoral dissertation, Duke University, 2007). See also the brief discussion in Ali, *Sexual Ethics and Islam,* 11–12.

73. Al-Khaṣṣāf, *Kitāb al-Nafaqāt,* "Bāb nafaqat al-marʾa ʿalā ʾl-zawj wa mā yajib lahā min dhālika," 35–36.

74. A pregnant divorcee's waiting period ended with delivery, whether this was shorter or longer than three months. Waiting periods also follow widowhood, but there is disagreement as to whether a pregnant widow must wait

the full four months and ten days specified for bereaved wives or whether she may remarry sooner if she delivers the child before that period is up.

75. Using some of these texts, G. R. Hawting has explored the issues of maintenance, and especially lodging, in his article "The Role of Qur'an and *Ḥadīth* in the Legal Controversy about the Rights of a Divorced Woman during her Waiting Period (*ʿIdda*)," *Bulletin of the School of Oriental and African Studies* 52:3 (1989): 430–445.

76. Exceptionally, a woman whose *maʿṣiya*, "sinful behavior," led to the divorce lost her claim to support during the waiting period. *Al-Jāmiʿ al-Kabīr*, K. al-Qaḍāʾ, "Bāb mā yanbaghī li ʾl-qāḍī an yaḍaʿahu ʿalā yaday ʿadlin idhā qaḍā," 193. If, however, she was a slave lodged with her master before the divorce, and the husband was not maintaining her, he did not have an obligation to do so after divorcing her.

77. *Kitāb al-Nafaqāt*, "Bāb nafaqat al-marʾa ʿalā ʾl-zawj wa mā yajib lahā min dhālika," 33.

78. Abū Yūsuf Yaʿqūb b. Ibrāhīm al-Anṣārī, *Kitāb al-Āthār*, ed. Abū ʾl-Wafāʾ (Hyderabad, India: Lajnat Iḥyāʾ al-Maʿārif al-Nuʿmāniyya, 1355 AH [1936 or 1937]) (hereafter Abū Yūsuf, *Kitāb al-Āthār*), "Bāb al-ʿIdda," 143, no. 645, where it is reported as the opinion of Ibrahīm al-Nakhaʿī. See also a slightly different formulation in *Al-Jāmiʿ al-Ṣaghīr*, K. al-Ẓihār, "Bāb al-ʿIdda," 231–232.

79. Also, Abū Ḥanīfa forbids him from marrying a slave woman if the wife in her waiting period was free, though Abū Yūsuf and Muḥammad al-Shaybānī allow it. *Al-Jāmiʿ al-Ṣaghīr*, K. al-Nikāḥ, "Bāb fī ʾl-nikāḥ al-fāsid," 177, 179; *Kitāb al-Ḥujja*, K. al-Nikāḥ, "Bāb al-rajul yakūn ʿindahu arbaʿ niswa fa yuṭalliqu wāḥida bāʾina innahu lā yatazawwaj ukhrā ḥattā tanqaḍī ʿiddat allatī ṭallaq," 3:406. See also Abū Yūsuf, *Kitāb al-Āthār*, "Bāb al-ʿidda," 147, nos. 671–672. Elsewhere, the jurists extensively discuss if and when a free man may marry an enslaved woman as well as the legality of combining free and slave women as wives.

80. See *Kitāb al-Ḥujja*, K. al-Nikāḥ, "Bāb al-rajul yakūn ʿindahu arbaʿ niswa fa yuṭalliq wāḥida bāʾina innahu lā yatazawwaj ukhrā ḥattā tanqaḍī ʿiddat allatī ṭallaq," 3:405–416, especially the citation of Saʿīd b. al-Musayyab on 3:411. See also *Ikhtilāf Abī Ḥanīfa*, "Bāb al-Ṭalāq," 209–210; Muḥammad al-Shaybānī, *Muwaṭṭaʾ al-Imām Mālik, bi riwayat Muḥammad b. al-Ḥasan al-Shaybānī* (Beirut: Al-Maṭbaʿa al-ʿIlmiyya, 1997) (hereafter *Muwaṭṭaʾ Shaybānī*), K. al-Nikāḥ, "Bāb al-rajul yakūn ʿindahu akthr min arbaʿ niswa fa yurīda an yatazzawaj," 178; and *Mudawwana*, K. al-Nikāḥ V, "Fī nikāḥ al-ukht ʿalā al-ukht fī ʿiddatihā," 2:283.

81. *Al-Umm*, K. al-Nafaqāt, "Al-khilāf fī hādha al-bāb," 5:216 and *Mudawwana*, K. al-Nikāḥ V, "Fī nikāḥ al-ukht ʿalā ʾl-ukht fī ʿiddatihā," 2:283; *Mukhtaṣar al-Muzanī*, "Mā yaḥillu min al-ḥarāʾir wa lā yatasarrā al-ʿabd wa

ghayr dhālika . . . ," 9:180; *Muwaṭṭa'*, K. al-Nikāḥ, "Bāb *Jāmiʿ* al-nikāḥ." There are possible exceptions in the case of a man who is ill when he repudiates his wife; at stake is how many wives will inherit from him.

82. *Mudawwana*, K. al-ʿIdda, "Mā jā'a fī nafaqat al-muṭallaqa wa suknāhā," 2:471.

83. See *Mudawwana*, K. al-Nikāḥ VII, "Fī nafaqat al-mukhtaliʿa al-ḥāmil wa ghayr al-ḥāmil wa 'l-mabtūta al-ḥāmil wa ghayr al-ḥāmil," 2:338–339.

84. *Al-Umm*, K. al-Nafaqāt, "Wujūb nafaqat al-mar'a," 5:128.

85. *Mudawwana*, K. al-ʿIdda, "Mā jā'a fī nafaqat al-muṭallaqa wa suknāhā," 2:471.

86. *Ikhtilāf*, "Bāb al-Ṭalāq," 195.

87. My emphasis. A variant reading of the Qur'an attributed to Ibn Masʿūd included "expend upon them" after "lodge them" in the first portion of the verse, but Hawting argues convincingly that its absence from these early texts proves that it was not in circulation at the time of Abū Ḥanīfa's teaching. See Hawting, "The Role of Qur'an and *Hadith*," 430–433. I am not convinced, though, by his suggestion (p. 432), following Burton, that deliberate falsification of the Qur'anic text was a routine practice for those who could not otherwise support their views.

88. Abū Yūsuf, *Kitāb al-Āthār*, "Abwāb al-Ṭalāq," 132, no. 608. On the question of the authoritativeness of prophetic hadith for early Ḥanafī authorities, see Benham Sadeki, "The Structure of Reasoning in Post-Formative Islamic Jurisprudence (Case Studies in Ḥanafī Laws on Women and Prayer)" (doctoral dissertation, Princeton University, 2006), 138–139; also 72–73. Using later sources, Sadeki notes the importance of *ikhtilāf* as "an arena where the roots of Ḥanafī law in the *Ḥadīth* could be demonstrated" (p. 139). Here again polemical exchange plays a key role in the development of doctrines and especially the rationales and evidence presented in defense of them.

89. *Mudawwana*, K. al-Nikāḥ IV, "Nafaqat al-ʿabīd ʿalā nisā'ihim," 2:256–258; *Al-Umm*, K. al-Nafaqāt, "Bāb nafaqat al-ʿabd ʿalā imra'atihi," 5:132. There were complicated exceptions when a slave was partially freed or party to *kitāba* (a contract to purchase his or her emancipation), or for an *umm walad* under certain limited circumstances. On the *umm walad* and the *mukātab*, see Jonathan Brockopp, *Early Mālikī Law: Ibn ʿAbd al-Ḥakam and His Major Compendium of Jurisprudence*, Studies in Islamic Law and Society, vol. 14 (Leiden, Netherlands: Brill, 2000).

90. *Mudawwana*, K. al-ʿIdda, "Mā jā'a fī nafaqat al-muṭallaqa wa suknāhā," 2:473–474. See similar passages in K. al-Nikāḥ IV, "Nafaqāt al-ʿabīd ʿalā nisā'ihim," 2:257. On the support of slaves in Ḥanafī doctrine, see al-Khaṣṣāf, *Kitāb al-Nafaqāt*.

91. Jennifer Glancy, *Slavery in Early Christianity* (Minneapolis: Fortress Press, 2006), 4, 25, 36. She notes on p. 9, "A male slave . . . had no legal con-

nection to his own offspring, thus excluding him from the cultural status of fatherhood."

92. De la Puente, "Esclavitud y matrimonio," misreads a key provision and argues against the notion that children resulting from marriage to enslaved women are slaves belonging to the mother's master.

93. *Mudawwana*, K. al-ʿIdda, "Mā jāʾa fī nafaqat al-muṭallaqa wa suknāhā," 2:473–474. See similar passages in K. al-Nikāḥ IV, "Nafaqāt al-ʿabīd ʿalā nisāʾihim," 2:257.

94. *Mudawwana*, K. al-ʿIdda, "Mā jāʾa fī nafaqat al-mukhtaliʿa wa ʾl-mubāriʾa wa suknāhuma," 2:474. Divorce through mutual imprecation can occur after delivery, as well. In all cases, *liʿān* absolves the husband of any duty to support his offspring and divests him of any legal rights associated with paternity.

95. *Mudawwana*, K. al-ʿIdda, "Mā jāʾa fī nafaqat al-muṭallaqa wa suknāhā," 2:471. Wet-nursing created fictive kin bonds. Legal works devote considerable space in their chapters on nursing to sorting out the marriage prohibitions created by milk fosterage.

96. *Al-Umm*, K. al-Nafaqāt, "Bāb nafaqat al-ʿabd ʿalā imraʾatihi," 5:132.

97. *Mukhtaṣar al-Muzanī*, K. al-ʿidad, "Imraʾat al-mafqūd wa ʿiddatihā idhā nakaḥat ghayrahu wa ghayr dhālika," 9:239. See also *Al-Umm*, K. al-ʿIdad, "ʿIddat al-ḥāmil," 5:320.

98. On legal maneuvering around this issue, see Tucker, *In the House of the Law*, 83–87.

99. *Mudawwana*, K. al-Nikāḥ IV, "Fī farḍ al-sulṭān al-nafaqa li ʾl-marʾa ʿalā zawjihā," 2:262–263.

100. Ibid., 2:258.

101. *Mudawwana*, K. al-ʿIdda, "Mā jāʾa fī nafaqat al-mukhtaliʿa wa ʾl-mubāriʾa wa suknāhumā," 2:474.

102. According to Ḥanafī doctrine, even if a slave wife is lodged with her husband and he is obligated to support her, she cannot get a divorce on grounds of nonsupport, whether her husband is free or slave, nor may her master obtain one on her behalf. Failure or inability to pay maintenance is no more grounds for marital dissolution in marriages of slaves than between free spouses. *Kitāb al-Ḥujja*, "Al-rajul yatazawwaj al-marʾa wa lā yajid mā yunfiq ʿalayhā," 3:451–452. However, the Mālikīs allow dissolution for nonsupport regardless of either spouse's freedom or enslavement. *Mudawwana*, K. al-Nikāḥ IV, "Fī nafaqat al-rajul ʿalā imraʾatihi," 2:255. The Shāfiʿīs hold that where the husband has an obligation to maintain his wife and fails to do so, if her master does not maintain her on the slave's behalf, the wife may choose to remain with a nonsupporting husband even against her master's wishes.

103. *Kitāb al-Ḥujja*, K. al-Nikāḥ, "Bāb al-rajul yatazawwaj al-marʾa wa lā yajid mā yunfiq ʿalā imraʾatihi," 3:451–452.

104. Ibid., 3:454.

105. Ibid., 3:459–462.

106. Ibid., 3:467.

107. Ibid., 3:456–457.

108. *Muwaṭṭaʾ*, K. al-Ṭalāq, "Bāb ajal alladhī lā yamassu imraʾatahu," 375; *Mudawwana*, K. Nikāḥ IV, "Fī ʾl-ʿinnīn," 2:265; *Muwaṭṭaʾ Shaybānī*, K. al-Nikāḥ, "Bāb al-rajul yankiḥu al-marʾa wa lā yaṣilu ilayhā li ʿilla bi ʾl-marʾa aw bi ʾl-rajul," 180; Abū Yūsuf, *Kitāb al-Āthār*, "Bāb al-khiyār," 141, nos. 640 and 642; *Al-Jāmiʿ al-Kabīr*, K. al-Nikāḥ, "Bāb min al-furqa min al-maraḍ," 107; *Mukhtaṣar al-Muzanī*, K. al-Wadīʿa, "Ajal al-ʿinnīn wa ʾl-khaṣī ghayr majbūb wa ʾl-khunthā," 9:191; *Al-Umm*, K. al-Nikāḥ, "Nikāḥ al-ʿinnīn wa ʾl-khaṣī wa ʾl-majbūb," 5:65. The Ẓāhirī Ibn Ḥazm held that impotence did not justify divorce, presumably on the basis that no textual support for this ruling exists. Jamal J. Nasir, *The Islamic Law of Personal Status*, 2nd ed. (London: Graham and Trotman, 1993), 131, citing *al-Muḥalla*.

109. *Al-Jāmiʿ al-Ṣaghīr*, K. al-Ẓihār, "Masāʾil min Kitāb al-Ṭalāq lam tadkhul fī ʾl-abwāb," 241–242.

110. *Al-Umm*, K. al-Nafaqāt, "Al-khilāf fī nafaqat al-marʾa," 5:154.

111. *Al-Umm*, K. al-Nafaqāt, "Al-khilāf fī nafaqat al-marʾa," 5:155. On "destruction of the self" *(itlāf li ʾl-nafs)* and the maintenance obligation, see also al-Khaṣṣāf, *Kitāb al-Nafaqāt*, "Bāb nafaqat al-marʾa ʿalā ʾl-zawj wa mā yajib lahā min dhālika," p. 20.

112. Gail Labovitz, *Marriage and Metaphor: Constructions of Gender in Rabbinic Literature* (Lanham, MD: Lexington Books, 2009), especially chapter 5, on property; Susan Treggiari, *Roman Marriage: Iusti Coniuges from the Time of Cicero to the Time of Ulpian* (Oxford: Oxford University Press, 1993).

113. Labovitz, *Marriage and Metaphor*, 168–171.

114. Daniel Boyarin, *Carnal Israel: Reading Sex in Talmudic Culture* (Berkeley: University of California Press, 1993), 142–146.

115. Judith Plaskow, edited with Donna Berman, *The Coming of Lilith: Essays on Feminism, Judaism, and Sexual Ethics, 1972–2003* (Boston: Beacon Press, 2005), 214-215.

116. Boyarin, *Carnal Israel*, 142.

117. *Qasm* is the verbal noun of *qasama*, to divide, apportion, or allot; a precise English rendering would result in the gerund "dividing," "apportioning," or "allotting." The noun describing the resulting quantity of time (or, infrequently, money) is *qism* or sometimes *qisma*, meaning "portion" or "allotment." *Qasm* is the husband's turn-taking and *qism* is each wife's allotted turn.

3. *Claiming Companionship*

1. [Saḥnūn b. Saʿīd al-Tanūkhī] Mālik b. Anas, *Al-Mudawwana al-Kubrā* (Beirut: Dār Ṣādir, 1323 AH [1905 or 1906]) (hereafter *Mudawwana*), K. al-

Nikāḥ VII, "Mā jā'a fī 'l-khulʿ," 2:335. See also Muḥammad al-Shaybānī, *Muwaṭṭa' al-Imām Mālik, bi riwāyat Muḥammad b. al-Ḥasan al-Shaybānī* (Beirut: Al-Maṭbaʿa al-ʿIlmiyya, 1997) (hereafter *Muwaṭṭa' Shaybānī*), K. al-Nikāḥ, 165.

2. *Mudawwana*, K. al-Nikāḥ IV, "Al-qasm bayna al-zawjāt," 2:270–271.

3. Ibid., 2:270.

4. Rachel Adler, *Engendering Judaism: An Inclusive Theology and Ethics* (Boston: Beacon, 1998), xix.

5. *Taʿaddud al-zawjāt*, plural marriage, looms large in modern discussions of Muslim marriage, both prescriptive and analytical. See Qasim Amin, *The Liberation of Women and the New Woman: Two Documents in the History of Egyptian Feminism*, trans. Samiha Sidhom Peterson (Cairo: American University in Cairo Press, 2000), 82–87, and Olivier Carré, *Mysticism and Politics: A Critical Reading of* Fī Ẓilāl al-Qur'ān *by Sayyid Quṭb*, trans. Carol Artigues, revised by W. Shepard (Leiden, Netherlands: Brill, 2003), 139–140, 145–147; Kate Zebiri, *Maḥmūd Shaltūt and Islamic Modernism* (Oxford: Clarendon, 1993), 63, 65–67; Judith E. Tucker, *Women, Family, and Gender in Islamic Law* (Cambridge: Cambridge University Press, 2008), 68, 75. For a typical example of popular literature, see Abdul Rahman al-Sheha, *Woman in the Shade of Islam*, trans. Mohammed Said Dabas (Khamis Mushait: Islamic Educational Center, 2000), 69–81, which centers on "western misconceptions." See also Azizah Y. Al-Hibri, "An Introduction to Muslim Women's Rights," in *Windows of Faith: Muslim Women Scholar-Activists in North America*, ed. Gisela Webb (Syracuse, NY: Syracuse University Press, 2000), 58–59. For a sampling of Indonesian discussion of the topic, see Pieternella van Doorn-Harder, *Women Shaping Islam: Reading the Qu'ran in Indonesia* (Urbana and Chicago: University of Illinois Press, 2006), 229–233, 255–258.

6. Nikki Keddie writes, "Most marriages were monogamous, with multiple wives reserved to a small elite." *Women in the Middle East: Past and Present* (Princeton: Princeton University Press, 2007), 42.

7. Muḥammad b. Idrīs al-Shāfiʿī, *Al-Umm* (Beirut: Dār al-Kutub al-ʿIlmiyya, 1993), K. al-Nafaqāt, "Tafrīʿ al-qism wa 'l-ʿadl baynahunna," 5:280; Mālik ibn Anas, *Al-Muwaṭṭa' li 'l-Imām Mālik b. Anas, bi riwāyat Yaḥyā b. Yaḥyā b. Kathīr al-Laythī al-Andalusī* (Beirut: Dār al-Fikr, 1989) (hereafter *Muwaṭṭa'*); K. al-Nikāḥ, "Bāb nikāḥ al-ama ʿalā al-ḥurra," 340; *Mudawwana*, K. al-Nikāḥ IV, "Al-qasm bayna al-zawjāt," 2:271, and K. al-Nikāḥ II, "Fī nikāḥ al-ama ʿalā 'l-ḥurra wa 'l-ḥurra ʿalā 'l-ama," 2:204–206; Muḥammad al-Shaybānī, *Kitāb al-Ḥujja ʿalā Ahl al-Madīna* (Hyderabad, India: Lajnat Iḥyā' al-Maʿārif al-Nuʿmāniyya, 1965)(hereafter *Kitāb al-Ḥujja*), K. al-Nikāḥ, "Al-ḥurra wa 'l-ama takūnān taḥta al-ḥurr," 3:254–263. Later texts attribute both views to Mālik. Unless otherwise noted, my discussion in the remainder of the chapter refers to free wives.

8. *Al-Umm,* K. al-Nafaqāt, "Tafrīʿ al-qism wa ʾl-ʿadl baynahunna," 5:281; Ismāʿīl b. Yaḥyā al-Muzanī, *Mukhtaṣar al-Muzanī (Al-Umm),* K. al-Wadīʿa, "Mukhtaṣar al-qasm wa nushūz al-rajul ʿalā al-marʾa," 9:198.

9. Except, of course, where Muḥammad's behavior is allowed exceptionally; then it may not set general precedent. For example, his having more than four wives does not mean that other male Muslims should or may take more than four wives.

10. *Mudawwana,* K. al-Nikāḥ IV, "Al-qasm bayna al-zawjāt," 2:268.

11. Ibid., 2:268–269.

12. Ibid., 2:272.

13. The fact that the *umm walad* came increasingly to be identified with a man's slaves rather than with his wife suggests a rigidifying of legal categories that merits further investigation.

14. *Al-Umm,* K. al-Nafaqāt, "Tafrīʿ al-qism wa ʾl-ʿadl baynahunna," 5:282. On the lack of claim of a slave concubine to a portion of her master's time, see also *Mukhtaṣar al-Muzanī,* K. al-Wadīʿa, "Mukhtaṣar al-qasm wa nushūz al-rajul ʿalā al-marʾa," 9:199.

15. *Mudawwana,* K. al-Nikāḥ IV, "Al-qasm bayna al-zawjāt," 2:269–270.

16. Ibid.

17. Ibid.

18. Ibid., 2:270.

19. *Al-Umm,* K. al-Nafaqāt, "Jummāʿ al-qasm li ʾl-nisāʾ," 5:280. For a later expression of the notion that one cannot control or "be held accountable" for love, see Khaled Al-Rouayheb, *Before Homosexuality in the Arab-Islamic World, 1500–1800* (Chicago: University of Chicago Press, 2005), 91.

20. Seeing the way early jurists treated some of the scriptural texts that are dragged into today's debates on matters such as polygamy can be helpful in highlighting the variability of interpretation. Some modern reformers have suggested that God forbids polygyny, because justice, required by Q. 4:3, is not attainable according to Q. 4:129 (the verse that figures in early discussions of partiality and justice). For a recent reading of Q. 4:3, see Ahmed Souaiaia, *Contesting Justice: Women, Islam, Law, and Society* (Albany: State University of New York Press, 2009), 50–57.

21. *Mudawwana,* K. al-Nikāḥ IV, "Al-qasm bayna al-zawjāt," 2:269–270.

22. Ibid., 2:272.

23. Ibid., 2:270.

24. *Al-Umm,* K. al-Nafaqāt, "Qasm al-nisāʾ idhā ḥaḍara al-safar," 5:160, and "Safar al-rajul bi ʾl-marʾa," 5:284.

25. *Al-Umm*'s section "Juristic disagreement on apportionment during travel" suggests that the Ḥanafī jurists held that a man could take whichever wife he wished but had to make up the days to those who remained behind. Even if he were to draw lots among his wives and take the one thus selected,

he would still have to compensate those who stayed home with an equivalent number of days. Without corroborating evidence from formative-period Ḥanafī sources, I would not draw any further conclusions. However, this is consistent with the Ḥanafī view about the wedding nights discussed later in this chapter. *Al-Umm*, K. al-Nafaqāt, "Al-khilāf fī 'l-qasm fī 'l-safar," 5:161. A similar view is found in at least one later Ḥanafī work, lending credence to the representation of the Ḥanafī position in *Al-Umm*. There, the Ḥanafī author criticizes the Shāfiʿī position. See Abū Bakr al-Kāsānī, *Badāʾiʿ al-Ṣanāʾiʿ fī Tartīb al-Sharāʾiʿ* (Beirut: Dār al-Kutub al-ʿIlmiyya, 1998), K. al-Nikāḥ, "Faṣl fī wujūb al-ʿadl bayna al-nisāʾ," 3:608. However, in the *Mabsūṭ*, al-Sarakhsī states, "If a man travels with one of his two wives for pilgrimage or another reason and, when he returns, the second [wife] requests that he stay with her the same amount of time that he spent with the other one on the journey, she is not due that. The days that he spent on his journey with the one who was with him are not counted against him. However, he does justice between the [two wives] in the future." Muḥammad ibn Aḥmad ibn Abī Sahl al-Sarakhsī, *Kitāb al-Mabsūṭ* (Beirut: Dār al-Kutub al-ʿIlmiyya, 2001), K. al-Nikāḥ, "Bāb al-qisma bayna al-nisāʾ," 5:206–207. This discussion makes no reference to drawing lots.

26. This is especially the case if he is absent during the nighttime portion of her turn. For example, if he visits one of his other wives during the day for anything but a necessity, or during the night for virtually any reason, he must make up this time. *Al-Umm*, K. al-Nafaqāt, "Tafrīʿ al-qasm wa 'l-ʿadl baynahunna," 5:282.

27. Assuming, of course, that the journey will not be too arduous or unsafe; he does not have the right to put her in jeopardy.

28. *Muwaṭṭaʾ*, K. al-Nikāḥ, "Bāb al-maqām ʿinda al-bikr wa 'l-thayyib," 334.

29. Shāfiʿī reports this hadith on Mālik's authority. *Al-Umm*, K. al-Nafaqāt, "Al-qasm li 'l-marʾa al-madkhūl bihā," 5:282–283.

30. *Mudawwana*, K. al-Nikāḥ IV, "Al-qasm bayna al-zawjāt," 2:269.

31. Behnam Sadeki, "The Structure of Reasoning in Post-Formative Islamic Jurisprudence (Case Studies in Ḥanafī Laws on Women and Prayer)" (doctoral dissertation, Princeton University, 2006).

32. *Muwaṭṭaʾ Shaybānī*, K. al-Nikāḥ, "Bāb al-rajul yakūn lahu niswah, kayfa yaqsim baynahunna," 176. This is the only discussion of apportionment in the *Muwaṭṭaʾ Shaybānī*'s sections on marriage and divorce.

33. *Kitāb al-Ḥujja*, K. al-Nikāḥ, "Bāb al-qasm bayna al-nisāʾ," 3:246. The passage goes on to describe the Medinan view: "The people of Medina say: If the one he married is a virgin, he stays seven with her, and if she is a non-virgin, he stays three with her before he apportions to the one who [already] was [married] to him, then he apportions his time between them both after it."

34. Ibid., 3:247.

35. The text provides another hadith that eliminates the second portion altogether: "Muḥammad said: And so Abū Ḥanīfa reported to us from al-Haytham b. Abī al-Haytham. He said: When the Messenger of God, may God's blessings and peace be upon him and his family, married Umm Salama and he consummated the marriage with her, he gave her barley gruel and dates and said "If you wish I will spend seven with you and seven with your companions."

36. *Kitāb al-Ḥujja,* K. al-Nikāḥ, "Bāb al-qasm bayna al-nisā'," 3:249–252.

37. At least one later (Shāfiʿī) text attempts to make sense of this vexing problem. According to *The Reliance of the Traveler,* if the non-virgin bride requests that the husband stay seven nights, then he must make up all seven to his other wife or wives. However, if he stays seven with her of his own accord, without her request that he do so, then he must only make up four nights to his other wives. This text also states that it is ultimately the husband's choice as to how many nights to stay with a non-virgin *(fa huwa bi 'l-khiyār).* Aḥmad b. Naqīb al-Miṣrī, *ʿUmdat al-Sālik,* in Nuh Ha Mim Keller, ed. and trans. (with parallel Arabic text), *Reliance of the Traveller: A Classic Manual of Islamic Sacred Law* (Beltsville, MD: Amana, 1999, 1991): 540.

38. *Kitāb al-Ḥujja,* K. al-Nikāḥ, "Bāb al-qasm bayna al-nisā'," 3:252–253.

39. See the treatment of the Umm Salama hadith in *al-Umm,* K. al-Nafaqāt, "Al-khilāf fī 'l-qasm li 'l-bikr wa li 'l-thayyib," 5:159–160.

40. *Al-Umm,* K. al-Nafaqāt, "Al-ḥāl allatī yakhtalifu fīhā ḥal al-nisā'," 5:159.

41. Ibid.

42. *Al-Umm,* K. al-Nafaqāt, "Al-qasm li 'l-mar'a al-madkhūl bihā," 5:283.

43. Ibid. The use of the feminine dual here means "they" are the brides in question.

44. The discrepancies in evidence here (and elsewhere) suggest that Norman Calder (in *Studies in Early Muslim Jurisprudence* [Oxford: Clarendon, 1993]) is correct in his assertion that al-Muzanī was working with a different version of Shāfiʿī's corpus than the finalized *Umm;* see also Jonathan Brockopp, "Early Islamic Jurisprudence in Egypt: Two Scholars and Their *Mukhtaṣars," International Journal of Middle Eastern Studies* 30:2 (1998): 167–182.

45. *Mukhtaṣar al-Muzanī,* K. al-Wadīʿa, "Bāb al-ḥāl allatī yakhtalifu fīhā ḥāl al-nisā'," 9:199.

46. Vardit Rispler-Chaim, "The Muslim Surgeon and Contemporary Ethical Dilemmas Surrounding the Restoration of Virginity," *Hawwa* 5:2–3:329.

47. See Rispler-Chaim, "The Muslim Surgeon," 327, for a modern take on the "state of mind" of a virgin bride on the wedding night.

48. Paul Powers, *Intent in Islamic Law: Motive and Meaning in Medieval Sunni Fiqh* (Leiden, Netherlands: Brill, 2005), 125.

49. Yossef Rapoport, *Marriage, Money, and Divorce in Medieval Islam* (Cambridge: Cambridge University Press, 2005), 61.

50. Maya Shatzmiller, *Her Day in Court: Women's Property Rights in Fifteenth-Century Granada*, Harvard Series in Islamic Law (Cambridge, MA: Islamic Legal Studies Program, Harvard Law School, 2007); Basim Musallam, *Sex and Society in Islam: Birth Control before the Nineteenth Century* (Cambridge: Cambridge University Press, 1983).

51. A vast and complicated array of ideas about female desire circulated in legal, moralistic, and literary works. See Fedwa Malti-Douglas, *Woman's Body, Woman's Word: Gender and Discourse in Arabo-Islamic Writing* (Princeton: Princeton University Press, 1991), and, briefly, Al-Rouayheb, *Before Homosexuality*, 66–67.

52. Ibn Ḥanbal is sometimes said to hold that a master must "fortress" his own female slave, meeting her need for sex or marrying her off, but this is far outside the mainstream.

53. These ambiguities are presented clearly in the writings of the fifth-/eleventh-century polymath al-Ghazali, who argued for men's responsibility to keep their wives satisfied: a deprived woman might become depraved. She might seek illicit satisfaction, incurring disastrous consequences. On the positive side, at the personal rather than social level, al-Ghazali noted that sex could increase affection between spouses. He added, almost as an afterthought, that women were people with needs and desires like men. Al-Ghazali, *Marriage and Sexuality in Islam: A Translation of Al-Ghazali's Book on the Etiquette of Marriage from the* Ihya', ed. and trans. Madelain Farah (Salt Lake City: University of Utah Press, 1984). See also Sadeki, "The Structure of Reasoning," 114–115, with regard to desire in prayer.

54. *Mukhtaṣar al-Muzanī*, K. al-Wadīʿa, "Mukhtaṣar al-qasm wa nushūz al-rajul ʿalā al-marʾa . . . ," 9:198.

55. Ibid.; *Al-Umm*, K. al-Nafaqāt, "Bāb ityān al-nisāʾ ḥayḍan," 5:132.

56. *Mudawwana*, K. al-Nikāḥ IV, "Al-qasm bayna al-zawjāt," 2:271–272.

57. *Al-Umm*, K. al-Nafaqāt, "Tafrīʿ al-qasm wa ʾl-ʿadl baynahunna," 5:281. See also *Mudawwana*, K. al-Nikāḥ IV, "Al-qasm bayna al-zawjāt," 2:272.

58. See Shaun Marmon, *Eunuchs and Sacred Boundaries in Islamic Society* (New York: Oxford University Press, 1995), and Paula Sanders, "Gendering the Ungendered Body: Hermaphrodites in Medieval Islamic Law," in Nikki R. Keddie and Beth Baron, eds., *Women in Middle Eastern History: Shifting Boundaries in Sex and Gender* (New Haven: Yale University Press, 1991), 74–95.

59. *Al-Umm*, K. al-Nafaqāt, "Tafrīʿ al-qasm wa ʾl-ʿadl baynahunna," 5:281.

60. *Mudawwana*, K. al-Nikāḥ IV, "Al-qasm bayna al-zawjāt," 2:271.

61. Ibid.

62. *Al-Umm*, K. al-Nafaqāt, "Tafrīʿ al-qasm wa ʾl-ʿadl baynahunna," 5:280–281.

63. *Al-Umm*, K. al-Nafaqāt, "Al-khulʿ wa ʾl-nushūz," 5:279.

64. *Al-Umm*, K. al-Nafaqāt, "Tafrīʿ al-qasm wa ʾl-ʿadl baynahunna," 5:281.

65. *Mudawwana,* K. al-Nikāḥ IV, "Al-qasm bayna al-zawjāt," 2:270; *Al-Umm,* K. al-Nafaqāt, Tafrīʿ al-qasm wa ʾl-ʿadl baynahunna," 5:281.

66. *Al-Umm,* K. al-Nafaqāt, "Nushūz al-rajul ʿalā imraʾatihi," 5:162.

67. Gerald Hawting has dealt with other aspects of these oaths in detail in "An Ascetic Vow and an Unseemly Oath? *Īlāʾ* and *Ẓihār* in Muslim Law," *Journal of the School for Oriental and African Studies* 57:1 (1994): 113–125. On the terminology of oaths and vows, see Norman Calder, "Ḥinth, Birr, Tabarrur, Taḥannuth: An Inquiry into the Arabic Vocabulary of Vows," *Journal of the School for Oriental and African Studies* 51:2 (1998): 214–239.

68. The Mālikīs hold that *ẓihār* may apply to any woman over whom a man has sexual rights, including a slave concubine; the Ḥanafīs and Shāfiʿīs hold that it can apply only to a wife. *Muwaṭṭaʾ,* K. al-Ṭalāq, "Bāb al-īlāʾ," 356; *Mudawwana,* K. al-Ẓihār, "Ẓihār al-rajul min amatihi wa umm waladihi wa mudabbiratihi," 3:51; *Al-Jāmiʿ al-Ṣaghīr,* K. al-Ẓihār, 223; *Al-Umm,* K. al-ʿIdad, "Al-Ẓihār," 5:396; *Mukhtaṣar al-Muzanī,* K. al-Ẓihār, "Bāb mā yakūn ẓihār wa mā lā yakūn ẓihār," 217. For further discussion of Mālikī perspectives on *ẓihār,* see Yasin Dutton, *The Origins of Islamic Law: The Qur'an, the* Muwaṭṭaʾ *and Madinan ʿAmal* (Surrey: Curzon Press, 1999), 65–68.

69. Q. 58:2–4; *ẓihār* is also mentioned briefly in 33:4.

70. *Al-Umm,* K. al-Nafaqāt, "Tafrīʿ al-qasm wa ʾl-ʿadl baynahunna," 5:282; *Mukhtaṣar al-Muzanī,* K. al-Wadīʿa, "Mukhtaṣar al-qasm wa nushūz al-rajul ʿalā al-marʾa . . . ," 9:198.

71. Q. 2:226–227.

72. Abū Yūsuf Yaʿqūb, *Ikhtilāf Abī Ḥanīfa wa Ibn Abī Laylā, li ʾl-imām Abī Yūsuf Yaʿqūb b. Ibrāhīm al-Anṣārī* (hereafter *Ikhtilāf Abī Ḥanīfa wa Ibn Abī Laylā*) (Cairo: Maṭbaʿat al-Wafāʾ, 1938), "Bāb al-Ṭalāq," 196–197; *Muwaṭṭaʾ,* K. al-Ṭalāq, "Bāb al-īlāʾ," 354. The *Muwaṭṭaʾ* records the opinion of some early Medinese authorities, including Saʿīd b. al-Musayyab, who held that forswearing automatically led to a revocable divorce if four months expired before the husband had intercourse with his wife. Mālik, however, held that nothing automatically happened after the expiry of four months, and his opinion was followed as authoritative.

73. Majid Khadduri, trans., *Islamic Jurisprudence: Shafiʾi's* Risala (Baltimore: Johns Hopkins University Press, 1961), 339–345.

74. *Mudawwana,* K. al-Īlāʾ wa ʾl-Liʿān, "Fī man ālā min imraʾatihi thumma sāfara ʿanhā," 3:98.

75. She had no legal recourse on grounds of forswearing. See, e.g., *Ikhtilāf Abī Hanīfa wa Ibn Abī Laylā,* "Bāb al-Ṭalāq," 196–197. Ibn Abī Laylā held that in such cases, an irrevocable divorce did occur.

76. Ibn Abī Laylā again differed; see ibid.

77. *Ikhtilāf Abī Hanīfa wa Ibn Abī Laylā,* "Bāb al-Ṭalāq," 198. See also *Al-Jāmiʿ al-Ṣaghīr,* "Kitāb al-īlāʾ," 219–221.

78. *Mukhtaṣar al-Muzanī,* K. al-Ṭalāq, "Bāb al-īlāʾ," 9:212.

79. *Mudawwana,* K. al-īlā' wa 'l-Li'ān, "Fī man qāla: Wa Allāhi, lā aṭa'uki fī dārī hādhihi sana aw fī hādhā al-miṣr," 3:87.

80. Ibn al-Qāsim gives a similar order in a related case; see *Mudawwana,* K. al-Īlā' wa 'l-Li'ān, "Fī man qāla: 'Alayya nadhr an lā aqrubaki," 3:87.

81. *Mukhtaṣar al-Muzanī,* K. al-Ṭalāq, "Bāb al-īlā'," 9:212.

82. See also *Mudawwana,* K. al-Īlā' wa 'l-Li'ān, "Fī man qāla: 'Alayya nadhr an lā aqrubaki," 3:87.

83. See *Muwaṭṭa',* K. al-Ṭalāq, "Bāb ẓihār al-ḥurr," 357; *Mudawwana,* K. al-Ẓihār, "Al-rajul yuẓāhir wa yūlī wa fī idkhāl al-īlā' 'alā 'l-ẓihār wa man arāda al-waṭ' qabla al-kaffāra," 3:61.

84. *Muwaṭṭa',* K. al-Ṭalāq, "Bāb al-īlā'," 357.

85. *Ikhtilāf Abī Hanīfa wa Ibn Abī Laylā,* "Bāb al-Ṭalāq," 198.

86. *Al-Umm,* K. al-'Idad, "Man yajib 'alayhi al-ẓihār wa man lā yajib 'alayhi," 5:395–396; *Mukhtaṣar al-Muzanī,* K. al-Ẓihār, Bāb mā yajib 'alayhi min al-ẓihār wa mā lā yajib 'alayhi . . . ," 9:216–217.

87. *Mukhtaṣar al-Muzanī,* K. al-Ẓihār, "Bāb mā yajib 'alayhi min al-ẓihār wa mā lā yajib 'alayhi . . . ," 9:216–217; see also *Al-Umm,* K. al-'Idad, "Man yajib 'alayhi al-ẓihār wa man lā yajib 'alayhi," 5:395–396, and *Ikhtilāf,* "Bāb al-Ṭalāq," 196–197.

88. *Mukhtaṣar al-Muzanī,* K. al-Ẓihār, "Bāb mā yajib 'alayhi min al-ẓihār wa mā lā yajib 'alayhi . . . ," 9:216–217; *Al-Umm,* K. al-'Idad, "Man yajib 'alayhi al-ẓihār wa man lā yajib 'alayhi," 5:395–396.

89. *Mukhtaṣar al-Muzanī,* K. al-Ẓihār, "Bāb mā yūjib 'alā al-mutaẓāhir al-kaffāra . . . ," 9:218.

90. *Mudawwana,* K. al-Īlā' wa 'l-Li'ān, "Fī man ālā min imra'atihi thumma sāfara 'anhā," 3:98.

91. Ibid., 3:101. Compare this with the Shāfi'ī view, presented in the *Mukhtaṣar al-Muzanī* (K. al-Ṭalāq, "Bāb īlā' al-khaṣī ghayr al-majbūb wa 'l-majbūb . . . ," 9:215): "Shāfi'ī, may God be pleased with him, said: If he forswears her while healthy then his penis is severed, she may choose at that time between remaining with him or separating from him."

92. *Mudawwana,* K. al-Īlā' wa 'l-Li'ān, "Fī man ālā min imra'atihi thumma sāfara 'anhā," 3:101.

93. *Mudawwana,* K. al-Nikāḥ VII, "Mā jā'a fī 'l-khul'," 2:335. This passage appears not in a passage about apportionment but rather in a discussion of female-initiated divorce.

94. *Muwaṭṭa' al-Shaybānī,* "K. al-Nikāḥ, "Bāb al-rajul yakūn 'indahu imra'atān fa yu'thir iḥdāhumā 'alā 'l-ukhrā," 198–199.

95. *Al-Umm,* K. al-Nafaqāt, "Al-khul' wa 'l-nushūz," 5:278.

96. Ibid., 5:279.

97. Abū Yūsuf, Abū Yūsuf Ya'qūb b. Ibrāhīm al-Anṣārī, *Kitāb al-Āthār,* ed. Abū 'l-Wafā' (Hyderabad, India: Lajnat Iḥyā' al-Ma'ārif al-Nu'māniyya, 1355 AH [1936 or 1937]) "Bāb al-'idda," 146, 667.

98. *Al-Umm,* K. al-Nafaqāt, "Al-khulʿ wa ʾl-nushūz," 5:278–279.

99. Ibid., 5:279.

100. *Muwaṭṭaʾ al-Shaybānī,* K. al-Nikāḥ, "Bāb al-rajul yakūn ʿindahu imraʾatān fa yuʾthir iḥdāhumā ʿalā ʾl-ukhrā," 198–199.

101. *Mudawwana,* K. al-Nikāḥ IV, "Al-qasm bayna al-zawjāt," 2:270.

102. *Al-Umm,* K. al-Nafaqāt, "Al-khulʿ wa ʾl-nushūz," 5:279. Aside from the question of justice to the wife, a jurisprudential issue was at stake: whether the wife could forgo a future claim. This seems to be for Shāfiʿī the critical issue; the wife could not waive all future rights to apportionment, just as she could not waive all future rights to maintenance, simply because those rights were not yet hers to forgo. Sherman A. Jackson, "*Kramer vs. Kramer* in a Tenth/Sixteenth Century Egyptian Court: Post-Formative Jurisprudence between Exigency and Law," *Islamic Law and Society* 8:1 (2001): 27–51, explores another case where the same issue (forgoing future rights) is at stake. Among other lessons from these parallels, we see the consistency of certain legal principles applied across subject matter areas within a *madhhab.*

103. *Al-Umm,* K. al-Nafaqāt, "Al-khulʿ wa ʾl-nushūz," 5:279.

104. Leila Ahmed, *Women and Gender in Islam: Historical Roots of a Modern Debate* (New Haven: Yale University Press, 1992).

4. Untying the Knot

1. Presumably he has witnesses who could attest to it, proving that he did take her back while he still had the right to do so. Mālikī and Ḥanafī jurists agreed that if the wife's waiting period had ended, the husband could not subsequently claim to have returned to her, even if she concurred, unless there was proof of some sort; to allow it would be tantamount to permitting a new marriage contract "without dower or a marriage guardian." [Saḥnūn b. Saʿīd al-Tanūkhī] Mālik b. Anas, *Al-Mudawwana al-Kubrā* (Beirut: Dār Ṣādir, 1323 AH [1905 or 1906]) (hereafter *Mudawwana*), K. Irkhāʾ al-Sutūr, "Al-rajʿa," 2:325; also see "Daʿwa al-marʾa inqiḍāʾ ʿiddatihā," 2:330. See also Abū Yūsuf Yaʿqūb b. Ibrāhīm al-Anṣārī, Kitāb al-Āthār, ed. Abū ʾl-Wafāʾ (Hyderabad, India: Lajnat Iḥyāʾ al-Maʿārif al-Nuʿmāniyya, 1355 AH [1936 or 1937]), "Abwāb al-ṭalāq," 128, no. 591; 130, no. 597; and, for a contrary view, 129, no. 549. In Muḥammad ibn Idrīs al-Shāfiʿī, *Al-Umm* (Beirut: Dār al-Kutub al-ʿIlmiyya, 1993) (hereafter *Al-Umm*), Al-ʿIdad, "Wajh al-rajʿa," 5:354, and K. al-Nikāḥ, 5:29, Shāfiʿī stated that if the wife denied that he had taken her back and he did not have witnesses, then the *ṭalāq* stood, but if she acknowledged the return, the resumption of marital relations was permissible.

2. Muḥammad al-Shaybānī, *Kitāb al-Ḥujja* (Hyderabad, India: Lajnat Iḥyāʾ al-Maʿārif al-Nuʿmāniyya, 1965) (hereafter *Kitāb al-Ḥujja*), K. al-Nikāḥ, "Bāb al-rajul yuṭalliq imraʾatahu thumma yurājiʿuhā fa yablughuhā ṭalāquhu wa lā yablughuhā rajʿatahu," 4:133.

3. *Kitāb al-Ḥujja*, K. al-Nikāḥ, "Bāb al-rajul yuṭalliq imra'atahu thumma yurājiʿuhā fa yablughuhā ṭalāquhu wa lā yablughuhā rajʿatahu," 4:133.

4. For a brief overview, see Noel Coulson, *A History of Islamic Law* (Edinburgh: Edinburgh University Press, 1964), 111–113.

5. Generally, Sunni jurists have held that triple divorces are valid and Shiʿi jurists have held that they are not. Some isolated Sunni opinions (e.g., Ibn Taymiyya) have rejected the consensus view on so-called triple repudiations, considering them to count only as a single *ṭalāq*. See Coulson, *A History of Islamic Law*, 111–113; on Ibn Taymiyya, see Yossef Rapoport, *Marriage, Money and Divorce in Medieval Islamic Society* (Cambridge: Cambridge University Press, 2005), 97ff. (and on p. 109 a fascinating discussion of the link between personal oaths and allegiance to the sultan); and see Frank E. Vogel, "The Complementarity of *Iftā'* and *Qaḍā'*: Three Saudi Fatwas on Divorce," in Muḥammad Khalid Masud, Brinkley Messick, and David S. Powers, eds., *Islamic Legal Interpretation: Muftis and Their Fatwas* (Cambridge, MA: Harvard University Press, 1996), 262–269, for contemporary application.

6. Paul R. Powers, *Intent in Islamic Law: Motive and Meaning in Medieval Sunnī* Fiqh (Leiden, Netherlands: Brill, 2006), 144. On intent in divorce more generally, see pp. 124 and 130–153.

7. Susan Spectorsky outlines the impact of various types of statements of divorce according to Ibn Ḥanbal and Ibn Rāhawayh. Though their views do not always coincide with those of the jurists studied here, Spectorsky's analysis gives the flavor of early legal discussions over *ṭalāq*. See Susan A. Spectorsky, ed. and trans., *Chapters on Marriage and Divorce: Responses of Ibn Ḥanbal and Ibn Rāhwayh* (Austin: University of Texas Press, 1993), 27–39. See also Scott C. Lucas, "Divorce, Hadith-Scholar Style: From al-Dārimī to al-Tirmidhī," *Journal of Islamic Studies* 19:3 (2008): 325–68.

8. Norman Calder, "Ḥinth, Birr, Tabarrur, Taḥannuth: An Inquiry into the Arabic Vocabulary of Vows," *Journal of the School for Oriental and African Studies* 51:2 (1998): 216.

9. Gail Labovitz, *Marriage and Metaphor: Constructions of Gender in Rabbinic Literature* (Lanham, MD: Lexington Books, 2009), 162. She qualifies the "male" agent (n. 38) here, but Jewish women's control over property including slaves was circumscribed by marriage in ways not sanctioned by the majority of Muslim jurists.

10. Labovitz, *Marriage and Metaphor*, 164.

11. Rapoport, *Marriage, Money, and Divorce*, 108–109.

12. Ibid., 110.

13. Muḥammad al-Shaybānī, *Al-Jāmiʿ al-Kabīr* (Lahore, Pakistan: Dār al-Maʿārif al-Nuʿmāniyya, 1967), K. al-Ṭalāq, "Bāb min al-amr yujʿalu fī yaday al-rajul fī 'l-ṭalāq wa ghayrihi," 180. For another analogy, with regard to the use of *istithnā'* in repudiation and manumission, see Abū Yūsuf Yaʿqūb, *Ikhtilāf Abī Ḥanīfa wa Ibn Abī Laylā, li 'l-imām Abī Yūsūf Yaʿqūb b. Ibrāhīm al-Anṣārī*

(Cairo: Maṭbaʿat al-Wafāʾ, 1938) (hereafter *Ikhtilāf Abī Ḥanīfa wa Ibn Abī Laylā*), Bāb al-Ṭalāq, 215–216; also Abū Yūsuf, *Kitāb al-Āthār*, "Abwāb al-Ṭalāq," 136–137, B620, B621.

14. In Ḥanafī (and Shāfiʿī) doctrine, only a free person can own slaves; under Mālikī *fiqh*, slaves can as well. See Chapter 5 in this book.

15. Muḥammad al-Shaybānī, *Al-Jāmiʿ al-Ṣaghīr* (Beirut: ʿĀlam al-Kutub, n.d.), K. al-Ṭalāq, "Bāb al-kināyāt," 206; Ismāʿīl b. Yaḥyā al-Muzanī, *Mukhtaṣar al-Muzanī* (*Al-Umm*), K. al-Ṭalāq, "Bāb mā yaqaʿ bihi al-ṭalāq min al-kalām wa mā lā yaqaʿ illā bi ʾl-niyya," 9:206.

16. *Mukhtaṣar al-Muzanī*, K. al-Ṭalāq, "Bāb mā yaqaʿ bihi al-ṭalāq min al-kalām wa mā lā yaqaʿ illā bi ʾl-niyya," 9:206.

17. *Al-Jāmiʿ al-Ṣaghīr*, K. al-Ṭalāq, "Bāb al-kināyāt," 206.

18. *Al-Jāmiʿ al-Ṣaghīr*, K. al-Ṭalāq, "Bāb al-aymān fī ʾl-ṭalāq," 202.

19. Ibid. See also *Al-Jāmiʿ al-Kabīr*, K. al-Ṭalāq, "Bāb fī ʾl-ṭalāq alladhī yaqaʿ bi ʾl-waqt wa alladhī lā yaqaʿ," 181. (Presumably, in the case of the manumitted slave, if a new penetration occurs he would owe her a compensatory dower.) Payment of a fair dower serves as an alternative to *ḥadd* punishment for extralegal sex where there is exculpatory doubt *(shubha)*. Similar examples of concern with an oath of *ṭalāq* that takes effect with intercourse can be found in other texts, including *Mukhtaṣar al-Muzanī*, K. al-Ṭalāq, "Bāb al-īlāʾ," 9:212.

20. *Mukhtaṣar al-Muzanī*, "Bāb al-ṭalāq qabla al-nikāḥ min al-Imlāʾ ʿalā Masāʾil Ibn al-Qāsim . . . ," 9:202.

21. *Mukhtaṣar al-Muzanī*, K. al-Khulʿ, "Bāb mā yaqaʿ wa mā lā yaqaʿ ʿalā imraʾatihi . . . ," 9:202. See parallel use in *Al-Umm*, K. al-Nafaqāt, "Ikhtilāf al-rajul wa ʾl-marʾa fī ʾl-khulʿ," 5:300. See the use by Ibn Ḥanbal—though he does not explicitly attribute this statement to the Prophet Muḥammad—in Spectorsky, *Chapters on Marriage and Divorce*, 123. Spectorsky explores this maxim in a bit more depth in Susan A. Spectorsky, "*Sunnah* in the Responses of Isḥāq b. Rāhwayh," in Bernard G. Weiss, ed., *Studies in Islamic Legal Theory* (Leiden, Netherlands: Brill, 2002), 68–70.

22. Mālik and his followers void general oaths such as "every woman I marry is divorced." However, if the husband makes the oath specific, limiting its application to a certain woman or women and leaving himself free to marry others, then the oath is valid. See Mālik ibn Anas, *Al-Muwaṭṭaʾ li ʾl-Imām Mālik b. Anas, bi riwāyat Yaḥyā b. Yaḥyā b. Kathīr al-Laythī al-Andalusī* (Beirut: Dār al-Fikr, 1989) (hereafter *Muwaṭṭaʾ*), K. al-Ṭalāq , "Bāb yamīn al-rajul bi ṭalāq mā lam yankiḥ," 374. The Ḥanafīs, however, hold that virtually all such oaths are permissible and binding, including those that are universal. See *Kitāb al-Ḥujja*, K. al-Nikāḥ, "Bāb al-rajul yaqūl: Kullu imraʾa atazawwajuhā min banī fulān fa hiya ṭāliq thalāthatan al-batta," 3:289–293; "Bāb al-rajul yaqūl li imraʾatihi: Kullu imraʾa atazawwajuhā ʿalayk fa hiya ṭāliq al-batta," 3:293–298; "Bāb al-

rajul yaqūl: Kullu imra'a atazawwajuhā mā ʿāsha fulān fa hiya ṭāliq al-batta," 3:305; Muḥammad al-Shaybānī, *Muwaṭṭa' al-Imām Mālik, bi riwāyat Muḥammad b. al-Ḥasan al-Shaybānī* (Beirut: Al-Maṭbaʿa al-ʿIlmiyya, 1997) (hereafter *Muwaṭṭa' Shaybānī*), K. al-Ṭalāq, "Bāb al-rajul yaqūl: Idhā nakaḥtu fulāna fa hiya ṭāliq," 189–190; *Al-Jāmiʿ al-Ṣaghīr*, K. al-Ṭalāq, "Bāb ṭalāq al-sunna," 192–193; *Ikhtilāf Abī Ḥanīfa wa Ibn Abī Laylā*, Bāb al-Ṭalāq, 202–203, 213–214. For various opinions of early authorities on this issue, see Abū Yūsuf, *Kitāb al-Āthār*, "Abwāb al-Ṭalāq," p. 137, no. 623.

23. The number of *ṭalāq*s necessary before a separation is absolute depends on the status of the spouses, just as the length of a wife's waiting period does. The Ḥanafīs consider both divorce and the waiting period to be calculated in accordance with the wife's status (two repudiations and two menstrual cycles if she is a slave; three of each if she is free). The Mālikīs and Shāfiʿīs consider the waiting period to depend on the wife's status and the number of divorces to depend on the husband's status.

24. On a woman's disputing her husband's right to return to her by asserting that her waiting period has ended, see *Mudawwana*, K. Irkhā' al-Sutūr, "Daʿwā al-mar'a inqiḍā' ʿiddatihā," 2:327–328; *Al-Umm*, K. al-ʿIdad, "Daʿwā al-mar'a inqiḍā' al-ʿidda," 5:355; and *Al-Jāmiʿ al-Ṣaghīr*, K. al-Ẓihār, "Bāb al-ʿidda," 230. As with all matters pertaining to menstruation the woman is believed if her assertion is plausible.

25. *Al-Umm*, K. al-ʿIdad, "Kayfa tathbut al-rajʿa," 5:352. The passage in question reads, in part, "Repudiated women wait concerning themselves for three periods . . . their husbands *(buʿūlatuhunna)* have more right to take them back *(raddihinna)* during [this period]."

26. Ibid. "She is not due any compensation for the taking back in any case, because it [i.e., the right to take back] is his [right] over her, not her [right] over him. She has no [say in the] matter that is his [alone], without her."

27. *Al-Umm*, Al-ʿIdad, "Wajh al-rajʿa," 5:354.

28. *Al-Umm*, K. al-ʿIdad, "Kayfa tathbutu al-rajʿa," 5:353.

29. *Mudawwana*, K. Irkhā' al-Sutūr, "Al-rajʿa," 2:324.

30. Ibid.

31. As legal scholar Catharine MacKinnon famously phrased it, "Man fucks woman; subject verb object." Catharine A. MacKinnon, "Feminism, Marxism, Method, and the State: An Agenda for Theory," *Signs* 7:3 (Spring 1982): 541.

32. *Mudawwana*, K. al-Aymān bi 'l-Ṭalāq wa Ṭalāq al-Marīḍ, "Al-aymān bi 'l-Ṭalāq," 3:3. Ibn al-Qāsim notes, "This is my opinion and I did not hear it from Mālik."

33. On intent in the resumption of marital relations following a revocable divorce, see Powers, *Intent in Islamic Law*, 143–144. On the intentions of "bodily action," see also p. 149.

34. Exceptionally, the Mālikī jurists, who allowed divorce for nonsupport, allowed him to take his wife back should his circumstances improve during the waiting period; see Chapter 2 in this book.

35. The jurists draw on Q. 2:229–230 for these provisions and attribute the requirement that this intervening marriage be consummated to prophetic tradition. See Lucas, "Divorce, Hadith-Scholar Style."

36. A pregnant woman could be repudiated at any time. See, for example, *Mudawwana,* K. al-ʿIdda wa Ṭalāq al-Sunna, "Fī ṭalāq al-ḥāmil," 2:420–422; K. al-ʿIdda wa Ṭalāq al-Sunna, "Mā jāʾa fī ṭalāq al-sunna," 2:419; and Abū Yūsuf, *Kitāb al-Āthār,* "Abwāb al-Ṭalāq," 129, no. 595.

37. Jurists disagreed over whether the onset of menstruation or its conclusion and the commencement of the third period of "purity" *(ṭuhr)* marked the end of the waiting period. This debate hinged on the meaning of *qurūʾ,* which some took to refer to menstruation and others to the intervals of purity between menstrual periods. See, e.g., *Mudawwana,* K. al-ʿIdda wa Ṭalāq al-Sunna, "Mā jāʾa fī ṭalāq al-ḥāʾiḍ wa ʾl-nufasāʾ," 2:422–423.

38. On intent in delegated divorce, see Powers, *Intent in Islamic Law,* 151–153.

39. *Muwaṭṭaʾ,* Bāb mā yabīn min al-tamlīk, 351.

40. Ibid.

41. *Muwaṭṭaʾ,* "Bāb mā yajibu fīhi taṭlīqa wāḥida min al-tamlīk," 351–352. See also *Al-Umm, Kitāb Ikhtilāf Mālik wa ʾl-Shāfiʿī,* "Bāb al-tamlīk," 7:437–438, and "Bāb khilāf Zayd b. Thābit fī ʾl-ṭalāq," 7:417–418.

42. *Mudawwana,* K. al-Takhyīr wa ʾl-Tamlīk, "Mā jāʾa fī ʾl-takhyīr, 2:373.

43. See, for instance, the discussion of retroactive authorization in *Al-Jāmiʿ al-Kabīr,* K. al-Ṭalāq, "Bāb al-ṭalāq alladhī yakūn min ghayri al-zawj fa yujīzuhu," 183.

44. For *khulʿ* in one early text, see Scott C. Lucas, "Where Are the Legal *Ḥadīth*? A Study of the *Muṣannaf* of Ibn Abī Shayba," *Islamic Law and Society* 15:3 (2008): 283–314.

45. The Shāfiʿīs hold that "*khulʿ* does not take effect *(lam yaqaʿ)* except with the husband's effecting it." *Al-Umm,* K. al-Nafaqāt, "Mā yaqaʿ bi ʾl-khulʿ min al-ṭalāq," 5:291. "Indeed, *khulʿ* is a *ṭalāq;* it does not take effect except by what *ṭalāq* takes effect." *Mukhtaṣar al-Muzanī,* K. al-Khulʿ, "Bāb al-wajh alladhī taḥill bihi al-fidya," 9:201; *Al-Umm,* K. al-Nafaqāt, "Al-kalām alladhī yaqaʿ bihi al-ṭalāq wa lā yaqaʿ," 5:290.

46. "If he specifies or intends a number [of divorces], it is that number." *Mukhtaṣar al-Muzanī,* K. al-Khulʿ, "Bāb al-wajh alladhī taḥill bihi al-fidya," 9:201; *Al-Umm,* K. al-Nafaqāt, "Al-kalām alladhī yaqaʿ bihi al-ṭalāq wa lā yaqaʿ," 5:290; "Muḥammad [al-Shaybānī] said: '. . . *Khulʿ* is a [single] irrevocable divorce *(taṭlīqa bāʾina)* unless they specify three or he intends it, then it is

three.'" *Muwaṭṭa' Shaybānī*, K. al-Ṭalāq, "Bāb al-khulʿ kam yakūn min al-ṭalāq," 189.

47. The analogy is imprecise in one respect: *kitāba* is generally a long-term transaction, with the slave paying for his or her freedom in installments over time (and gaining the status of *mukātab/mukātaba* during the intervening period), but *khulʿ* results in immediate release in exchange for payment. On *kitāba*, see Jonathan E. Brockopp, *Early Mālikī Law: Ibn ʿAbd al-Ḥakam and His Major Compendium of Jurisprudence* (Leiden, Netherlands: Brill, 2000), 165–192.

48. *Al-Jāmiʿ al-Ṣaghīr*, K. al-Ṭalāq, "Bāb al-khulʿ," 215–216. The regulations for *khulʿ* and *kitāba* (p. 214) do not always precisely agree.

49. *Mudawwana*, K. Irkhā' al-Sutūr, "Mā jā'a fī khulʿ ghayr al-madkhūl bihā," 2:340; *Muwaṭṭa'*, K. al-Ṭalāq, "Bāb mā jā'a fī 'l-khulʿ," 359. Al-Muzanī discusses the case of a pair who contract *khulʿ* for a dinar with the stipulation that the husband has the right to return to the wife. Al-Muzanī rejects the stipulation, stating that the husband may not own both the dinar and the right to return. *Mukhtaṣar al-Muzanī*, K. al-Khulʿ, "Bāb al-wajh alladhī taḥill bihi al-fidya," 9:201.

50. See Ibn Rushd, *The Distinguished Jurist's Primer, a translation of* Bidāyat al-Mujtahid, trans. Imran Ahsan Khan Nyazee (Reading, UK: Centre for Muslim Contribution to Civilization, Garnet Publishing, 1996), 2:82, for Abū Thawr's view that "if it has been transacted with the use of the word 'divorce', he has this right [i.e., "to take her back in the waiting period"]."

51. *Al-Umm*, K. al-Nafaqāt, "Mā taḥill bihi al-fidya," 5:289; "Mālik said: There is no problem with a woman ransoming herself from her husband for more than he gave her." *Muwaṭṭa'*, K. al-Ṭalāq, "Bāb mā jā'a fī 'l-khulʿ," 359–360.

52. *Mudawwana*, K. Irkhā' al-Sutūr, "Mā jā'a fī 'l-khulʿ," 2:336.

53. *Mudawwana*, K. Irkhā' al-Sutūr, "Mā jā'a fī khulʿ ghayr al-madkhūl bihā," 2:341–342.

54. *Muwaṭṭa' Shaybānī*, K. al-Ṭalāq, "Bāb al-mar'a takhtalaʿ min zawjihā bi akthār mimmā aʿṭāhā aw aqall," 188–189. See also Lucas, "Where Are the Legal *Ḥadīth*?"

55. Lucas, "Where Are the Legal *Ḥadīth*?" 306. This formulation is Lucas's, not a direct quote from Ibrāhīm.

56. *Al-Jāmiʿ al-Ṣaghīr*, K. al-Ṭalāq, "Bāb al-khulʿ," 216.

57. *Mudawwana*, K. Irkhā' al-Sutūr, "Mā jā'a fī 'l-khulʿ," 2:336–337; see *Al-Jāmiʿ al-Ṣaghīr*, K. al-Ṭalāq, "Bāb al-khulʿ," 214.

58. *Mudawwana*, K. Irkhā' al-Sutūr, "Mā jā'a fī khulʿ ghayr al-madkhūl bihā," 346.

59. *Mukhtaṣar al-Muzanī*, K. al-Khulʿ, "Bāb mukhāṭabat al-mar'a bimā yalzamuhā min al-khulʿ wa mā lā yalzamuhā . . . ," 9:202–203.

60. *Al-Umm,* K. al-Nafaqāt, "Al-khulʿ fī ʾl-maraḍ," 5:293. See also *Mukhtaṣar al-Muzanī,* K. al-Khulʿ, "Bāb al-khulʿ fī ʾl-maraḍ," 9:204. "Sickness and health" matter because specific regulations govern *ṭalāq* during illness; these rules aim to protect wives from being disinherited.

61. *Al-Umm,* K. al-Nafaqāt, "Mā yaqaʿ bi ʾl-khulʿ min al-ṭalāq," 5:291. Numerous similar statements are found in other sections on *khulʿ*.

62. Ibid., 5:292.

63. *Mudawwana,* K. Irkhāʾ al-Sutūr, "Mā jāʾa fī ʾl-khulʿ," 2:337.

64. *Al-Umm,* K. al-Nafaqāt, "Al-khulʿ fī ʾl-maraḍ," 5:293.

65. *Al-Umm,* K. al-Nafaqāt, "Ikhtilāf al-rajul wa ʾl-marʾa fī ʾl-khulʿ," 5:300.

66. *Al-Umm,* K. al-Ṣadāq, "Fī ʾl-ṣadāq bi ʿaynihi yatlafu qabla dafʿihi," 5:92.

67. *Mudawwana,* K. Irkhāʾ al-Sutūr, "Mā jāʾa fī ʾl-khulʿ," 2:337.

68. Of course, the dower actually need never be paid if the wife agrees to delay or even waive payment after the marriage is contracted or consummated.

69. Formative-period Ḥanafī sources are largely silent on the topic of compensation for *khulʿ*.

70. *Mukhtaṣar al-Muzanī,* K. al-Khulʿ, "Bāb mukhāṭabat al-marʾa bi mā yalzamuhā min al-khulʿ wa mā lā yalzamuhā . . . ," 9:203–204.

71. Ibid., 204.

72. "Kull man jāza amruhu fī mālihi, fanujīz khulʿahu." Though a male pronoun is used in the Arabic, the text makes clear that control of one's financial assets is a requirement only for a wife to contract *khulʿ*. The relevant criterion for a husband is whether he is capable of pronouncing a valid repudiation; control over his assets is not necessary.

73. *Al-Umm,* K. al-Nafaqāt, "Mā yajūz khulʿuhu wa mā lā yajūz," 5:292.

74. Ibid., 5:292–293.

75. Ibid.

76. This is a section title in the *Muṣannaf* of ʿAbd al-Razzāq al-Ṣanʿānī: "Bāb ṭalāq al- ʿabd bi yad sayyidihi," 7:187.

77. Ibid., 7:188.

78. Ibid.

79. *Muṣannaf ʿAbd al-Razzāq,* "Bāb nikāḥ al-ʿabd bi ghayri idhn sayyidihi," 7:190.

80. One authority explains that Shurayḥ "considered the slave's divorce binding, but did not consider his marriage binding" (or "permitted the slave's divorce, but did not permit his marriage"), meaning "that [the male slave] may not marry except with his master's permission, but if he marries, then the divorce is in the slave's hand." *Muṣannaf ʿAbd al-Razzāq,* "Bāb ṭalāq al-ʿabd bi yad sayyidihi," 7:189.

81. See also the assumption that the male slave can exercise *ṭalāq* in queries that presuppose this power while discussing specific aspects of the divorce, such as its revocability. *Muṣannaf Ibn Abī Shayba,* 5:258; also 5:81–82.

82. *Muwaṭṭa'*, K. al-Ṭalāq, "Bāb mā jā'a fī ṭalāq al-ʿabd," 367. See later in this section, where the *Muwaṭṭa' Shaybānī* treats the same tradition. Ibn Ḥanbal likewise does not address this issue in his response. "[H]e has control over it [and] his master's divorcing [on his behalf] has no legal effect." Spectorsky, *Chapters on Marriage and Divorce,* 101. One Ḥanafī text posed a scenario in which a male slave was absent for an extended period of time on his master's business. The absent slave was married to another family's female slave; her masters wished to obtain a divorce for her. However, they asserted very clearly that husband's right could not be terminated without his consent: "They may not separate them unless the slave divorces her, because since they consented to her marriage, they do not have [any rights] to separation, unless the slave divorces her." The jurists thus reject any attempt to encroach on the husband's unilateral right to control the termination of his marriage. This text does not address the motivations of the parties in this matter. Perhaps the slave wife herself wanted to be free to remarry; more likely, her male owner wanted to reinstate his sexual access to her or marry her off again for another dower. *Kitāb al-Ḥujja,* 4:61

83. *Innahu laysa li 'l-ʿabd ṭalāq wa 'l-ṭalāq bi yad al-sayyid. Al-Umm,* K. al-ʿIdad, "Ṭalāq al-muwallā ʿalayhi wa 'l-ʿabd," 5:370–371. Shāfiʿī treats the case of the male slave in conjunction with the issue of the freed client *(al-muwallā ʿalayhi).*

84. *Al-Umm,* K. al-ʿIdad, "Ṭalāq al-muwallā ʿalayhi wa 'l-ʿabd," 5:371.

85. *Muṣannaf Ibn Abī Shayba* 4:265–267.

86. *Muṣannaf ʿAbd al-Razzāq,* "Bāb al-ama tubāʿ wa lahā zawj," 7:222, no. 297/13236.

87. Ibid., 7:221–222, no. 297/13230, 13231, 13232, 13233, 13234, 13235, 13236, and 13237.

88. For an opinion that the sale of the husband does not result in divorce, see ibid., 7:222, no. 297/13234, 13235; that it does, see ibid., no. 13236.

89. Ibid., 7:221–222, no. 297/13240. The immediately preceding entry tells a similar story, but leaves off the purchase at the end, closing with ʿAlī returning her.

90. Spectorsky, *Chapters on Marriage and Divorce,* 236.

91. *Muṣannaf ʿAbd al-Razzāq,* "Bāb al-ama tubāʿ wa lahā zawj," 7:222, no. 297/13238.

92. *Muṣannaf Ibn Abī Shayba,* 5:86.

93. Asked whether "a female slave who is sold and who has a husband remains married to him," Ibn Ḥanbal replies in the affirmative (Spectorsky,

Chapters on Marriage and Divorce, p. 81; see also p. 236, where he states simply, "Her sale is not her divorce"). He adduces the earlier views of two Companions that sale does force a divorce only when asked whether a particular account about a female slave named Barīra is the evidence for his position. He states that it is not, but does not provide alternate evidence for his view. On the question of Barīra, see also Spectorsky, "Sunnah in the Responses."

94. Ibn Rushd, *The Distinguished Jurist's Primer*, 2:56, notes the past existence of dispute on this question.

95. Aḥmad b. ʿUmar al-Khaṣṣāf, *Kitāb al-Nafaqāt* (Beirut: Dār al-Kitāb al-ʿArabī, 1984), 26.

96. Jennifer Glancy, *Slavery in Early Christianity* (Minneapolis: Fortress Press, 2006), 24.

97. Rapoport, *Marriage, Money, and Divorce*, 112.

98. Azizah Al-Hibri, "Muslim Women's Rights in the Global Village: Challenges and Opportunities," *Journal of Law and Religion* 15:1/2 (2000–2001): 40.

99. Maysam J. al-Faruqi, "Women's Self-Identity in the Qur'an and Islamic Law," in Gisela Webb, ed., *Windows of Faith: Muslim Women Scholar-Activists in North America* (Syracuse, NY: Syracuse University Press, 2000), 99.

100. Ibid., 77.

101. Ibid., 98.

102. Ibid.

103. Mona Zulficar, "The Islamic Marriage Contract in Egypt," in Asifa Quraishi and Frank Vogel, eds., *The Islamic Marriage Contract: Case Studies in Islamic Family Law*, Harvard Series in Islamic Law (Cambridge, MA: Islamic Legal Studies Program, Harvard Law School, 2008), 252.

104. Zulficar, "The Islamic Marriage Contract in Egypt," 252.

5. Marriage and Dominion

1. Mona Siddiqui, "The Defective Marriage in Classical Ḥanafī Law: Issues of Form and Validity," in G. R. Hawting, J. A. Mojaddedi, and A. Someli, eds., *Studies in Islamic and Middle Eastern Texts and Traditions in Memory of Norman Calder* (Oxford: Oxford University Press, 2000), 282.

2. Ibn Ḥanbal also permitted it. See Susan A. Spectorsky, ed. and trans., *Chapters on Marriage and Divorce: Responses of Ibn Ḥanbal and Ibn Rāhwayh* (Austin: University of Texas Press, 1992), 69.

3. Some later texts distinguish between a man's own female slave and a wife who is someone else's slave by referring to *ama mamlūka* and *ama mankūḥa*.

4. See Azizah Y. Al-Hibri, "Muslim Women's Rights in the Global Village: Challenges and Opportunities," *Journal of Law and Religion* 15:1/2 (2000–2001): 57, especially n. 11.

5. Shāfiʿī was an exception here. Basim Musallam, *Sex and Society in Islam: Birth Control before the Nineteenth Century* (Cambridge: Cambridge University Press, 1983), 31.

6. For a discussion of some of these issues in later Ḥanafī thought, see Baber Johansen, "The Valorization of the Body in Muslim Sunni Law," in Devin J. Stewart, Baber Johansen, and Amy Singer, eds., *Law and Society in Islam* (Princeton: Markus Wiener, 1996), 89.

7. See, e.g., Spectorsky, *Chapters on Marriage and Divorce,* 161.

8. Ibid.

9. However, even if he manumitted her with the agreement that she marry him, she could refuse. In Mālik's view, "the manumission is permitted and there is nothing due from her." [Saḥnūn b. Saʿīd al-Tanūkhī] Mālik b. Anas, *Al-Mudawwana al-Kubrā* (Beirut: Dār Ṣādir, 1323 AH [1905 or 1906]) (hereafter *Mudawwana*), K. al-ʿItq II, "Fī ʾl-rajul yuʿtiqu amatahu ʿalā an tankiḥahu aw ghayrahu," 3:208. Other authorities hold that she owes him her value. Muḥammad al-Shaybānī, *Kitāb al-Ḥujja ʿalā Ahl al-Madīna* (Hyderabad, India: Lajnat Iḥyāʾ al-Maʿārif al-Nuʿmāniyya, 1965) (hereafter *Kitāb al-Ḥujja*), "Bāb al-rajul yuʿtiqu amatahu ʿalā an yatazawwajahā wa yajʿala ṣadāqahā ʿitqahā," 3:421; Ismāʿīl b. Yaḥyā al-Muzanī, *Mukhtaṣar al-Muzanī* (Muḥammad b. Idrīs al-Shāfiʿī, *Al-Umm* [Beirut: Dār al-Kutub al-ʿIlmiyya, 1993], K. al-Wadīʿa, "Bāb mā ʿalā ʾl-awliyāʾ wa inkāḥ al-ab al-bikra bi ghayri idhnihā . . . ," 9:177.

10. Muḥammad al-Shaybānī, *Al-Jāmiʿ al-Ṣaghīr* (Beirut: ʿĀlam al-Kutub, n.d.), K. al-Ṭalāq, "Bāb īqāʿat al-ṭalāq," 199.

11. In normal circumstances a man was allowed sexual access to his former wife whom he had come to own, but if there was a barrier to licit intercourse before he came to own her as a slave, this continued to affect the legitimacy of intercourse between the pair. The most common example of such an obstacle was absolute divorce. (See, e.g., Mālik ibn Anas, *Al-Muwaṭṭaʾ li ʾl-Imām Mālik b. Anas, bi riwāyat Yaḥyā b. Yaḥyā b. Kathīr al-Laythī al-Andalusī* [Beirut: Dār al-Fikr, 1989] [hereafter *Muwaṭṭaʾ*], K. al-Nikāḥ, "Milk al-rajul al-ama allatī qad zawwaja wa ṭallaqa," 341.) As evidence for the prohibition of sex with a concubine whom a man had absolutely divorced when she was a wife, the jurists relied on Q. 2:230, which requires an intervening marriage before an absolutely divorced woman is lawful to her former husband. Remarriage and purchase are explicitly compared, with the verdict that "she is not lawful to him by ownership *(bi ʾl-milk)* until she marries a husband other than him, just as she would be forbidden by that [absolute divorce] to one who marries." *Mudawwana,* K. al-ʿIdda wa Ṭalāq al-Sunna, "Mā jāʾa fī ʿiddat al-muṭallaqa tatazawwaju fī ʿiddatihā," 2:442. See also Muḥammad al-Shaybānī, *Muwaṭṭaʾ al-Imām Mālik, bi riwāyat Muḥammad b. al-Ḥasan al-Shaybānī* (Beirut: Al-Maṭbaʿa

al-ʿIlmiyya, 1997) (hereafter *Muwaṭṭaʾ Shaybānī*), "Bāb al-rajul yakūn taḥtahu ama fa yuṭalliquhā thumma yashtarīhā," 192–193. The *Mudawwana* (K. al-Ẓihār, "Fī man ẓāhara min imraʾatihi thumma ishtarāhā . . . ," 3:58) extends this prohibition to *ẓihār*, as does Muḥammad b. Idrīs al-Shāfiʿī in *Al-Umm* (K. al-ʿIdad, "Man yajib ʿalayhi al-ẓihār wa man lā yajib ʿalayhi," 5:395); *Mukhtaṣar al-Muzanī*, K. al-Ẓihār, "Bāb mā yajib ʿalayhi al-ẓihār wa mā lā yajib ʿalayhi," 9:216.

12. *Mudawwana*, K. al-Nikāḥ IV, "Milk al-rajul imraʾatahu wa milk al-marʾa zawjahā," 2:251.

13. Ibid. For another example where, though marriage and *milk al-yamīn* are explicitly placed in parallel to one another, the use of *milk* implicitly defines marriage as not-*milk*, see *Mudawwana*, K. al-ʿIdda wa Ṭalāq al-Sunna, "Mā jāʾa fī ʿiddat al-muṭallaqa tatazawwaj fī ʿiddatihā," 2:442.

14. *Al-Umm*, Al-ʿIdad, "Ṭalāq al-muwallā ʿalayhi wa ʾl-ʿabd," 5:370. For a Ḥanafī treatment of Ibn ʿUmar's statement, see Abū Yūsuf Yaʿqūb b. Ibrāhīm al-Anṣārī, *Kitāb al-Āthār*, ed. Abū ʾl-Wafāʾ (Hyderabad, India: Lajnat Iḥyāʾ al-Maʿārif al-Nuʿmāniyya, 1355 AH [1936 or 1937]), "Abwāb al-Ṭalāq," 137, no. 624. See also no. 625, which suggests that Ibn ʿUmar's actions may have differed from his explicit statement of principle on the subject.

15. Khalil ʿAthamina, "How Did Islam Contribute to Change the Legal Status of Women? The Case of the *Jawārī*, or the *Female Slaves*," *Al-Qantara* 28:2 (July–December 2007): 383–408.

16. *Mudawwana*, "Fī khulʿ al-ama wa umm al-walad wa ʾl-mukātaba," 2:351; *Al-Umm*, Al-ʿIdad, "Ṭalāq al-muwallā ʿalayhi wa ʾl-ʿabd," 5:370.

17. *Mudawwana*, K. al-Nikāḥ IV, "Milk al-rajul imraʾatahu wa milk al-marʾa zawjahā," 2:251.

18. Baber Johansen has argued that this inability of a free person to be commercial property means that we must consider the dower a gift rather than a purchase price; what he does not consider is the possibility that what is being "sold" is not full ownership over her. As for the line between marriage and ownership, he makes a slightly different point: "But there is one thing that the slave-owner cannot do: he cannot marry his female slave." Johansen, "The Valorization of the Body," 89.

19. *Mudawwana*, K. al-Nikāḥ IV, "Milk al-rajul imraʾatahu wa milk al-marʾa zawjahā," 2:251.

20. See, e.g., *Al-Umm*, K. al-Nikāḥ, "Ma jāʾa fī manʿ imāʾ al-muslimīn," 5:15–18.

21. *Al-Umm*, K. al-Nafaqāt, "Bab al-rajul lā yajid mā yunfiq ʿalā imraʾatihi," 5:133.

22. Judith Evans-Grubbs notes (as with much of the epigraphic evidence provided and analyzed in Susan Treggiari, "'Contubernales' in 'Cil' 6," *Phoenix* 35:1 [Spring 1981]: 42–69), that "most *patrona-libertus* unions were cases

where the woman, freed first, had been able to buy her *contubernalis* out of slavery or had been left him as a legacy by her former master." Judith Evans-Grubbs, "'Marriage More Shameful than Adultery': Slave-Mistress Relationships, 'Mixed Marriages,' and Late Roman Law," *Phoenix* 47:2 (Summer 1993): 131.

23. Aḥmad b. ʿUmar al-Khaṣṣāf, *Kitāb al-Nafaqāt* (Beirut: Dār al-Kitāb al-ʿArabī, 1984), "Bāb al-ʿabd yatazawwaj bi amr mawlāhu mā yalzamuhu min al-nafaqa," 75.

24. Ibn Rushd summarizes the general view that such marriages are permissible if the women's guardians agree, assuming of course that the slaves in question do not belong to the women themselves. Ibn Rushd, Imran Ahsan Khan Nyazee, trans., *The Distinguished Jurist's Primer, a translation of* Bidāyat al-Mujtahid, trans. Imran Ahsan Khan Nyazee (Reading, UK: Centre for Muslim Contribution to Civilization, Garnet Publishing, 2000), 2:49, 51.

25. Evans-Grubbs, "'Marriage More Shameful than Adultery,'" 128–129; see also Bruce W. Frier and Thomas A. J. McGinn, *A Casebook on Roman Family Law* (Oxford and New York: Oxford University Press, 2004), 42–43, 51.

26. Evans-Grubbs, "'Marriage More Shameful than Adultery,'" 126.

27. *Mudawwana*, K. al-Nikāḥ IV, "Milk al-rajul imra'atahu wa milk al-marʾa zawjahā," 2:251–253; *Kitāb al-Ḥujja*, K. al-Nikāḥ, "Inkāḥ al-rajul amatahu ibnahu wa ʿabdahu ibnatahu," 3:267; *Mukhtaṣar al-Muzanī*, K. al-Wadīʿa, "Bāb mā ʿalā ʾl-awliyāʾ wa inkāḥ al-ab al-bikra bi ghayri idhnihā . . . ," 9:177. See also *Al-Jāmiʿ al-Ṣaghīr*, K. al-Nikāḥ, "Bāb fī tazwīj al-ʿabd wa ʾl-ama," 190.

28. *Al-Umm*, K. al-ʿIdad, "Al-jimāʿ alladhī taḥill bihi al-marʾa li-zawjihā," 5:358.

29. *Muwaṭṭaʾ*, K. al-Nikāḥ, "Bāb nikāḥ al-ʿabīd," 341.

30. *Mudawwana*, K. al-Nikāḥ IV, "Milk al-rajul imra'atahu wa milk al-marʾa zawjahā," 2:151–152.

31. Baber Johansen, "Secular and Religious Elements in Hanafite Law: Function and Limits of the Absolute Character of Government Authority," in *Contingency in a Sacred Law: Legal and Ethical Norms in the Muslim Fiqh* (Leiden, Netherlands: Brill, 1999 [1981]), 204.

32. Ibid. See also p. 207: "Indeed, the woman has the capacity to own the property of goods, but not the property of marriage," while "the male person combines the capacity to be a proprietor of marriage and of property. The female person has the capacity to be a proprietor of property and not of marriage." See also Shaun E. Marmon, "Domestic Slavery in the Mamluk Empire: A Preliminary Sketch," in Shaun E. Marmon, ed., *Slavery in the Islamic Middle East* (Princeton: Markus Wiener, 1999), 6.

33. *Mudawwana*, K. al-Nikāḥ IV, "Milk al-rajul imra'atahu wa milk al-marʾa zawjahā," 2:251.

34. *Muwaṭṭa'*, K. al-Nikāḥ, "Bāb mā jā'a fī 'l-rajul yamlik imra'atahu wa qad kānat taḥtahu fa fāraqahā," 340.

35. *Mudawwana*, K. al-Nikāḥ II, "Fī istisrār al-ʿabd wa 'l-mukātab min amwālihimā wa nikāḥihimā bi ghayri idhn al-sayyid," 2:206.

36. *Muwaṭṭa'*, K. al-Ṭalāq, "Bāb mā jā'a fī ṭalāq al-ʿabd," 367; see also *Mudawwana*, K. al-Nikāḥ II, "Fi inkāḥ al-rajul ʿabdahu amatahu," 2:20, and *Muwaṭṭa' Shaybānī*, "Bāb al-rajul ya'dhan li ʿabdihi fī 'l -tazwīj, hal yajūz ṭalāq al-mawlā ʿalayhi?" 188. Note that when a female slave owns another female slave, there is no suggestion that she has any sexual rights over her. Silence on female homoeroticism again prevails; heteronormative assumptions govern not only the way questions are answered but also how they are formulated.

37. *Muwaṭṭa'*, K. al-Ṭalāq, "Bāb mā jā'a fī ṭalāq al-ʿabd," 367.

38. For instance, see the discussion of judging of partiality as a motive for apportionment between wives, discussed in Chapter 2, and that of intent to return, in Chapter 4. For another case in which internal states matter, see Marion Katz, *Body of Text: The Emergence of the Sunni Law of Ritual Purity* (Albany: State University of New York Press, 2002), 154–155, where the Māliki ruling on "the purity implications of skin-to-skin touching" may depend "on the subjective erotic charge of the act." See also Ze'ev Maghen, *Virtues of the Flesh: Passion and Purity in Early Islamic Jurisprudence* (Leiden, Netherlands: Brill, 2004), 253–264.

39. *Al-Umm*, K. al-Nikāḥ, "Tasarrī al-ʿabd," 5:70.

40. *Mukhtaṣar al-Muzanī*, K. al-Wadīʿa, "Mā yaḥill min al-ḥarā'ir wa lā yatasarrā al-ʿabd wa ghayr dhālika," 9:179–180.

41. *Kitāb al-Ḥujja*, "Bāb al-ʿabd takūn taḥtahu ama fa yahib al-mawlā al-ama li 'l-ʿabd fa yaqbaluhā," 3:515.

42. Ibid.

43. *Kitāb al-Ḥujja*, "Bāb nikāḥ al-ʿabd," 3:360. See also Abū Yūsuf, *Kitāb al-Āthār*, "Abwāb al-Ṭalāq," 130, 598: "Yūsuf related to me from his father [Abū Yūsuf] from Abū Ḥanīfa from Ḥammād from Ibrāhīm. He said: The male slave does not take a concubine *(lā yatasarrā)*." He goes on to cite the same verse as justification, concluding that "the slave does not own anything." Interestingly, the section ends with a less categorical statement attributed to Ibrāhīm [al-Nakhaʿī]: "It is reprehensible for a slave to take a concubine." It remains an open question to what extent this lesser degree of prohibition actually represents a different view on the permissibility of slaves taking concubines, or whether it merely reflects a pious unwillingness to declare forbidden something that is not directly prohibited by revelation.

44. *Kitāb al-Ḥujja*, "Bāb nikāḥ al-ʿabd," 3:360.

45. The same issue emerges in the case of a woman married off by two guardians (the second not knowing of the first marriage). Both Shāfiʿī and Abū

Ḥanīfa (and their followers) hold that the first marriage is always upheld, even if the second has been consummated. Mālik, however, and a number of other Medinan authorities hold that if the later marriage has been consummated, it stands and the first is void.

46. This principle originates in the Qurʾanic penalty for illicit sex (Q. 24:2 specifies one hundred lashes). Punishment is halved for female slaves. The jurists apply this principle—or choose not to apply it—consistently in marital matters. As noted in Chapter 3, Mālik grants an enslaved wife an equal share of her husband's time, while the others grant her one night for every two given to a free wife.

47. Joseph Schacht, *An Introduction to Islamic Law* (Oxford: Clarendon, 1964), 127.

48. Jonathan Brockopp, *Early Mālikī Law: Ibn ʿAbd al-Ḥakam and His Major Compendium of Jurisprudence* (Leiden, Netherlands: Brill, 2000), 195, n. 150. On women's sexual use of their male slaves in ancient Rome, see, briefly, Jennifer Glancy, *Slavery in Early Christianity* (Minneapolis: Fortress Press, 2006), 21: "Although some matrons exploited their male slaves sexually, constraints on the sexuality of freeborn women rendered this practice less acceptable than the sexual exploitation of male or female slaves by male slaveholders. . . . A matron who gave birth to the child of a slave disrupted the household; the event would likely be the occasion for a divorce. The child, though freeborn, would be illegitimate."

49. Johansen, "Valorization of the Body," 91.

50. See Kecia Ali, *Sexual Ethics and Islam: Feminist Reflections on Qur'an, Hadith, and Jurisprudence* (Oxford: Oneworld Publications, 2006), chapter 1.

51. I owe this apt phrase to Peter C. Hennigan, *The Birth of a Legal Institution: The Formation of the Waqf in Third Century A. H. Ḥanafī Legal Discourse* (Leiden, Netherlands: Brill, 2004), 26.

52. *Al-Umm,* K. al-Nafaqāt, "Ma jāʾa fī ʿadad mā yaḥill min al-ḥarāʾir wa ʾl-imāʾ wa mā taḥill bihi al-furūj," 5:215.

53. *Al-Umm,* K. al-Nikāḥ, "Tasarrī al-ʿabd," 5:69–70.

54. *Al-Umm,* K. al-Nafaqāt, "Ma jāʾa fī ʿadad mā yaḥillu min al-ḥarāʾir wa ʾl-immāʾ wa mā taḥill bihi al-furūj," 5:215.

55. On *qiwāma,* see Karen Bauer, "Room for Interpretation: Qur'anic Exegesis and Gender" (doctoral dissertation, Princeton University, 2007), and her "'Traditional' Exegesis and Q 4:34," *Comparative Islamic Studies* 2:2 (2006): 129–142.

56. The terminology for sexual acts, especially penetrative intercourse, used in these texts cries out for interpretation. For the most part, I translate *jimāʿ* (coupling, joining) as intercourse and *waṭʾ* as sex, though the latter term has a forceful overtone that does not come through in English. These texts also use various other terms, including *ityān* (for which Khaled Al-Rouayheb offers

the rendering "carnal penetration of." See Khaled Al-Rouayheb, *Before Homosexuality in the Arab-Islamic World, 1500–1800* [Chicago: University of Chicago Press, 2005], 165, n. 15). On the gendering of active and passive roles in intercourse, see ibid., pp. 13–17, describing sex as an act of domination and possession, and p. 90 ("Sexual roles as a rule mirrored nonsexual relations of power, the sexually dominant [the penetrator] also being socially dominant [the man, the husband, the master.]" He goes on to note, however, that "love . . . tended to overturn the established social order." This distinction between sex and love deserves further exploration in the context of juristic discourses—as in the case of a husband's division of time and sex among his wives according to the engagement of his affections.

57. *Al-Umm*, K. al-Nafaqat, "Bāb al-istimnāʾ," 5:138.

58. *Muṣannaf ʿAbd al-Razzāq*, "Bāb al-ʿabd yankiḥu sayyidatahu," 6:164

59. Marmon, "Domestic Slavery."

60. For broader discussion of same-sex intimacy, including nonconsensual relations, see Al-Rouayheb, *Before Homosexuality;* Scott Kugle, *Homosexuality in Islam* (Oxford: Oneworld Publications, 2009); and Ali, *Sexual Ethics and Islam*, chapter 5.

61. Everett Rowson, "The Categorization of Gender and Sexual Irregularity in Medieval Arabic Vice Lists," in Julia Epstein and Kristina Straub. eds., *Body Guards: The Cultural Politics of Gender Ambiguity* (New York: Routledge, 1991), 76, n. 23. See also Arno Schmitt, "*Liwāṭ* im *Fiqh*: Männliche Homosexualität?" *Journal of Arabic and Islamic Studies* 4 (2001–2002): 49–110, especially 80–87.

62. On sex between male owners and male slaves, see Al-Rouayheb, *Before Homosexuality*, 39–41, 124.

63. *Muṣannaf ʿAbd al-Razzāq*, "Bāb al-marʾa tuṣaddiqu al-rajul," 6:162, nos. 10548–10549.

64. W. Robertson Smith, *Kinship and Marriage in Early Arabia* (Boston: Beacon, 1903 [1885?]), 92; on patrilineal marriage more generally, see 88–95. The term *baʿl* appears in the Qurʾan in two pivotal verses related to spousal rights (Q. 2:228; 4:128), as well as elsewhere (e.g., 24:31). The usage of the term in scripture deserves further investigation.

65. Glancy, *Slavery in Early Christianity*, 11.

66. This rule, of course, also complies with the Shāfiʿī stance disallowing the forfeiture of rights before they are due. See Sherman A. Jackson, "*Kramer versus Kramer* in a Tenth/Sixteenth Century Egyptian Court: Post-Formative Jurisprudence between Exigency and Law," *Islamic Law and Society* 8:1 (2001): 27–51.

Conclusion

1. John Kelsay, *Arguing the Just War in Islam* (Cambridge, MA: Harvard University Press, 2007).

2. John L. Esposito and Dalia Mogahed, *Who Speaks for Islam? What a Billion Muslims Really Think* (New York: Gallup Press, 2007).

3. Peter J. Awn, "Indian Islam: The Shah Bano Affair," in John Stratton Hawley, ed., *Fundamentalism and Gender* (New York and Oxford: Oxford University Press, 1994), 63–78.

4. Amira El Azhary Sonbol, "Introduction," in Amira El Azhary Sonbol, eds., *Women, the Family, and Divorce Laws in Islamic History* (Syracuse, NY: Syracuse University Press, 1996), 1.

5. Wael B. Hallaq, *An Introduction to Islamic Law* (Cambridge: Cambridge University Press, 2009), 70.

6. Suzanne Dixon, *The Roman Family* (Baltimore: Johns Hopkins University Press, 1992), 55.

7. Judith E. Tucker, *Women, Family, and Gender in Islamic Law* (Cambridge: Cambridge University Press, 2008).

8. Muḥammad b. Idrīs al-Shāfiʿī, *Al-Umm* (Beirut: Dār al-Kutub al-ʿIlmiyya, 1993) (hereafter *Al-Umm*), K. al-Nikāḥ, "Mā jāʾa fī nikāḥ al-ābāʾ," 5:29: "Istiʾmāruhā aḥsan fī ʾl-iḥtiyāṭ wa aṭyabu li nafsihā wa ajmal fī ʾl-akhlāq."

9. Baber Johansen, "Secular and Religious Elements in Hanafite Law: Function and Limits of the Absolute Character of Government Authority," in *Contingency in a Sacred Law: Legal and Ethical Norms in the Muslim Fiqh* (Leiden, Netherlands: Brill, 1999 [1981]), 204.

10. Tucker, *Women, Family, and Gender*, 222.

11. Sandra R. Joshel and Sheila Murnaghan, "Introduction: Differential Equations," in Joshel and Murnaghan, eds., *Women and Slaves in Greco-Roman Culture: Differential Equations* (London: Routledge, 2001), 3.

12. Maya Shatzmiller, *Her Day in Court: Women's Property Rights in Fifteenth-Century Granada*, Harvard Series in Islamic Law (Cambridge, MA: Islamic Legal Studies Program, Harvard Law School, 2007).

13. Fedwa Malti-Douglas, *Woman's Body, Woman's Word: Gender and Discourse in Arabo-Islamic Writing* (Princeton: Princeton University Press, 1991), 4.

14. Khaled Abou El Fadl, *Speaking in God's Name: Islamic Law, Authority, and Women* (Oxford: Oneworld Publications, 2003).

15. Khaled Abou El Fadl, *The Great Theft: Wrestling Islam from the Extremists* (New York: Harper One, 2005), 258–259.

16. Ibid., 39.

17. *Al-Umm*, K. al-Ṣadāq, "Al-sharṭ fī ʾl-nikāḥ," 5:108.

18. Judith Plaskow, edited with Donna Berman, *The Coming of Lilith: Essays on Feminism, Judaism, and Sexual Ethics, 1972–2003* (Boston: Beacon Press, 2005), 199, discussing a 1983 essay by Rachel Adler.

19. Gail Labovitz, *Marriage and Metaphor: Constructions of Gender in Rabbinic Literature* (Lanham, MD: Lexington Books, 2009), 250.

20. Rachel Adler, *Engendering Judaism: An Inclusive Theology and Ethics* (Boston: Beacon, 1998), 169.

21. Tucker, *Women, Family, and Gender*, 7.

22. Gabriele Marranci, *Anthropology of Islam* (Oxford: Berg, 2008), 127–128. On the lack of attention to masculinity in Islamic studies, see pp. 122, 127–130.

Index

ʿAbd Allāh ibn Abī Salama, 169
ʿAbd Allāh ibn Masʿūd. *See* Ibn Masʿūd, ʿAbd Allāh
ʿAbd al-Razzāq. See *Muṣannaf* of ʿAbd al-Razzāq al-Ṣanʿānī
Abou El Fadl, Khaled, 193–194
Absolute divorce. *See* Irrevocable divorce
Abū Bakr, 35, 230n25
Abū Ḥanīfa, 18, 30; on paternal compulsion to marry, 32–33, 36–37; on virginity in marriage consent, 34; on female consent to marriage, 37, 41–43, 211n59; on female legal capacity, 44–47; on dower, 49, 55–56, 59, 83, 213n88; on exchange marriage, 58; on maintenance obligations, 65–67, 72, 78–79, 86–87, 221n48; on stipulations in marriage contracts, 72–73; on *nushūz*, 82–83, 224n70; on divorce, 86–87, 133–135; on companionship rights, 99, 101, 107–111, 231n33, 232n35; on oaths of abstention, 122–123; on compensated divorce, 147–148, 150; on slave ownership, 165–166; on property rights of slaves, 174–176, 248n45. *See also* Ḥanafī jurisprudence
Abū Yūsuf, 18–19; on dower, 78, 83, 214n105; on divorce, 87, 147–148; on maintenance obligations, 87; on abandoned claims of companionship, 127–128; on property rights of slaves, 248n43
Adler, Rachel, 98, 195–196
Aga Khan, 62
Age: of consummation, 33, 35, 76, 78, 208n21, 220n40; of marriage, 62–63. *See also* Majority
Aḥmad b. ʿUmar al-Khaṣṣāf. *See* al-Khaṣṣāf, Aḥmad b. ʿUmar
Ahmed, Leila, 22, 130
ʿĀʾisha: on pre-Islamic marriage, 13–14; authority of, 21, 37; marriage of, 31, 35, 76, 208n21
Anal intercourse, 182
Analogies, 15–20, 26, 52–53, 203n38; of wives with slaves, 8, 10–12, 16–17, 24–26, 53–56, 164–165, 191, 209n34; of fathers with slave owners, 37–40; of slaves with women and children, 47–48; of dower with price, 49–55, 59, 61–62, 214n99, 246n18; of divorce with manumission, 51, 135–146; of delegated divorce with commerce, 143–146; of compensated divorce with slave purchase of emancipation, 146–147, 241n47
Anas b. Mālik, 107
Antoun, Richard, 215n115
Apportionment between wives. *See* Companionship rights
Arabi, Oussama, 212n76
Arranged marriage. *See* Consent to marriage

Bano, Shah, 188
Beyond the Veil (Mernissi), 202n31

Bodily rights, 24
Body of Text (Katz), 202n30, 206n73, 248n38
Brockopp, Jonathan, 177, 203n42

Calder, Norman, 136, 203n42, 204n48, 206n73
Cantor, Norman, 7
Castration, 23, 116
Chattel or Person? (Romney-Wegner), 51
Child support, 86–89, 227nn94–95
Cohabitation, 100
Companionship rights, 97–132, 196, 228n117; androcentric nature of, 99–102, 114–116, 130–132; applications of fairness in, 100–106, 131, 230–231nn25–27; one-in-four standard in, 101–102; travel and illness in, 102–106, 118, 230–231nn25–27; wedding night exemptions in, 106–114, 231n33, 232nn35,37; sexual obligations in, 114–120, 131–132, 194–195, 233nn51–53; impotence in, 116, 196; female desire in, 116–120, 233nn51–53; oaths of abstention in, 121–126, 234nn68,72,75; abandoned claims of, 126–132, 234n75, 236n102; male *nushūz* in, 128–131
Companions of Muḥammad, 13, 16, 35, 154–158
Compulsion to marry, 31–37, 58, 207n8, 216n122
Concubines/concubinage, 8, 22, 167–168, 245n9; children of, 8, 39, 67, 102, 168–169, 200n20, 230n13; gender prerogatives in, 12–15, 165–166, 176–184, 201n26, 202n32; companionship rights of, 102, 118, 230n13; transitions to and from marriage of, 167, 245nn9,11; of enslaved men, 172–176; male concubines, 12–15, 174–186, 249n48; housework obligations of, 200n20
Conditional divorce, 74–75
Consensual divorce, 84. See also *Khulʿ* divorce
Consensus, 52
Consent to marriage, 29–49, 30; marriage guardians *(walī)* in, 30, 35, 36, 42–47, 208n27; parental compulsion in, 31–37, 58, 216n122; role of virginity in, 32–36, 41, 210n47; majority in, 33–34; analogy of fathers with slave owners in, 37–40; of slaves, 37–40, 44–46, 48, 209n41, 210nn44–45, 212nn71–72,76; female control in, 37–46; suitability in, 42, 211n61; women's sexual incapacity in, 46–47, 212n80; financial rights in, 57–58; in modern Muslim discourses, 62–63. *See also* Dower
Consummation: age of, 33, 35, 76, 78, 208n21, 220n40; connection of dower obligation with, 49, 78, 83, 220n34; in annulment decisions, 74, 91–92; link with maintenance obligations of, 75–78, 91–95, 221n48; impotence, 92, 228n108; wedding night obligations, 106–114; in irrevocable divorce, 142. *See also* Virginity
Contraception, 166
Contubernium, 209n36
Coulson, Noel, 18
Courts as a sphere of negotiation. *See* Jurists' project

De Bellefonds, Yves Linant, 54–55
De la Puente, Christina, 5, 44
Delegated divorce, 143–146, 162–163
Diversity of legal doctrine, 3–5, 190. *See also* Legal texts
Divorce, 4–6, 133–163, 196; unilateral nature of, 17, 84, 135–136, 140–141, 144–145, 160–163, 186, 197; analogy with manumission of, 51, 135–146; role of travel in, 52–53; maintenance obligations in, 66–67, 83–89, 224n74, 225n76, 226nn87–89, 227nn94–95,102; conditional divorce, 74–75; in polygamous households, 79; types of, 84; revocation of, 84–85, 135, 140–142; waiting periods in, 84–86, 135, 224n74, 225n76, 239n23, 240n37; remarriage restrictions in, 85, 95, 130, 135, 142, 225n76; child support in, 86–88; for nonsupport, 89–93, 227n102; for abstention, 121–125, 234n75; for *nushūz*, 130, 149–150; *khulʿ* and compensation for, 135, 146–154, 197, 241nn47–50, 242nn69,72; in slave contexts, 135, 153–160, 172, 227n102, 242–243nn80–82, 243n93; regulations of, 135–146, 238n21; statements of, 136, 237n7, 238n22; triple divorce, 136, 138, 143, 237n5; model divorce, 142; pronounced during menstruation,

142–143; delegated divorce, 143–146, 162–163; in modern Muslim discourses, 160–163, 188
Divorce for compensation. See *Khulʿ* divorce
Divorce Iranian Style, 63
Dixon, Suzanne, 188–189
Dominion. See *Milk* (ownership, control)
Dower, 49–62, 55; for enslaved females, 49, 213n88; purchase of consummation through, 49, 53, 55–56, 59–62, 78, 83, 151–152, 215n111, 217n132; analogies with commerce and ownership in, 49–53, 59, 61–62, 214n99, 246n18; basic rules of, 53–62, 94; failure to specify an amount in, 54–55, 214nn105–106; minimum acceptable amounts in, 55–59, 215nn111,113; in exchange marriage, 56–58, 215nn114–115, 216nn118,121; undeliverable payment in, 58–60, 216n125; in modern Muslim discourses, 62, 63; inheritance of, 220n34

Egalitarianism, 190
Enslaved females, 183; illicit sexual activity of, 11, 67, 168; licit sexual activity of, 11, 25–26, 38–40, 53, 156–157, 164–167; virginity as factor for, 32, 40; commodification of bodies of, 39, 52, 56, 209n39, 212n71, 215n113; consent to marriage by, 39–40, 43–47, 212nn71–72; dower for, 49, 213n88; spousal obligations of, 66, 67–72; legal status of children of, 87–88, 226–227nn91–92; companionship rights of, 100–102; divorce rights of, 135, 153–154, 227n102; as wives of enslaved men, 165–166, 172–176; as wives of free men, 167, 245n9; maintenance obligations for, 227n102. *See also* Concubines/concubinage
Eunuchs, 23, 116
Evans-Grubb, Judith, 170, 246n22
Exchange marriage, 56–58, 215nn114–115, 216nn118,121

Al-Faruqi, Maysam, 161–162
Fatawa-i-Kazee-Khan, 35
Fāṭima bint Qays, 86–87
Fatwas, 23, 205n66
Favoritism. *See* Companionship rights
Female homosexuality, 248n36
Females. *See* Enslaved females; Free females
Forand, Paul, 38
Forswearing, 121–122, 234nn72,75, 235n91. *See also* Oaths of abstention
Free females, 4–6; ownership of male concubines by, 14, 16, 165, 176–186, 249n48; transition from virginity to experience of, 41–42; property rights of, 43–44, 48–49, 57–58, 165–166, 191–193, 247n32; legal capacity of, 43–48; consent for slaves' marriages by, 44–46, 170–172; domestic duties of, 94; apportionment rights of, 100–101, 196; role of *milk* in marriages of, 165–172, 183–185; marriage to male slaves of, 169–170, 246n22, 247n24. See also *Nushūz*

Gendered rights, 8, 21–22, 188–197; of concubinage, 12–15, 22, 165–166, 176–184, 201n26, 202n32; of legal capacity, 15, 26, 43–49, 57–58, 165–166, 184–186, 190–192; of domination over female sexuality, 15–17, 32–33, 63, 164–186; of divorce, 17, 67, 75, 84, 135–136, 140–141, 186, 197; in slave marriages, 39, 40, 48, 212nn71–72, 76; of mobility, 65–66, 70–73, 85, 91, 95, 189–190, 192; of maintenance obligations, 66, 74, 79–83; of sexual desire, 70, 116–120, 233nn51–53; of annulment, 74; of companionship, 99–102, 114–116, 130–132; of male *nushūz*, 128–130; in language about marriage and sex, 141, 179–181, 239n31, 249n56. *See also* Enslaved females; Free females; *Milk* (ownership, control)
Al-Ghazali, 233n53
Glancy, Jennifer, 45, 48, 160, 184, 210n44, 249n48
Greek law, 130

Hadith, 16, 25; on consent to marriage, 62; on urgency of male desire, 70; on permission to fast, 73, 95, 194; on age of consummation, 76; on physical discipline, 166
Ḥafṣa, 77
Hallaq, Wael, 10–11, 188

Ḥanafī jurisprudence, 16–20; on social equality in marriage, 21; on consent to marriage, 35, 37, 40–44, 209n41; on virginity, 35; on paternal compulsion to marry, 35–37; on female sexual experience, 41–42; on legal capacity of women, 44–46; on witnesses to marriage, 46; on marriage as a commercial transaction, 51; Transoxanian texts of, 51; on divorce, 52–53, 84–89, 137–140, 143–144, 236n1, 238–239nn22–23, 243n82; on exchange marriage, 58; on maintenance obligations, 71, 84–93, 95, 227n102; on stipulations in marriage contracts, 74–75, 220n31; on *nushūz*, 82–83, 224n72; on companionship rights, 105, 113–114, 120, 129–130, 230n25; on oaths of abstention, 121–126; on compensated divorce, 147–150, 242n69; on marriage between free women and enslaved men, 170; on property rights of slaves, 174–176; on property rights of women, 176, 181; on slave marriage and divorce, 185, 243n82; in India, 188; use of analogy in, 203n38. *See also* Abū Ḥanīfa
Ḥanbalī jurisprudence, 17, 100
Harems, 22
Al-Ḥasan al-Baṣrī, 35, 156
Hawting, G. R., 225n76, 226n87
Hennigan, Peter, 20
Al-Hibri, Azizah, 161
Hierarchical social structures, 10, 21–26, 170, 188–190. *See also* Kinship structures
Hirsch, Susan, 2
Homosexual activities, 182, 248n36

Ibn ʿAbbās, 154, 156
Ibn ʿAbd al-Barr, 81
Ibn Abī Laylā, 18–19, 36, 86, 234n75
Ibn Abī Shayba, 154–155, 183
Ibn al-Ḥājj, 23
Ibn al-Qāsim, 17–18; on paternal compulsion to marry, 33, 207n8; on female consent to marriage, 41; on dower, 53–54, 59; on maintenance obligations, 70, 87; on *nushūz*, 81, 222n58; on divorce, 87, 141, 143; on companionship rights, 98, 101–105, 107, 115–118; on compensated divorce, 152
Ibn Buṭlān, 7
Ibn Ḥanbal, 17, 22, 66, 208n21, 237n7, 243n93
Ibn Ḥazm, 222n58, 228n108
Ibn Masʿūd, ʿAbd Allāh, 29–31, 226n87
Ibn Qasīṭ, 169
Ibn Rāhawayh, 157, 237n7
Ibn Rushd, 247n24
Ibn Shihāb al-Zuhrī, 81, 149
Ibn Wahb, 35, 171
Ibrāhīm al-Nakhaʿī, 150, 220n32, 225n78
Ikhtilāf al-ʿIrāqiyayn, 19, 36
Ikhtilāf Mālik wa ʾl-Shāfiʿī, 56
Īlāʾ. *See* Forswearing
Ilkkaracan, Pinar, 215n115
Illicit sexual activity: involving slaves, 11–12, 25–26, 67–68, 168, 245n11; punishments for, 32, 238n19; in paternal compulsion to marry, 33, 207n8; with sister of wife, 78–79; in revocable divorce, 140–142; of free females with male concubines, 176–184, 249n48; of masturbation, 180; of homosexual activities, 182, 248n36
Impotence, 92, 116, 196, 228n108
India, 188
Individual freedom, 24
Inheritance rights, 4–5, 66, 220n34
Intermarriage, 177
Iraqi practice. *See* Ḥanafī jurisprudence
Irrevocable divorce, 84–85, 91, 95, 140; triple divorce, 136, 138, 143, 237n5; remarriage following, 142; in compensated divorce, 146–154
Isḥāq b. Rāhwayh. *See* Ibn Rāhawayh
Islamic kinship systems, 8–12, 202–203nn29–34; pre-Islamic Arabs customs in, 9, 11, 56–57, 184; outside influences on, 9–10; relationship between marriage and slavery in, 10–12; licit sexual activity in, 11–15
Islamic law, 3–5, 187–197. *See also* Jurists' project

Jābir b. ʿAbd Allāh, 154
Jābir b. Zayd, 154–155
Jaʿfar al-Ṣādiq, 18–19, 41–42, 211n61
Al-Jāmiʿ al-Kabīr, 18, 137–138, 204n44, 223n62, 225n76, 238n19
Al-Jāmiʿ al-Ṣaghīr, 18, 204n44; internal disputations in, 20; on dower, 59; on

divorce in unconsummated marriages, 91–92; on compensated divorce, 147–148, 150; on concubines, 167
Jewish law *(halakha)*, 4, 195–196; on acquisition and marriage *(kinyan)*, 10, 49–50, 51; analogies of women and slaves in, 47–48, 137; on minimum dower amounts, 55; on maintenance obligations, 94–95; on legal categories, 98; on conjugal obligations, 114; on polygyny, 130; on divorce, 137, 237n9
Johansen, Baber, 51, 61–62, 171–172, 191–192, 246n18
Johnson, Mark, 25
Judd, Steven, 19
Jurists' project, 2–5, 28, 187–197, 198n3; diversity of legal opinion in, 3–5, 190; personal-status laws under, 4–5, 187–189; survival of core ideas from, 5–6, 193–197; hierarchy of normative marriages in, 6–7, 170; analogy in, 15–20, 26, 52–53, 203n38; primary sources for, 16, 25; major schools of, 17–20. *See also* Gendered rights; Legal texts

Kafā'a. *See* Suitability
Katz, Marion, 202n30, 206n73
Khansā' bint Khidhām, 41
al-Khaṣṣāf, Aḥmad b. ʿUmar: on maintenance obligations, 65, 76, 85; on *nushūz*, 82, 83, 224n67; on companionship rights, 120; on slave marriage and divorce, 158–159
Khulʿ divorce, 135, 146–154, 197
Kinship and Marriage in Early Arabia (Smith), 184
Kinship structures, 8–14, 24, 202–203nn29–34; of pre-Islamic Arabs, 9, 11, 13–14, 56–57, 184, 202n31; in Mediterranean cultures, 9–11; in patriarchal systems, 11, 13–14; of slaves, 11–12, 39–40. *See also* Islamic kinship systems
Kitāb al-Āthār, 18, 87, 127–128, 204n44
Kitāb al-Ḥujja, 18, 19, 29–30, 37, 206n73; on female consent to marriage, 41–43; on dower, 55; on age of consummation, 76; on maintenance obligations, 90–91, 227n102; on companionship rights, 107–109, 114; on divorce, 133–135, 236n1; on slave divorce, 155; on property rights of slaves, 175–176; on stipulations in marriage contracts, 220n32
Kitāb al-Mabsūt, 230n25
Kitāb al-Nafaqāt, 65, 75–76
Kitāb al-Umm, 14–16, 19, 202n32, 204n48; reliance on hadith in, 35; on female consent to marry, 35–36; on paternal compulsion to marry, 36; on exchange marriage, 57, 58; on dower, 60, 214n106; on maintenance obligations for slaves, 72; on stipulations in marriage contracts, 72–73; on consummation, 76, 92–93; on divorce, 92–93; on companionship rights, 104, 111–114, 128, 236n102; on compensated divorce, 151, 153; on slave divorce, 155; on male concubines, 165–166, 179–181; on marriage between free women and enslaved men, 171

Labovitz, Gail, 25, 137, 195, 237n9; on female control over marriage consent, 37; on Jewish analogies of women with slaves, 47–48; on marriage as ownership, 51
Lakoff, George, 25
Legal personhood of women, 15, 26, 184–186, 190–192; in control over property, 43–44, 48–49, 57–58, 165–166; in rights to contract marriage, 44–48
Legal texts, 17–26, 190–191, 202–203nn29–34; diversity of opinion in, 3–5, 190; interconnected discourse and disputations in, 20–21, 30, 134–135, 161–162; influence of social practices on, 21–23; as evidence of social history, 23–24; as prescriptive, 24; genres of thought and argumentation in, 24–26; logical consistency in, 26, 191; authorship and chronology of, 27–28, 206n73; translations and transliteration of, 28; creation of legal categories in, 98, 164–166, 196, 230n13, 244n3. *See also* *names of specific texts*, e.g., *Mudawanna*
Legislative codes, 4
Lewis, Bernard, 7
Licit sexual activity, 165; in marriage, 6, 10–15, 25–26, 46–47, 53; of slaves, 11, 25–26, 38–39, 53, 56, 67–68, 156–158, 164, 166–167, 209n39, 245n9; in pre-Islamic Arabia, 13–14, 56–57, 184; male domination of, 15, 25–26; age

Licit sexual activity *(continued)*
of consummation in, 33, 35, 76, 78, 208n21; women's incapacity to convey, 46–47, 212n80; purchase by dower of, 49, 53, 56, 59–62, 151–152; role of *milk* in, 63, 138–139, 171–172, 181–192, 238n19, 245n9; links with maintenance obligations of, 65–67, 93–96, 218n5, 222n50, 228n108; of nonpenetrative activities, 82, 115–116, 224nn67–68; as companionship right, 114–120, 131–132, 194–195; female desire in, 116–120, 233nn51–53; of forced intercourse, 120, 224n72; abstention, 121–126, 234n75; in revocable divorce, 140–142; purchase in compensated divorce of, 151–152. *See also* Companionship rights; Concubines/concubinage; Gendered rights; Illicit sexual activity; *Nushūz*

Longino, Kim, 63

MacIntyre, Alasdair, 20

MacKinnon, Catharine, 239n31

Maghen, Ze'ev, 70

Maintenance obligations, 65–96, 189–190; link with sexual availability of, 65–67, 75–83, 93–96, 218n5, 222n50, 228n108; link with consummation of, 66, 74–78, 91–93; in *nushūz* contexts, 66, 79–83, 120, 222n53, 223nn61–62; in slavery contexts, 66, 67–72, 219nn17,22, 227n102; wives' rights to support in, 66, 89–94, 227n102; in divorce, 66–67, 83–89, 224n74, 225n76, 226nn87–89, 227nn94–95,102; stipulations in marriage contracts on, 72–75, 220nn31–33

Majority, 32; in age of consummation, 33, 35, 76, 208n21, 220n40; in paternal compulsion to marry, 33–34; in female consent to marriage, 37, 39–41; in maintenance obligations, 66, 78; in female property rights, 192–193

Makhrama, 169

Male concubinage, 12–15, 165–166, 176–186, 201n26, 202n32

Male dominion *(milk)*. See *Milk* (ownership, control)

Male homosexuality, 182

Male *nushūz*, 128–131

Mālik ibn Anas, 17–20, 22, 30; ownership of concubines by, 22; on paternal compulsion to marry, 32–33, 37, 58; on female consent to marriage, 34–35; analogy of fathers with slave owners of, 38; on women's sexual incapacity, 46–47; on dower, 49, 53–54, 55–56, 61–62, 78, 213n88; on exchange marriage, 57–58; on maintenance obligations, 65–67, 69–71, 76–78, 84–85, 89; on stipulations in marriage contracts, 72–73; on divorce, 84–85, 89, 135, 143–145, 238n22; on companionship rights, 97–106, 115–118; on oaths of abstention, 122–123; on compensated divorce, 148–149; on slave ownership, 165; on concubines, 168; on marriage between free women and enslaved men, 171; on property rights of slaves, 173–174, 248n45; on male concubines, 176; on marriage between free men with enslaved women, 245n9

Mālikī jurisprudence, 16–19, 203nn41–42; on rights of slaves, 21, 40, 210n45; on paternal compulsion to marry, 35–37; on female consent to marriage, 41, 43–44; on female legal capacity, 44–45; on dower, 53–54; on maintenance obligations, 70–71, 84–93, 95; on stipulations in marriage contracts, 74–75, 220nn31,33; on *nushūz*, 81, 126; on divorce, 84–89, 139–141, 236n1, 239n23, 240n34; on companionship rights, 97, 107–111, 113–114, 117–118, 120, 131; on oaths of abstention, 121–125, 234nn68,72; on abandoned claims of companionship, 126, 129–130; on compensated divorce, 148–152; on male concubines, 181; on homosexual activity, 182; on slave marriage, 185; on female property rights, 192–193; on waiting periods, 239n23. *See also* Mālik ibn Anas

Malti-Douglas, Fedwa, 193

Manumission, 7–8, 192; analogies to divorce of, 51, 139–146; for marriage purposes, 167, 170, 245n9

Māriya, 77

Marranci, Gabriele, 197

Marriage, 4–17, 189–190; licit sexual activity in, 6, 10–15, 25–26, 46–47, 53; in analogies of wives with slaves, 8, 10–12, 16–17, 24–26, 53–56, 164–165, 191, 209n34; control over mobility in, 65–66, 70–73, 85, 91, 95, 189–190, 192; inter-

section with property rights of, 153–160, 165; gendered language of, 179–181, 249n56. *See also* Companionship rights; Consent to marriage; Consummation; Maintenance obligations; *Milk* (ownership, control); Spousal rights
Marriage contracts: male authority *(milk)* in, 6–7, 12, 152; as commercial transactions, 51; on inheritance rights, 66; stipulations in, 66, 72–75, 197, 220nn31–33; challenges to validity of, 67. *See also* Dower
Marriage guardians *(walī)*, 30, 35, 36, 42–47, 208n27
Masturbation, 180
Matrilineal kinship, 184
Medinan practice. *See* Mālikī jurisprudence
Melchert, Christopher, 17, 204n45
Mernissi, Fatima, 202n31
Metaphor, 26
Milk (ownership, control), 164–186, 189–190; ownership aspects of, 6–7, 12, 27, 164, 166–172, 245n11, 246nn13,18; in female ownership of male concubines, 12–15, 176–184, 249n48; role in marriage of, 49, 50–51, 53, 63, 136, 152; sexual aspects of, 63, 138–139, 171–172, 181–192, 238n19, 245nn9,11; wives' purchase of *(khulʿ)*, 146–154; in slave contexts, 165–176; in free female marriage to male slaves, 169–170, 246n22, 247n24
Milk al-nikāḥ, 171–176, 181
Milk al-yamīn (ownership by the right hand), 10, 12–15, 53, 164, 167, 173–174, 202n28
Mir-Hosseini, Ziba, 2, 63
Mobility, 65–66, 70–73, 85, 91, 95, 189–190, 192
Model divorce, 142
Modern Muslim discourses, 5–6, 193–197; rhetoric of female domesticity and virtue in, 6; on dower, 62, 63; on consent to marriage, 62–63; on divorce, 160–163, 188; on polygyny, 230n20
Monogamy, 100, 229n6
Motzki, Harald, 202n29
Mudawwana, 17–18, 20, 202n30, 204n43; on paternal compulsion to marry, 32–33, 207n8; on female consent to marriage, 34–35, 41; reliance on hadith in, 34–35; analogy of fathers with slave owners in, 38; on women's sexual incapacity, 46; on dower, 53–54, 59, 213n88, 214n106; on exchange marriage, 57; on maintenance obligations, 68–71, 76–78, 87, 89–90; on urgency of male desire, 70; on stipulations in marriage contracts, 73, 74; on *nushūz*, 81, 126; on divorce, 87; on companionship rights, 97–98, 101–105, 107, 117–118, 128, 129; on oaths of abstention, 123–124; on compensated divorce, 149; on concubines, 167; on *milk*, 168–169; on marriage between free women and enslaved men, 171; on property rights of slaves, 173
Muḥammad, 9; Companions of, 13; marriage to ʿĀʾisha of, 31, 35, 76; on exchange marriage, 57, 216n118; on consent to marriage, 62; wives and concubines of, 77, 100–101, 167, 221n42; apportionment of time with wives by, 107, 109–110, 112, 127–129, 232n35; on divorce, 143; on divorce for compensation, 147–148; exceptionalism of, 230n9
Muḥammad b. al-Ḥasan al-Shāybanī, 30, 204nn44–45; on female consent to marriage, 41, 42–43; on exchange marriage, 57; on dower, 59, 78, 83; on maintenance obligations, 90–91; on companionship rights, 108–110, 114, 126–127; on divorce, 134–135, 137–138; on property rights of slaves, 175–176. See also *Muwaṭṭaʾ Shāybanī*
Muḥammad ibn Idrīs al-Shāfiʿī. *See* Shāfiʿi, Muḥammad b. Idrīs
Mujāhid, 157
Mukhtaṣar of al-Muzanī, 19, 46, 204n48; on dower, 54, 60; on maintenance obligations for slaves, 72; on companionship rights, 111, 114; on divorce, 138–139; on compensated divorce, 150–151, 241n49; on *nushūz*, 223nn61–62; on oaths of abstention, 235n91. *See also* Al-Muzanī, Ismaʿīl b. Yaḥyā
Muṣannaf of ʿAbd al-Razzāq al-Ṣanʿānī, 13, 15–16, 202n29; on consent to marriage, 34; on female consent to marriage, 43; on slave rights of marriage and divorce, 154–155, 157, 201n26; on female sexual activity with male concubines, 182, 202n32

Muṣannaf of Ibn Abī Shayba, 154–155, 183
Al-Musayyab ibn Najaba, 29–31
Al-Mutawakkil, 22
Muwaṭṭa', 17–18, 28, 34, 203n42; on female consent to marriage, 34–35, 41; on stipulations in marriage contracts, 73; on *nushūz*, 81; on companionship rights, 107, 109, 129; on divorce, 144–145, 155, 243n82; on compensated divorce, 149; on slave rights of marriage and divorce, 155; on marriage between free women and enslaved men, 171; on oaths of abstention, 234n72
Muwaṭṭa' Shāybanī, 18, 28, 204n45, 206n73; on female consent to marriage, 42–43; on companionship rights, 107–110, 126–127; on compensated divorce, 149–150; on slave divorce, 243n82
Al-Muzanī, Ismāʿīl b. Yaḥyā, 19, 204n48; on women's sexual incapacity, 46–47, 212n80; on dower, 54, 60; on maintenance obligations in divorce, 89; on companionship rights, 102, 110–114; on divorce, 138–139; on property rights of slaves, 174; on oaths of abstention, 235n91. See also *Mukhtaṣar* of al-Muzanī

Nonconsensual sex, 224n72
Nondower marriage, 56–58
Non-vaginal intercourse, 82, 224nn67–68
Notarial manuals, 23
Nursing, 227n95
Nushūz: in maintenance obligations, 66, 79–83, 222n53, 223nn61–62, 224nn67–72; in companionship claims, 120, 126, 129; male *nushūz*, 128–130; in divorce compensation claims, 149–150

Oaths of abstention, 121–126, 234nn68,72,75
The Origins of Islamic Jurisprudence (Motzki), 202n29
Ownership, 24, 182–184; terminology of, 6–7, 37; overlap in marriage and slavery of, 25–26, 139; role in marriage of, 49, 50–51, 53, 63–64; in slave marriage and divorce decisions, 156–160. *See also Milk* (ownership, control); Slaves/slavery

Passive language, 179–181, 249n56
Paternal compulsion to marry, 31–37, 58, 207n8, 216n122
Patriarchal marriage and kinship systems, 11, 13–14, 184
Patronage systems, 24
Peirce, Leslie, 2, 220n40
Personal-status laws, 4–5, 187–189. *See also* Legal personhood of women
Pilgrimage, 82, 223n64
Plaskow, Judith, 94
Polygyny, 77, 196; maintenance obligations under, 66; marriage contract stipulations on, 72–73; divorce in, 74–75, 79; as normative, 100, 229nn5–6. *See also* Companionship rights
Powers, Paul, 114, 136, 210n47
Pregnancy: waiting periods, 83–86, 135, 224n74; child support, 86–89, 227nn94–95; status of child, 87–88, 226–227nn91–92
Property rights, 24; of women, 43–44, 48–49, 57–58, 165–166, 191–193, 247n32; in dower arrangements, 49, 57–58; intersection with marriage of, 153–160, 165; of slaves, 165–176, 192–193, 248nn43,45; in female ownership of male concubines, 176–184, 249n48. *See also* Ownership

Qasm. *See* Companionship rights
Qur'an (Koran), 16, 25; terminology of commerce in, 50; in Sunni jurisprudence, 52; on consent to marriage, 62; on *nushūz*, 79–81, 222n53; on divorce, 86–87, 140, 161–162, 240n35; on maintenance obligations, 86–87; on fairness in apportionment, 104; on female sexual desire, 116–117; on slave marriage, 156; on marriage of free men with enslaved women, 169; on licit sexual activity, 180–181; on dower, 214n106
Qurayʿa bint Ḥibbān, 29–31

Rabbinic law. *See* Jewish law *(halakha)*
Al-Rabīʿ ibn Sulaymān al-Murādī, 19
Rāfiʿ b. Khadīj, 97, 127, 128
Rape, 120, 224n72
Rapoport, Yossef, 49, 137, 160
Remarriage, 77, 95, 130, 135, 142, 225n76
Revocable divorce, 84–85, 135, 140–142

Ricoeur, Paul, 25
Risāla (Shāfiʿī), 36
Roman law: on acquisition and marriage, 10, 214n99; on slavery, 11, 45, 188–189, 210n44; on rights of marriage, 38, 68, 170, 209n36; on polygyny, 130
Romney-Wegner, Judith, 51

Sadeki, Benham, 108, 226n88
Ṣafiyya, 77, 167, 221n42
Saḥnūn al-Tanūkhī, 17–18, 202n30; on dower, 53–54; on companionship rights, 117–118; on oaths of abstention, 123; on divorce, 141
Saʿīd b. al-Musayyab, 73; on companionship rights, 101, 122; on divorce, 148, 155, 157; on slavery, 157; on oaths of abstention, 234n72
Saʿīd b. Jubayr, 155
Santillana, David, 81
Al-Sarakhsī, Muḥammad ibn Aḥmad ibn Abī Sahl, 209n41, 230n25
Savage, Eric, 7
Sawda, 77, 127–129
Schact, Joseph, 177
Schneider, Irene, 218n5
Segregation of women. *See* Gendered rights
Separation. *See* Divorce
Sexual crimes, 4–5
Sexuality, 192; as key to regulation of marriage, 6, 10–12; urgency of male desire, 70; in revocable divorces, 84–86, 140–142; gendered language of, 141, 179–181, 239n23, 249n56; homosexual activities, 182, 248n36. *See also* Illicit sexual activity; Licit sexual activity
Shāfiʿī, Muḥammad b. Idrīs: on female ownership of male concubines, 14–15, 176–186; ownership of concubine by, 22; on paternal compulsion to marry, 32–33, 207n8; on female consent to marriage, 34–36, 191; on ʿĀʾisha's marriage, 35, 76, 208n21; analogy of fathers with slave owners by, 38; on slave rights of marriage and divorce, 40, 155, 165–166, 185, 250n66; on female legal capacity, 44–46; on dower, 49, 54–56, 60–61, 78, 213n88; on exchange marriage, 58; on maintenance obligations, 65–67, 78, 84–85, 87–88; on stipulations in marriage contracts, 72–73; on *nushūz*, 81–82, 120; on divorce, 84–85, 87–88, 93, 140, 143, 155, 236n1; on companionship rights, 99, 101–106, 110–114, 116, 118–120, 127–129, 194, 236n102; on oaths of abstention, 122–123, 235n91; on divorce for compensation, 148, 150–153; on concubines, 167–168; on marriage between free women and enslaved men, 169–170; on property rights of slaves, 174, 248n45; on legal personhood, 184–186; works of, 202n32, 204n48
Shāfiʿī jurisprudence, 16–19; on paternal compulsion to marry, 35–37; on female consent to marriage, 41, 43; on legal capacity of women, 44–46; on maintenance obligations, 71–72, 77–78, 84–93, 95; on rights of slaves, 71–72, 174–175, 210n45; on stipulations in marriage contracts, 74–75, 220n31; on *nushūz*, 82, 223nn61–62; on divorce, 84–89, 137–140, 143, 239n23; on companionship rights, 113–114, 120, 129–130, 232n37; on oaths of abstention, 121–125, 235n91; on compensated divorce, 150–153; on waiting periods, 239n23. *See also* Muḥammad ibn Idrīs al-Shāfiʿī
Sharīʿa, 3–5, 187–197. *See also* Jurists' project
Shatzmiller, Maya, 220n40
Shāybanī. *See* Muḥammad b. al-Hasan al-Shāybanī
Shiʿi jurisprudence, 18–19, 41–42, 211n61
Siddiqui, Mona, 42
Sisters, 57, 78–79, 215n115
Slavery in Early Christianity (Glancy), 184
Slaves/slavery, 6–8, 238n15; manumission of, 7–8, 139–141, 167, 170, 192; as nonfungible commodity, 7–8; legal rights of, 8; *milk al-yamīn* in, 10, 12–15, 39–40, 156–160, 164, 202n27; licit sexual activity of, 11, 25–26, 38–40, 56, 67–68, 164–165, 209n39; illicit sexual activity of, 11–12, 25–26, 67–68, 245n11; kinship systems in, 11–12; consent to marriage in, 37–40, 44–46, 48, 209nn36,41, 210nn44–45, 212nn71–72; access to bodies of, 45, 177, 184–185; analogies with women of, 47–48; analogies with

Slaves/slavery *(continued)*
children of, 48; sexual agency of, 48; in modern Muslim world, 63; as patronage relationship, 63–64; maintenance obligations in, 66–72, 219nn17,22, 227n102; children of, 87–88, 102, 168–169, 200n20, 226–227nn91–92, 230n13; rights of marriage and divorce in, 135, 153–160, 165, 172–173, 182, 185, 227n102, 242–243nn80–82, 243n93, 248n46, 250n66; property and ownership rights *(milk al-nikāḥ)* of, 165–176, 192–193, 248nn3,43,45. *See also* Concubines/concubinage; Enslaved females
Smith, W. Robertson, 184
Social structures. *See* Hierarchical social structures
Sonbol, Amira, 23, 188
Spectorsky, Susan, 17, 203n40, 237n7, 238n21, 243n82
Spousal rights, 6–7, 10–12, 15, 66, 166. *See also* Companionship rights; Consummation; Dower; Licit sexual activity; Maintenance obligations
Stipulations in marriage contracts, 66, 72–75, 197, 220nn31–33
Subordination of women. *See* Gendered rights
Suitability, 42, 211n61
Sunna, 5, 34–35, 42, 52, 81, 183
Sunni jurisprudence, 16–17, 52
Support. *See* Maintenance obligations

Ṭalāq. *See* Divorce
Toledano, Ehud, 63–64, 69, 209n34
Torrey, Charles, 50
Travel, 52–53, 102–106, 118, 230–231nn25–27
Triple divorce, 136, 138, 143, 237n5
Trousseaux, 49
Tsafrir, Nurit, 19
Tucker, Judith, 4–5, 189, 196

ʿUmar b. ʿAbd al-ʿAzīz, 13–16, 101
ʿUmar ibn al-Khaṭṭāb, 12–13, 77, 200n20, 201n26; on female consent to marriage, 42, 211n59; on sexuality and ritual purity, 70; on stipulations in marriage contracts, 73; on divorce, 86–87, 91–92, 144–145, 155; on maintenance obligations, 86–87; on consummation, 91–92; on slave marriage and divorce, 155; on concubines, 167–168
Al-Umm. See *Kitāb al-Umm*
Umm Salama, 77, 107, 109–110, 112, 232n35
Umm walad, 102, 168–169, 200n20, 230n13
Unilateral divorce, 17, 84, 135–136, 140–141, 144–145, 186, 197
ʿUthmān b. ʿAffān, 35

The Veil and the Male Elite (Mernissi), 202n31
Virginity: of enslaved females, 32, 40; in consent to marriage, 32–36, 41, 210n47; in dower contexts, 56; in determining companionship rights, 107–111, 232n37. *See also* Consummation

Waiting periods, 84–86, 135, 224n74, 225n76, 239n23, 240n37
Walī. *See* Marriage guardians
Wedding nights, 106–114, 231n33, 232n35
Wet-nursing, 227n95
Widows, 107–110
Willis, John Ralph, 50–51
Witnesses: to marriage, 46; to divorce, 136; to resumption of marital relations, 140–141
Women. *See* Enslaved females; Free females
Women, Family, and Gender in Islamic Law (Tucker), 189, 199n1, 215n115, 217n136, 220n40, 229n5

Yad (hand), 10, 144, 155, 173–175, 180
Yitzhak, Ronen, 221n42

Ẓāhiri jurisprudence, 222n58, 228n108. *See also* Ibn Ḥazm
Zeʾevi, Dror, 209n39, 215n115
Ẓihār, 121, 234n68. *See also* Oaths of abstention
Zināʾ. *See* Illicit sexual activity
Zomeño, Amalia, 49
Zulficar, Mona, 162–163

Harvard University Press is a member of Green Press Initiative (greenpressinitiative.org), a nonprofit organization working to help publishers and printers increase their use of recycled paper and decrease their use of fiber derived from endangered forests. This book was printed on recycled paper containing 30% post-consumer waste and processed chlorine free.